John Man is a historian with a special interest in Mongolia. He has travelled widely across the lands that formed the Mongol Empire, becoming one of the few Western writers to explore the hidden valley where Genghis may have died, climb the sacred mountain on which he is supposedly buried and explore the ruins of Xanadu, the first capital of Genghis's grandson, Kublai Khan. His books, published in over twenty languages, include the bestselling *Genghis Khan: Life, Death and Resurrection* and *Kublai Khan*.

www.transworldbooks.co.uk

Praise for *Genghis Khan*:

'Absorbing and beautifully written . . . a thrilling account of Genghis Khan's life, death and his continuing influence . . . a gripping present-day quest' *Guardian*

'A first-rate travel book, not so much a life of the Khan but a search for him . . . Man has scholarly gifts as well as acute intelligence and a winning way with words. This is a fine introduction to the subject, as well as a rattling good read' Felipe Fernandez-Armesto, *Independent*

'A fine, well-written and well-researched book' *Mail on Sunday*

'Compelling . . . Man's perspective is as clearsighted and invigorating as that of the Mongol horsemen he travels with . . . this is an eloquent account, not only of a fascinating historical figure and his people, but of the resonance of history itself' *Waterstones Books Quarterly*

'Enthralling and colourful' *Independent on Sunday*

'This is a great story' *Spectator*

'Fascinating . . . every bit as gripping as its subject deserves . . . vividly captures the warlord's charisma, together with the mixture of ruthlessness, military genius and self-belief which, Man argues, made him the greatest leader ever . . . History doesn't come much more enthralling than this' *Yorkshire Evening Post*

'Man's excellent writing breathes new life into a character whose spirit lives on in China and Mongolia today' *Historical Novels Review*

'Man is an excellent guide . . . well-versed in Mongolian, he has travelled extensively in the country while researching the more mysterious elements of Genghis' life, and this experience shines through the book . . . he writes knowledgeably' *Literary Review*

'Fascinating . . . a wonderfully diverting study' *Ink*

THE
MONGOL
EMPIRE

Genghis Khan, His Heirs and
the Founding of Modern China

JOHN MAN

CORGI BOOKS

TRANSWORLD PUBLISHERS
61–63 Uxbridge Road, London W5 5SA
www.transworldbooks.co.uk

Transworld is part of the Penguin Random House group of companies
whose addresses can be found at global.penguinrandomhouse.com

First published in Great Britain in 2014 by Bantam Press
an imprint of Transworld Publishers
Corgi edition published 2015

Maps by Tom Coulson, Encompass Graphics

A CIP catalogue record for this book
is available from the British Library.

ISBN
9780552168809

Typeset in Sabon by Falcon Oast Graphic Art Ltd.
Printed and bound by CPI Group (UK) Ltd, Croydon, CR0 4YY

Penguin Random House is committed to a sustainable
future for our business, our readers and our planet. This book is made
from Forest Stewardship Council® certified paper.

1 3 5 7 9 10 8 6 4 2

For TW and DW-M

CONTENTS

MAPS

ACKNOWLEDGEMENTS

With thanks to: Chris Atwood, Professor of Mongolian History, Indiana University; Charles Bawden, Emeritus Professor, and former Professor of Mongolian at the School of Oriental and African Studies, London, who started it all; Dr Dambyn Bazargur and Badraa; Siqin Brown, SOAS; Yuefan Deng, Stonybrook University, NY; Dalai, historian, Ulaanbaatar; Ruth Dunnell, Associate Professor of Asian History and Director of International Studies, Kenyon College, Gambier, Ohio; Erdenebaatar, Institute of Animal Husbandry, Ulaanbaatar; Stephen Haw, for vital guidance on Marco Polo's China; 'Helen', Renmin University, Beijing, for wonderful interpreting; Professor Tsogt-Ochir Ishdorj, Head, Department of Historiography, History Institute, Mongolian Academy of Science; Jorigt and Nasanbayar of the Mongolian Language Institute, School of Mongolian Studies, Inner Mongolia University, Hohhot; Luc Kwanten and Lilly Chen, Big Apple-Tuttle Mori, Beijing and Shanghai; Professor Yao Dali, History Department, Fudan University, Shanghai; Lars Laaman, History Department, SOAS, for his help with Sharaldai (see Bibliography) and his translator, Geok Hoon Williams; Yuan-chu Ruby Lam, Department of Chinese, Wellesley College, MA; Du Jian Lu, Xi Xia Institute, Ningxia University; Richard John Lynn, for his Xanadu verse translations; Tom Man, of Perioli-Man, Oxford, for putting flesh on the Pleasure Dome; David Morgan, formerly Professor of History, University of

Wisconsin-Madison; Nachug, Director, Institute for Genghis Khan Studies, Edsen Khoroo (Genghis Khan Mausoleum); Oyun Sanjaasuren, MP, leader of Citizens' Will-Republican Party, Head of Zorig Foundation; Igor de Rachewiltz, School of Pacific and Asian Studies, Australian National University, for vital and unstinting guidance; Panoramic Journeys, together with Esee, two Nyamas, Ravi, Refika, Nancy and Joan; my Mongol guides, Goyotsetseg Reston (Goyo) and Tumen; Randall Sasaki, Texas A&M University, and Kenzo Hayashida for an introduction to Kublai's lost fleet; Sainjirgal, researcher, Genghis Khan Mausoleum; Sharaldai, theologian, Genghis Khan Mausoleum; Professor Noriyuki Shiraishi, Niigata University, for his comments and guidance in Avraga; Professor Chris Tyler-Smith, formerly at the Department of Biochemistry, Oxford University, for his help on Genghis's genetic legacy; Professor Wei Jian, Renmin University, Beijing, for unique insights and inspirational guidance; 'William' Shou for the Xanadu trip; Jack Weatherford, Macalester College, MN; Graham Taylor, Karakorum Expeditions, Ulaanbaatar; Frances Wood, British Library; Lijia Zhang, Beijing, for friendship; as always, Felicity Bryan and her team; and in Transworld Doug Young, Henry Vines and Sheila Lee.

The quotations from *The Secret History* are from de Rachewiltz's version (see Bibliography), with permission from Koninklijke Brill NV, Leiden, Netherlands.

A note on spelling
In transliterating Chinese, pinyin is now standard, but it still overlaps the old Wade–Giles system. I use whichever seems more appropriate. Spellings of personal names vary widely. 'Genghis' is pronounced 'Chingis' in Mongol, and should really be spelled like that in English (to overcome a common fault: the G is soft, as in 'George', not hard, as in 'good'). I retain 'Genghis' out of deference to tradition. I use the more familiar 'Kublai' rather than 'Khubilai', 'Qubilai' or 'Kubla'. Xanadu is 'Shangdu' (Upper Capital) in Chinese; but Xanadu is traditional in English, thanks to Coleridge.

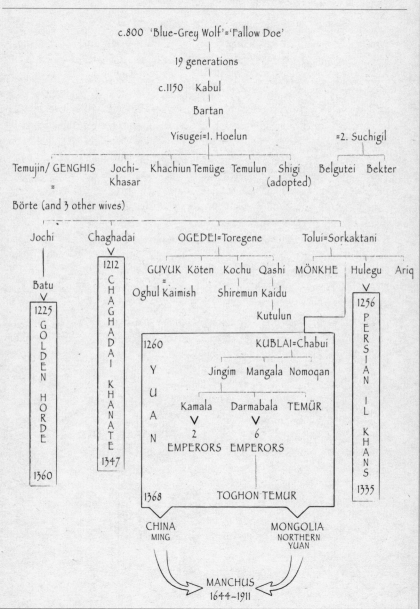

THE EMPIRE: RULERS AND REGIONS

A guide to the main characters, their relationships, their domains and a rough chronology

GREAT KHANS in CAPITALS

c.800 'Blue-Grey Wolf'='Fallow Doe'

19 generations

c.1150 Kabul

Bartan

Yisugei=1. Hoelun   =2. Suchigil

Temujin/ GENGHIS   Jochi-   Khachiun Temüge Temulun Shigi   Belgutei Bekter
=   Khasar   (adopted)

Börte (and 3 other wives)

Jochi   Chaghadai   OGEDEI=Toregene   Tolui=Sorkaktani

Jochi	Chaghadai	OGEDEI=Toregene	Tolui=Sorkaktani
Batu	**1212**	GUYUK Köten Kochu Qashi MÖNKHE Hulegu Ariq	

1212
C H A G H A D A I   K H A N A T E
1347

GUYUK Köten Kochu Qashi   MÖNKHE Hulegu Ariq
=
Oghul Kaimish   Shiremun Kaidu

Kutulun

Batu
1225
G O L D E N   H O R D E
1360

1256
P E R S I A N   I L   K H A N S
1335

1260
Y U A N
1368

KUBLAI=Chabui

Jingim Mangala Nomoqan

Kamala   Darmabala TEMÜR
2   6
EMPERORS EMPERORS

TOGHON TEMUR

CHINA   MONGOLIA
MING   NORTHERN YUAN

MANCHUS
1644–1911

INTRODUCTION

THE IDEA FOR THIS BOOK CAME FROM WORKING ON A PROPOSAL FOR A series of films. I was in Hohhot, Inner Mongolia, with a corporate boss who was interested in promoting Mongol culture. One of his ambitions was to commission a feature film to tell the story of Genghis Khan. It would be big budget, $100 million in Hollywood terms, appealing to audiences worldwide. Never mind other films on the same subject – no one had done Genghis's whole life. He had already discussed the project with three Hollywood scriptwriters. Things had not gone well. I could see why. He was interested in history, but knew little about narrative techniques; Hollywood scriptwriters know a lot about narrative, but care little about history. I saw one script by a well-known writer. It had this body-copy in an opening scene:

> The desert giving way to grass – sparse and flat. A woman, solitary, a symbol of sensuous feminine grace, carries water balanced on her head. Her hips sway timelessly.

It would never work, not just because in Mongolia no woman ever carried water on her head, let alone doing so while symbolizing grace with hips swaying timelessly. It would not work because of the history. Genghis's story is too big to be contained in a single film, even for a brilliant scriptwriter willing to become familiar with medieval Mongolia, China, Korea, Tibet, Japan, Russia, Georgia, Hungary, shamanism, Islam, Buddhism and Daoism. You could no more compress it into a hundred or so minutes than you could the Second World War.

It's not just the range of material that makes it impossible. It wouldn't work because Genghis's empire is only part of the story. He died halfway through. His grandson Kublai took up where Genghis left off, doubling the empire's size over the next seventy years. A single book, possibly; a single film, no.

So, I told him, he would have to think *really* big. How about not one film, but nine? How about not $100 million, but $1 *billion*? That would give scope to tell the full story.

He loved the idea. The problem is it will never happen, not because of the history, which divides quite neatly into nine self-contained stories, but because of its scope. How on earth do you write nine films all at once – and they have to be all written together, because they interrelate – let alone shoot them?

The discussion had a positive outcome. It made me take the long view and look back on the Mongol empire from today, with Asia dominated by the empire's top successor-state, China.

On the map, China is, as its name says, *zhong guo*, or Central Nation, a singularity, a unity, linking the Pacific to Central Asia, the gravelly wastes of the Gobi to subtropical Hong Kong. But the view from inner space suggests otherwise. Open Google Earth, find China, drift from west to east for 4,000-plus kilometres, and you will see that ecologically the nation is divided. The west and north are all browns and greys, marking the deserts of Xinjiang, the ice-bound wrinkles of the Tibetan plateau and the grasslands of Mongolia. There are few picture-icons on screen. Click on some and you will see why – huge skies, lunar landscapes, unnamed mountains, hardly a city and not many people.

Wandering very roughly from south-west to north-east, a colour change makes a fuzzy boundary. The browns of high and sparse wastelands tumble into lowland greenery. Along with China's two great rivers, the Yellow River and the Yangtze, the green surges east, over fertile lowlands, until it bulges into the Pacific like a well-fed paunch. This half is veined with roads, crammed with cities, exuberant with pictures and teeming with about a fifth of all humanity.

From Earth orbit, China looks as if it is made of two different parts.

In history, there were many more than two. Once upon a time, 850 years ago, China was not today's China. It was divided into six.[1] Before that, down the centuries, other parts came and went, sometimes a dozen or more, seldom fewer than six, sometimes thrusting westwards as if feeling a way towards India, sometimes scrabbling to the north-east into Manchuria and Korea. In fast-forward, the map of Chinese history looks like a cell-culture dividing, growing, dying back, but always a plurality, united only by an idea of unity that in the early days definitely did not include the very non-Chinese areas of Tibet or the deserts and grasslands beyond the Great Wall.

What brought these parts together?

For the start of the answer, stay on Google Earth, mouse your way up to Beijing, in the top right part of the green bit, then on northwest, across the grey-brown grasslands that span China's northern border into what is now Mongolia proper. If you search around for a focal point, you may find the twin border towns where the only railway comes through. There's not much to see. You are now over the Gobi, where the grass is so scattered on the gravel plains that only a camel would consider it as food. In summer, ramshackle trucks with two trailers belch their way northwards across wastelands that you might call trackless, except that the Gobi has many tracks and no roads. The tracks remain through the winter, because they are frozen. The desert may become temporarily trackless in early summer, when it is flayed by dust storms that could strip away your eyelids.

Head north-west, following the railway line. Halfway to the capital, Ulaanbaatar, go northwards for 80 kilometres until you come to a river, the Kherlen, which you can't miss because it sweeps round in a great bend, running in from the north and heading away

[1] Jin, Song, Yunnan, Tibet, Xinjiang and part of Mongolia (though the last is complicated in ways we'll get to later).

north-east. Follow it upstream, and you come to forested ridges and mountains known collectively as the Khentii.

If you want to understand why China is politically united and the shape it is today, this is where the story starts, on a mountainside where, in the year 1180 or thereabouts, a young man, hardly more than a teenager, has been hiding from enemies who want to kill him. The boy's name is Temujin, and at this moment very few people have heard of him, because he is down, and very nearly out. But not quite. Soon, he will become rather better known as Genghis Khan.

He is the key – his character, his vision, his beliefs, his ideology and his talent as a leader. Everyone knows about his ruthlessness, of course: millions dead, dozens of cities ruined. Less widely known is his genius for leadership, and less still the religious ideology with which his heirs justified their conquests. To them, Heaven was very much on their side, and every success, every city destroyed, every conquest, every submission, proved it.

History is not always just one damn thing after another; sometimes it is a story that makes sense. This one, the story of the Mongol empire, has a narrative arc unified by an ambition that now seems quite mad. Genghis created the belief – perhaps in himself, certainly in his followers – that Heaven had given the world to the Mongols and that their task was to do everything possible to turn divine will into reality. The story of how this ambition ran its course spans almost two centuries, much ground and astonishing changes – from 1180 to the late fourteenth century; from nothing much to the world's largest land empire; from an insignificant young warrior to the world's most powerful ruler; from a dream of world conquest to the discovery that the dream was mere fantasy.

But from that dream came something real: today's China. Inheriting the vision of world conquest from his grandfather, Kublai conquered all old China, added vast new territories, united east and west, doubled the country's size, gave it its capital, ruled from it as a Chinese emperor and created a new sense of national unity. Of course, the empire of which he was indirect head reached much further, to the borders of Europe, but his China – essentially today's China plus Mongolia – was under his direct rule. No subsequent ruler thought of backtracking. That Mongolia itself became independent a century ago was simply an unfortunate aberration.

Of the many ironies in this story, two of the strangest are that today's China owes its shape and size – its geographical self-image – to a barbarian non-Chinese who was its greatest enemy; and that the same barbarian is now honoured as an insider, the founder of a Chinese dynasty.

All of this still governs the geopolitics of Inner Asia. Mongolia has vast and untapped resources. China is hungry for them. The frontier between them, until recently nothing but expanses of gravel, sand and rock, is rapidly yielding unheard-of quantities of copper, coal, gold and many other minerals. These are, of course, technically on Mongolian soil. But Mongolia has been independent of its Chinese colonial masters for only a century, and to many Chinese the region is 'really' Chinese, on the grounds that it was once united by Kublai Khan, the Mongolian emperor who founded China's Yuan dynasty. And who inspired Kublai Khan? Why, his grandfather Genghis, which in Chinese eyes turns Genghis into a Chinese.

Did Mongolia rule China? Did China rule Mongolia? Much depends on the answers. To understand what is happening and what will happen here over the next few decades, there is no choice but to go back 840 years, to that young man hiding on a mountain in a wilderness, unknown to the outside world.

PART I
GENGHIS

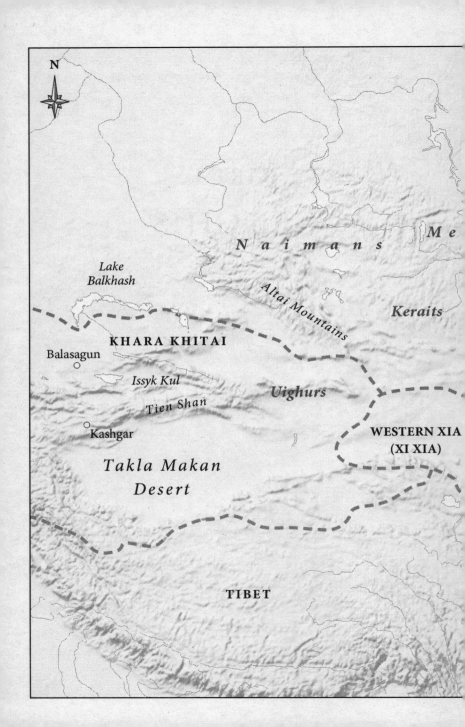

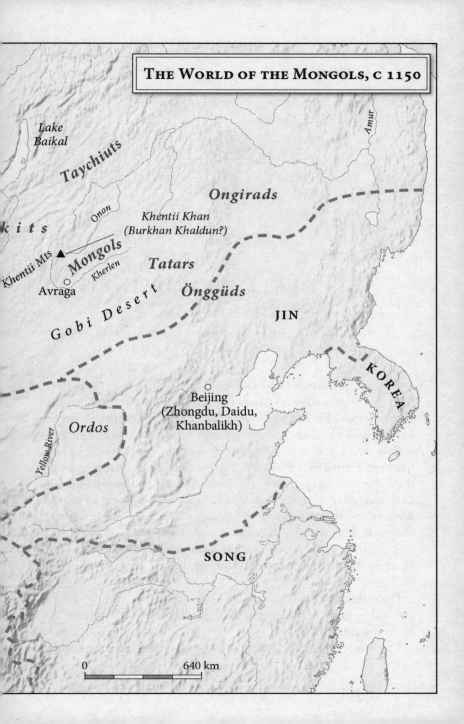

THE WORLD OF THE MONGOLS, C 1150

Lake Baikal

Amur

Taychiuts

Ongirads

kits

Onon

Khentii Khan
(Burkhan Khaldun?)

Khentii Mts

Mongols

Kherlen

Tatars

Avraga

Önggüds

JIN

Gobi Desert

KOREA

Beijing
(Zhongdu, Daidu,
Khanbalikh)

Ordos

Yellow River

SONG

0   640 km

1

'HIS DESTINY ORDAINED
BY HEAVEN'

1180, ON A MOUNTAIN IN NORTHERN MONGOLIA: IT ALL STARTS HERE, with the young man who would become Genghis Khan surviving an enemy attack. He has been lying low, following deer-trails he has known since childhood, sleeping rough beneath shelters of elm and willow twigs. His new wife, with whom he is very much in love, has been carried off. When the coast is clear on the morning of the third day, he emerges. Only days before, with his enemies hunting him over scree-covered slopes and through fir forests, he seemed doomed to an early death in obscurity. Yet here he is, alive. It occurs to him that his survival is not solely down to good luck and his own skills. Surely he has been protected. Heaven – Blue Heaven, the ancient god of the Mongols – must have had a hand in it.

From this tiny event – a down-and-out warrior grateful for his survival – grew a leader, an ideology, a dream of conquest, an empire, a new world.

But before we get into the consequences, there are questions to answer. How and why did he get into this fix in the first place? Who wanted him dead?

One answer is: Nature herself, for he had been born into a harsh way of life. These mountains and fir forests run across what is now the Russian border. A hunter with a good bow could shoot deer and elk, but there was not much to eat in the forests but pinenuts and berries. Real food was found in the broad valleys and the flatlands to the south, where grass for horses, cattle and sheep underpinned a herding economy. Or rather, real food *is* found: this should really be in a mix of past and present, because life in the Mongolian countryside is much as it was, with the exception of motorcycles and solar-powered TVs. It is from their animals that the herders must meet their needs: meat, skins, wool and the dozens of different products made from milk. There's not much variety. Life is good in the summer, of course, when you can shoot marmots or gazelle, and your animals fatten on lush grasses, and there is plenty of fermented mare's milk, the mildly alcoholic *airag* (otherwise known by its Turkish name, *kumiss*). Possibly, summers were even better in Genghis's day. Recent research suggests that his success depended on 15 warm and wet years, which promoted 'high grassland productivity and favoured the formation of Mongol political and military power'.[1] But the winters are Siberian. The main river, the Kherlen, and the many small ones that run out of the Khentii Mountains, are frozen for half the year. Occasionally, ice-storms seal the grass in an armour of ice, killing animals by the million. Wolves take sheep. To the south, conditions are even harsher. Grasslands give way to the Gobi's sparse and gravelly wastes.

To cope with these challenges, herders, who have been developing their skills for over 2,000 years, are experts. The Mongolian *ger* (better known to westerners by the Turkish term *yurt*) is domed to shoulder strong winds, and thick woollen felt over wooden roof-spokes keeps out rain and snow. To stay warm and to cook, you burn dried dung. In winters gone by, without today's iron stoves,

[1] Pedersen et al., see Bibliography.

you either coughed in a fog of smoke or opened the roof-flap and let in the cold. In summer, the smoke was a defence against the pestering flies. *Gers* and the carts that carry them, and the powerful little bows of wood and bone acted as reminders that these sailors on the ocean of grass needed their forest roots.

The trouble was not so much the climate, the need to keep moving to fresh pasture and the lack of luxuries, but the feuding. Clans and tribes had their traditional allies, but with wealth and power measured in herds and everyone on the move twice a year between summer and winter pastures, clan fought clan and vengeance followed injury down the generations. At best, young men had glorious assets: huge blue skies, horses galore, powerful bows, shoulder muscles like slabs of stone. But there were costs. A raid put an arrow in your back or left you wifeless, childless, motherless or horseless, facing winter with not a sheep to your unwritten name. Girls, as good in the wooden saddles as boys, grew up tough in mind and body, but were still in need of strong men.

The downside of steppe life was anarchy. Everyone knew this. All but the wildest wanted peace. The trouble was that every would-be leader wanted it on his own terms, without any of the give-and-take imposed by a central government. The only recourse was power, which was what the young Genghis lacked, but which he hoped for, because his great-grandfather had had it.

Earlier in the same century, when the old were young, a tribal chief named Kabul had crossed the Gobi, ridden through the mountain passes where the Great Wall now runs, down to the city now known as Beijing. In a film, this would be part of the back-story, sung by a bard, because by Genghis's time everyone would know what happened. Kabul, Genghis's great-grandfather, was the source of the very idea of national unity. He had united the Mongol tribes as their khan,[2] and the emperor of the northern Chinese empire of

---

[2] The nature of Mongolia's unity before Genghis created the nation is much debated. In brief, Kabul's realm was not a state but a unity of clans. He was master of a confederation of chiefdoms.

Jin had invited him to Beijing in the hope of winning him over with silks and wine. Kabul was not to be won. He got drunk, had the temerity to tweak the emperor's beard, and barely escaped with his life. Vengeance fell on Kabul's heir – his cousin, Ambakai, captured and crucified on a frame known as a 'wooden donkey'. His last message acted as a rallying-cry to his heirs: 'Until the nails of your five fingers are ground down, until your ten fingers are worn away, strive to avenge me!' Kutula, one of Kabul's sons, responded, launching a series of raids, earning himself a reputation as a Mongol Hercules, with a voice like thunder and hands like bear paws. But his strength did not guarantee victory. In about 1160, the Mongols, as hard to unify as a herd of cats, fell back to raiding and revenge killing and wife-stealing.

Kabul's grandson Yisugei dreamed of restoring unity, and so, unfortunately, did his cousins. The Mongols now consisted of some eighteen clans, two of whom claimed the khanship. To do so successfully, each needed the loyalty of all. This was the Catch 22 of steppe politics: leadership needed loyalty, which depended on wealth and power, to acquire which needed leadership.

To secure followers, Yisugei's first task was to get a wife.

This story and many others are told in the epic known as *The Secret History of the Mongols*, our main source for the events that produced Yisugei's son, the nation's founder, the future Genghis Khan. It is not only the prime source; it is the only one in Mongolian, and it is crucial because the incidents it describes are selected for their importance in explaining the rise of its hero. This 'foundation epic' was written in a mixture of prose and poetry within two years of Genghis's death in 1227, when the new nation's leaders gathered to crown his heir, his third son, Ogedei. Memories were still fresh, and the best stories were already being turned into song by bards (though not the conquests, perhaps because bards did not accompany the armies; *The Secret History* is pretty hopeless on military matters). Its disparate elements include snatches of epic verse, paeans of praise, ancient precepts and elegies, none of which were secret, by the way: the epithet was applied by modern scholars because it was kept private by Genghis's family. It contains many adventures – all the chaotic ebb and flow of the struggle for survival and dominance on the vast canvas of grassland and forest. At the time they happened, these events would have seemed of only local significance. But by the time *The Secret History* was written, everyone knew they were much more than that, because from the chaos had arisen a hero, a leader, a national founder, an emperor.

The Secret History has two agendas. The first is to turn the chaos into a coherent account of state-creation, with frequent identifi- cation of the year according to the widely used twelve-year cycle of animals common in east Asia (the *History* itself is dated the Year of the Rat, 1228), with the anonymous writer[3] choosing those incidents that make sense of Genghis's rise. For instance, it retells a clichéd incident in which a mother gathers her disputatious sons and has them break first one arrow then try to break a bundle, which they can't do; moral – to survive and conquer, stick together! Secondly, the *History* tells us about the qualities that were essential for leadership: bravery, decisiveness, judgement, generosity of spirit, ruthlessness, a vision of what had to be achieved. There are many obscurities. But often the incidents – almost certainly those that had already been popularized by bards – have a dramatic intensity that makes them as good as treatments for movie scenes, complete with dialogue.

Yet it's more than a narrative. It is also a political manifesto, showing how divine will has been at work to produce Genghis, back for twenty-three generations to animal ancestors, which were – as its opening lines state – a deer and a wolf, 'born with his destiny ordained by Heaven Above'. It tells how this worked in practice. Twelve generations back, there was a woman, Alan the Fair, who

[3] Possibly a Tatar, Shigi, who was adopted into Genghis's family and became head of his bureaucracy. The *History* was written for Genghis's heir, Ogedei, almost certainly with his collaboration. The year of composition is much debated. Other Rat years have their supporters. Atwood (2007) favours 1252 on the basis of many anachronisms, de Rachewiltz argues (2008) that the author conflated two years, 1228–9, and the *History* should be dated 1229, the year of the Ox.

bore two sons, then after the death of her husband became pregnant three more times. Her two older sons accuse her of impropriety. Not at all, she says: 'a resplendent yellow man' came into her tent through the smoke-hole or the gap at the top of the door and 'his radiance penetrated my womb', then 'he crept out on a moonbeam or a ray of sun in the guise of a yellow dog'. It's not quite a virgin birth, but at least an immaculate conception. Alan the Fair knows a messenger from Heaven when she sees one, because the bright yellow, or golden, light symbolizes supreme power and the dog is an oblique way of talking about a wolf, the Mongols' totemic animal and a symbol of fierceness. 'The sign is clear,' she says. 'They are the sons of Heaven', destined to 'become rulers of all'.

Twelve generations later Genghis appears, followed by his heirs and family – the Golden Clan as they called themselves. It was for them that *The Secret History* was written. That was why it was secret. It remained so because the original was lost. It was preserved only because the Mongols' Chinese-speaking successors trans-literated the Mongol into Chinese syllables as an aid to learning the language, but that version also vanished from the imperial archives. It was rediscovered in private hands in the late nineteenth century, and scholars set about the task of restoring the Mongolian text, back-transliterating it from the Chinese signs.

With the theme stated in the first few lines – a destiny 'ordained by Heaven Above' – many of the incidents incorporate a religious ideology, based on the Mongolian deity Blue Heaven. As time and *The Secret History* go on, we will learn more about this concept and its evolving complexities.

So here we have a document carefully constructed for its narrative power and ideology to present the past in a way that explains the present and foresees the future. It's not exactly the most objec-tive of historical sources. Historians are confronted with this problem all the time, but usually there are many alternative sources that allow scholars to work towards 'objective' truth, assuming there is such a thing. In this case, it is the first and only written account in Mongolian, on which all later sources draw (though there are Chinese and Persian sources, which add details that both corroborate and conflict with the Mongolian). All we can do is make the best of it, admiring it as part history, part folklore and part hagiography, and being extremely careful about taking it at face value.

A chance meeting changed the course of Yisugei's life, and that of world events. One day, according to *The Secret History*, he was out hawking on the banks of the River Onon when he came across a man riding beside a little black, two-wheeled cart pulled by a camel, a form of transport reserved for wealthy women. Perhaps Yisugei recognized him as Chiledu, the younger brother of the chief of a neighbouring tribe, the Merkits, who lived in the forests to the north-west, up towards Lake Baikal. A glimpse of the girl in the cart inspired him – she was a beauty. Moreover, her clothing showed she was of a clan traditionally linked to his by marriage. He fetched his two brothers, overtook the slow-moving procession, chased off the Merkits, grabbed the camel's tether, and set off slowly across the grassland, with the young woman, Hoelun, bewailing her fate, throwing herself back and forth, plaits flying, in an agony of grief at the loss of her husband. Oh, shut up, said one of the men riding beside her. Forget him. He's history. This was not quite true, as things turned out, for the incident provides crucial motivation for later events, but Hoelun accepted Yisugei as her new husband and protector. Six months later, after Yisugei returned from a raid, she greeted him with the news that she was pregnant.

Yisugei's task now was to regain the authority once wielded by his grandfather, Kabul Khan. He needed help. One potential ally was a Turkish tribe, the Keraits,[4] his neighbours to the west (remnants of a region-wide community of Turks who had migrated westwards, eventually reaching a new homeland, today's Turkey).

The Keraits had been nominally Christian for almost two centuries. They owed their Christianity to a 'heretical' sect named after the fifth-century patriarch Nestorius, who was banished from

[4] The simplest of many spellings, among them Kereyid, Kereit and Khereit.

Constantinople for asserting the equality of Christ's two natures, god and man. This meant opposing the official cult of the Virgin as the Mother of God, which Nestorius said denied Christ's humanity. His followers fled, and thrived, spreading eastwards to China and into Central Asia, where they converted several tribes, including the Keraits.[5]

The Keraits' current leader, Toghril, had had a colourful career, having been abducted and ransomed twice in childhood, before slaying several uncles to secure the throne. When Toghril was forced to flee by a vengeful relative, Yisugei helped him regain the leadership. (The remains of his HQ – a mound, a few stones – can still be seen a short drive west from Ulaanbaatar.) Toghril and Yisugei became 'sworn brothers', an alliance which would later prove of peculiar importance in Genghis's career.

Three months later, another raid, a victory, in Manchuria, home of the Mongols' old rivals, the Tatars.[6] Yisugei returned with a captive, a senior Tatar named Temujin. It was around this time, probably in 1162, that Hoelun's baby was born, close to the River Onon, near a hill called Spleen Hillock.[7] If later practices are anything to go by, Hoelun's *ger* would have been off-limits to almost everyone, with a female shaman as midwife looking closely at the baby for some omen, for this was after all the great-grandchild of a khan. Lo and behold, a son, with a clot of blood 'the size of a knucklebone' in his right hand. Later, in folklore, this was seen as an omen of fierceness – but only because the baby turned out fiercely successful. Some babies wielding blood clots turn out gentle failures.

---

[5] Vague echoes of this in the west started a rumour that there lived in Central Asia a Christian king referred to as 'Prester John', Prester being a contraction of Presbyter (priest). Supposedly Prester John would gallop to the aid of the Christian Crusaders in the Holy Land. It was a disappointment when the 'Christians' turned out to be the Mongols.

[6] Often spelled Tartar in English, because it was confused with Tartarus, a region of Hell. It was then applied to the Mongols as a whole. To Europeans, Mongols were a people from Hell.

[7] Where this happened is disputed. In 1962, for Genghis's 800th birthday, the government opted for a site in Dadal, on the basis of not very good evidence. More likely it was near Binder.

Following tradition, Yisugei named the boy after his captured foe, Temujin (who vanishes from the story, presumably killed or ransomed). So the future Genghis entered life with a Tatar name, quite a suitable one actually, because it derives from the Mongolian word for 'iron' and means 'iron-man' (i.e. blacksmith), not that the original Temujin was a smith any more than anyone named Smith is today. Anyway, his parents liked the connotations of iron – two later children bore names with the same root.

When the boy was eight, Yisugei set out to find a future wife for Temujin from Hoelun's clan, the Ongirad, with whom the Mongols traditionally arranged marriages. They lived several hundred kilometres away to the east, on the grasslands that flow over today's Chinese border. Near his destination, he came across an Ongirad couple who had a daughter, Börte, a year older than Temujin, and were keen for a match. The two fathers agreed, in a stock phrase, that both their children had fire in their eyes and light in their faces. To seal the bond and ensure mutual trust, Yisugei left his son with his future in-laws, Dei and Chotan. On leaving he told Dei to look after Temujin, and urged 'Don't let him be frightened by dogs!' This may seem odd – the future ruler of all Eurasia afraid of dogs? – but dogs were bred big and fierce. Even today, when you approach a *ger*, you shout 'Keep the dogs down!' Genghis himself must have approved the anecdote as a nice human touch.

During the journey home Yisugei came across a group of Tatars feasting and, in accordance with the rules of hospitality on the steppe, he was offered food and drink. They must have recognized him, and seized the chance to take revenge for his previous attacks by mixing poison into his drink. By the time he reached home three days later, he was sick, and dying.

This is the real beginning of the story, because just before Yisugei died, he summoned Temujin home. Everything before is back-story, given significance only by what happened next. If Yisugei had not died, little Temujin would probably have been left with his prospective in-laws for years, would have married his intended, Börte, and lived happily ever after, or not, unknown to the outside world. His destiny would have been very different, and so would that of Mongolia, China and all Eurasia.

Hoelun was left without a protector, and with seven young children between three and nine, five of her own and two by a second wife, Suchigil. Their hopes for success in war, their insurance against catastrophe, had suddenly vanished. Another clan, the Taychiuts, direct descendants of Ambakai, whose khanship had ended on a 'wooden donkey', now bid for power. Seeing a chance to dispense with possible rivals – in particular Yisugei's boy Temujin – they abandoned Hoelun, even spearing an old man who remonstrated with them. Hoelun was left without herds to almost certain death.

But she was a woman of spirit. She became a hunter-gatherer. *The Secret History* depicts her, skirts hoisted, noblewoman's tall hat firmly on her head, grubbing with a sharpened stick for berries and roots: burnet, silverweed, garlic, onion, lily bulbs, leeks. Suchigil must have been doing much the same, but she plays no role in the story. The boys learned to make hooks from needles and use nets to catch 'mean and paltry' fish.

So for three or four crucial years, Temujin knew what it was like to be at the bottom of the heap, to be without the protective network of family, companions and close friends, without enough animals to provide meat, milk or felt for a new *ger* covering. He must have grown up feeling trapped in the brutal hand-to-mouth existence of down-and-out hunter-gatherers, longing for security, herds, and vengeance.

During this harsh time, Temujin found a best friend, a boy named Jamukha. At the age of ten, the two exchanged gifts. In winter, swaddled in furs against the cold, they played at dice with animal ankle-bones, as people still do today. In the spring, as the grass grew sweet through the melting snow, Jamukha made Temujin a whistling arrowhead in exchange for an arrow tipped with horn. Twice the boys swore they would be *anda* – blood-brothers.

This was a family under stress – two women raising seven children. It was hardly surprising if the two eldest boys, Temujin and his half-brother Bekter, felt a growing sense of rivalry. One autumn, when Temujin was thirteen, his two half-brothers stole a small fish and a bird Temujin and their brother Khasar had caught. When Temujin and Khasar complained to their mother about the thefts, Hoelun reproached them. How could they say such things at a time when 'We have no friends but our shadows'? The two boys stormed out, seething. Then, bows at the ready, they crept up on Bekter, who was on a rise watching over some light-bay geldings. Bekter yelled at them: We need to be together, taking revenge on our Taychiut kinsmen; why 'regard me as a lash in the eye, a thorn in the mouth?' Don't touch Belgutei, he added, and sat cross-legged, as if calling his half-brother's bluff.

Temujin and Khasar shot Bekter and killed him, in cold blood.

You have to ask: if *The Secret History* is about the rise of our hero, what is this foolish and cowardly act doing in there? The answer is that it is a lesson, spelled out by Hoelun. She is distraught, and delivers a scathing condemnation. 'You who have destroyed life!' she yells, and compares her sons to a roll-call of destructive beasts, 'citing old sayings, quoting ancient words'. She goes on and on, in verse, which suggests it was well known and sanctioned by Genghis himself. It's there to make two points. First, no leader should undermine the family network, the core to survival and future strength. Her children have disobeyed the ancient injunction taught by the tale of the unbreakable bundle of arrows: stick together. Second, listen to the women. They often know what's right.

Not long after this, perhaps the following May, the Taychiuts paid a call. Against the odds, Temujin had survived, thanks to his mother. It was time to deal with him properly by kidnapping him, showing him off and executing him. When they came, the children escaped across the melting snow into a narrow valley, where they remained, trapped. 'Send out Temujin!' called the attackers. 'We have no need for the rest of you!' Instead, his two brothers and sister put him on a horse and sent him off alone into dense forest, where he hid for three days.

At this point, trying to work his way out on foot, leading his horse, his saddle became loose and fell off. Looking at the straps, he couldn't understand how this had happened, or – more significantly – why, for in cultures with a belief in spirit worlds, otherwise inexplicable events are often ascribed to other-worldly influences. So Temujin wonders, for the first time in *The Secret History*, whether he is under divine protection: 'Is this a warning from Heaven?' He's not sure – with good reason, as it turns out – but is not going to take a risk. He turns back and hides for three more days. Then he tries again, only to be stopped by another odd occurrence: a white boulder the size of a tent tumbles in front of him, blocking his path. Again he wonders, 'Is this a warning from Heaven?' Again he retreats, for another three days, until hunger drives him out – right into the arms of the waiting Taychiut. If Heaven is protecting him (as suggested by the auspicious use of threes, and the triply auspicious nine, and the colour white) it has not yet become very effective.

This episode and the adventure that follows are powerfully told in *The Secret History*; it makes a good story, it shows that Heaven is on his side, and it contains a number of insights into Temujin's character. He himself must have told it many times, and approved its retelling as a way of showing his growing strength, maturity and Heaven-sent luck.

For a week or two, Temujin was held prisoner by the Taychiut chief, Targutai,[8] under whose orders he was passed from camp to camp as proof of his captor's dominance. He was made to wear a heavy wooden collar, a portable pillory known as a cangue, fixed round his neck and wrists.

His prospects could hardly have been worse, for humiliation would precede execution. In fact, character and chance were about to come to his aid. The previous night Temujin had been billeted with a man named Sorkan-shira, who was a member of one of the Taychiut's subject clans, and not as loyal to its leader as he might have been. He allowed his two sons to loosen Temujin's cangue in order to let him sleep more comfortably. Here was a tiny foundation for friendship, which could be built upon if and when the time came.

---

[8] Literally 'Fatty', which suggests he was nicknamed for being fat. More likely, he belonged to a sub-clan, the Targut.

The next night was the first full moon of summer, in mid-May – Red Circle Day, as the Mongols called it. The Taychiut had gathered for a celebration. Imagine the broad valley of the Onon, ice-free at last, scattered trees overlooked by still-snowy ridges, horses and sheep grazing the fresh pastures, dozens of round tents, smoke curling from the smoke-holes, horses tethered in lines outside each tent, hundreds of people from the surrounding encampments, an air of rejoicing. Among the crowds that afternoon is Temujin, in his cangue, guarded by a 'weak young man' holding the prisoner's rope.

After dark, the people head for their tents under the full moon. All is quiet. Temujin seizes the moment. He jerks the rope free, swings his wooden collar, clouts the guard on the head and flees into the woods. Behind him he hears a plaintive yell – 'I let the prisoner escape!' – and knows they will be after him. He runs to the river, staggers in and lies down, his head raised clear of the near-freezing water by the wooden cangue.

His pursuers stick to the woods, but someone is on his way home downriver. It is Sorkan-shira, who spots Temujin. Astonished, he mutters that the Taychiut are jealous because there's 'fire in your eyes and light in your face . . . Lie just so; I shall not tell them.' Wait until the coast is clear, he says, then go off to your mother's.

Temujin, though, has a better idea. He is in a dire state. His hands are fixed in the cumbersome cangue, which has rubbed his neck and wrists raw. He is in woollen clothes, in icy water. Flight would mean death by exposure, or recapture. So he totters after Sorkan-shira downstream, looking out for the tent where he passed the previous night, pausing now and then to listen for the slop-slop of paddles in leather buckets as women churn mare's milk late into the night to make *airag*.

He hears the noise, finds the tent and enters. At the sight of the shivering and dripping fugitive, Sorkan-shira is horrified, and urges Temujin to be off at once. His family though – his wife, two sons and daughter – are as sympathetic as before. They untie the cangue and burn it. They dry Temujin's clothes, feed him and hide him in a cart of sheep's wool. He sleeps.

The next day is hot. The Taychiut continue their hunt,

turning from the forest to the tents, and at last to Sorkan-shira's. They poke about, looking under the beds, and then in the cart with its pile of wool. They are just on the point of revealing Temujin's foot – a detail surely added by some bard to increase tension – when Sorkan-shira can stand it no longer.

'In such heat,' he says, 'how could one stand it amidst the wool?' Feeling foolish, the searchers leave.

Sorkan-shira sighs with relief, and tells Temujin to get out, giving him food and drink, a horse and a bow with two arrows. Temujin rides upstream and rejoins his family.

The story portrays the experiences and reveals the reactions that form Temujin's character. He knows what it is like to be poor and outcast. He knows the crucial importance of family. He sees when to act, and acts decisively, but he has steady nerves and knows how to contain himself. Crucially, he can spot a potential ally. All of this will be vital if he is to fulfil his fundamental need: security.

The Secret History continues with another epic adventure. Temujin is gathering companions, as Toshiro Mifune does in *The Seven Samurai* (or Yul Brynner in the Hollywood version, *The Magnificent Seven*). A year passes. The family has herds, and nine horses, enough for their needs, but not enough to count as wealth. One day, when Temujin's surviving half-brother, Belgutei, is out hunting marmots on the best horse, thieves steal the other eight. Temujin and the others can only watch in helpless rage. Towards evening, when Belgutei returns on the one remaining horse, Temujin, the eldest, gallops off, tracking the thieves across the grass for the next three days.

On the fourth morning, he comes across a tent and a large herd of horses being tended by a teenager named Boorchu. Yes, he saw Temujin's light-bay geldings being driven past earlier. Insisting that Temujin leave his own exhausted horse and take a new one, a black-backed grey, Boorchu shows Temujin the tracks, and takes a sudden decision. 'Men's troubles are the same for all,' he says. 'I will be your companion.' He doesn't bother to return to his tent to tell his father what is happening. Off they go together.

Four days later, the two catch up with the robbers and their herds, and the missing horses. The two companions act instantly, riding into the herd, cutting out their own horses and galloping off. The thieves follow, but night falls and they give up.

Another four days later, approaching Boorchu's father's camp, Temujin makes a generous gesture: 'Friend, would I ever have got these horses back without you? Let's share them.' No, no, Boorchu replies. He wouldn't think of it. His father is rich and Boorchu is an only son. He has all he needs. Besides, he acted in friendship. He couldn't possibly take a reward, as if the horses were mere booty.

Arriving back at Boorchu's tent, there is an emotional reunion between son and father, who has been devastated by Boorchu's disappearance and presumed death. Boorchu is unrepentant, typical of a teenage boy. He's back, so what's the problem? After the scolding and the tears of relief, father and son give Temujin food, and the father, Naku, seals the bond between the two boys: 'You two young men, never abandon each other.' Temujin will remember Boorchu's selfless nobility, and Boorchu will later become one of the greatest of Mongol generals.

There remained a promise to be fulfilled and a ready-made ally to be rediscovered. Temujin, now sixteen, returned to Dei's tent to marry his betrothed, Börte, as arranged by his father some seven years previously. Börte was seventeen, quite ready for marriage, and her parents were delighted. After the marriage, Dei and his wife accompanied their daughter back to Temujin's home, bearing a present for Hoelun – a sable gown. It must have been a magnificent object, jet black, sleek as oil, with sleeves long enough to cover the hands in cold weather and a hem reaching down to mid-calf. Hoelun would have been thrilled – except that her eldest, now master of the house, had seen a good use for it.

He could already count on his own family, two 'sworn brothers' and another Mongol clan – Börte's and Hoelun's people, the Ongirad. He could do with more help, though, and knew where to find it – from his father's blood-brother, Toghril, the Kerait leader, now master of a domain that stretched from central Mongolia to the Chinese border south of the Gobi.

To back his plea, he offered the black sable gown. Toghril was delighted. 'In return for the black sable coat,' he said, 'I will bring together for you your divided people.'

A good move, because not long afterwards came the attack which forced Temujin to flee to the flanks of his sacred mountain.

The raid comes soon after dawn, when Temujin's family are camping in a broad valley near the headwaters of the Kherlen, the river that embraced their homeland. An old serving woman, Khoagchin, woken by the beat of galloping hooves, yells a warning. Temujin and his brothers leap on their horses and ride to safety on the flanks of the Mongols' sacred mountain, Burkhan Khaldun.[9]

Here's a problem. Everyone today thinks they know this mountain. Its name is Khentii Khan – the King of the Khentii – and it is closely connected to Genghis in Mongol minds. Ordinary people, officials and most academics believe that this is the mountain where he roamed as a youngster, escaped his enemies, and is buried (a subject we will return to later). They believe it for many good reasons – because for centuries it has been the focus of Genghis-worship; because one third of the way up there was once a temple, the remains of which can still be found today; and because on the summit there are dozens of shrines. So every four years the government mounts an expedition to it, and up it. It is all very persuasive; except that there is no hard evidence that today's Burkhan Khaldun is yesterday's Burkhan Khaldun. Possibly the name referred to a complex of half a dozen peaks, or even to the whole mountainous region.[10] Possibly each clan had its own sacred mountain. If so, no one knows which young Temujin's was.

In any event, Temujin escapes on to a Burkhan Khaldun, if not *the* Burkhan Khaldun. Hoelun snatches up her five-year-old daughter, Temulun, puts her in front of her on a horse, and gallops off with others, but 'there was no horse left for Lady Börte'. The old servant

[9] 'Burkhan' means 'sacred', 'holy'. 'Khaldun' may possibly derive from a word meaning 'cliff' or 'willow'. Frankly, no one knows.
[10] The arguments are summarized by de Rachewiltz in his *Secret History*, pp. 229–30. He is (almost) certain that yesterday's Burkhan Khaldun is today's Khentii Khan. I'm not so sure (see p. 303).

pushes Börte into an enclosed ox-drawn carriage. She might have got away, but the rough ground snaps the cart's wooden axle. The Merkit raiders gather again, wondering what's in the cart. Young men dismount, open the door, and 'sure enough they found a lady inside'. They haul Börte and the old woman up on to their horses' rumps, and join in the search for Temujin on Burkhan Kaldun's forbidding flanks, squelching through peat bogs and forests thick enough 'to stop a well-fed snake'. For three days they circle the mountain, in vain. At last, they withdraw with their women captives. 'We have had our revenge,' they tell each other, and begin the week-long haul back home. Once there, Börte is handed over to a chief.

Temujin does not act the hero in this incident, galloping to safety, leaving his young wife to be kidnapped. But by the time *The Secret History* was written the story was famous, and – we can assume – sanctioned by the hero himself. Everyone had the advantage of hindsight and knew that he was the leader-in-waiting, so his survival was paramount. Besides, the story needs her to be kidnapped, because the kidnapping provides a motivation for what is to come.

Temujin is hiding out in thickets, sleeping rough. He has lost his beloved Börte. His friends will vanish if he is seen to be a loser. When it is safe for him to come out on the morning of the third day, Temujin re-emerges, and is overcome with gratitude for his survival. This is not the first time he has found shelter in the woods and defiles of Burkhan Khaldun. *The Secret History* breaks into verse to capture his feelings:

> Thanks to Burkhan Khaldun
> I escaped with my life, a louse's life,
> Fearing for my life, my only life,
> I climbed the Khaldun
> On one horse, following elk tracks;
> A shelter of broken willow twigs
> I made my home.
> Thanks to Khaldun Burkhan[11]

[11] The name's elements are reversed for stylistic reasons. This is verse, after all.

> My life, a grasshopper's life,
> Was indeed shielded!

Though all high places are sacred, this mountain deserves special reverence. He vows he will honour it always by remembering it in his prayers every morning; and so will his children, and his children's children. Then, in actions representing total submission to a higher power, he faces the rising sun, drapes his belt and hat – both symbols of power and authority – over his shoulders, beats his chest, makes a ninefold obeisance towards the sun and prepares a libation of *airag*, fermented mare's milk.

Temujin's life was shielded – by what? There is only one possibility: by the power that he had been near while on the mountain, the Heaven of *The Secret History*'s opening lines. It is time to take a closer look at what this power was.

'Heaven' is the translation of the Mongol god, Tengri, who was also the god of several other Central Asian peoples, for belief in Tengri went back centuries before the Mongols arrived in Mongolia. Possibly the word derives from the same root as the Chinese for 'Heaven', *tien*, as in Tien Shan, the Heavenly Mountains, or Beijing's Tiananmen, the Gate of Heavenly Peace. In any event, Tengri was used by the Xiongnu, who may or may not have been the Huns, and who ruled an empire that covered a good deal of east Asia from 200 BC to AD 200.[12] Turkish tribes adopted the name, recording it in various spellings on numerous stone inscriptions in central Mongolia and then carrying it with them as they migrated westwards, until they converted to Islam. It was also inherited by the Mongols when they arrived in their homeland in the late first millennium (which, in the words of Igor de Rachewiltz, suggests that 'the Turks played vis-à-vis the Mongols a role similar to that of Greece vis-à-vis Rome'[13]). Like the word 'heaven' in many languages, it refers both to the sky

---

[12] The Chinese and Mongolians say they are one and the same, but the evidence is lacking. See my *Attila*, Chapter 2.
[13] In de Rachewiltz, 'Heaven, Earth and the Mongols'. See Bibliography.

and its divine aspect: 'the heavens opened', 'Heavens above!' There is also a sense (possibly, though nothing in its etymology is certain) of a force, 'the power that makes the sky turn'.[14]

So far, Tengri looks like an equivalent of the Old Testament god, though the Jewish god often interfered in human affairs, guiding and punishing, while the ancient Turkish-Mongol one was impersonal, not involved in the petty feuds of the steppe. It was and is natural, therefore, for Muslims and Christians to equate Tengri with Allah and God. The term is also used to refer to Hindu gods and Buddhist spiritual entities. Like all the main monotheisms, Tengrism was rooted in beliefs in a universe of spirits. Tengri presided over numerous lesser *tengris* (ninety-nine of them in later Buddhist theology) and over the uncountable spirits of rocks, trees, rivers, springs, groves, storms and almost any natural manifestation you can think of. That's why today, as you drive around Mongolia, you see on mounds and hills and ridge-tops stones piled into shrines (*ovoos*), on which lie offerings of bottles, blue silk and valueless banknotes.

This brings us into the system known as animism, the belief not only in the existence of countless spirits, but also in the ability of certain people – shamans – to contact and control them, and use them to heal. There is something fundamental in these beliefs. Spirits and shamans are common to pre-literate, pre-urban cultures across the world, from Siberia (where the word 'shaman' comes from) to Africa, Australia and the Americas. There were many ways to contact the spirit world, through hallucinogens, drugs, trances, music, drumming, rituals and/or by climbing something that approached the place where the spirits and/or the Great Spirit, Zeus, Allah, God or Tengri lived, like a tower or a mountain. This is why mountains sacred to prehistoric peoples have shrines on them; why they are hard but not too hard to climb; why cultures as separate as the Mayas, the Sumerians and the Egyptians built pyramids; and why religious buildings in many faiths have towers.

So it is on a sacred mountain that Temujin has his first inkling of being under the protection of Heaven, the universe's supreme power.

[14] Jean-Paul Roux, *Tängri*.

It was the power that kept the stars turning, the power that all mankind sensed, and which therefore underlay all religions.

As conquest followed conquest, Tengri underwent refinements, gradually strengthening to become what some scholars call an ideology, Tengrism. Possibly this happened under the influence of the great monotheisms of Islam and Christianity. Originally merely a spiritual version of the sky, Blue Heaven, Tengrism became both more universal and more involved with human affairs – *Eternal* Heaven. Eternal Heaven grants protection, good fortune and success. It is the source of strength, with the power to inspire the correct decision at times of crisis, and to impose its will. Later, when the empire was established and expanding, edicts usually began with an invocation: 'By the power of Eternal Heaven . . .' or 'Relying on the strength of Eternal Heaven . . .' The problem lay in deciding what was decreed and what wasn't.

Superficially, to claim Heaven's backing looks like nothing more than a reflection of the Chinese imperial tradition of claiming to rule by the 'Mandate of Heaven'. But perhaps there's more to it. The Mandate of Heaven could, by definition, be granted by the gods to an emperor only retrospectively, after he or his dynasty had come to power. Before conquest or seizure of power, Heaven may be on your side, but you cannot know it for sure until you ascend the Dragon Throne. The corollary is that if you fail, Heaven withdraws its mandate; but you cannot know this until you fall from power. Young Temujin's future followers believed that Heaven was on his side in advance of any success, not only when he was still a louse on the side of a mountain but back for centuries to the emergence of the Mongols.

But why? Young Temujin had no idea, and nor did the later Genghis. Nor, come to that, did his heirs. No one had anything sensible to say on the subject. From this mystery sprang one of the Mongols' most surprising traits – tolerance, in the sense of an absence of religious bigotry, which we will see in action in due course.

Later, successful conquests inspired a rather less attractive trait – arrogance. True, you have to be strong to begin with. But to be truly successful, Heaven must increase your inborn strength. Then you will be successful in whatever you do. Success proves that Heaven is with you. On the basis of this circular argument, Temujin/Genghis's heirs acquired a certainty their famous forefather never had. For if you have been appointed by Heaven, then any conquest is by Heaven's order and Heaven's will. In a famous letter to the Pope, Genghis's grandson Guyuk asked in effect, 'How do you think we achieved all this, except by Heaven's command? So Heaven must be on our side. That being so, you cannot possibly claim God's backing. Accept, and submit.'

In the Christian West, there is a traditional belief that God can be influenced by prayer. Even today, church services pray for peace and good health, the implication being that if Christians do not do this, the things they pray for may slip God's mind. Originally, Tengri was too remote to be influenced. But as conquest succeeded conquest, beliefs changed. If the Mongols were world-rulers, perhaps they had some influence over the deity that backed them. On one occasion Genghis asks Heaven for strength to do what is necessary, namely start a war in risky circumstances. The Persian historian Rashid al-Din, writing in his encyclopaedic *Collected Chronicles*[15] some seventy-five years after Genghis's death, tells of another occasion when Genghis prayed 'Oh Eternal Heaven, lend me help from on high and permit that here on earth men, as well as spirits good and bad, assist me.'

The concept of Tengri had an additional subtlety, again deriving from Turkish beliefs. Heaven Above was the more powerful half of a duality, the other, weaker half being the Earth Below, or Mother Earth as the Mongolians called it. It had a name taken from a Turkic source: Etügen, with various spellings.[16] To be truly *truly* successful, you need not only Heaven, but Heaven and Earth working together. Naturally, success proved that the Mongols had the backing of both, a belief that was yet to evolve its most outrageous tenet – that the

---

[15] Other versions of the name are *Compendium of* or *Collection of Histories*.
[16] Marco Polo mentions this god as Natigay, a corruption of Etügen, though he thought she was male. So did John of Pian di Carpine, who transcribed the name as Itoga.

whole world already actually belonged to the Mongols, and that it was their job to make everyone on earth realize this astonishing fact.

2

THE FOUNDER OF
HIS NATION

TEMUJIN'S NEXT TASK WAS TO RESCUE BÖRTE. HE HAD NO CHOICE: IF
he accepted her loss, his prestige, such as it was, would plummet,
and there would be no chance of ruling anyone, let alone believing
that he was under divine protection. He would be destined for
nothing but a quick end. He turns to the man he calls 'father',
Toghril, and is not disappointed.

> In return for the black sable coat
> We shall crush all the Merkit,
> We shall cause your wife Börte to return

For additional help Temujin called on his childhood friend and
sworn brother, Jamukha, now head of his own clan. Four divisions
– 12,000 men or more – worked their way north over the mountains
towards Lake Baikal and approached the tributary of the Selenga,
the Khilok, beyond which the Merkits were camped. They crossed
by night, each man building a float of reeds and swimming across

with a horse. The operation was too huge to achieve total surprise. Huntsmen ranging the Khilok's further banks saw what was happening and galloped off with a warning. The Merkit fled, scattering in panic down to the Selenga and along its banks.

Amongst those in pursuit of the refugees rode Temujin, calling for Börte. A prized hostage, she was in one of the fleeing carts. She heard the call, jumped down, came running, seized his bridle, and 'they fell into each other's arms'. It makes a romantic picture, two teenagers in a moonlight embrace. That was enough for Temujin. 'I have found what I was looking for,' he said, and called off the chase.

It was a famous victory, and later *The Secret History* knew how it had been achieved. Temujin had been backed by his two allies, but there was more, the lesson emphasized by repetition and by verse: 'with my strength increased by Heaven and Earth',

> Called by Mighty Heaven
> Carried through by Mother Earth,
> We emptied the breasts of the Merkit people.

The only shadow was that Börte returned pregnant with her first-born, Jochi. Though Temujin accepted the child as his own, Jochi was stigmatized by his possible illegitimacy, so that when the time came to name a successor he would not be accepted as heir.

For eighteen months after the successful campaign against the Merkit, Temujin's family lived with Jamukha's. They were the best of friends, exchanging gifts, feasting together, even sleeping under the same quilt (though this does not imply homosexuality).

But in mid-April, as family groups of Mongols were moving to spring pastures along the Onon River, the two friends were riding along in front of the carts when Jamukha suggested that they should each make his own camp. Temujin paused, puzzled, wondering if Jamukha was suggesting a separation. He asked Hoelun's advice, but it was Börte who spoke: everyone knew Jamukha tired of things quickly, she said, a stock phrase suggesting that he should not be trusted.

From this hint, suspicion grew to a startling conclusion. If the two were not one, then who was the leader? Jamukha was the more influential, but Temujin was not prepared to become a mere follower. In that case, he had to part from his friend. But if they parted, they could not be companions; if not companions, then rivals; if rivals, then enemies, for one or other must surely dominate.

Temujin made his decision, and led his own group onwards, without camping at all, right through the night.

He might have simply marched away into isolation, and remained a footnote of history. But the gamble paid off. By the time the stories were written, there was much to be explained, and *The Secret History* does so by condensing a drawn-out process into a drama.

At dawn, three brothers and their families, leading members of a minor clan, catch up with Temujin. Then another five appear, then more men, more families of more clans, some breaking from their family groups, all opting for Temujin rather than for Jamukha. They have come because rumours have spread that young Temujin is destined for leadership, and rumour strengthens into hope, hope into prophecy. One man says that he is related to Jamukha and would never have left him, 'but a heavenly sign appeared before my very eyes, revealing the future to me'. In his vision, a cow butted Jamukha and broke a horn. Then an ox harnessed itself to a tent-cart, a symbol of the whole nation, and headed after Temujin, bringing the nation to him 'on the wide road' – the royal road to supreme power. Symbols, portents, signs, dreams, visions and prophecies – all combine to assert one great truth bellowed out by the ox: 'Together Heaven and Earth have agreed: Temujin shall be the lord of the people!'

And still they come, all pitching their tents nearby, many above Temujin in the family hierarchy, yet all drawn by the feeling that here at last was the man the Mongols needed to restore their lost unity. Three senior relatives choose to serve, and swear an oath to pursue their new khan's enemies, to bring him the finest women and the best horses, and to hunt for him. If they ever disobey him, let Temujin take all their possessions and 'cast us out into the wilderness'. One main body of Mongols had their new khan – half a nation, with Jamukha's people still to be absorbed.

There is a problem. *The Secret History* slips in a note to say that at this point, after the swearing of the great oath of loyalty, they 'made Temujin khan, naming him Genghis Khan'. This is probably in the late 1180s. Yet it also says he was named khan later, in a much larger gathering in 1206. What exactly happened, and when? The short answer is that no one knows. It is odd that *The Secret History* does not tell us. True, it is often shaky on facts, but years are sometimes mentioned. Yet there is no date for something as significant as Temujin being renamed Genghis. Could it be that this was a very private affair, arranged by the family for the family? If so, perhaps the author of *The Secret History* kept the information private out of respect.

Most authorities nowadays say this event took place in 1189, at Blue Lake, where Temujin's family had been based. Indeed, if you go there today, you are left almost convinced. It is a beautiful place. The lake is blue if the sky is, and if you see it at the right angle; otherwise it looks brown because it lies in peaty soil. Above it looms a little mountain named Black Heart. When I first visited, in 2003, there was nothing much to mark it out but a shoulder-high pillar with a small bas-relief of Genghis. On Black Heart, white-painted boulders spelled out 'Genghis Khan' in the old vertical script. It was silent, beautiful, intimate, a perfect spot for a family to raise herds in secrecy.

On my next visit, six years later, much had changed. Someone had fenced the eastern shore of the lake and built a wooden house. On a flat area along the southern shore stood tourist dachas. The pillar had gone, and in its place was a semicircle of what looked like totem poles ready for some American Indian ritual. The 4-metre fir trunks were capped by portraits of all thirty-four Mongol khans, from Genghis's father through the emperors who claimed descent from Genghis. They faced inwards to a granite slab sporting a new portrait of Genghis, made of plastic. It was an unsettling combination of tackiness, commercialism and grandeur. Under the portrait ran a caption, carved into the granite in the old vertical script: 'In the Heaven-sent year 1189 at Black Heart Blue Lake, in the presence of all the Mongol khans, the title of Genghis Khan was awarded.'

Is it true? Perhaps. It's the perfect spot. Though there is no evidence for the date in *The Secret History*, from 1189 it refers to him more as Genghis than Temujin.

If the timing is controversial, so is the new name – or title, as it may have been. The Mongols could have chosen any of several available titles. Gur or 'Universal' Khan was chosen by Jamukha; Toghril would become the Wang (Chinese for 'prince') Khan. But no traditional titles, whether Turkish, Mongol or Chinese, would have seemed appropriate for a man of Temujin's stature. Something new was called for.

'Genghis', whether title or name, was unique. Strangely, no one recorded its origin. Until recently, no one could explain it convincingly, which allowed unlikely theories to multiply. Some claimed it was related to the word for 'sea', *tengis*, for the sea was an object of veneration; or to Tengri. Others say the name was given by a shaman after hearing the cry of a bird. Nothing worked, until a recent suggestion, increasingly accepted by scholars, that Genghis derives from an obsolete Turkish word, *chingis*, meaning 'fierce, hard, tough' – indeed this is its spelling in Mongolia's Cyrillic script. At the time, the origin must have been self-evident, but it was also perhaps a private, family name, being granted in circumstances that did not filter into the public world of the storytellers. If so, Temujin was proclaimed privately as 'the Fierce Ruler'.

The Secret History now embarks on the chaotic few years (1190–1206) during which Genghis works his way towards what is generally regarded as the founding of the nation. It is like the emergence of a solar system, with many bodies – Mongols, Tatars, Naiman, Keraits, Taychiuts and Jin – in and out of allegiance, with Jamukha as a sort of planetoid colliding with this one or sticking to that. At one point, Genghis linked with Toghril to destroy the Tatars, killing all the male members of the leading clan who were taller than 'the linch-pin of a cart', which meant all but the youngest children. Since this avenged his father's murder and suited the Jin as well, both Mongolian and Chinese sources provide a date: the Year of the Dog, 1202. In thanks, the Jin commander awarded both Genghis and Toghril honorary titles (this was when Toghril became the *wang*, the 'princely' ruler, mongolized as Ong). Soon afterwards the Mongols and Jin were at each other's throats again. Several incidents provide lessons in character and leadership.

One constant in the *History*'s confused account is that Genghis emerges as the true leader, Jamukha as the false one. Once, Jamukha overcame Genghis, who fled to hide on the upper reaches of the River Onon. Jamukha had his captives, 'the princes of the Chinos [Wolves] boiled alive in 70 cauldrons'. Scholars argue about what this means. Most assume that it refers to the male leaders of a small clan loyal to Genghis, whose legendary totemic forefather had been a wolf, or a leader of that name. Boiling alive was indeed an established form of execution, though it is fair to assume that seventy is not an exact number and simply means 'many'. In addition, Jamukha cut off the head of an enemy chief and dragged it away tied to his horse's tail. These two examples of deliberate brutality and humiliation are in implied contrast to Genghis's style of leadership. If Jamukha, even in victory, is a brutal murderer eager to rule by terror, then Genghis, even in defeat, is the opposite.

But there is another lesson hidden here. Later, Genghis, as national leader, would be a master of terror, unleashing death and destruction in truly horrific ways. So what, one may ask, is wrong with boiling seventy of his colleagues alive and dragging a decapitated head about behind a horse? What's wrong is that it doesn't work. Genghis and his gang are not cast down, do not surrender. Just the opposite. The atrocity spurs him to greater efforts to achieve vengeance and victory. Jamukha's action is that of a poor leader, not because he perpetrates an atrocity, but because he perpetrates the *wrong sort of atrocity*. Terror must be applied so that the advantages outweigh the disadvantages – a strategy Genghis would use with appalling effectiveness in China and the world of Islam.

Battle followed battle, alliances were made and betrayed and re-formed, leaving Jamukha still at large at the head of an alliance of tribes and Toghril vacillating between friendship and enmity. *The Secret History* skimps on politics, strategy and military details, but records several examples of the one trait that Temujin valued above all – loyalty, the most fundamental of virtues for life on the steppe.

During one battle with Jamukha's coalition, Temujin had two narrow escapes, which opened the way for shows of loyalty that bound him and his followers as if with a sacred vow.

At one point in the battle, an arrow just missed Temujin, but pierced his horse's neck, killing it. After changing mounts, another arrow, a poisoned one, actually hit him, in the neck. In camp that night, with no food or drink to sustain him, he lapsed into unconsciousness. His No. 2, Jelme, sucked the wound clean, then sneaked into Jamukha's camp and stole some curds. When Temujin came to, Jelme fed him with curds and water. At dawn, as Temujin's strength returned, he saw that he owed Jelme his life.

Later, with the battle won, old Sorkan-shira himself appeared, along with a companion. Temujin asks if Sorkan by any chance knew who had fired the arrow that killed his horse. It is Sorkan's companion, Jirko, who speaks up: it was he who fired the arrow. Having almost killed Temujin, he courted instant execution. So he dedicates himself to his leader. If you kill me, he says, I'll only rot away in a plot of earth the size of your hand; but if you show mercy, I'll cut through oceans and mountains for you. On other occasions, later in life, Temujin had no time for turncoats. But there is no betrayal involved here. He is swayed by Sorkan's presence and impressed by Jirko's honesty and courage. 'This is a man to have as a companion,' he says, and renames him on the spot in memory of his deed. 'He shall be named Jebe ["Arrow-point"] and I will use him as my arrow.'

Both Jebe and Jelme would become two of the khan's greatest generals.

After the battle, the Taychiut chief who had held Temujin captive – Targutai – was himself captured by a man of a subordinate clan and his two sons. The three shoved him on his back in a cart and then, while the father of the two young men sat on his captive's paunch, they set off to give themselves up with their prize. On the way, however, they recalled Temujin's un-compromising views on loyalty and began to wonder if they were doing the right thing. They had, after all, sworn to serve the man who was now their prisoner. Rather than reveal themselves as traitors to Temujin, they let their captive go, and presented themselves to Temujin. It was a good move. Even though Temujin would have sent Targutai to a terrible death, he placed loyalty to a leader above his own desire for revenge. 'You were unable to forsake your rightful khan. Your heart was right,' he told the three men, and took them into his service. (Targutai got his come-uppance anyway. He was killed later by one of Sorkan-shira's sons.)

At one point, in the summer of 1203, Genghis was again down, and nearly out. With a mere 2,600 men, he retreated along the Khalkha River to the shores of an unidentified lake (or possibly a river) called Baljuna.

What followed assumed huge significance, not because it marked Genghis's nadir in military terms, but because it was a turning point in terms of leadership. According to several Chinese sources, Genghis endured extreme deprivation with nineteen loyal commanders, who, in a ritual that bound them to Genghis and to each other, all drank the muddy waters of Lake Baljuna. As one account puts it:

> Upon arrival at the Baljuna, the provisions were used up. It happened that a wild horse came northward. Khasar brought it down. From its skin they made a kettle; with a stone they got fire, and from the river, water. They boiled the flesh of the horse and ate it. Genghis Khan, raising his hand toward the sky, swore thus: 'If I finish the Great Work, then I shall share with you men for better or for worse; if I break my word, then let me be as this water.' Among the officers and men, there was none who was not moved to tears.

This was the moment at which a leader willing to share suffering, defeat and death with his companions forged a bond like no other. And who were these Baljunans, as they became known? Not an inward-looking *cosa nostra* of top Mongolians. Almost half of them were outsiders who might just as easily have been Genghis's enemies, a mix of clans, races and religions – three Christian Keraits, a Merkit (shamanistic), two Khitans (possibly Buddhists) and three Muslims, who would have been traders, not herders, and one of whom was a descendant of the Prophet. This was the proto-government of a proto-nation.[1]

Despite its significance, the incident is mentioned only obliquely in *The Secret History*. Genghis sets up camp on Lake Baljuna, but there's no 'covenant'. Clearly, the omission was deliberate. Yet it's a great story, and well known, as proved by the many references in Chinese sources. Surely it would not have been ignored by the Mongolian storytellers; surely Genghis would not have disapproved. That leaves only one likely explanation: the author deliberately left it out. His motive? The mixed ethnicity of the Baljunans gives us a probable clue. It looks as if the author, writing for Genghis's family, wished to downplay the role of non-family, non-Mongol members.

From Baljuna, where Genghis and his loyal band regain their strength over the summer of 1203, Genghis sends a long and moving message to Toghril, his old ally, in effect suggesting national unity. It seizes the moral high ground. Khan, my father, he asks in sorrow, why turn against me? Don't you recall how we swore allegiance? Were we not like oxen together on a two-shaft cart, like the wheels on a two-wheeled cart? Did not Yisugei, my father, come to your help? Were you not sworn brothers? And more of the same, all designed to wrack Toghril's soul while Genghis regains his strength and awaits the arrival of reinforcements from his wife's people, the Ongirat, and other local clans.

He was right to wait. In his absence, Toghril's alliance fell apart. Jamukha, always impatient with Toghril's rule, planned his assassination. Toghril discovered the plot. The plotters fled to join the Naimans, a powerful, independent khanate that dominated the far west of present-day Mongolia. Genghis fell upon the hapless Toghril, and after a three-day battle was victorious. Toghril and his son also sought refuge with the Naimans. There Toghril was killed by a guard

---

[1] The incident is analysed in detail by Cleaves in 'The Historicity of the Baljuna Covenant' (see Bibliography).

who refused to believe the refugee was the great khan of the Keraits. His son was killed later in the depths of Central Asia.

Now it was the turn of the Naimans, who were sheltering Jamukha. In mid-May 1204, Genghis began his march up the Kherlen towards the Khentii range, where the Naimans, under the leadership of their chief, Tayang, were camped. By the time they encountered the enemy, an overwhelmingly superior force, the Mongol horses were exhausted. A commander suggested making camp to regain strength, and at the same time scare the opposition by having each man light five fires. It worked. That night Naiman guards, posted on the heights ahead, reported to Tayang that the Mongols 'had more fires than the stars'.

Tayang became twitchy and suggested withdrawal to fight another day. Now for the first time we hear of Tayang's fiery son, Kuchlug, who would have none of it, saying that his father was as useless as a tethered calf or 'a pregnant woman who doesn't go beyond her pissing place'. Driven into a rage, Tayang gave the order to fight.

And now *The Secret History* starts to revel in the coming victory with a poetic flow of metaphors. When Tayang asks why his men are fleeing, Jamukha reminds him of Genghis's 'four hounds', the generals Jebe, Jelme, Subedei and Kublai, who were raised on human flesh. With foreheads of hardened copper and chisels for snouts,

> They advance feeding on dew
> And riding on the wind.

And who is that over there? Tayang asks.

The one whose body is stitched with cast copper and wrought iron? replies Jamukha. That is Genghis, my sworn brother. And see Khasar, Genghis's brother? He eats three-year-old bulls. He can swallow a man whole, quiver and all, without it even touching the sides of his throat. He can shoot straight through ten or twenty people, even if they are on the other side of a mountain.

In short, Tayang was doomed, Genghis victorious, and Kuchlug fled to the west, where he would build a new life for himself and play a significant role in Genghis's future. Jamukha also fled, into the mountains of the far north-west with five other survivors, seeking the help of the Merkits, the people who had captured Börte twenty years before. A final campaign ended with the Merkits' defeat and Jamukha captured, betrayed by companions.

According to *The Secret History*, Genghis executed Jamukha's companions for their treachery: 'How can we let men live who have raised their hands against their rightful lord?' He then gave Jamukha an opportunity to recant, looking for a chance to show mercy. But Jamukha accepts his fate. 'O my sworn friend,' he says,

> I would be a louse in your collar, I would be a thorn in the inner lapel of your coat. Let me die swiftly, let them kill me without shedding blood. When I lie dead, my bones buried in a high place, for ever and ever I will protect you and be a blessing to the offspring of your offspring.

This is *The Secret History*'s spin on events, rounding off a classic tale of two sworn friends who fell out. Jamukha emerges as a man who went astray, but in the end regains the nobility that justifies Genghis's earlier trust. And Genghis is the generous leader, who would never willingly abandon the bonds of blood-brotherhood. Jamukha condemns himself, and is granted a princely – namely, bloodless – death.

Genghis was now absolute master of all the tribes of Mongolia, the man who had 'unified the people of the felt-walled tents'. At a national assembly, a *khuriltai*,[2] he was proclaimed leader of the newly united nation.

Where this happened is, of course, as disputed as everything else to do with Genghis. But one place makes sense, because it is almost exactly where baby Genghis may have come into the world, just

---

[2] The first two syllables, *khural* (with a sound-shift of *i* to *a*), are used today for the Mongolian Parliament.

beside the River Onon, at the junction with its winding tributary, the Khorkh. Now the wooden shacks of Binder ramble across the plain's northern end, but 800 years ago it was a huge open pasture running between river and hills, with Spleen Hillock rising gently from its centre. The place was marked by a wooden pillar by an octogenarian geographer named Bazargur, who had made it his business to commemorate all sites connected with Genghis, and a former prime minister and local businessman had built a fenced area that included a solid, 3-metre stupa with a portrait of Genghis and the self-confident statement: 'In 1206 Genghis Khan convened the Great Meeting here and proclaimed the Mongol nation.' Others had seen, and believed, for there were old joss-sticks in the brazier and little gifts – vodka bottles, small-denomination notes – on the stupa. Who, seeing these memorials, would doubt they were close to the spirit of their hero and the roots of their nation?

This was the moment his loyal companions had been working, fighting and waiting for. Rewards came in plenty, as *The Secret History* records at length, reviewing the adventures and campaigns that had brought them all to this point. Those who stood by him – eighty-eight of them are named – became commanders of one or more 'thousands', making ninety-five 'thousands' in all. Those especially favoured would be forgiven for up to nine crimes. The names mount in a litany of praise. Old companions and their sons as generals, royal aides, quiver-bearers, day-guards and night-guards.

The appointments marked something new in nomadic imperial administrations. In the past, unity had always been undermined by tribal rivalries. Genghis's own childhood had been blighted by them, and his slow rise to power constantly threatened by them. Now came a revolution, with appointments made not on the basis of inherited position within a tribal hierarchy, but of services rendered.

Genghis's new society needed new rules, and new ways of administration. In particular, it needed *written* administration. Genghis had foreseen the need for this as his conquests grew, for one of those captured from the Naiman was a Uighur named Tatar-Tonga, who had been Tayang's chief administrator. Two years before, after the defeat of Tayang, he had been found wandering the battlefield, holding the state seal, looking for his lord and master. The Uighurs, once masters of Mongolia, had been driven out in the ninth century, had settled in what is now Xinjiang, north-western China, and had adopted a script from further west along the Silk Road. Many of their scribes had become, in effect, freelance secretaries. Now Genghis ordered Tatar-Tonga to adapt the script for Mongolian and teach it to the princes.[3]

To oversee the embryonic chancellery, Genghis required someone closer to him than a captured functionary. The choice fell upon a young man called Shigi, who had been seized from the Tatars several years previously and adopted by Genghis's family, either by his mother or his wife, no one knows which. In any event, he was now a trusted family member. 'While I am setting in order the entire nation under the protection of Eternal Heaven, you have become my seeing eyes, my hearing ears,' Genghis told Shigi. 'Divide up the people of the felt-walled tents . . . punish those who deserve to be punished', and record the division of possessions, the laws and the judgements 'on white paper in a blue book'. This would be a permanent record for future generations, and anyone who tried to change it would be punished. Shigi's Blue Book became famous as the 'Great Yasa', or *jasagh* (transliterations vary of the Mongol word for government or legal code, which sounds like *dzassag*). Scholars often refer to this as a grand body of law, a sort of Mongolian Code Napoléon. In fact, no one knows what it was. The book vanished, which is odd if it really was a written code of law. Possibly it was just a collection of off-the-cuff rulings, regulations and decrees – precedents from which laws might have been derived in time, but weren't.[4]

The previous paragraph mentions another novelty, hinting at

---

[3] This script is still in use today in Inner Mongolia, little changed.
[4] David Morgan (in his 'Great Yasa' paper, see Bibliography) points out that Juvaini, the Persian historian who worked for the Mongols a generation after Genghis's death, refers to the contents of the Yasa as *qawā'id*, the plural of *qā'ida*, the word adopted by Osama bin Laden for his organization. It means many things – base, foundation, pedestal, capital, rule, custom, regulation among others, but (Morgan writes) '"law" is not an available option'.

Genghis's growing confidence in his destiny. Traditionally, the Mongols honoured the Blue Heaven. This is the moment when we are told that Genghis is under the protection of *Eternal* Heaven. It seems that the khan and his followers had begun to see faith as justified, dreams becoming reality. A clan's brief success, achieved with the fickle backing of the Blue Heaven, might last for a season; the founding of a nation suggested the support of something rather more enduring; and what could be a better help in achieving empire than an eternal deity?

Genghis's revolution penetrated right the way through society. Out went tribal regiments; in came regiments that owed loyalty to their commanders. True, some regiments remained tribal; but only if loyalty was assured. Switching regiments became a capital offence; and commanders who failed to measure up could be fired. The whole military and social structure was underpinned by Genghis's decision to form his own elite bodyguard of 10,000, with special privileges. This was a masterstroke, for the corps included the sons of the regimental commanders, who had a rank equal to that of their fathers; except that in the event of a dispute, the son would be preferred above the father. Very clever. Before a commander entertained thoughts of disloyalty, he would recall that his son was a hostage to the khan, and that treachery would have to involve the two of them. Personal loyalty and blood ties superseded tribal bonds, weaving a new and enduring social texture, devoted to one purpose: conquest.

And conquest was vital, for this was not a money economy. Troops could not be paid, except in kind. Power itself bought nothing. Once the conquered tribes had been absorbed – the elite killed or ransomed, ordinary men allocated to regiments, young women distributed, the children taken as slaves, the silks, goblets, saddles, bows, horses and herds all shared out – the warriors would look at their leader with new expectations. Old ways had been broken, new ones forged – to be served how, exactly? Only by looking to the ultimate source of wealth: the settled lands to the south, beyond the Gobi.

*

Genghis's strategy brings us to Avraga, the forward base from which he could look south, the place where *The Secret History* would be written in the year or two after his death.[5] The first time I went there, it was nothing but a few enigmatic bumps in an immense landscape of flowing grass. That I learned anything at all about it was the result of a remarkable stroke of luck. On my second visit I arrived with four adventure tourists one evening in the late summer of 2009, to find a new museum, a big fence around the site, and signs of much archaeology.

By chance, our timing was perfect. A group of archaeologists were winding up their day's work, shouldering spades and wheeling barrows towards us. A Japanese man with professorial glasses and a wispy beard shook my hand as if he were Livingstone meeting Stanley, and said, in good English: 'My name is Shiraishi.' Seeing my blank look, he added: 'I am your editor.'

It was an astonishing coincidence. Noriyuki Shiraishi, Professor of Archaeology at Niigata University, had added a long note to the Japanese version of my biography of Genghis, counteracting some of my naïve judgements. I had no idea that he was also head of the archaeological work done at Avraga over the previous nine years. It was he who was responsible for the museum and the protective fence, and he, in all the world, who was the best person to reveal what Avraga was about.

The site, 1,200 by 500 metres, consisted of houses cheek by jowl along a single street, running parallel with a rampart about 250 metres to the north. Street and rampart bracketed the main stone-wall structure, which was some 11 metres across, with a little 3-by-3-metre niche. Not an impressive building by the standards of town-dwellers; but Mongols hardly ever built houses, so this one was of some significance, not because of its size but because of its

---

[5] The name derives from *a'uruq*, meaning a base camp or military household 'where old people, womenfolk, children, servants with baggage and supplies were left when the men went to fight and where they returned' (de Rachewiltz, *Secret History*, p. 499). The word dropped from use, and the name became confused with *avraga*, meaning both 'champion' and something big, thus suitable for Genghis's HQ.

purpose. In the floor of the building were four stones that had been the bases of pillars. These had supported a huge square tent, 17 metres across and probably some 9 metres high, assuming standard proportions. As Shiraishi says in the papers recording his work, Chinese sources mentioned Genghis's 'Great [or Main] Palace-Tent', but no one knew what or where it was. Shiraishi is sure he has found it: 'There is no doubt that Platform No. 1 [the main building] is the remains of this palace' – built (probably, possibly, maybe, perhaps) on Genghis's orders immediately after unification in 1206.

A word about the palace-tent. It is an *ord* in modern Mongolian, and something similar in Turkish. English-speakers should know about this because, by extension, it also means the territory and the people ruled from it. The semi-desert region of Inner Mongolia, once Mongol, now part of China, is called Ordos, the plural of *ord*, after the many palace-tents that used to be there. Spellings varied. Outsiders sometimes put an 'h' at the beginning, giving the English *horde* and equivalents in many other languages. So anyone speaking of barbarian 'hordes' is voicing a direct, if unconscious, linguistic link across Asia and back in time to Genghis.

The discoveries by Shiraishi and his team of Japanese and Mongolian archaeologists have revealed much more about Genghis's palace-tent and its surroundings. The remains are on several levels, the first dating back to the early thirteenth century. This, the original palace-tent, was surrounded by a scattering of offices, houses and a temple or two. Then, after about 1230, came a new palace-tent replacing the first one, built by Genghis's heir, Ogedei, shortly after his enthronement in 1229. Ogedei, following his father's orders, moved 380 kilometres westwards to the new and much larger capital of Karakorum in 1235. His palace there had the same proportions as the one at Avraga and, according to the Chinese official history of the Yuan dynasty, he used the same architect, Liu Ming.

In its day Avraga was a town dedicated to the service of Genghis. The proof? Shiraishi guessed that Genghis would need vast amounts of weapons, and indeed one of Shiraishi's colleagues, Yasuyuki Murakami, found bits of slag on and under the surface scattered over some 10,000 square metres – 'a garbage dump for an iron factory'.

Finds dating from later periods suggest that Avraga remained a religious site, maintained for two centuries or so after Genghis's death to worship the souls of the Mongol khans. In the late thirteenth century, it seems, the site became open pasture. But then a new palace-tent was built, perhaps to act as a shrine for Genghis, as suggested by the discovery of pieces of fine white porcelain bowls 'thought to have been used by people of the emperor's class'. Around 1450 the shrine vanished for good. Avraga's mud-brick walls sank back into the earth, grass grew over its stones, and the town vanished from sight and local memory.

As a result, Shiraishi recalled, something appalling happened. In 2006, locals held their National Day celebrations right on top of it, leaving wheel marks, glass, plastic bottles and the remains of campfires everywhere. Something had to be done, and was. Appeals went to the local government, UNESCO and Japan's Cultural Grasslands Programme. Money flowed, the site was fenced, the museum built, a sign raised to record the groups involved in this 'Project to Protect the Avraga Ruins'.

Work continued. In 2007, Shiraishi's team discovered the remains of five furnaces. Also a solid 5-by-5-metre building with underfloor heating, like the system used in China for *kàngs* (heated communal sleeping-platforms). It was perhaps an inn, where a few could escape the rigours of a winter night. Dating the ash from the stove revealed that the house was in use when Genghis was still a boy, which suggests that he did not choose the site himself, but inherited it or took it over.

When we were there, Shiraishi was supervising the excavation of a building which, he guessed, had been a little temple, with a central area and a little side-chapel. It was a simple structure, floored with clay, not tiles. Shiraishi pointed out some small holes, where long-vanished wooden pillars had been. The stone footings were still there, but Avraga seemed to have lacked stonemasons: the bases were improvised from slabs of undressed rock or small millstones. But Genghis's religion was shamanism, which had no temples. What was this for?

It was maybe Daoist, Shiraishi said, probably built by Jurchens, the people then ruling north China, because the basic unit was a Chinese *chi* (about 0.3 metre, or 12 inches). The whole temple was 30 by 30 *chi*, about 100 square metres – not impressive in the eyes of a Jurchen trader from Beijing, but a surprise in a region of tents and grass.

'Why was it here?'

'For visiting Jurchens, perhaps,' he replied. 'Or a group of Jurchen residents.'

All of this threw a new light on Genghis and his times. He is often seen by his victims as springing from the dark, an unknown barbarian ignorant of the world outside his own, eager only for booty. But here was proof that the pre-imperial Mongols knew their southern neighbours intimately, through trade, architecture, religious practices and diplomacy. Any resident southerners must surely have reacted to Genghis's revolution with a mixture of delight and suspicion: delight in the possibilities for trade presented by a strong, united nation, and suspicion of what the Mongols' new khan intended with all those horses and men and blacksmiths busy forging swords and arrowheads.

But no outsider could possibly have known what Genghis himself did not yet know – that wealth, though vital, was not going to be enough; that conquest would suggest something far grander: the idea that Heaven itself had ordained the spread of Mongol rule way beyond the Gobi's gravelly wastes. In Avraga's palace-tent, Genghis was already planning the first of the campaigns that would, over the next twenty years, re-form most of Asia.

3

TO THE SOUTH

WE NOW FOLLOW GENGHIS'S GAZE SOUTH, ACROSS 600 KILOMETRES OF grassland and Gobi to the broad and silt-laden Yellow River, and then on upriver for another 250 kilometres, to the city of Yinchuan.

Today, Yinchuan, capital of Ningxia province, has a population of 2 million. Hemmed by mountains to the west and the Yellow River to the east, it is surrounded by fields, orchards and a network of ancient canals. Two tall pagodas are reminders that this city was once a centre of Buddhism, with roots going back 1,500 years. Yinchuan lies just one third of the way across present-day China, but in Genghis's day it was the capital of a culture apart, whose enigmatic relics stagger tourists. If you drive for half an hour westwards, hazy mountains harden into a rugged wall of rock: the Helan Shan, or Alashan. In front of them loom odd cone-shaped structures, 30 metres high, that look like the noses of rockets pock-marked by nasty encounters with asteroids. There are nine of them, but at first glance you can see only three or four. The others are swallowed by the space around them, an apron of gravel and soil that runs for 10 kilometres along the lower slopes of the mountains. The cones are the ruined tombs of emperors, destroyed by Genghis.

They and their huge site assert the power and prestige of a culture that for over 200 years dominated an area the size of France and Germany put together.

Why would Genghis cast predatory eyes on these people, rather than on their wealthier neighbours, the Jin, the Mongols' traditional enemy? To understand Genghis's strategy, look at his choices.

China in the early thirteenth century was a land divided.

The central and southern regions had long been under the control of the Song dynasty, which had presided over an artistic and intellectual renaissance. Its southern portion was still in Song hands, but the north – modern China's north-east – had fallen to Jin, the kingdom founded a century before by the Jurchen from Manchuria. Genghis's great-grandfather Kabul and his great-uncle Katula had fought Jin, and it would eventually be Genghis's main target. But Jin was a tough nut. It had forgotten its barbarian origins and ruled its millions of Chinese peasants and its dozens of well-defended cities from behind the formidable walls of the city that is now Beijing.

Next door to the west lay a second 'barbarian' kingdom, the one with the nine cone-shaped tombs, which was far more promising. It is best known by its Chinese name, Western Xia (Xi Xia), to distinguish it from another Xia kingdom that had existed further east in the fifth century.

Here were three powers – Jin, Song and Western Xia – in a precarious balance. In the wings were two other regions, Tibet and Khara Khitai, both too distant to be considered for conquest (yet). Now add in various semi-independent tribes and clans, many bound by the network of trade routes that linked China to Central Asia and ultimately Europe. Imagine the differences of religion – Islam in the west, Buddhism, Confucianism, Nestorian Christianity and shamanism; and of major languages – Chinese, Tibetan, Turkic, Arabic, Tangut. This was the cauldron into which Genghis was about to cast himself and his people, aliens in language, culture and religion. The consequences were utterly unknowable.

Not that Genghis could worry about the long-term consequences. His immediate task was to find the weakest point for an assault that would bring the quickest and most lucrative returns. Which of his two neighbours to attack first? Jin was too strong, with walled cities guarded by mountains. Western Xia was by comparison an open house, guarded by deserts that Mongols could cross in days; its cities were few; its armies smaller. Better to secure victory over the weaker, then turn on the stronger.

Western Xia is hardly known to anyone beyond a few specialists, because Genghis would eventually do his best to wipe state, culture and people from the face of the earth. Its successor cultures, Mongol and Chinese, had no interest in saving its records, understanding its script or restoring its monuments. Only recently has it re-emerged on to the stage from which it was so violently ejected.

You can see the consequences today. The strange, weather-worn cones near Yinchuan, marking the graves of the Western Xia emperors, are patterned by eight centuries of rain and punctuated with holes, which once held rafters. The rafters had supported tiled roofs, over-lapping each other and curving upwards in the style of Chinese pagodas. At the peak of Western Xia's power, in the early thirteenth century, this place would have looked spectacular, with its nine pagodas glowing with colour, in their own courtyards, with attendant 'companion tombs', and all guarded and tended by contingents of troops.

The people of Western Xia referred to themselves by their Tibetan name, the Mi, and to their empire as the Great White and High Nation. But, as usual, the terminology of the dominant culture comes out top. The Chinese called them the Dang Xiang, while in Mongol they became Tangut (Dang plus a Mongolian -*ut* plural). The Tanguts of Western Xia: that's how they are known today. The ancestral Tanguts had migrated from eastern Tibet in the seventh century, settling in the Ordos, the sweep of territory within the bend of the Yellow River. In 1020, they built a new capital near or on present-day Yinchuan, and thrust further westwards, building an empire 1,500 kilometres across and 600 kilometres deep. The spine of their domain was the narrow, pasture-rich route running between the northern foothills of the Tibetan massif and the hideous wastes of the Alashan Desert, which is geographically a southern extension of the

Gobi. These pastures run all the way to Dunhuang and its fourth-century complex of Buddhist caves and temples on the eastern edge of the Takla Makan Desert. This part of the Silk Road, 1,000 kilometres long and in parts a mere 15 kilometres wide, was known as the Hexi Corridor (*He-xi* meaning 'River-West', i.e. west of the Yellow River); today it is more commonly called the Gansu Corridor, after the province of which it is part. A side-road led across the desert north-wards along a river, the Ruo Shui, known to historians as the Etsin, which flows north through desert to a border fortress known as Etsina (to Marco Polo) or Khara Khot ('Black City', its Mongol name).

The true founder of Western Xia, Yuanhao, was an ambitious and talented ruler who – like Genghis 200 years later – saw that the new nation needed effective administration, which demanded written records, using a script which was to be a supreme expression of civilization, yet also unique. His model was Chinese. But to assert Tangut individuality, Yuanhao told his scholars to devise signs that were totally original. Tangut characters *look* Chinese to those who don't read Chinese; but they are not.

It was this script that was used to record laws and translate the texts of Buddhism, which from the start had been not only the official religion, but also an ideology to assert Tangut nationalism. The output was prodigious. A Tangut edition of the 6,000-chapter *Tripitaka*, the corpus of Buddhist canonical writing, required 130,000 printing blocks. This was just one of thousands of works that were bought, stolen or saved – depending on one's point of view – by the British archaeologist Sir Aurel Stein in 1907 and the Russian explorer Petr Kozlov in 1908–9, which gave the West a head start in Tangut studies. It took Chinese scholars decades to catch up.[1] For two centuries, Tangut emperors succeeded each other in ruling what was on the whole a stable, sophisticated, prosperous realm, until it developed a major weakness. Its last great emperor,

[1] The work continues as part of the International Dunhuang Project, which links researchers and institutes in the UK, Germany, France, Russia, Sweden, Japan, Korea and China (www.idp.bl.uk).

Renxiao, died in 1193, leaving inexperienced successors in the hands of scholars and bureaucrats, and defended by an army supported not by herders but by farmers and city-based traders.

Genghis already knew a good deal about Western Xia, because Mongols and Tanguts were as interlocked as related families. The Tanguts had close links with his old ally and enemy, Toghril, the khan of the Keraits. Toghril's brother, Jakha, had been captured and raised by the Tanguts as a boy; later, they even made him a *gambu* (general, or counsellor). One of Jakha's daughters became one of Genghis's daughters-in-law, and in due course the mother of two emperors and a ruler of Persia. As perhaps the greatest woman of her age, she will be the focus of later chapters. And when Toghril's son fled, he did so through Tangut territory, which in 1205 became an excuse for the first Mongol raids. So they knew all about the Tanguts: their sophistication, their scholarship, their deep Buddhist faith, their wealth, the trade caravans that funnelled through the Hexi Corridor and, crucially, their weaknesses.

There was as yet no imperial aim. Genghis needed booty for his troops, with extended payments if possible; Western Xia was the obvious source; which meant turning Western Xia into a tribute-paying vassal state before Jin stepped in. There would have been no thought of occupation, only a vague plan, probably, to use Western Xia as a stepping-stone to seize yet more wealth from Jin.

In spring 1209 came the invasion proper. Genghis marched 500 kilometres south-west, to the Three Beauties ranges, where the Altai Mountains peter out into peaks, valleys and sheltered pastures before merging into gravelly plains. From there, the route led on south another 300 kilometres to the Helan (or Alashan) Mountains, which form the eastern edge of a desert ideal for fast-moving cavalrymen. When the Mongols seized a little fortress-town, the Tanguts sent an urgent request for help to the Jin. Luckily, Jin was in the hands of a new leader, Prince Wei, who complacently told the Tangut ruler: 'It is to our advantage when our enemies attack one another. Wherein lies the danger to us?'

Marching southwards over desert, mountains to the left, the

Mongols came to a fortress defending the only pass leading through the mountains to the Tangut capital, present-day Yinchuan. Today you can drive through this pass in a few minutes. In Genghis's day the track would have been along a dry riverbed in summer, or along the mountain flanks at times of flood, except that the route was blocked by the fortress and an army of perhaps 70,000.

Genghis's only hope was to lure the Tanguts out on to the plain. After a two-month stand-off, the Mongols used their usual tactics, pretending to retreat, but in fact holing up in the foothills, leaving a small contingent to act as bait. When the Tanguts duly attacked, the Mongols leaped on them, and won a stunning victory. The way to Yinchuan was open.

Now they faced a problem. Yinchuan was a well-defended city, and the Mongols were fast-moving nomadic cavalrymen. They had never tried to take a city before. They had no siege bows, catapults, incendiary bombs or flamethrowers. A remedy lay to hand: Yinchuan's ancient canal system, which led water from the Yellow River to irrigate Western Xia's fields. The Mongols broke the dykes and tried to flood the city into surrender. This was not a good idea. Yinchuan's surrounding agricultural land is as flat as Holland. Flood waters spread far, but remain shallow. Buildings stand clear of shallow floods. But tents and horses and carts do not. The Mongols flooded themselves out, and were forced back to higher ground.

The Tangut leaders were also in a quandary. Their enemies were still close by, their crops were ruined, and they were not going to get help from the Jin.

To break the impasse, both gave ground. The Tangut emperor submitted, giving a daughter in marriage to Genghis, and handing over camels, falcons and textiles as tribute. Genghis, certain that he now had a compliant vassal who would supply tribute and troops as required, ordered a withdrawal.

But this was his first international agreement, and it lacked bite. As events would show, he was a victim of his own wishful thinking. The Tanguts assumed the storm had passed, unaware that the real storm had not yet struck.

*

Genghis's power as leader – his charisma – derived from success in war, which in turn derived from Heaven's backing, or rather from his followers' belief that he had Heaven's backing. This presented a problem: he was not the only one with such a claim. The other one was the top shaman, a man named Kököchü, who was so eminent he was known as Teb Tengri, which means something like 'Very Divine' or 'Wholly Heavenly' (no one is sure because the term was unique). Moreover, Genghis owed him support for both personal and political reasons. Kököchü's father had been so close to Genghis's father, Yisugei, that he may have actually married his mother, Hoelun, after Yisugei's death. If so, the shaman was in effect Genghis's stepfather. It was probably Kököchü who gave Genghis his new name or title. Ata-Malik Juvaini, the great thirteenth-century Persian historian of Genghis's age, was in no doubt about his significance and self-importance: 'There arose a man of whom I have heard from trustworthy Mongols that during the severe cold that prevails in those regions he used to walk naked through the desert and the mountains and then to return and say: "God has spoken with me and has said: 'I have given all the face of the earth to Genghis and his children.' " '

The problem was that Genghis himself claimed to have a direct line to Heaven. This did not matter when Kököchü and he were close and in total agreement. But Kököchü became ambitious on his own account. In Juvaini's words, 'There arose in him the desire for sovereignty.'

Genghis would have to assert himself. What drove him to act was a fight between Kököchü and Genghis's brother, Khasar, in which Khasar was beaten up and humiliated. At first Genghis upbraided his brother for his weakness. Then Kököchü raised the stakes by saying that Heaven had told him Khasar would rival Genghis, at which Genghis arrested Khasar, tied him up and started to interrogate him. His mother, Hoelun, was furious, 'so angered that she was unable to contain her fury' – which, as we know from the time Genghis killed Bekter, could be formidable. How could Genghis treat Khasar like this, she raged, he who had been raised on the same milk as Genghis? 'She sat cross-legged, took out both her breasts, laid them over her knees and said, "Have you seen them? They are the breasts that suckled you." ' *The Secret History* quotes Genghis as if he himself is telling the story, emphasizing the authority and wisdom of the women in his life: 'I was afraid of mother getting so angry and really became frightened.'

Eventually, he was reconciled to his brother. But the split seemed to encourage Kököchü to make trouble by enticing some of Genghis's followers. Another of Genghis's brothers, Temüge, was threatened and made to kneel before Kököchü. He reports the incident to Genghis, with dramatic results. Börte sits up in bed, 'covering her breasts with the blanket', and breaks in, weeping: 'What kind of behaviour is this?' Something has to be done, and Genghis tells his brother he can take whatever action he wants.[2]

As it happens, Kököchü is on his way, with his father and six brothers. Temüge briefs three sturdy helpers, who stand outside the tent. When the eight enter, Temüge grabs Kököchü by the collar and challenges him to a wrestling match. Genghis tells them to fight out-side – where, as arranged, the three strong men seize Kököchü, drag him away and break his back. Temüge goes back into the tent and announces the murder in an oddly indirect way: 'He was not willing to wrestle and lay down pretending that he could not get up. Not much of a companion, is he!' But Kököchü's father and six brothers understand. There is almost a riot. Genghis shoulders his way out-side, to the safety of his guards.

Later, he makes arrangements to dispose of the body, which is placed in a tent and simply vanishes. Genghis puts an outrageous spin on these events. Since Kököchü had laid hands on Genghis's brothers and spread baseless slanders, 'he was no longer loved by Heaven, and his life, together with his body, has been taken away'.

Thus ended a conflict between the old shamanist traditions and the new regime. Genghis, as ruthless and devious when necessary as many another dictator, had an old but dangerous family friend murdered, made himself into Heaven's only representative, united

[2] This was a well-known story. Juvaini has similar details. It seems that he and the author of *The Secret History* used the same sources, perhaps written, probably oral.

church and state, and became the unchallenged ruler of his new nation.

With Western Xia as a compliant ally, Genghis could turn to the conquest of Jin. It looked doable. The new Jin emperor, Wei, ruled an insecure state in which his 3 million Jurchen dominated 40 million Chinese peasants made restless by famine and economic collapse. Several top officials had defected to Genghis with valuable information. A border tribe, the Önggüds, who straddled the transition zone between herders and farmers, had offered unimpeded passage to the Mongols. Information on Jin defences also flowed from Muslim merchants, grateful for the security provided by Genghis's expanding empire. You may ask: What of the Great Wall? Yes, there had been a wall, or several walls, built across north China to keep out the 'northern barbarians' from the time of the First Emperor in 210 BC. But the Great Wall as we know it today dates from the fifteenth century. The Mongols faced only several border 'walls', which were nothing but low ridges, easily ridden over.

Still, the attack would not be easy. From a population ten times that of the Mongols, the Jin emperor could command cavalry and infantry numbering several hundred thousand, and his cities were well fortified. Two immense fortresses guarded the approaches to Beijing, which was virtually impregnable to a direct assault.

Genghis's invasion was meticulous in planning, and audacious in execution. In spring 1211, the Mongols gathered in the valleys south of the Khentii and advanced across the Gobi in three parallel columns, well spread in order not to drain the scattered waterholes. This was a huge operation by any standards: imagine something like 100,000 warriors with 300,000 horses, strung out in perhaps 10–20 groups of 5,000–10,000, each with camel-drawn carts, and all linked by fast-moving messengers as the army crossed 800 kilometres of gravel plain. Yet all sources ignore it, quite rightly, because nothing went wrong. The crossing had been done before by both nomadic armies and Chinese, and would be done again.

As the Mongol army spilled into Jin in the summer of 1211, Genghis took the city of Fuchou (today's Zhangbei), where he set up camp to allow the horses to regain their strength. A few kilometres away, the Jin commander, 'an irascible ruffian named Hushahu',[3] was guarding the mouth of the defile known as Yehuling (Wild Fox Ridge), which leads from the high grasslands down to present-day Zhangjiakou. Each seemed to be waiting for the other to move. Hushahu had a chance of launching a surprise attack when the Mongols were busy looting. Instead, perhaps to win time, he sent for a Khitan officer, Ming-an, and gave him a foolish order: 'You have often been sent to the north, you are familiar with Genghis Khan; go and enquire of him why he is warring against us; ask what grudge he bears the Jin, and if he fails to give you a bold answer, upbraid him.' Ming-an promptly defected, with vital information about the disposition of the Jin army. The defile they were holding ended in a pass called Young Badger's Mouth,[4] though the name later dropped from use. Squashed into the pass with no room to manoeuvre, the tight-packed cavalry was overwhelmed by arrows and a Mongol charge. The Jin horsemen turned, and trampled their own infantry. Bodies 'piled like rotten logs', as *The Secret History* says, lay scattered for 30 kilometres along the valley that drops to Zhangjiakou. The Mongols would always consider the Battle of Young Badger's Mouth one of their greatest victories.

Follow-on skirmishes drove the Jin generals fleeing back to Beijing and captured several major cities and fortresses. Beijing held out, isolated, leaving the Mongols free to roam and loot at will. Genghis headed southwards for another 300 kilometres to the Yellow River.

Meanwhile, the western column had secured the land along the Yellow River, while in the east one of his star generals, Jebe, struck 300 kilometres into Manchuria, crossing the frozen Liao River to attack today's Shenyang, the old Manchurian capital of Mukden, Jin's second city after Beijing. It proved impregnable by direct assault, so Jebe did what Mongols often did. He pretended to flee,

---

[3] The words are from Mote, *Imperial China*, p. 244 (see Bibliography).
[4] Huan Er Zui (獾兒嘴). Today the defile and pass are hidden by a new highway, which skirts the twisting old road with tunnels and cuttings.

leaving baggage scattered as if in panic. When Jin scouts confirmed that the Mongols were 150 kilometres away, the delighted citizens started celebrations for the New Year of 1212 by gathering up their unexpected windfall, which lured them ever further from the city. The Mongols sprang: after a non-stop 24-hour ride, they found the city open and the inhabitants partying. Surprise was total. They plucked Shenyang like a ripe plum.

Content with his victories, Genghis withdrew northwards to the borderlands between grass and Gobi. Victory to him and his troops still meant no more than booty, and destruction, and prestige. He was still little more than a gang leader, with no interest in occupation and administration. But he had entered, unawares, upon a new sort of warfare – the taking of cities – which would turn him into another sort of leader altogether.

In the autumn of 1212, the Mongols came back for more loot, and would have driven on to the capital, if Genghis had not been wounded by an arrow and ordered a withdrawal. He returned the following summer, retaking towns along the route, with renewed attacks on the Wild Fox Ridge and its two massive fortresses. Records speak of the ground being strewn with caltrops – devices with four spikes intended to pierce horses' feet – but two of Genghis's greatest generals, Jebe and Subedei, rode along the mountain crests to seize the fort at the far end of the pass. This time, the road to Beijing was open.

Jin was an empire under apocalyptic strains. Thousands of soldiers died in battle, and with the Mongols seizing food wherever they went, civilians starved. Beijing sank into political turmoil. The erratic general Hushahu, a favourite of Emperor Wei, had been pardoned for losing so disastrously at Young Badger's Mouth, and had shown his disdain for the Mongol threat by organizing hunts outside the capital with his own private army. As the Mongols approached, he realized that such panache was likely to prove suicidal. But he had no intention of placing himself in the unreliable hands of his emperor. He staged a coup, slew the 500 soldiers guarding the Forbidden City, murdered the emperor, placed his own uncle on the throne and proclaimed himself regent, celebrating these astonishing acts with a banquet attended by the capital's most famous and beautiful courtesans.

When two months later the Mongol army surrounded the city, Hushahu despatched some 6,000 men to oppose them, threatening death for the commander, Gaoqi, should he fail; which he did. To avoid the fate he knew awaited him, Gaoqi turned assassin. He rode back at full tilt ahead of the bad news, presumably with a small band of men, cornered his commander, and beheaded him. Still carrying the head, Gaoqi ran to the new emperor, Xuanzong, and confessed all. Whether out of relief at his own escape or terror at the gruesome sight, the emperor instantly made Gaoqi vice-commander of the empire.

Not that there was much of an empire. With the emperor pinned in his capital and most towns frozen by fear, Genghis sent off all but a small force to ravage the country and seize cities. This was still a nomad army, without heavy-duty siege gear, but Genghis was learning. Corralling prisoners by the thousand, the Mongols forced them to head assaults. The besieged, often recognizing relatives in the seething masses below their walls, could not bear to attack their own, and capitulated. Thus an army of 100,000, divided into three columns, rode south and west to the Yellow River and eastwards to the Pacific, blotting up towns by the dozen across an area the size of Germany. 'Everywhere north of the Yellow River,' wrote the Chinese biographer of the great Mongol general Mukhali, 'there could be seen dust and smoke, and the sound of drums rose to Heaven.'

But Beijing still held out. A century before, it had been turned into a very tough nut, even for a regular army. Outside the walls were four fortress-villages, each with its own granary and arsenal, each linked to the capital by a tunnel. Three moats fed from Kunming Lake protected the walls themselves, which formed a rectangle some 15 kilometres around and some 15 metres thick at the base. A crenellated parapet rose 12 metres above the ground, with thirteen gates and a guard tower every 15 metres – over 900 of them in all.

Inside these formidable defences, the inhabitants deployed equally formidable weapons. Double- and triple-bow crossbows could fire

3-metre arrows a kilometre. Artillery was in the form of catapults known as traction trebuchets. All of these weapons could be adapted to fire a weird variety of incendiary devices, for these were the early days of gunpowder. Fire-arrows from siege bows and fire-balls from trebuchets were used to set alight scaling ladders and assault towers. Naphtha could be tossed in pots or thrown in bottles, like Molotov cocktails. Another means of defence was to use distilled petroleum, known as Greek fire in the West, to make crude but effective flamethrowers. To take and hold cities, the Mongols would have to capture and master these weapons.

The siege that followed lasted a year, into the spring of 1214. It was a hard winter for the Mongols, who are said to have suffered an epidemic of some kind. But by the spring those within the walls were far worse off. Genghis offered to withdraw in exchange for the right concessions. The emperor agreed to hand over a princess, 500 boys and girls, 3,000 horses, and an astonishing 10,000 bolts of silk (which, if rolled out, would stretch to about 90 kilometres). Promising to retreat in peace, Genghis ordered his booty-laden troops back northwards to the welcoming grasslands.

The emperor had learned a bitter lesson. Beijing, surrounded by devastation, threatened by nomads now familiar with siege warfare, could never again be considered invulnerable. There could be safety only beyond the true geographical frontier between him and the nomads: the Yellow River. He decided to move his capital way south, to the ancient Chinese capital of Kaifeng.

This was an immense undertaking. Sources mention 3,000 camels laden with treasure and 30,000 cartloads of documents and royal possessions, trailing 600 kilometres southwards for two months, all in pursuit of security beyond the Yellow River. It achieved the exact opposite. Some 2,000 of the imperial army were Khitans, from Manchuria, who did not like the idea of moving even further from their ancestral home into the Chinese heartland. Fifty kilometres out of Beijing, they mutinied, galloped back, set up their tents, and sent a message of submission to Genghis.

The Mongol army was camped some 400 kilometres to the north, at a lake in the grasslands of Inner Mongolia. Genghis was aghast at the news. A Chinese source records his words: 'The Jin Emperor mistrusts my word! He has used the peace to deceive me!' It would also have struck him that he had been granted a terrific opportunity: Beijing abandoned by its emperor, and mutinous troops ready to fight for the Mongols. But he had to act instantly. A new capital in Kaifeng could be a base for a future Jin offensive, and much, much harder to subdue. By September, the Mongols were back at the walls of Beijing.

There was no attempt at assault. As autumn turned to winter, the Mongol army just sat tight. In the spring, the emperor in Kaifeng sent two relief columns. The Mongols smashed both, seizing 1,000 cartloads of food. More of Beijing's outlying towns fell into Mongol hands. Beijing began to starve. The living took to eating the dead, leaders argued, the city's civilian commander committed suicide, the military commander sneaked away (he reached Kaifeng, where he was executed for treachery). In June 1215, the leaderless and starving citizens opened the gates in surrender.

Genghis, meanwhile, had decamped to the edge of the grasslands, 150 kilometres north, and was on his way back to the Kherlen, near Avraga. Without his restraining influence, the Mongols ran wild. They ransacked the city and killed thousands. A palace went up in flames and part of the city burned for a month.

A few months later, an ambassador from Genghis's next opponent, the shah of Khwarezm, came to find out if it was really true that such a great and well-defended city had fallen to a mere nomad. The evidence was all too apparent. He reported that the bones of the slaughtered formed mountains, that the soil was greasy with human fat, and that some of his entourage had died from the diseases spread by rotting bodies.

Now the Mongols were masters of all north-east China, reducing the Jin empire by a third, and cutting it in half, leaving two rumps, south of the Yellow River and Manchuria. In the newly conquered territories, the few towns still holding out surrendered. Surviving garrisons revolted against their former masters and declared for the new ones. A million fled south, through devastation and famine. The Jin heartland collapsed into chaos.

*

Genghis was not yet content, for the Jin emperor in Kaifeng refused a final submission. A knock-out blow was needed, actually a double blow – the total reduction of Jin power in Manchuria and a final assault on Kaifeng.

Manchuria was a rural backwater of farmers, herders and hunters, in which the strongest Khitan leader, Liuke, had declared allegiance to Genghis in 1212 and made himself warlord of most of Manchuria, master of 600,000 families. The rest of the region had long sent young men off to the Jin army. Manchuria would be a walkover.

So it proved, when Mukhali and Genghis's brother Khasar swept across all Manchuria in 1214–16. Mukhali was already one of Genghis's greatest generals, having been with him for fifteen years, and he would become the anchorman in the long struggle to subdue north China. A small force raced to the end of the Liaodong peninsula, reaching the Pacific by autumn 1216, leaving another column to pursue several thousand Khitan insurgents across the Yalu River into Korea. A brash Mongol emissary journeyed on to the Korean court in Kaesong, coming away with gifts that included 100,000 sheets of paper: it seems that Genghis wished to keep his newly literate officials well supplied with stationery.

When news of these conquests reached Genghis, he demanded and received 30,000 troops from his new vassal, Western Xia, and despatched a force into the Ordos, heading south along the Yellow River, in a drive to take Kaifeng from the rear. In an immense, year-long campaign, an army of 60,000 advanced 1,000 kilometres against vastly superior forces, through territory bristling with strongholds, to the very outskirts of Kaifeng. They fought half a dozen major battles, most of them in winter, before finally retreating when Jin defences proved too much. The war would go on, though complete victory would take almost twenty years.

It would have come a lot quicker if events far to the west had not claimed Genghis's attention, and opened another chapter in the history of Mongol conquests.

4

THE GATES OF HELL

THE CONQUESTS HAVE ALREADY INVOLVED TWO DISTINCT CULTURES, taking us from the Mongolian grasslands to the urbanized wealth of Western Xia and north China. So far, the effects have been bloody, though not entirely unprecedented. Now the story is about to involve a third culture, Islam, with a human and cultural impact utterly new in world history. Deaths in China must have been in the tens of thousands. Events now about to unfold multiply that figure at least tenfold.

The numbers – almost certainly exaggerated by Islamic writers, but appallingly high nevertheless – suggest the release of some terrible racial or religious hatred. Yet it was not like that; there was no crusading ambition to assert the grand truths of shamanism over other beliefs, no determination to annihilate lesser breeds. Yes, of course, the Mongols would be the masters. But everyone else was welcome to serve, once they acknowledged Mongol superiority. The overriding consideration was conquest, because, for whatever obscure reason, that was the destiny imposed on Genghis by Heaven. Destruction was a matter of strategy. Cities, regions, kingdoms and empires tumbled for no other purpose than to make way for the next victory. Deaths were entirely incidental.

*

The first link in this chain of events had been forged years before when the scion of the Naiman ruling house, Kuchlug, had escaped westwards, at the head of his few surviving troops. He had ended up in another vast realm, obscured from modern eyes by its remoteness in time and space. Yet Kuchlug and his new base play a vital role in this story, because they drew Genghis into the world of Islam.

To understand what happened, we have to go back a century. In 1124, the Jurchen, in establishing the Jin empire, chased out the former rulers, the Khitan. Two hundred top Khitans fled westwards for 2,500 kilometres, beyond the deserts of Xinjiang and over the Tien Shan mountains, far beyond the reach of the new rulers of north China. Here, a decade later, in an anarchic section of Inner Asia inhabited by a mixture of mainly Turkic and Islamic peoples, they carved out a realm of grass, mountain and desert the size of western Europe. It covered present-day Kyrgyzstan, part of present-day western China, southern Kazakhstan and Tadjikistan. The kingdom was known as Khara Khitai – Black Cathay – after its Khitan founders.

When, seventy years later, Kuchlug arrived, he was welcomed by the current ruler, securing his position by marrying his daughter. Then, in the words of the historian Juvaini, he 'leaped forth like an arrow from a strong bow' to seize power. His treachery won him few friends. And he made things worse: at the behest of his new wife, he turned Buddhist and violently anti-Islamic, thus alienating his new subjects. When the imam of Khotan in southern Xinjiang reviled him, Kuchlug had him crucified on the door of his own madrassa. In Genghis's eyes, this unstable fanatic would one day wish to avenge his father and grandfather. For the sake of the future security of the Mongol nation, he had to be eliminated.

Genghis entrusted the task to Jebe. Geography was the greatest challenge: a 2,600-kilometre march, first across Mongolia's grass-lands, a climb over the 3,000-metre Altai Mountains, and then through the rugged heights of the Tien Shan to Issyk Kul, the world's second largest alpine lake. Some 80 kilometres from Issyk Kul's western end lay Kuchlug's capital, Balasagun.

Militarily, success came easily, as Genghis had foreseen. At the Mongols' approach, Kuchlug fled south to the Silk Route emporium of Kashgar, on the western edge of the Takla Makan Desert. When Jebe went in pursuit, he banned pillaging, which meant that Kashgar's Uighur inhabitants were happy to see him. Kuchlug fled again, over the desert towards the Pamirs, perhaps aiming for what is now Pakistan. Being 'chased like a mad dog' by the Mongols, as Juvaini relates, Kuchlug and his followers were cornered by hunters, who handed him over. The Mongols paid the hunters, cut off Kuchlug's head and paraded it through the cities of their new domains.

The Mongol campaign brought them into contact with Kuchlug's Islamic neighbour, a kingdom straddling much of present-day Uzbekistan and Turkmenistan, and overlapping into Iran and Afghanistan. It was known as Khwarezm (as it is in one common transliteration; there are half a dozen), after its core province. This unruly region on Islam's eastern borderlands had been taken from its nominal overlord, the caliph in Baghdad, half a century before. It controlled the great Silk Road emporia – Samarkand, Bukhara, Urgench, Khojend, Merv, Nishapur – as well as the traditional frontier river, the Syrdarya, and the region beyond, which reached for almost 500 barren kilometres over the Kyzyl Kum Desert to the Amudarya (the ancient Oxus). It was a confused and brutal time: Samarkand alone endured seventy attacks by Khara Khitai forces, almost one a year. Under this pressure, in about 1210 Khwarezm's shah, Muhammad, had concluded a brief alliance with Kuchlug, with the result that when Kuchlug seized power in Khara Khitai, Muhammad emerged as 'a second Alexander' in Khwarezm, thus starting a train of events that led to the next stage in Genghis's journey towards a trans-continental empire.

The key to what follows was the character of Muhammad. No one has a good word to say of the man who brought to his people and his religion their greatest disaster. His mother, Terken, who ran her own court, also bears a good deal of the blame. It was perhaps on her initiative that he, a volatile and insecure Turk, had tried to impose his will on his mainly Iranian people by imprisoning several chiefs. Ten thousand died when Muhammad seized Samarkand. According to Juvaini, he was a notorious libertine, 'constantly satisfying his desires in the company of fair songstresses and in continual drinking of purple wine'. This may be a libel, because Juvaini, writing for his Mongol overlords, was eager to explain the Mongol invasion as a punishment for Muslim sins; but there's no doubting Muhammad's failures as a leader.

Genghis had no interest in embroiling himself in this mess, claiming that all he wanted was a trade link. Three merchants from Bukhara had arrived in Mongolia, eager to exploit the route that had suddenly opened up with the Mongol advances into north China. In response, Genghis sent a trade delegation to Muhammad, with gifts including walrus and narwhal tusks, jade, musk and a nugget of Chinese gold as big as a camel's hump. They also bore a message of supposed goodwill, saying Genghis would place Muhammad 'on a level with the dearest of his sons'. Muhammad feared the worst. He had just heard of Genghis's seizure of Beijing, complete with skeletal remains, which stymied his own ambitions to expand into China. Now here was Genghis asserting fatherly dominance, as if he, the shah, was nothing more than a vassal. The leader of the trade delegation, a local Muslim, tried to reassure Muhammad that Genghis's forces were outnumbered by the shah's. But the damage was done.

So when in 1218 Genghis followed up with a huge trade delegation of 100 (as *The Secret History* records), or more (according to other sources), suspicion turned to hostility, mixed perhaps with greed. The delegation – 500 camels carrying gold, silver, beaver skins and sables – chose to head for Otrar, in the south of today's Kazakhstan, because the town was right on the border and because it was rich, having been a thriving link on the east–west trade route later known as the Silk Road for over 1,000 years. It was rich, too, in its own farmland, the fertile flood plain created by the Syrdarya and a tributary, the Arys, as they wound their way from the Tien Shan to the Aral Sea. In a sense, the floods made the city. To rise above the annual flood of meltwater rushing from the Tien Shan, locals had always built themselves mounds of earth to live on.

Known as *tobes*, there were some 200 of them, some big enough only for a family, many village-sized, and a few evolving into towns. The most imposing was Otrar, an artificial plateau with 15-metre bulwarks covered in earth-brick walls, four gates, a moat and a suburban halo, which had a wall of its own.

Some of this is visible today, thanks to forty years of archaeological work,[1] which has revealed layer upon cultural layer, houses upon earthen houses, all the way down, and back, to 100 BC. Now, the rivers have been sucked almost dry by the irrigation of cotton-fields, turning the Aral Sea into salt-puddles,[2] the once-fertile plains into semi-desert and their canals into dried-up ditches. At the time the Mongols arrived, the town had one of the finest libraries in the Muslim world, bath-houses to rival Rome's, 70,000 households, honeycombs of two- and three-room houses, communities of artisans, even a system of public toilets.

Sophisticated, rich – but precariously placed. Once a proudly independent city-state, Otrar had been turned by Muhammad's expansion into a border town between Khwarezm and Khara Khitai eight years previously. Muhammad's governor was the other villain in this story, usually known by his nickname, Inalchuk ('Little Lord').

No sooner had the delegation arrived than there followed the event that, in Juvaini's words, 'laid waste a whole world', and poured forth rivers of blood. Inalchuk arrested the whole delegation and reported what he had done to his boss, the shah. Then, 'without thinking or reflecting, the Sultan at once gave orders for that party of Muslims [Genghis's merchants in Otrar] . . . to be put to death', and their goods to be seized. Inalchuk killed the whole delegation – all of them Muslim except for the leader.

Why? Did Inalchuk think that Genghis's people were all spies? Were the two of them greedy and/or paranoid? No one knows.

At first, Genghis refused to be provoked. He sent three envoys,

[1] Mostly under the direction of Karl Baipakov, Institute of Archaeology, Almaty.
[2] The water level has now stabilized, and may soon be rising, thanks to conservation work.

who gave Muhammad a chance to make amends. Instead, Muhammad killed the envoys, or – according to another account – only the top man, the other two being freed with their beards cut off.

To kill a single envoy would have been enough for war, let alone 100 or more. When the news reached Genghis, Juvaini describes him flying into a whirlwind of rage. There is more than a personal insult involved, more than a diplomatic outrage. 'How can my "golden halter" be broken?' demands Genghis, meaning that Muhammad has broken the bonds of allegiance. It seems that by now, in 1218, he took it for granted that all leaders were bound to acknowledge him as overlord. He 'went alone to the summit of a hill' – surely his sacred mountain, Burkhan Kaldun – 'bared his head, turned his face towards the earth and for three days and nights offered up prayer, saying: "I am not the author of this trouble; grant me strength to exact vengeance."'

This marked a new phase in Genghis's career. Up to this point, tradition had ruled. His predecessors had aspired to unite tribes and invade north China. In Genghis's case this had also meant dealing with Western Xia. But no nomad chief would have dared invade an empire so far from home, let alone one that was the dominant power of Inner Asia. But he had no choice. He had been humiliated and directly challenged. As *The Secret History* says, he had to attack Khwarezm 'to take revenge, to requite the wrong'.

His decision inspired a discussion among his family on the subject of succession. The problem was posed by Yisui, one of his wives, of whom there were now several. In words placed in Yisui's mouth by *The Secret History*,

> When your body, like a great old tree,
> Will fall down,
> To whom will you bequeath your people

Genghis saw the point: 'Yisui's words are more right than right.' He opened the problem to all four of his sons, in public. The mantle might have fallen naturally to Jochi, the eldest; but Jochi could have been fathered by a Merkit when his mother was a captive. The suggestion started a heated argument.

Chaghadai, the second son, burst out: 'How can we let ourselves be ruled by this bastard?'

Jochi seized his brother by the collar. 'I have never been told by my father the khan that I was different from my brothers. How can you discriminate against me? In what skill are you better than I? Only in your obstinacy!'

Boorchu and Mukhali held them apart, while a senior adviser calmed things by recalling the dangers surmounted by Genghis to found the nation: when he had only his spit to drink, he struggled on until the sweat of his brow soaked his feet. And what about their mother? She went hungry for you, and hauled you up by the necks to make you the equal of others.

Chaghadai accepted the rebuke. OK, he would work with Jochi, he said, and suggested the third son, Ogedei, as a compromise. Genghis further defused the tension. Mother Earth was wide and her rivers many; each would get his own portion of the estate. Tolui, the youngest, said he would stand by his elder brother with advice.

What had Ogedei to say? Ogedei knew he was not the obvious choice. But he mumbled, 'I will certainly try according to my ability.' Not much of a speech, but enough. The heir was chosen, the clan and nation still united, with the decision being confirmed in writing. It was a tribute to Genghis's openness – transparency, as we would now call it – his willingness to face a difficult decision, and his growing sophistication in government.

The political foundations were laid for expansion westwards.

Genghis, taking personal charge of a campaign that needed meticulous planning, sought all the help he could get.

Help, in particular, with something no Mongol leader had ever tackled before: the administration of conquered territory. It must already have struck Genghis as foolish to undertake the same conquest over and over again, as he had in China, where some cities had been besieged and taken three times. A few of the Mongol princes had a rudimentary idea of administration, having learned the Uighur script adopted a few years previously. But there was as yet no bureaucracy. He would need one, if he did not wish to repeat the pattern of the Chinese campaigns.

He, or someone, recalled one of the prisoners taken in Beijing three years before, when his adopted relative Shigi had made an inventory of the imperial treasure and any notable captives. Among the Jin officials one had stood out, literally – a very tall young man of twenty-five with a beard reaching to his waist and a magnificent, sonorous voice. He was a Khitan, one of the people who, as the Liao, had once ruled in north-east China and been displaced by the Jin. His name was Chucai, and his family, the Yelu, was one of the most eminent in the Liao empire. His father worked for the Jin, becoming rich and influential. Chucai, born with every advantage, was a brilliant student, poet and, at the time Genghis invaded, a provincial vice-prefect. Recalled to the capital, he served throughout the siege. The sack of Beijing was a horrific experience. To make sense of it, he went into retreat for three years, and emerged strengthened in his belief that truth and virtue were best served by combining the doctrines of the Three Sages, Confucius, Buddha and Laozi (Lao-tsu), the founder of Daoism. Now he found himself summoned to Genghis, who needed someone to set up and run an imperial bureaucracy. It was an honour; and Chucai was expected to show due humility for his release from his previous masters.

In an exchange that became famous, Genghis addressed him: 'The Liao and the Jin have been enemies for generations. I have avenged you.'

Chucai replied calmly: 'My father and grandfather both served the Jin respectfully. How can I, as a subject and a son, be so insincere at heart as to regard my sovereign and my father as enemies?'

Genghis was impressed, and offered this self-possessed and clever young man the job. And Long Beard, as Genghis called him, saw that conquest was proof that Heaven's Mandate had settled upon Genghis. From now on, Chucai would play an important role in moulding the character of the khan and his empire.

It was probably Chucai's influence, therefore, that guided Genghis towards spirituality, or at least a display of it. In 1219, just before the invasion of Khwarezm, Genghis commissioned a stele, whose engraved words embody feelings typical of a Daoist philosopher, as they might be adopted by a nomadic sage:

> Heaven has wearied of the sentiments of arrogance and luxury carried to their extreme in China. As for me, I live in the wild regions of the North, where covetousness cannot arise. I return to simplicity, I turn again to purity, I observe moderation. In the clothes I wear or the meats I eat, I have the same rags and the same food as the cowherd or the groom in the stables. I have for the common people the solicitude I would have for a little child, and the soldiers I treat as my brothers. Present at 100 battles, I have ever ridden personally in the forefront. In the space of seven years I have accomplished a great work, and in the six directions of space all is subject to a single law.

A return to simplicity? Not quite yet. First there was a campaign to be planned and fought.

Genghis sent out requests for troops to his vassals, including Western Xia. He had conquered the region; he had received tribute; its Buddhist king, the Burkhan, the Holy One, had promised aid when necessary. Genghis sent off his request to the king: Remember your promise? 'You said that you would be my right wing.'

What Genghis received, however, was a slap in the face as sharp as the one from Khwarezm's sultan, Muhammad. The slap came not directly from Western Xia's ruler, but from his military commander, or *gambu*, the power behind the throne, Asha. It must have seemed to Asha that he had been presented with a terrific opportunity to regain Western Xia's independence. The Mongols had yet to crush north China, and were now facing another war. Surely no power on earth could fight a war on two such widely separated fronts. Asha pre-empted his king with a contemptuous rejection: 'Since Genghis Khan's forces are incapable of subjugating others, why did he go as far as becoming khan?'

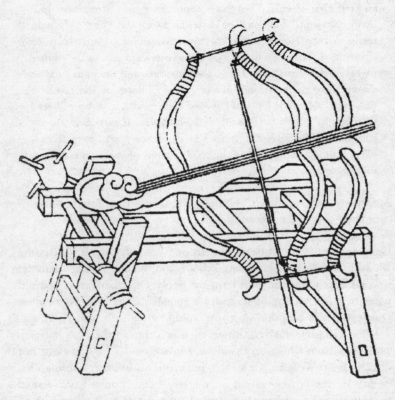

The Chinese triple-bow crossbow, which had to be primed with a two-man winch, was used to defend cities by shooting fire-arrows at siege towers. It was one of the many weapons that fell into the hands of the Mongols after they took Beijing in 1215.

When the reply came, Genghis could do nothing to express his anger as he wished. His first task was to march against Muhammad. But then, 'if I am protected by Eternal Heaven', there would be a reckoning indeed.

In 1219, Genghis led his army westwards, blotting up minor tribes along the way. This was a different sort of army from the one that had swept into Western Xia and northern China. With something like 100,000–150,000 soldiers, each with two or three horses, it retained the fast-moving, hard-riding flexibility of long-established nomadic armies, but with a hard new core. The sieges of Chinese cities had provided the best in siege technology and expertise: battering rams, scaling ladders, four-wheeled mobile shields, trebuchets with fire- and smoke-bombs, flamethrowing tubes, and the huge double- and triple-bowed siege bows, which could fire arrows like small telegraph poles.

There was more. Armies on the move had always lived off the land, by robbery and pillage. They could do nothing much with their victims, except send artisans back to HQ, kill the men, rape the women, enslave the children. They had little interest in prisoners, for prisoners would undermine the very flexibility that made conquest possible. But now prisoners had a triple use: as a slave-labour force of specialist artisans; as soldiers to man the army's non-nomadic core; and as cannon fodder – a particularly nasty expedient in which civilians could be driven ahead of the army to fill in moats with their bodies, take the full force of the defences, and possibly blunt them as defenders held back from killing their own flesh and blood.

This was a juggernaut, which demanded the building of roads and bridges, self-sustaining and, with every city taken, growing in wealth, numbers, weapons and power. It would roll on explosively, driven by the agenda of its supreme commander: to redress wrongs, pay his troops and guarantee security. It was still the agenda of a nomad warrior. He could not have realized that he was embarking on something which would demand a far grander vision.

Against them, when the army arrived at the borders of Khwarezm, was ranged a potentially much greater force. But the sultan was unloved, and could not risk creating a unified command structure under a general who might simply turn against him. So when the Mongols surrounded Otrar, the sultan's forces were scattered among the major cities. All of this Genghis knew from disaffected Muslim officials who came over to the Mongols. He exploited these divisions to the full, offering towns and fortresses the chance to surrender peacefully without any pillaging by the Mongol troops.

Centres of resistance were another matter. Otrar, whose governor had sparked this bloody war, received special attention, in an assault known in Kazakhstan as the Otrar Catastrophe. Genghis wanted the governor taken alive, to ensure him a gruesome death. The siege lasted for five months, until a senior commander tried to flee through a side-gate. His action hastened both his end and the city's. The Mongols forced entry through the same gateway used by the fleeing commander. Their quarry, Inalchuk, barricaded himself in the inner sanctum with several hundred defenders. Since the Mongols had orders to take Inalchuk alive, there followed a slow, methodical attack that lasted another month. Realizing they were doomed, the defenders staged suicide assaults, fifty at a time, until finally Inalchuk and his few surviving bodyguards were trapped on upper floors, where they tore bricks from the walls to throw at their attackers. It ended with Inalchuk being led away in chains to a lingering and painful execution.

From a first look at Otrar today – a rough, bare platform of dusty earth, not a tower remaining, hardly a trace of a wall – you might assume that the Mongols destroyed the place. Not so. Why would they, when it was such an important link on the Silk Road, which was exactly what drew Genghis there in the first place? It was Inalchuk they wanted. With him dead, the town could live, which it did very well for another 500 years, as the archaeological finds reveal: several metres of 'cultural layers', and hundreds of artefacts – jewellery, bronze objects, glassware, ceramics, copper and silver coins – many of which were made in local workshops. It acquired a huge mosque and a 2-hectare suburb devoted to pottery. In brief, it became one of the major centres from which sprang modern Kazakh culture. What destroyed Otrar had nothing to do with Genghis. The region fell to non-Genghisid Mongols from western Mongolia in the first half of the eighteenth century, an invasion that cut the trade routes and killed many of the Silk Road cities. The people left. Wind, rain, snow and frost turned Otrar into the wreck it is today.

Meanwhile, Genghis had divided his army, sending Jochi northwards to sweep round in a vast pincer movement that would eventually snip off all Khwarezm's northern regions. During January 1220, Genghis left a second force to mop up Otrar, while he himself led the other pincer-arm straight across the Kyzyl Kum Desert – a mere 450 kilometres of bitter, sand-and-tussock wilderness – towards Bukhara.

As the Mongol army approached Bukhara in February or March 1220, a 20,000-strong garrison made a pre-emptive attack and was overwhelmed on the banks of the Amu Darya. The remaining troops made a hasty retreat into the citadel, the Ark, while the townspeople, unwilling to be killed for the sake of a sultan they despised, opened the gates. Genghis rode in, through alleys lined with the wooden houses of the common people, past palaces of baked-earth brick, into the inner city, the Shahristan, and to the city's largest building, its mosque; thus finding himself in the heart of a culture rich in ways he was just beginning to appreciate.

The civilization that lay at his feet was a glory comparable to China's, though a newcomer by comparison. It had been founded over 500 years before, when Arabs, drawing inspiration from Islam's founder, Mohammed, swept outwards over Persia, Syria, Iraq, Egypt, North Africa, Central Asia, even across the Straits of Gibraltar, until Arab armies briefly linked the Pyrenees and Kashgar in western China. For a while, this empire was unified by its new religion and Islam's holy book, the Koran, as well as by a second doctrinal source, the *sunnah*, the deeds and sayings of both the Prophet and his successors.

But ruling an empire was very different from building it. Territories and sects took wealth and power for themselves. The Shi'ites claimed a right to rule based on 'Shi'at Ali', the Party of Ali,

Mohammed's son-in-law. Another faction, favouring the claims of Mohammed's uncle, Abbas, arose on the empire's fringes, notably in Iraq. Under the Abbasids, the empire's centre of gravity jumped again, eastwards this time, to Baghdad. By 1000 the Islamic world, created as one imperial river by the Arabs, had divided into a delta of five major streams and dozens of minor ones. At the imperial heart, local rulers turned the Abbasid domains into a shifting kaleidoscope of petty dynasts. But unity of a sort endured. All Islam worshipped the same god, honoured the same prophet, shared Arabic as a lingua franca, shared trade, inherited the same astonishingly rich intellectual mantle.

Fuelled by staggering wealth from its conquests, medieval Islam hungered for learning and inspired brilliant scholarship (the idea that Europe would ever amount to anything would have struck Islamic scholars as bizarre). Paper displaced papyrus, bookshops thrived, libraries graced the homes of the rich. Since Arabic was the language of divine revelation, the written word was venerated and calligraphy became an art form. Medieval Islam, assured of its superiority, was innovative, curious and surprisingly tolerant. The Arabs, looking back to the Greeks for the foundations of science and philosophy, translated Greek classics en masse. Many other languages and creeds – Persian, Sanskrit and Syriac, Christianity, Judaism and Zoroastrianism – also formed part of this rich amalgam.

The arts flourished. Urbanized literati patronized the ornate and elegant creations of poets. Though Islam discouraged (and later banned) human likenesses in art, there was nothing to inhibit design and architecture. Wonderful domed mosques arose, pre-dating Italian Renaissance domes by centuries. Potters, though failing to match Chinese porcelain, created lustrous, beautifully decorated glazes. Stuccoed and frescoed palaces set an ornate style emulated throughout Islam.

Science, too, blossomed. Arabic numerals, derived from Indian ones, provided a far more powerful mathematical tool than any previous system, as Europe later discovered. Though Arab scientists remained convinced that gold could be produced by the transformation of metals, their rigorous search for the 'philosopher's stone' that would cause this to happen created the bridge between alchemy (*al-kimiya*, 'transmutation') and modern chemistry. Muslim travellers wrote reports of China, Europe and much of Africa. European languages, enriched by translations from Arabic into Latin, still contain many other tributes to Arab scientific predominance: zero, algebra, star names (such as Betelgeuse), zenith, nadir, azimuth.

Among the great centres, Baghdad was the greatest. Straddling the Tigris, it was planned as a perfect circle: a triple rampart guarded by 360 towers. The Round City, as it was known, became a magnet for traders, scholars and artists from as far afield as Spain and northern India, growing to become one of the largest cities in the world, equalling Constantinople – about the same size as Paris at the end of the nineteenth century – with wealth to match. Porcelain came from China; silk, musk and ivory from east Africa; spices and pearls from Malaya; Russian slaves, wax and furs.

For four centuries the ancient oasis cities of Samarkand, Bukhara, Merv and Gurganj, the eastern outposts of Islam, were worthy if lesser counterparts to Baghdad. The four cities were all on rivers running from the Pamirs into the wastes of the Kyzyl Kum, all sustained by intricate canal systems and underground channels (*qanat*), all walled against enemies and the encroaching sand. They had long been the rich bulwarks of the provinces of Khurasan and Transoxiana (the land beyond the River Oxus, today's Amu Darya). All were trade emporia linking east and west. Watermelons packed in snow were couriered to Baghdad. Paper from Samarkand was in demand all over the Muslim world. Caravans the size of small armies ranged back and forth to eastern Europe.

Bukhara, Khwarezm's capital, with a population of 300,000, almost rivalled Baghdad itself. Its scholars and poets, writing in both Arabic and Persian, made it the 'dome of Islam in the east', in a common epithet. Its royal library, with 45,000 volumes, had a suite of rooms each devoted to a different discipline. Perhaps the greatest of the great scholars was the philosopher-physician ibn-Sina, known in Europe by the Spanish version of his name, Avicenna (980–1037), who was born not far from the spot where Genghis now stood, in front of the town's mosque. He poured out over 200 books, most famously his medical encyclopedia, *Canons of Medicine*, which when translated into Latin became Europe's pre-eminent medical textbook for five centuries.

All of this came briefly under threat when the Turks arrived, part of a westward drift of Turkish tribes that had been going on for centuries. But Islamic civilization endured because, as they settled, the Turks converted to Sunni Islam, and acquired Muslim names and titles. In the early thirteenth century Khwarezm, under its uninspiring leadership, had inherited these religious, artistic and intellectual traditions, of which Genghis knew little; and its wealth, of which he had heard much.

Juvaini records what happened next in vivid detail. Genghis asks if the mosque is the palace. No, he is told, it is the house of God. Dismounting, he goes to the pulpit and climbs two or three steps, and exclaims infamous words: 'The countryside is empty of fodder; fill our horses' bellies.'

While the horrified imams and other notables held the Mongols' horses, troops emptied grain stores, tossing Korans from their wooden cases to make feeding troughs.

After a couple of hours, the contingents began to return to their camps outside the walls to prepare for the assault on the citadel; the Korans were torn and trampled beneath the horses' hooves. Some historians have seen this as deliberate desecration, inspired by Genghis himself. But that doesn't fit. He had already humbled Buddhists and Confucians. Now it was the turn of Muslims. But there was no ideology at work. Juvaini himself makes no judgement on the trampled Korans. It was just that Genghis and his unheeding troops focused on the practical concerns of nomads and warriors. He wasn't against Islam. It was just that he didn't care about it one way or the other.

Yet there was a lesson in this casual exercise of dominance, and Genghis saw it instantly. Here was yet more evidence that he was right to believe in Heaven's backing, and he was keen that his

BECOMING GENGHIS

Blue Lake, one of Genghis's family camp-sites, is widely accepted as the spot where Genghis received his title in 1189.

Above: *A new plaque commemorates the occasion. Seen here with Black Heart mountain behind, it is flanked by totemic portraits of later khans.*

Below: *Blue Lake seen from Black Heart mountain.*

'All of them having agreed among themselves, they said to Temujin, "We shall make you khan . . . If we violate your counsel, cast us out into the wilderness!" In this way they swore and made Temujin khan, naming him Genghis Khan.' – adapted from *The Secret History*.

Conquest

Today's reminders of Genghis's early conquests include the tombs of the Western Xia emperors outside Yinchuan; the ruins of Otrar in Kazakhstan, the entry point into the world of Islam; the sand-blasted remnants of old Merv; and a few pre-conquest buildings that survived the onslaught.

The Western Xia imperial tombs once had exotic tiled roofs, until stripped by the Mongols in 1211.

*Today's Otrar (**right and below**), though long abandoned, preserves its old shape – a mound that once stood clear of its surrounding flood plain. In Genghis's day, it was a thriving city. Its steam-baths (**below right**) had a sophisticated system of under-floor heating. Sources spoke of total destruction, but in fact Otrar kept on thriving for another 400 years.*

Above: *The Great Kyz Kala in Merv, once one of Islam's greatest cities, was already centuries old when the Mongols destroyed it. Its name means Girls' Castle, because (according to legend) 40 girls saw the destruction and committed suicide by jumping from the roof. The building's organ-pipe structure is still unexplained.*

Right: *The mausoleum of the dynastic founder Ismail Samani, in Bukhara, is a 10th-century jewel of Islamic architecture. It is one of the few buildings that existed when Genghis invaded in 1219–20. Tradition claims it survived because it was buried in sand.*

Below: *In a Muslim illustration, Genghis delivers a famous speech to Bukhara's leaders, proclaiming that they must be sinful, for otherwise Heaven would not have allowed him to defeat them.*

A SECRET DEATH, A SECRET BURIAL

Genghis's illness in August 1227 came just when he was on the verge of defeating Western Xia. It had to remain a secret. Possibly he was taken to a hidden valley in the Liupan mountains, where he died. His body was then carried to his homeland in the Khentii mountains and given a secret burial. It is widely believed, without evidence, that his grave is on the mountain known as Khentii Khan, which may or may not be the sacred mountain of Burkhan Khaldun, much mentioned in *The Secret History*.

Above: *The valley in the Liupan, which is rich in medicinal plants, holds an abandoned village that is still used seasonally by locals. They gather plants that may have been used in an attempt to cure the ailing Genghis.*

Below: *In a Muslim painting, mourners gather round Genghis's coffin.*

Above: *Khentii Khan, widely thought to be Burkhan Khaldun, is a bare summit that attracts many pilgrims.*

Below: *On top, scores of small shrines encircle a large one above which waves Genghis's horse-tail standard. Pilgrims honour Genghis here, with observances that owe much to Buddhism and shamanism, but there is no firm evidence that he is buried on the mountain – at least, not yet.*

Above: *The new front of Mongolia's parliament has him as its enthroned guardian.*

IN MEMORIAM

Across Mongolian lands past and present, Genghis is recalled in folklore, religion, institutions, objects and memorials. In Mongolia, he is the nation's founder. Chinese revere him as the First Progenitor of the Yuan Dynasty. Many worship his spirit, praying to him for protection and guidance.

Above: *In the Chinese town of Edsen Khoroo – the 'Lord's Enclosure' – in Inner Mongolia, this 1950s temple, the so-called Mausoleum of Genghis Khan, is home to a cult that worships Genghis's spirit with pseudo-Buddhist rituals.*

Above: *A modern statue of Genghis dominates the Mausoleum's entrance, backed by a map of the empire.*

Above: *In a new tourist attraction near Holingol, in Inner Mongolia, now part of China, Genghis looms over a Mongol army. In China, he is not so much a conqueror as a Chinese emperor, and a symbol of Chinese unity.*

Near the Mongol capital, Ulaanbaatar, Genghis towers 40 metres over his home pastures in the form of the world's biggest equestrian statue – further proof of his heroic stature.

CONQUERING ISLAM

In this Muslim view, Mongols gather to assault a moated city. Note the powerful recurved bows possessed by both sides. Well-dressed leaders seem to be making an escape across the moat. Mongols beat a war-drum (bottom right) and a counterweight trebuchet – a novelty taken over from Muslim armies – stands ready to bombard walls, its sling dangling.

enemies should understand, and comply. On his departure, he went into the *musalla*, a courtyard for prayers during festivals held outside the city walls. Here he decided to give a speech to a carefully selected audience.[3] First, he told the assembled citizens to select the wealthiest and most eminent among them, and 280 men gathered inside the *musalla*'s simple walls. Juvaini is explicit about the number: 190 were residents, 90 merchants from other cities. Genghis mounted the pulpit and gave them his explanation for his rise and their fall:

> O people, know that you have committed great sins, and that the great ones among you have committed these sins. If you ask me what proof I have for these words, I say it is because I am the punishment of God. If you had not committed great sins, God would not have sent a punishment like me upon you.

These are famous words, often repeated, widely accepted as true. But are they? Juvaini's agenda was to please his Mongol masters and justify their success by emphasizing the sins of the Muslims. As the eminent Mongolian historian Shagdaryn Bira puts it, 'Juvaini finds in Genghis Khan and his deeds . . . a genuine confirmation of the prophecies of almighty Allah, who, as he writes, once said, "Those are my horsemen; through them shall I avenge me on those who rebelled against me." ' Bira concludes that for Juvaini 'The guilty parties were not the initiators of aggression, but its victims.'[4]

For the next few days, with the sultan's soldiers and their families penned in the citadel and the townspeople cowed in their houses, the rich and their escorts filed out of the city to Genghis's tent, where they handed over their wealth – cash, jewellery, clothing, fabrics.

Two matters remained: the capture of the citadel and the disposal of the population. First, the Ark, which the soldiers were using as a base for night attacks. To clear the ground for the assault, the

---

[3] Many writers have transposed the event to the mosque, perhaps because it adds to the drama.
[4] *Mongolian Historical Writing*, pp. 87–8 (see Bibliography).

surrounding wooden houses were burned. Now the catapults and great siege bows could be wheeled into position. Below the walls, locals were driven forward beneath bombardments of flaming naphtha to fill in the moat. For days the battle raged, until the Ark was battered and burned into submission, and its defenders lay dead, killed in action or executed, including all males 'who stood higher than the butt of a whip'. The surviving citizens were herded together to be distributed, the young men into military service, women into slavery with their children, the blacksmiths, carpenters and gold-workers to teams of Mongol artisans.

Then the Mongol juggernaut rolled on eastwards towards Samarkand, the new capital. It was defended by between 40,000 and 110,000 troops (the sources vary hugely) sheltering inside a moat, and city walls, and a citadel, all hastily strengthened in the weeks since the siege of Otrar began. The defences included a brigade of twenty elephants, presumably brought by some enter-prising merchant from India. Driving crowds of prisoners, the Mongols set up camp right around the town. In one engagement, the defenders sent out their elephants, which panicked, turned and trampled their own men before escaping on to the open plain. Again, it was Muhammad's hopeless leadership that did for the city. He fled, urging everyone along his route to get out, because resistance was useless. The merchant princes and clerics of Samarkand, unprepared to risk death for such a man, sued for peace and received similar treatment to the inhabitants of Bukhara, with Mongol commanders and their families taking their pick of possessions, women and artisans.

Khwarezm's *coup de grâce* would, of course, include the capture or death of the fleeing Muhammad, a task given to Jebe and Subedei, who hounded him across present-day Uzbekistan, Turkmenistan and Iran. Desperately searching for a place of safety, with the Mongols one day's gallop behind him, he arrived at the shores of the Caspian, where local emirs advised him to hole up on a small island. Leaving his treasures to be seized, he and a small retinue rowed to the island, where he died of shock and despair. His dreadful mother had followed in his footsteps, ending up in a fortress just south of the Caspian, to be starved out by her pursuers and carted off to many years of abysmal captivity in Mongolia.

Meanwhile, the Mongol pincers closed on the remaining great city, Gurganj, or Urgench as it later became (and still is). From the north, in late 1220, came Genghis's son Jochi, now conqueror of half a dozen lesser towns. From the south-east came Jochi's brothers Chaghadai and Ogedei, reinforced by Boorchu with Genghis's personal corps. Together, there could have been 100,000; not enough, however, to cow the inhabitants, who settled in for a battle that lasted five months. This was the Mongols' hardest fight. Here, on the flood plain of the Amu Darya, there were no stones for the catapults, so the Mongols logged mulberry trees to make ammunition. Prisoners, as usual, were forced to fill in the moats and then undermine the walls. With the walls down, the Mongols had to fight for the city street by street, razing houses as they went by lobbing flaming naphtha into them. When this proved too slow, they tried to flood the city by diverting the river, an attempt that ended in disaster when the locals surprised and killed 3,000 Mongols working on the dam. By the time victory came in early 1221, the invaders were in no mood for mercy. Citizens with any skill – 100,000 of them – were led away as captives, the rest slaughtered. Juvaini speaks of 50,000 soldiers killing twenty-four men each. That makes 1.2 million.

Finally, with the whole empire almost his, Genghis designated Tolui, his youngest son, to mop up in the western regions, beyond the Amu Darya. It took him just three months to deal with the three main cities of Merv, Nishapur and Herat. Nishapur fell in April, its people killed, the town razed and ploughed over. Herat wisely surrendered, and its inhabitants were spared, except for its 12,000-strong garrison. It is Merv that deserves attention.

In the early thirteenth century, this oasis city was the pearl of Central Asia, a city of mosques and mansions, of walls within walls, of mud-brick suburbs covering 100 square kilometres, all sustained by cool water flowing through tunnels from a dam across the River Murgab. Its ten libraries contained 150,000 volumes, the greatest collection in Central Asia. Today, Old Merv is a shadow. If you stand on one of the little mounds near its centre, you are surrounded by dusty ridges and mounds of rubble by the acre. The only resurrection here occurred 20 miles away to the west, where new Merv – Mary – casts its industrial pall into the sky. Old Merv is the very image of desolation.

Much of this is down to wind and rain, but the process started in January 1221, when the Mongols arrived outside the city walls. It was the city's commander, a puffed-up aristocrat named Mujir al-Mulk, who condemned it. When 800 Mongols probed Merv's defences, they were chased off, but sixty of them were captured and executed, which, when Genghis and Tolui heard of it, ensured a terrible fate.

The army was not large, some 7,000 men, each with his bow, arrows and knife, each in his toughened leather armour, each with several remounts. As often, they were vastly outnumbered. They faced an army of 12,000, and a city whose normal population was about 70,000 swollen to over ten times that figure by refugees from the surrounding villages. They all knew their fate. They bolted the doors and waited, hypnotized by fear.

For six days, the Mongol commander patrolled the walls. Seeing no alternative, Mujir al-Mulk sued for peace. The Mongols demanded 200 of the wealthiest and most influential citizens, who were duly delivered and interrogated about their wealth. Then the Mongols entered the city, unopposed, set upon vengeance. For four days, they drove the docile crowds out on to the plain, taking care to separate out 400 craftsmen and a crowd of children to act as slaves.

Then the killing started. The place was ransacked, the buildings mined, the books burned or buried. Merv died in days, and lost almost everything and almost everyone. As Juvaini records, the Mongols ordered that, apart from the 400 captured artisans, 'the whole population, including the women and children should be killed, and no one, whether man or woman be spared. The people of Merv were then distributed among the soldiers and levies and, in short, to each man was allotted the execution of three or four hundred persons.'

After the Mongols departed came the reckoning, conducted by an eminent cleric. 'He now together with some other persons passed 13 days and nights in counting the people slain within the town. Taking into account only those that were plain to see and leaving aside those that had been killed in holes and cavities and in the villages and deserts, they arrived at a figure of more than one million three hundred thousand.'

One million three hundred thousand? In addition to the 1.2 million supposedly killed in Urgench? It sounds simply incredible. But we know from the last century's horrors that mass slaughter comes easily to those with the will, leadership and technology. In the Armenian massacres of 1915, Turks killed 60 per cent of the Armenian population (1.4 million out of 2.1 million); the Holocaust saw 6 million slain; in the Khmer Rouge atrocities in Cambodia in the mid-1970s, 1.7 million (out of about 8 million) died; 800,000 were killed in the Rwandan genocide of 1994 (out of a total population of 5.8 million).

Juvaini's figure actually understates: 7,000 x 300 makes 2,100,000. So 1.3 million is more than possible, and in far less time than in any of the foregoing examples. The Rwandan genocide took just three months, which UN Ambassador Samantha Power called 'the most rapid genocide the world has ever known'.[5] But for a Mongol, an unresisting prisoner would have been as easy to despatch as a sheep, and had far less value. It takes only seconds to slit a throat. For 7,000 men, the slaughter of a million would have been an easy two hours' work.

This was undoubtedly a holocaust on an unprecedented scale. Technically, it was possible for the Mongols to have killed many millions in the two-year course of the invasion. Gibbon concludes, naming French sources:[6] 'The exact account which was taken of the slain amounted to 4,347,000.'

But are these figures accurate?

It's instructive to look at the fate of Merv as recorded by Juvaini after the massacre. One million three hundred thousand was –

[5] *New York Review of Books*, 6 January 2003.
[6] Pétit de la Croix, *Vie de Gengiscan*, and Antoine Gaubil, *Histoire de Gentchiscan*.

supposedly – everyone. That was in February 1221. Yet in November of the same year, rumours of resistance sparked a rebellion. The Mongol commander, Barmas, ordered the artisans and skilled workers into a camp outside the walls, tried to summon the notables, failed, 'slew numbers of people whom he found at the gate', and took many more off to Bukhara. Rebels and pro-Mongol forces struggled for dominance. When one rebel came, 'the common people revolted and went over to him', and he in his turn undertook agricultural schemes and dam-building. Shigi himself arrived to quell the revolt, for 'strangers from all parts, attracted by its abundance of wealth, had risen from their corners and turned their faces towards Merv', joined by the townspeople. The new siege ended: 'putting camel-halters on believers [the Mongols] led them off in strings of ten and twenty and cast them into a trough of blood [i.e. executed them]; in this way they martyred 100,000 persons'. A local governor had the sneaky idea of calling survivors to prayer, 'and all that came out of the holes, were seized, imprisoned, being finally cast down from the roof. In this manner many more people perished' until 'in the whole town there remained not four persons alive'. Rebellion followed massacre, massacre followed rebellion, with always more people to kill, always an economy worth robbing.

How to resolve these discrepancies? There was no census, and all numbers are little more than guesses. But here's a thought. In the early twentieth century the area covered by Khwarezm – roughly Uzbekistan, Turkmenistan, eastern Iran and western Afghanistan – held about 3 million people in all, against a current population of the whole region of about 30 million. So if Juvaini is correct, assuming numbers were then much the same as they were a century ago, the Mongols killed *the whole population* of their new domain.

But obviously they didn't. Even in the most extreme cases, the cities went on operating, with rebellions crushed, armies raised, taxes paid and reconstruction undertaken. So the assumptions must be wrong. More work is needed. Perhaps all we can do is assume a higher level of population and a lower level of death – something like 25 per cent of 5 million, a level that would allow a crushed and brutalized society to continue life, of a sort, and recover with the passing of the years.

That still leaves 1.25 million deaths in two years.

Which is still one of the biggest mass killings in absolute terms in history.

That suggests a comparison with the Holocaust itself, for there are some terrible similarities in the attitude of Tolui's Mongols and the Nazi perpetrators of the Final Solution. The Mongols were, one and all, master-slaughterers, of sheep, of people, as proficient as those managing gas chambers and ovens. But the comparison is not exact. The Holocaust was the consequence of state policy, carried through by thousands over several years, with no purpose other than to fulfil Hitler's anti-Semitic obsession. The Khwarezmian massacres were all one-off applications of a decision to use terror for strategic purposes; not genocide, the killing of a people, but the killing of towns – a tactic that deserves its own term: urbicide. It wasn't personal or obsessive. It was dispassionate, cold-blooded murder, with one purpose: to win as quickly and as cheaply as possible.

That was not quite the end. Muhammad's son, Jalal ad-Din, was very different from his father. He rallied the surviving forces and retreated southwards, into present-day Afghanistan, pursued by Genghis. At Parvan, just north of Kabul, he inflicted the first defeat the Mongols had suffered in this campaign. (The Mongol general, by the way, was Genghis's adopted son and possible author of *The Secret History*, Shigi. Genghis was understanding. Shigi had never experienced fate's cruel knocks, he said. This was a salutary lesson for him.) Jalal, trying to preserve a core of resistance, fought on, even as he retreated another 400 kilometres, through the Hindu Kush and down via the Khyber Pass to northern India's stifling plains, until he was trapped between the Indus and the advancing Mongols. It was the end for his army, but not for Jalal, who forced his horse into the water and reached safety on the far bank. Marvelling at his courage, Genghis let him go. Jalal lived to fight again, though to no great effect, writing himself into legend as a hero. Rumours of him continued for years. No one knows how he died.

Genghis did not follow up his victory by advancing into India. He had more immediate claims on his attention: Western Xia, the rebellious vassals who had dared defy him before the campaign began. But first he took time to give further thought to his destiny.

5

THE GREAT RAID

AT THE FAR WESTERN END OF THE MONGOL ADVANCE, EXTRAORDINARY events had been unfolding which demand that we wind the clock back six months, to the spring of 1221. With the Khwarezmian empire almost conquered, Subedei, Jebe and their victorious troops on the shores of the Caspian stared around for some new challenge. What and who lay beyond? Whatever and whoever, they were all part of Genghis's 'golden halter' and should be informed of their duties: immediate submission and the rendering of tribute. Genghis agreed. He himself was just off to chase Jalal ad-Din southwards, and Tolui was about to give Merv his close attention. Genghis could spare Subedei for a year or two. No one was better qualified than the forty-five-year-old veteran of China, Manchuria, Khara Khitai and Khwarezm. He and Jebe could meet up with Jochi, and the three of them could ride around the Caspian and see what they could pick up in vassals, loot and information.

Thus was born one of the most astonishing adventures in military history – a 7,500-kilometre gallop through southern Russia which for the first time brought the Mongols into contact with mainstream Christianity.

*

The first kingdom in the line of march was Georgia, Christian for almost 1,000 years, independent for 100. It was at this moment at the height of its power and prestige, thanks to the country's heroine-queen, Tamara. Georgians look back to Tamara's reign (1184–1213) as a Golden Age, a renaissance of literature, architecture, scholarship and art, funded by trade linking Europe, Russia and Khwarezm.

In fact, it was in that very year, 1221, that Christian Europe had its first rumour of what was happening in Central Asia. Christianity needed help. For the past three years, the French and German armies of the Fifth Crusade had been trying to conquer Egypt and had been cut to pieces by the Saracens. The Pope had turned to the Georgians, while other Christian leaders looked further east, from which, as if by a miracle, help was apparently on its way in the form of King David of India, the grandson of that legendary Christian king Prester John, a name he might also have taken for himself. David/Prester John, a Nestorian Christian, had already allegedly defeated the hordes of Islam and was on his way to rescue Christian Europe. This nonsense conflated several facts: there had been a Nestorian king (Toghril); and there *had* been victories over Islamic powers (by Genghis).

Then came confusing and contradictory news from Georgia. The Mongols were first believed to be of Christian origin, because their falcon flag was mistaken for a cross. Disillusion followed swiftly. Random as a whirlwind, the Mongols rode almost to Tbilisi, cut the flower of Georgian knighthood to bits, vanished back briefly into northern Iran, swung north again, shattered the Georgian army for a second time, killing the king, Giorgi the Resplendent, and then moved on, through the Caucasus, leaving the Georgians wondering why they had been spared a further onslaught. Giorgi's heir, his sister Rusudan, wrote a stunned apology to the Pope. 'A savage people of Tartars, hellish of aspect, as voracious as wolves, have invaded my country,' she wrote. 'Alas, we are no longer in a position to take up the Cross.'

On the lowlands north of the Caucasus, in present-day Chechnya, the Mongols came up against another, greater enemy. Though they had no political unity, these nomadic Turkish tribes – known to the Russians as Polovtsy, to Turks as Kipchaks, and to Europeans as Kumans, all with various spellings – dominated the grasslands north of the Black Sea, across the Don, to the borderlands of the Russian state and its capital, Kiev. The Polovtsy were more than a match for the Mongols, with a flexible mix of heavy-duty war machines and horse-archers. Besides, they were on their home ground and had more warriors. Jebe and Subedei turned to duplicity. They sent an envoy to the Polovtsy with herds laden with treasures picked up in Georgia. The Polovtsy departed with their windfall overnight. The Mongols, unburdened by carts, treasure or war machines, caught up with the laden Polovtsy, defeated them, and snatched their treasures back again. The survivors fled on into Russia, leaving the Mongols in charge of the steppe north of the Crimea.

Now Jebe and Subedei divided their forces. While Jebe secured a new base on the banks of the Dnieper – probing Russia, interrogating prisoners, gaining information of all lands further west – Subedei headed south into the Crimea, where, for the first time, Mongols met Europeans. These Europeans were from an empire of a different sort, the merchant empire of Venice. Their enclave, which spanned the entry to the Sea of Azov, was one of two in the Crimea, with two Genoese outposts nearby. The Venetian merchantmen at once saw the potential of the new arrivals. They were rich, with silvered saddles and harnesses, and silks beneath their chainmail; they had a virtual army of interpreters; they had a corps of eager Muslim merchants; they even had with them an Englishman, who is worth a long footnote.[1] And the Venetians, with their sailing ships and trade contacts, had access to a new world of goods. A deal was done.

[1] The unnamed Englishman was almost certainly Robert, of unknown origins, who had been the chaplain of Robert Fitzwalter, leader of the Barons' Rebellion against King John in 1215, which ended with the signing of Magna Carta. Banished from England, Robert the ex-chaplain fled to the Holy Land, where he gambled his wealth away, but discovered a gift for language. This brought him to the attention of Muslim merchants acting as intelligence-gatherers for the Mongols. The Mongols took him to Batu's HQ on the Volga. He would be with them for twenty years, as Gabriel Ronay brilliantly relates (see Bibliography).

Subedei burned the Genoans out, gave the Venetians a monopoly of the Black Sea trade, and in spring 1223 headed back to join Jebe for a renewed advance into what is now southern Russia.

The Polovotsian khan Köten had secured his position by becoming an ally, indeed the son-in-law, of a local Russian warlord, Mstislav Mstislavich the Daring. Princes of other Russian provinces came on side, from Volynia, Kursk, Kiev, Chernigov, Suzdal, Rostov, all massing on the Dnieper's west bank that spring.

Confronted by this immense force, the Mongols hesitated. Word came that Jochi, working his way westwards north of the Caspian, had been ordered to join them; but Jochi was keen to retain his independence, and anyway was ill. In his continued absence, Subedei and Jebe sent a peace delegation to the Russian princes. The princes rejected the proposal, accused the Mongols of being spies and killed them, an affront that of course demanded vengeance.

The Russian force slowly gathered on the banks of the Dnieper where it spreads out below rapids (now drowned behind a hydro-electric dam). It amounted to some 80,000 men: the mounted archers of the Polovtsy, Galician foot-soldiers arriving by boat, heavily armoured Russian cavalrymen with their conical helmets and iron face-masks, long-swords, maces and iconic banners. They outnumbered the Mongols, but were, at heart, disparate forces used to fighting European-style, with setpiece engagements backed by castles. Compare this to the rigid discipline of the 20,000–25,000 Mongols, their speed in the field and their unity of purpose, secured by a messenger service that was in constant touch with Genghis's headquarters. Moreover, they were now superbly armed, not only with their own bows, but with Muslim swords of Damascene steel.

For the Russians lined up on the west bank of the Dnieper, their first sight of the Mongols inspired nothing but disdain. Groups of Mongols, armed only with bows and sabres, loosed off a few shots and then fled across the open steppe when a detachment of Russian cavalry crossed the river. The main army hastened to cross, using a bridge of boats. Still the Mongols retreated, abandoning their herds and local prisoners, which the advancing army swept up in its triumphant progress.

For nine days, the Mongols fled ever deeper into the grasslands, the Russians ever more confident of victory, the Polovtsy delighted to get their lands back. On 31 May, the Russians reached a little river, the Kalka, flowing over steppe-land to the Sea of Azov, 40 kilometres to the south. First across were the Polovtsy, for they equalled the Mongols in speed. Behind came the Russian cavalry, and then the foot-soldiers, with the carts and heavy gear left on the far bank of the little defile. Soon, the army was like a smear of water being dragged into a line of droplets.

Now the Mongols attacked, in an utterly unconventional way, heavier cavalry routing the lightly armed Polovtsian archers, the horsemen then assaulting the Russian cavalry, moving in with their lances, spears and lightweight swords, until both advance forces were in chaotic flight, sweeping through their rearguards, pressing the lot into the shallow river valley. Six princes and seventy nobles soon lay dead. Across the river, the stolid Kievans just had time to begin a slow retreat with the wagons, as the other forces galloped and ran for their lives across the steppe, until they were cut down.

Eventually, the surviving leaders, including Prince Mstislav Romanovich of Kiev, surrendered, on the understanding that no blood would be shed. Subedei and Jebe had no intention of forgoing vengeance, but they kept their promise with a slow and bloodless execution, to send a grim warning to the waiting west. The captives were tied up and became the foundation for a heavy wooden platform, on which Subedei, Jebe and their officers feasted, while Prince Mstislav and his allies suffocated beneath them.

At this moment, in early June, Jochi, who had lingered north of the Caspian, was on his way with reinforcements. After one brief foray across the Dnieper, Subedei and Jebe turned back towards the Volga, where the two forces met. Working their way upriver for 700 kilometres, they came up against the Bulgars, a group who had settled on the Volga in the eighth century, whose relatives later gave their name to Bulgaria. The clash proved a near disaster. The sources give no details, but the Bulgars proved too tough, and the Mongols, having suffered their first and only defeat, backed off – though the memory of the humiliation would remain until revenge became possible fifteen years later.

The Great Raid, as it deserves to be called, and its crucial encounter on the Kalka River had extraordinary consequences. As the Mongols rode back to rejoin Genghis on the Irtish River, they brought with them excellent knowledge of the land, its resources and the opposition. They knew that the Russians, lacking a unified command, could be picked off province by province, city by city. And beyond, as they now knew from Polovtsy prisoners, was enough grassland to sustain any Mongol army driving westwards. With proper planning, Genghis could pursue his manifest destiny by creating a third focal point for his nomad empire. In the centre, his homeland; in the far east, the rich cities of China; in the far west, new objectives: the rich plains of southern Russia, and beyond them – Hungary.

It took little imagination to see the Russian and Hungarian grasslands as the new Mongolia, Europe as another China, ripe for the plucking.

6

EMPEROR AND SAGE

BUT WHAT WAS THE MEANING OF IT ALL? OBVIOUSLY, EVENTS PROVED that Genghis was destined for conquests way beyond his Mongolian homeland. But what was the nature of the Power that had elevated him, and through him his nation? How puzzling to be snatched from obscurity, protected, and rewarded with unprecedented conquests, and then granted no insight into the underlying nature of the universe.

Religious speculation was in the air he had breathed from childhood, when shamanism and Nestorian Christianity were rivals among Mongol and Turkish groups. As a young man, he knew that other rulers made similar claims of divine backing. The Chinese emperor ruled by the Mandate of Heaven; the king of Western Xia was a Burkhan, a Holy One, a Living Buddha. Everywhere he saw monuments to faith – the pagodas and royal tombs of Yinchuan, the temples of Datong and Beijing. Now, from the reports of Subedei and Jebe, he heard of the Christian cathedrals of Georgia. Perhaps all these faiths – shamanism, Confucianism, Buddhism, Christianity – might be groping towards the same obscure godhead. This is one conclusion to be drawn from an edict in which he ordered that all religions were to be granted equal respect, a law that underlay one of the most remarkable qualities of the Mongol emperors from the time of Genghis onwards: their religious toleration.

Gibbon, writing in the late eighteenth century in his *Decline and Fall of the Roman Empire*, was much struck by Genghis's 'enlightened' attitude:

> It is the religion of Zingis that best deserves our wonder and applause. The Catholic inquisitors of Europe, who defended nonsense by cruelty, might have been confounded by the example of a barbarian, who anticipated the lessons of philosophy [at which point he adds a footnote: 'A singular conformity may be found between the religious laws of Zingis Khan and Mr Locke'], and established by his laws a system of pure theism and perfect toleration.

But things are not so simple. Gibbon and Locke, both Enlightenment figures, saw Genghis as a primitive precursor of their own views, tolerating other religions despite their differences from Christianity. In fact Genghis tolerated them for practical reasons. Shamanism was not antagonistic to other religions. It was just that religious oppression alienated people. Better to keep new subjects on side if possible. And were not religions, at heart, all worshipping the same god? Genghis accepted any priest of any religion, happily granting them privileges and exemption from taxes, as long as they accepted Mongol sovereignty and prayed for him.

An example: when in 1214 he first heard of the Buddhist priest Haiyun, later tutor to his grandson Kublai, he instructed the shaven-headed teenager to grow his hair and adopt a Mongol hairstyle. Haiyun objected that if he did he could no longer be a monk. Genghis backtracked and allowed all Buddhist monks to keep their heads shaven. When in 1219 the great general Mukhali again brought Haiyun to Genghis's attention, this time with his master, Genghis decreed: 'They truly are men who pray to Heaven. I should like to support them with clothes and food and make them chiefs. I am planning on gathering many of this kind of people.'

An awareness of the influence wielded by religions also seems to have woken in Genghis other rather less spiritual thoughts. If religion could support empires and monuments, what power could he wield if he could get access to the ultimate Truth? Perhaps deeper knowledge would secure him (a) influence over religious groups and their followers; and (b) an ability to prolong his life.

Genghis had with him two men who were better qualified than most to encourage such speculation. One was the Khitan Yelu Chucai, 'Long Beard', who had endured the siege of Beijing and then sought enlightenment in a Buddhist retreat before joining Genghis in 1218. The other was his Chinese minister, Liu Wen, also renowned for his skills as a herbalist and in whittling bone into whistling arrowheads.

It was from these two, while he was gathering his forces for the invasion of Khwarezm – and incidentally commissioning the stela in which he proclaimed his simplicity and purity – that Genghis first heard of a Daoist sect known as Quanzhen ('Complete Perfection'), and its eminent head, the sage Changchun.

The Complete Perfection sect, rooted in a combination of high-mindedness and eccentricity, was founded by Wang Zhe, nicknamed Wang the Madman, to whom the doctrine was revealed in 1159 by two mysterious strangers when he was out walking. It was, in essence, a form of Daoism, which had evolved over 1,700 years from the teachings of the semi-legendary Laozi (Lao-tsu). Daoists believe that life is best lived in finding and following the Way – the Dao – by which they mean understanding the original purity of people and things; knowing their destiny as decreed by Heaven; and then regaining purity by fulfilling that destiny. After years of isolation and self-imposed suffering, Wang founded a sect to promote his syncretic teachings – the Three Doctrines, which united China's three main religions, Confucianism, Buddhism and Daoism, with Daoism as the fundamental faith. He was well-versed in Dao's huge body of alchemical literature, and the belief that certain substances – jade, pearl, mother-of-pearl, cinnabar, gold – could be used to make a life-prolonging elixir. The idea of a longer life, together with the sect's philanthropic principles, won converts among the common people. One of Wang's disciples was a teenager who won wide acclaim for his prodigious memory and elegant verses. When Wang died in 1170, the twenty-two-year-old, now styling himself Changchun ('Everlasting Spring'), took on his mantle.

Such a man would have been of interest to Genghis and some of his officials for several reasons. Chucai's agenda included educating Genghis in spirituality. Politically, Genghis would have seen the sense in co-opting a man with such a benign influence over his restless Chinese subjects. But it was alchemy's practical application that clinched matters. Perhaps what he heard about Changchun was true – that he was 300 years old and could teach others the secret of his long life. From the heart of Central Asia, Genghis sent orders to fetch Changchun, now seventy-one.

To his temple 500 kilometres from Beijing, in Laizhou, on the Shandong peninsula, came a delegation led by Liu Wen, accompanied by twenty Mongols. Liu Wen had been in central Mongolia when he received Genghis's order. It had taken seven months to cross the grasslands, the Gobi and the war-torn countryside of north China. His orders, he told Changchun, were 'whether it takes months or years, on no account to return without you'.

Clearly, it was the will of Heaven. Changchun prepared for a journey that would cover 10,000 kilometres and take almost four years. A record of his journey was made by a disciple, Li Chih-ch'ang (Li Zhichang), beautifully translated by the orientalist Arthur Waley in *The Travels of an Alchemist*, from which the quotes in this chapter come. It provides a unique survey of Inner Asia at a crucial moment. Never before had it been possible for anyone, let alone an ageing monk, to travel from the Pacific to the heart of Islam while under the protection of a single authority. The 'Mongol Peace' would eventually make it possible for several western travellers to cross Eurasia from west to east, the most famous being Marco Polo. But the first to make the crossing came in the other direction, at the behest of Genghis himself.

A few days later, with nineteen followers and a mounted escort of fifteen, Changchun set out for wherever Genghis might be in however many months it would take to get there – Afghanistan, in two years' time, as it turned out.

In the third week of May 1222, with early summer beginning to warm the Afghan highlands, the monk and the khan met at last, speaking through an interpreter. The two old men were almost equals, each a master in his own domain, each recognizing the other's hard-won authority. After the pleasantries, Genghis came right to the point:

'Adept, what Medicine of Long Life have you brought me from afar?'

The Master did not miss a beat.

'I have means of protecting life,' he said, 'but no elixir that will prolong it.'

Genghis swallowed his disappointment. Tents were set up, questions asked about what to call his guest (Genghis settled on 'Holy Immortal'). Now for the main purpose of the trip, as conceived by Chucai and adopted by Changchun himself. The Holy Immortal would give the ruler of Asia's heartland a tutorial on good living and good ruling. But these regions were still not properly tamed. Genghis still had to deal with bandits in the mountains, a task that would take a month or so. The Master said that in that case it would be best to return to Samarkand, only a three-week journey there and back, nothing to one who had already travelled 10,000 *li*.[1]

In September came the return trip into Afghanistan, by which time Genghis was about to set off for home. On the way, the two old men had several chats, culminating in a discourse by Changchun on the Dao, the Way that underpins all things in Heaven and Earth. Genghis had the Master's words recorded in Mongol and dated 20 November 1222. 'Most men only know the greatness of Heaven,' explained the Master, with A-hai, Samarkand's governor, acting as interpreter. 'They do not understand the greatness of Dao.' When Man was first born, he shone with a holy radiance but, agitated by sensuality and emotional attachment, his life essence became unbalanced. Those who study Dao seek to regain that balance by

[1] A *li* is about half a kilometre. But 10,000 (*wan*) was the equivalent of 'a lot'. Traditionally, the Great Wall is *wan li* long.

asceticism and meditation. In this lay the true elixir of long life. The khan should curb his appetites, live without desire, reject luscious tastes and abstain from lust. Try sleeping alone for a month, he advised. Banish base sexual impulses.

During the return journey, with Genghis and the Master travelling a little apart to avoid the din of an army on the move, the lessons continued, with a few more raps over the knuckles. 'It is said that of the 3,000 sins the worst is ill-treatment of one's father and mother. Now in this respect I believe your subjects to be gravely at fault, and it would be well if Your Majesty could use his influence to reform them.'

The khan was pleased: 'Holy Immortal, your words are exceedingly true. Such is indeed my own belief.' Then to his ministers and officers he said: 'Heaven sent this Holy Immortal to tell me these things. Do you engrave them upon your hearts.' But they didn't. Changchun is not mentioned in *The Secret History*, perhaps because there were no bards present to turn the occasion into a story, more likely because the history was written to promote Genghis's family, and foreigners get short shrift.

Now the Master begged to be allowed to return home. In a final interview came the reward for which he and his followers must have been hoping. Genghis ordered that Changchun's whole organization should be free from tax, setting in train a minor revolution that would serve both of them.

As soon as Changchun arrived home in 1224, Buddhism retreated in the face of a new, centralized and highly ambitious form of Daoism. The Master, eager to put Genghis's edict into effect, urged his followers to accept Mongol rule with equanimity. Tax relief had a wonderful effect on recruitment. From being a small sect, dominated by its parent and rival, Buddhism, Daoism boomed, its growing bands of disciples taking over decaying Buddhist temples and building new ones. In 1227, Changchun was made head of the whole expanding, tax-exempt Daoist movement, in effect becoming a sort of Daoist pope.

But he knew his time was near. On 22 August, six months short of his eightieth birthday, the Master wrote a poem on the fleeting nature of life and its enduring essence:

The transient foam comes and vanishes;
but the stream goes on untroubled.

'He then went up to the Pao-hsuan hall and returned to Purity.'
By a strange coincidence, it was the very month and year in which
his greatest pupil also died; but that is a story for another chapter.

7

DEATH AND SECRECY

GENGHIS COULD AT LAST TURN TO WESTERN XIA, THE TANGUT kingdom that had refused him reinforcements five years previously – an unforgivable insult, a direct contradiction to Heaven's will, and a threat to the empire's future. Western Xia was the key to Inner Asia, and thus the key to future expansion in China. Western Xia had to be destroyed.

But he faced a strategist's nightmare. Four powers were now battling for supremacy in Inner Asia: the Mongols, Western Xia, the Jin in northern China (still only partially defeated by the Mongols) and the Song in the south. While the main Mongol force had been crushing Khwarezm, these four – Mongols, Xia, Jin and Song – had been fighting, making peace, allying and re-allying, without resolution. The next stage in this struggle came to a head in 1227, the crucial year of two turning points which occurred almost simultaneously – the death of Genghis and the final solution to the problem of Western Xia.

Western Xia had a new young ruler, Li Dewang, who was not the man to steer his state back to its former pre-Mongol stability. Perhaps guessing what was coming, he signed a peace treaty with his rivals and neighbours the Jin, who needed a respite from conflict on three fronts. Genghis's war machine shifted gear to prevent the two allied enemies joining forces. In the autumn of 1225 Genghis advanced south, across the Gobi and through the Three Beauties ranges. Here, as active as ever at about sixty-three, he went hunting wild asses and fell, sustaining an injury that demanded rest.[1]

That night, Genghis developed a fever. Plans had to change. Leaders met and talked. Tolun, who was one of the chamberlains who had administered Genghis's household since the invasion of China thirteen years before, advised withdrawing. Genghis refused: it would look like cowardice. Better to stay and play for time, sending a message hinting that it was still not too late for the Tanguts to make peace if they wanted it.

But the acerbic Tangut commander-in-chief, Asha, was set on war, sending a message which said, in effect, 'Bring it on! Come to my encampment in the Alashan!' Genghis, still recovering from his fever, was incensed. The arrogance of it! The Tanguts were meant to be vassals! Now this – insult upon insult. 'This is enough!' he said. 'Even if we die, let us challenge their boasts!' There could be no mistake this time. There was more than imperial strategy at stake. This was personal. And, of course, Heaven was with him in his righteous anger. 'Eternal Heaven, you be the judge!' he said, and prepared to advance.

Asha's challenge implied the strategy that he expected the Mongols to follow: a fast sweep in from the north across the Gobi, and a good clean fight in the Xia backyard, where the Tanguts could draw on their two main cities, Yinchuan and Wuwei, for reserves. Genghis, therefore, would do the exact opposite – on his own terms, in his own time, which was not yet, because winter was upon them.

In spring the forces regathered. Genghis was well enough to lead his army, not to the Alashan, but across 160 kilometres of sand and gravel to Western Xia's northern stronghold, the city the Mongols

---

[1] Actually where and when he had his accident is not clear. Some say it was a, or the, cause of his death. But he remained campaigning almost to the last.

knew as Khara Khot, the Black City. This had been a fortress for over 1,000 years. It guarded a grim landscape of gravel and sand, but it was a thriving outpost on the Etsin River, as the Mongols called it (the Ruo Shui today), which flowed northwards through the desert from the soft, green foothills of the Qilian Shan, the Snowy Mountains, 300 kilometres to the south.[2]

The Mongol army was now adept at siege warfare. Khara Khot didn't stand a chance. Its seizure was the first step in a round-about approach to ensure that Xia would have no reserves when the show-down came. And if Asha dared send a force across 500 kilometres of desert from Yinchuan, his troops would arrive exhausted, at the limit of their supply lines, and utterly unfit for battle. The Tanguts, heirs to a refined and urbanized culture, preferred to place their faith in the strong walls of their capital. No army swept westwards.

This was a policy that suited the Mongols perfectly. Once one city had fallen, the Mongols would as usual be able to draw on prisoners, defectors, supplies and weapons to take the next one, by negotiation if possible, by force if necessary. As in Khwarezm, this was no Blitzkrieg, but a steady advance that fuelled itself, with the momentum of a slow-motion avalanche.

Two months later and 300 kilometres further south, where the Etsin runs in from the Qilian Shan, Genghis could afford to divide his growing army. Subedei headed west to oversee the assault on the most distant cities, while the main force struck east towards the heart of Western Xia.

To the east, 160 kilometres away, lay the Silk Road city of Zhangye, an oasis town famed then and now for its Buddhist temple, with its 34-metre-long reclining Buddha. Genghis had been here before, briefly, in 1205. At that time a young Tangut boy, the son of the city's commander, had been captured and adopted (one source calls him Genghis's 'fifth son'). The boy had acquired a Mongol name – Tsagaan (White) – risen through the ranks, and now commanded Genghis's personal guard. Tsagaan's father, however,

---

[2] The details of this campaign are much disputed. *The Secret History* is even worse than usual as a source, and other sources conflict.

was still the city's commander. Tsagaan shot over the walls an arrow carrying a message to his father, requesting a meeting. His father agreed. Representatives were talking terms when the Tangut second-in-command discovered what was afoot, staged a coup, killed Tsagaan's father, and rejected the very idea of submission. Furious, Genghis threatened to bury the whole population alive. But when the town fell, Tsagaan interceded to save the inhabitants – all except the thirty-five who had killed his father.

In August, while Genghis escaped the heat in the Snowy Mountains, his troops were at the gates of Wuwei, Western Xia's second greatest city, which wisely surrendered and escaped annihilation. In the autumn Genghis rejoined his army at the Yellow River, crossed it (probably near today's Zhongwei, where the river spreads out and breaks up into shallow side-streams) and circled north, approaching Yinchuan from the south-east – a direction precisely opposite to the one Asha had proposed in his challenge. As if scared into an early grave, the ineffective emperor, Li Dewang, died and the poisoned chalice of kingship fell to another, Li Xian, though his reign was so brief and what followed so destructive that he is virtually nothing but a wraith.

In November, the Mongols encircled today's Lingwu,[3] a mere 30 kilometres south of Yinchuan. Now, at last, the Tanguts made their move. Lingwu was a place watered by a large system of canals, which were frozen solid, as was the river. As the Tangut army approached along the opposite bank, the Mongols galloped across the frozen river, shattered the demoralized Tanguts and returned to their siege. No details of the battle survive, but it must have been clear to both sides that the Tanguts were finished.

Lingwu fell in December. The only detail we have of this episode is that the troops went down with some sort of disease, typhus or dysentery perhaps. We know this because the scholar, humanitarian and imperial aide Chucai, returning from Central Asia, witnessed the scenes of pillage and suffering, and did his best to minimize both. While 'all the Mongol officers contended with each other to

[3] Then Lingzhou, it was known to the Mongols as Turemgii – The Aggressive [City].

seize children, women and valuables, His Excellency [Chucai] took only a few books and two camel-loads of rhubarb', which was used as medicine to treat so many conditions it was practically a panacea.

Then, while one Mongol force besieged Yinchuan, another went off to secure other smaller cities to the east and south, while Genghis, now rejoined by Subedei, headed south and west, over the Jin border just 100 kilometres away. The purpose of this advance was to prevent Jin troops coming to the rescue of their Tangut allies, and to prepare for the final conquest of the Jin heartland. Subedei crossed the Liupan Mountains to seize a 150-kilometre-wide strip of western Jin, celebrating his success by sending his lord and master 5,000 horses as a gift. Genghis, meanwhile, struck due south.

A few weeks later, directing the siege of Longde, Genghis sent his Tangut officer, Tsagaan, to report on the situation in Yinchuan. Tsagaan found that after six months of starvation and sickness the Tangut emperor was prepared to give up. All he needed, he said, was a month's grace to prepare suitable gifts. They would not save him. Genghis intended total, brutal victory. 'While I take my meals,' he told his followers, 'you must talk about the killing and destruction of the Tangut.' As a first step in this dreadful process, the Tangut ruler had to die. So Genghis agreed to a formal capitulation, told Tolun to make the arrangements, and kept his real plans to himself.

Now it was summer. Genghis based himself in the Liupan Mountains, south of present-day Guyuan, where he continued to juggle war with politics, striking where necessary, always staying open to the possibility of getting his way by negotiation.

Western Xia was as good as finished, and Jin knew it. In the same month that the devastated nation agreed to capitulate, the Jin, according to the official Yuan history, the *Yuan Shi*, sent an embassy to sue for peace, to which Genghis agreed. Not that it stopped his advance through Jin. But 100 kilometres to the south of the Liupan Mountains, just short of the Jin–Song border, Genghis fell ill, so seriously ill that he was rushed north again, setting off the odd series of events that put his life's work in jeopardy, and ended in his death.

*

Where the final drama of Genghis's life unfolded has always been a matter of dispute among scholars. When researching these events, it struck me that I might find out more on the ground. In Yinchuan, archaeologists told me that there really was no problem. Locals had always known where Genghis had died. I should go to Guyuan, in the south of Ningxia, and beyond to the Liupan Mountains.

Guyuan is the poorest city in China's poorest province, with a Muslim minority, the Hui, who are the poorest of the poor. As you drive south beyond the Yellow River, the fertile plains give way to problem areas. The soil is rich – a thick layer of dark earth dumped over millennia by the winds of the Gobi – but it does not stay around to be cultivated. Rains wash it away, sun bakes it solid, winds whip it into dust clouds, torrents carve out unstable ravines.

Yet Guyuan had a rather wealthy past. Once upon a time it was an entrepot on the Silk Road, with a 13-kilometre double wall around it and ten gates. But Guyuan fell to the Mongols without a murmur. Genghis would have known exactly why he wanted it. He already controlled the central portion of the Silk Road – Otrar, Samarkand and the other great emporia of Central Asia. If things worked out, he would soon control the Silk Road's eastern end as well. And 70 kilometres south there was the most perfect military base, deep inside what has recently become the Liupan Shan State Forest Park.

The park's gateway is a white concrete dragon, its spiny backbone straddling the road. Beyond lies a wilderness of astonishing beauty, and – despite being popular with daytrippers – equally astonishing isolation. It is totally unknown to foreigners, not rating a mention in any guide book and hardly any on the internet. Yet it is glory: 6,790 square kilometres of forested ridges and peaks and stream-carved ravines. Inside the park, the new road swirls up and down in hairpin bends, and finally ends at what is billed as Genghis Khan's last camp – three 'Mongolian tents' made of nice, new, smooth concrete, their pointed domes strung with a streamer of little coloured flags.

But when I was there in 2002 with two Chinese archaeologists and Jorigt, a friend who taught at the Inner Mongolia University in

Hohhot, I found myself staring at something that didn't fit with concrete tents and tourists. It was a table with eight seats, a table made of one huge, circular stone and seats that were stool-sized cylinders of stone, all apparently ancient. They were in fact millstones, perhaps a century or two old, but I didn't know that at the time.

The others joined me.

'What on earth are these old stones?' I asked.

'Yuan dynasty,' said the young guide, a twenty-two-year-old Hui named Ma. 'You see the hole in the middle? It's a flag support. Genghis Khan used this.'

Ma, a graduate of Yinchuan's Tourism College, told the story with utter assurance, pointing to an official guide book as evidence. 'In 1227, Genghis stayed here for the summer. When he attacked Western Xia, he fell from his horse and was injured. But he had a duty to fight, so he came here, and trained his forces here, and hunted, and looked after his body. But this had no effect. So he died here. It was hot so his body began to decay. So he was buried here. Only his saddle and his other equipment was taken away for burial elsewhere.'

This was an astonishing claim. Dying here was one thing; no other source suggested that Genghis might actually be *buried* here. I began to doubt that he had even been to this secret, overgrown, hard-to-get-to valley.

Oh, he was definitely here, said Ma. 'It's cool in summer, and a very good place for training, a very important military position, central for Mongolian forces from Gansu and Shaanxi provinces. If you occupy this place,' Ma waved a hand at the surrounding hills, 'no enemy forces can get you, and you can control all the surrounding region. And just up the road there is the place where Genghis called his generals together to brief them. This was the Training Centre. And there is another place called the Command Centre.'

I still doubted. Was it really likely that a whole army could make its way over the precipitous pass? And once here, how would they camp? The place was all forest, no pasture. I needed evidence.

The stones were evidence, said Ma. Archaeologists found them just up the road.

The sky was clear, the sun not too hot, and lunch was hours away. Ma led Jorigt and me uphill. The road turned into a track rising through fir forest to the place where the stones had been found. 'But soon no one will know where they found them, because these trees will all be fully grown.'

I began to understand. The area, being newly declared a national park, was to become a forest. The valleys had once been open, with farmers raising crops, breeding animals, hunting for boar, rabbit and deer, keeping in contact with the outside world along the steep pass we had just crossed – an ancient path for horses and wagons. In 1227, this valley might have been a huge glade of crops and pastures, a perfectly wonderful base to hide an army.

I needed something to make sense of all this. Maybe folklore would help. Perhaps there were some local elders to talk to.

'Oh, no. There is no one here. Because this is a State Forest Park, everyone was moved out. The last people left four years ago.'

By now, we had wandered further up, beyond the firs and into the cool, gentle embrace of deciduous woodland. By chance, I glanced through a gap in the slender birches, and saw what looked like dark spots a couple of kilometres away.

'But look. Aren't those houses?' Houses that were standing in remarkably open countryside, which was pale green as if with a mantle of ripening grain. 'And aren't those fields? Maybe there *are* people.'

'No people!' Ma was adamant. 'All people have been moved!'

This was agonizing. If there were houses and crops, that meant people, and people meant information and folklore, and maybe evidence about what really happened here.

'Look, a path.' I pointed to a gap in the roadside bushes. 'And wheel tracks.'

There was a silence. Despite himself, Ma was obviously intrigued. The three of us set off, finding ourselves in a woodland idyll: an open path leading over sweet streams pure as bottled water, beneath a canopy that filtered sunlight into a dappling of green. The tracks, only a few days old, were made by one of those small, two-wheeled tractors with long handlebars.

When we arrived, skirting fields of young flax, we entered a ghost village. The half-dozen stone houses were tumbledown and over-grown, their roofs of grey, curved tiles misshapen by age.

'*You ren ma?*' yelled Jorigt. 'Anyone there?'

No echo came from the hills beyond, and no answering voices. All was silence, decay, collapse. But a cultivated field spoke of people. We would have to return and find them. We set off back in thought-ful silence.

And there, suddenly, right in our way, was a woman, a reserved and dignified figure in a grey shirt, dark trousers and a white head-dress shaped like a chef's hat, marking her as a Muslim Hui. She carried a three-year-old with cheeks as red as her overalls and held the hand of a five-year-old boy in a frayed grey jacket faintly printed all over with the name 'Snoopy'. Over her shoulder was a bag. She was collecting an edible, asparagus-like fern. In an instant, she solved many mysteries. Her name was Li Bocheng, and it was her husband and brothers-in-law who farmed the fields. They had once lived here, but every summer they returned to plant and harvest. Oh, yes, she had heard about Genghis Khan, but if we wanted to know about him we had better talk to the men. They would return with the cows later.

By mid-afternoon we were back, to find six men, along with the woman and her two children. A house stood open, revealing a brick oven and a stone sleeping-platform scattered with mattresses. In front of the house was a plastic apron, neatly laid with medicinal roots. We squatted down on bits of stone and old sacking, while Li Bocheng brought green tea in jam-jars. Her husband, a wiry man in his thirties, wearing a shirt of black-and-white stripes, took on the role of spokesman, telling us of Genghis as if he had been the previous tenant.

All this – with a sweep of his arm towards the valley – belonged to Genghis. This was the Training Place, where his bodyguard lived, and up there, where the cattle are, that's where he lived, the Meeting

Place. Down there, below the flax field, was the Command Centre. 'That's what my father told me, because that's what the old people told him, when he came here, fifty years ago. And right up there, that was what they called the Sitting Place of Genghis Khan. There's a platform; you can see over everything.'

He could show us. We set off at eight the next morning, over the terrace above the house, with two brothers, Yu Wuho and Yu Wuse, as guides. While we walked through firs, the Yu brothers told their story.

When their parents came, this had been a community of thirty families. Once, 100 years ago, there had been a Buddhist temple here, though with the influx of the Muslim Hui it had been cannibalized for building materials and farm use (hence the grain-rollers and millstones). Then the valley had been deliberately overgrown. Now everyone else had gone. They were the last, coming in the summer over the mountains with a few dozen sheep and cattle to tend the fields and collect medicinal roots in the forests. They would go on farming as long as they could, pending compensation from the government.

We were into thick woods by now. We crossed a stream and climbed a near-vertical slope soft with mulch, at the top of which the ground, shadowed by birch trees, flattened into a confusion of odd little rock mesas. 'The road used to come up here,' said Yu Wuho. It was hard to make sense of the contorted, dappled ground, but I could see where a track might have run, past an overgrown outcrop about 5 metres high that might have been natural, or not.

There was a shout from further uphill, and a flurry of conversation. A man was on his knees scrabbling with his hands at the soft earth, and others in the shadows, ten of them altogether. They were collecting medicinal plants. They had walked in before dawn from their village 25 kilometres away, along one of the many paths over the mountains, and would work all day.

And so the wilderness revealed more of itself, suggesting what had made it so attractive over centuries to farmers and hunters – and, for a few months perhaps, to nomadic warriors. This place was famous for its medicinal plants. I saw a list later: there were thirty-nine of them. They were collecting one in particular, called *chang-bo* locally. Each of this party could harvest 2–3 kilos a day. What the little onion-like root was for and how it was prepared, though, no one had a clue. All they did was collect it and sell it.

Yu Wuho gestured at the surrounding forest: 'This we call Genghis Khan's Medical Treatment Place.'

Damp earth, teetering saplings and rampant bushes made an ever-changing ecosystem, so it was hard to tell natural from artificial. But if there had been a track, and the rocky pinnacle had been some sort of guard tower, perhaps this place had been a kind of pharmacy, where the sick and injured could come for special treatment with medicinal plants.

By mid-morning we were out of the woods, walking on carpets of grass, buttercups and blue gentians across an open ridge, where the saplings were small and scattered. On the crest were the remains of a wall, which had once, I supposed, marked an all-round lookout over wave upon wave of forested mountain. But a hilltop lookout was no base from which to watch army manoeuvres. I wanted to find the promised 'platform'. We descended, and struck thorn bushes. We made a wary circuit, then the ground levelled out.

'This is it,' said Yu Wuho, 'the Sitting Place of Genghis Khan. The Lord's Place.'

There was to be no rock platform, I realized. It was of grass, or had been. I paced it out: the Sitting Place was about 250 metres long and 50 metres wide.

Well, no one would bother to sit there now. When the Yus were children, it was open and you could see stone equipment scattered across the grass, and you had a wonderful view down to the village. Now we were hemmed in by monoculture, and the rocks were buried. At the edge of the flat space, you could just see down the valley and imagine an immense parade ground, with tents and herds and formations of troops.

Back at the houses, I tried to make sense of what I had seen. It was all a slurry of raw material, artefacts and folklore carrying me back 50 years, 100 years, 800 years, but with nothing to anchor the talk to history. That left the legends, and the place itself – a secret valley with its medicinal plants, one of them perhaps considered powerful enough to save the life of an ailing conqueror.

I was lucky. But if you, reader, go there, I'm afraid you will be too late. Those who remember what was once said about this place will be gone to villages and towns outside the valley. The paths will overgrow, the fields will vanish under saplings, the houses will fall, the blight of firs will claim the open spaces. Even if historians and archaeologists come, who will remember, who will show them where the Training Place, the Command Centre, the Medical Treatment Place and the Sitting Place once were?

For a few days in the summer of 1227 the fate of Eurasia hung in the balance. The murder of one emperor, the death of Genghis, the destruction of a whole culture – these are events of great significance. Unfortunately, they are wrapped in secrecy. It was the need for secrecy, foreseen by Genghis, imposed by his entourage, that allowed his aims to be fulfilled. Had news leaked out, all could have been lost, enemies heartened, conquests reversed, the half-formed Mongol empire strangled almost at birth, the whole course of Eurasian history turned in a different direction. What follows is a possible scenario based on the scanty information.

To review, in the second week of August 1227 Genghis is on the verge of the final conquest of Western Xia and has just occupied western Jin. This is to be a base from which to complete the conquest of all north China, which will give him an empire running from the Pacific almost to Baghdad. The work of a lifetime is about to pay off, if all goes well. The emperor of Western Xia is already on his way to capitulate. At this crucial moment, Genghis falls ill, perhaps with typhus caught from his troops. Historians generally agree that the illness struck some 100 kilometres south, in the county of Qing Shui, in today's Gansu province; but there is room for doubt, because the county's name is the same as that of the river that flows north to the Yellow River. Some claim that he died in Qing Shui county, a suggestion rejected by two scholars who have immersed themselves in the evidence, Xu Cheng and Yu Jun of

Ningxia University.[4] Their approach, based on historical sources and archaeological findings, supports the folk memories of the farmers in the Liupan Shan.

Wherever the illness struck, it's serious; but no hint of its seriousness must leak out. So, on the first day of the last week of his life, Genghis is rushed in a closed cart into the hidden valley in the Liupan Shan, where secrecy can be guaranteed, and where he can be given remedies made from the forest's medicinal plants.

Nothing works. Death approaches.

But for a few days, according to the major Chinese source, the *Yuan Shi*, the official history established by Genghis's grandson Kublai, Genghis is still the strategist, planning for the future. His instructions were clear. In one version of these events, written by the Persian historian Rashid al-Din a couple of generations later, Genghis says: 'Do not let my death be known. Do not weep or lament in any way, so that the enemy shall not know anything about it. But when the ruler of the Tanguts and the population leave the city at the appointed hour, annihilate them all.'

And then, as Chinese sources record, Genghis lays out the strategy by which Jin must be defeated. It means taking the new capital, Kaifeng. To do that, the Mongols should first outflank the mighty fortress of Tongguan, which guarded the Yellow River some 400 kilometres upriver from Kaifeng. He knew what he was talking about: the Mongols had taken the fortress once before in 1216, only to lose it again when they retreated from Kaifeng. Both the fortress and Kaifeng itself were near Jin's southern border with Song. Best therefore to get Song's permission to march around Tongguan and approach Kaifeng from the south: 'Since Jin and Song have been enemies for generations, Song will certainly agree.' This would force the Jin to send reinforcements in a forced march from Tongguan, exhausting the troops, weakening the fortress, exposing Kaifeng. This was exactly the plan of campaign that Genghis's successors used in their final defeat of Jin a few years later.

---

[4] Xu Cheng and Yu Jun, 'Genghis Khan's Palace in the Liupan Shan', *Journal of Ningxia University*, Yinchuan, 1993/3.

Now, suddenly, his entourage is face to face with possible catastrophe, the consequences of which would be dire indeed. Li Xian, the emperor of Western Xia, on his way from Yinchuan, may well have no victor to surrender to. If he hears that Genghis is dying or dead, he will at once turn round, and consider how to save himself and his kingdom. His best chance would be to turn instantly to Jin. Western Xia and Jin had been allies before; true, Jin had recently rejected Li's advances, but that was before the Mongols had taken the war into Jin territory. What would there be to stop him offering to kowtow to Jin, joining forces against a common enemy, destroying what had been achieved, and killing Genghis's grand strategy for future conquest stone dead?

There is only one possible course of action. Everything must go forward as planned. No hint of the truth must leak out. It is vital, therefore, that the Western Xia emperor arrive, capitulate, and then become the first of his treacherous people to die.

Where is this to be played out?[5] It so happens that there is a suitable site on open ground close by, which, I believe, had already been set up for an entirely different purpose.

Between Guyuan and the Liupan Shan, the road passes over low terraced hills and through a line of baked-earth houses, which is about all there is to the village of Kaicheng. It was not always such a backwater. A sign in English and Chinese points up a track to the right: 'Ancient Ruins of Kaicheng'.

The vague shapes beneath the flowing wheat were once walls, making a square some 3–4 kilometres in circumference. In the thirteenth century, Genghis's grandson, Kublai, built this into a provincial headquarters that must have rivalled Guyuan, 20 kilometres away. By 1300, it had a garrison of 10,000 troops. But in 1306 an earthquake destroyed it, killing 5,000. The survivors fled, and it vanished from sight and memory. Now Chinese archaeologists are working to reveal it once again.

But why would Kublai build himself a headquarters in Kaicheng,

---

[5] *The Secret History* says Lingwu, near Yinchuan, but its account is confusing, and Lingwu is 200 kilometres from where Genghis was taken ill.

when Guyuan was already there 20 kilometres away, with its walls and gatehouses? Possibly because Kaicheng was in effect a sacred site, chosen by his grandfather in the spring of 1227. There were sound reasons for Genghis's choice: it was safely away from Guyuan's intrusive inhabitants, within easy reach of the troops secluded in the Liupan Shan a day's ride away, and out in the open, where a vast army could gather. Here, possibly, Genghis decreed a temporary palace where the Mongols could receive the embassy that came from Jin seeking peace. And then, by happy chance, this new HQ, with its tent-palaces and garrison, found a second use, as a base for the meeting with the emperor of Western Xia when he arrived to make his final capitulation, and meet his doom.

This whole charade would have been carefully orchestrated. Sources agree that four things happened in quick succession:

- the Tangut emperor submitted;
- he came for an audience with Genghis;
- Genghis had him killed;
- and Genghis himself died.

The order in which these things happened is unclear. What follows is only the most likely of several possible scenarios.

Li Xian arrives at the tent-palace in Kaicheng and is greeted with a strange circumstance: during his audience with the khan, Genghis 'kept the door closed and made Burkhan pay homage outside the tent'. And during the audience, *The Secret History* relates, Genghis 'felt sick' or – in de Rachewiltz's translation – 'felt revulsion within his heart'. This is odd. Surely the khan would not willingly deal with his vanquished foe in such a fashion, when by doing so he must have raised suspicions in the emperor's mind, and in the minds of his entourage? There is one possible conclusion. Neither Genghis nor his entourage had any choice, because Genghis was simply not fit enough to hold an audience. Of course, the Tangut emperor was going to be killed anyway. But it was important that he make his submission and offer his gifts, completing the ritual of formal surrender. And it was important that everyone, Tangut and ordinary

Mongols, believed Genghis was still in control. This extraordinary drama makes the best sense if we assume that behind the curtain Genghis is so near death that he cannot be seen.

Li Xian, puzzled but compliant, lays out his offerings, the first being a set of golden Buddhas, followed by a museum-full of other gifts, each one in sets of nine, the most auspicious number: golden and silver bowls, boys, girls, geldings, camels and much more, all set out according to 'colour and form'.

Then Tolun saw to the execution. The killing of rulers, like the killing of all nobles, demanded the observance of a ritual long recognized by the Mongols. No blood was to be shed. Death could be by trampling or strangulation. However it was done, it was done in secret.

Everything worked out perfectly, because after all, as Genghis tells Tolun in *The Secret History*, 'We came here on account of the poisonous words of an enemy and with Our strength increased by Eternal Heaven, who gave him into Our hands, we took Our revenge.'

The sources provide few details about the death. According to one Chinese history, Genghis died in the Year of the Pig (1227), on the twelfth day of the seventh lunar month: 25 August. But other accounts do not agree on the exact day. *The Secret History*, the most intimate source, is the least helpful. It says only that Genghis 'ascended to Heaven' – proof enough that his death and burial were to remain a state secret.

So perhaps – who knows? – he was never in his royal tent during the surrender. Perhaps his words are an interpolation, designed to disinform. Perhaps he was back in the hidden valley, too ill to move; or actually dead, because after all he survived only a week after the onset of his illness. And perhaps only in the security of that valley could his grieving entourage make the arrangements to keep his death secret, and then prepare for the showdown in Kaicheng.

The Tanguts fell easy prey to their conquerors. Yinchuan was looted, tiles torn from the roofs of the royal tombs, the people scattered, Genghis's ruthless will meticulously fulfilled. What that meant is not recorded. Neither the Mongols nor any later Chinese dynasty would have mourned the disappearance of a rival empire. The Tanguts almost vanished from history, along with most of their records, and their script, and their language.[6] Perhaps still hidden in some desert cave is a Tangut account of the carnage, recorded by a survivor. In the meantime, you can imagine the destruction by visiting or checking online the strange, bare-earth tombs jutting from Yinchuan's desolate gravel plain.

The secrecy ensured that rumour conquered all. Stories multiplied that Genghis died besieging some city or other; or survived until the surrender of Western Xia. And later – decades later, centuries later – poets marked the great man's passing, turning rumour and folk tales into verse. The few facts became hidden by a tangle of post-Genghis lore, much of it Buddhist. In one account, Genghis takes Gurbelchin, the Tangut emperor's wife, who wounds Genghis and then drowns herself in the Yellow River; in another, Gurbelchin is a royal daughter, who castrates Genghis with a hidden knife. In a version told to the great Mongolist Owen Lattimore by his Mongol companion Arash in the 1930s, 'Genghis cried out when he felt the cut, and people came in, but he only said to them: Take this girl away; I wish to sleep. He slept and from that sleep he has never wakened – but that was six hundred or seven hundred years ago, and would not Holy Genghis heal himself? When he is healed he will awake and save his people.'

From this morass of Tibetan, Chinese, Buddhist and Mongolian lore, the only firm information to be gleaned is the enormity of the loss. Apparently, as time went by, people had been unwilling to accept their god-king's death as natural, and turned it into a tragedy with their hero undone, like Samson, by a woman and a foreigner. Today, all Mongols know the tale of how the evil queen wounded the lord and then cast herself into the Yellow River, which they still call the Queen's River.

*

[6] Almost, but not quite. Later, sixteen Tanguts were among the 150-odd overseers (*darugachi*) who served the Yuan dynasty, and several small Tangut communities survived in other parts of China.

As a leader, Genghis was one of the greatest ever. Modern leadership theory gives an idea of his qualities.

There are two dimensions to Genghis as leader: the particular and the general. He was, like his empire, unique, a character rooted in time and place. But he also had qualities that apply much more widely, making him in many ways a leader if not for all time then at least for many times.

He was of his time in two ways:

1. His belief in Heaven's backing

It's a historical commonplace for rulers to claim divine support. But most limit the claim to their own people, nation or empire (as Chinese emperors did). Religious leaders have often aimed to spread their word universally, but world rule is reserved for world's end. Yet Genghis himself perhaps believed, and his heirs certainly did, that Heaven really had given the world to them, and their job was to have everyone acknowledge this. With hindsight, it's completely crazy. But since at the time no one, let alone a Mongol, had any idea of what the world was like and how impossible the vision was, the belief was a vital element in Genghis's charismatic appeal.

2. Focused ruthlessness

Throughout the course of history there have been genocides, attempted genocides, massacres and outrages galore; but never anything like those unleashed by Genghis and his heirs. He achieved what others could only dream of: annihilation of those who opposed him. First in line were enemy clans and tribes; then many enemy cities. But, as we've seen, unlike many modern genocides, this was not racist. True, Mongols considered themselves the top nation among lesser breeds. But three factors limited the spirit of destruction. First, Genghis appreciated talent, from whatever ethnic background (more on this later). Second, his prime purpose was not total destruction but eternal rule, which is hard to achieve with devastated lands and alienated populations. Third, this meant that his aim was purely strategic – to force capitulation. Opposition meant death, but (vengeance apart) surrender meant life as part of Genghis's Heaven-backed empire.

These two important elements in his leadership are, I suggest, unique to him, and to his time. They would not work today, and certainly would not apply to any of the ways in which leadership is exercised in the modern world.

Other traits do apply. Here is a quick survey of those elements of Genghis's leadership that might be envied and imitated by leaders today.

Genghis controlled his image – becoming in effect his own spin-doctor – by vetting the stories circulating in his lifetime and retold in *The Secret History*. He had a rare ability to accept criticism; he kept his word; he encouraged and rewarded loyalty; he shared his army's hardships, insisting on his austere nomadic roots; unlike his compatriots, he saw the dangers of alcohol;[7] he rejected luxury; he recognized his own limitations (for instance, although illiterate, he saw that government demanded literacy, and introduced a script); he gave clear rules and stuck to them; he was a realist, but also when necessary a risk-taker; he had no interest in gratuitous violence against individuals – there is no record of torture under Genghis (though his heirs sometimes disgraced themselves by using it).

Genghis had a remarkable lack of ego, equating his interests with those of the state; he chose an heir (a challenge that many lesser bosses never face); he employed talent wherever he found it, never mind the ethnic background; he was magnanimous, even to enemies; he was meticulous in planning; he was a deep thinker, as his relationship with both Yelu Chucai and Changchun showed; he was tolerant of different religions; and finally – perhaps the most surprising trait in a world conqueror – he was never arrogant, displaying remarkable humility in the face of the immensity of the task which, for whatever incomprehensible reason, had been imposed upon him.

To come at the matter from another direction, many of these traits are elements in what Daniel Goleman, one of the most successful of leadership theorists, calls 'emotional intelligence'. Goleman lists eighteen so-called 'competencies' that are displayed by top leaders. Effective leaders, he says, display four of them; highly effective ones

---

[7] 'A drunkard is like one who is blind, deaf and insane,' he is supposed to have said.

display six or more. There is no totally convincing way to compare present-day requirements with those needed 800 years ago, but Genghis can be said to have had fifteen of the eighteen (lacking only the modern 'competencies' of commitment to service, conflict management and teamwork). However you assess him, Genghis ranks as a leader of genius.

Leadership competencies	
Personal competencies	*Social competencies*
emotional self-awareness	empathy
accurate self-assessment	organizational skills
self-confidence	commitment to service
self-control	inspiration
integrity	persuasiveness
adaptability	an interest in cultivating the abilities of others
drive	recognizing the need for change
optimism	conflict management
	teamwork
Source: Goleman et al., *The New Leaders*.	

What of Genghis's body? The question has no final answer, because there is no grave. Instead there are two separate traditions, which underlie two competing claims by China and Mongolia, each determined to be the true heirs of Genghis.

The tradition in China focuses mainly on Genghis's accoutrements. It is in direct conflict with that of Mongolia, which deals mainly with his body, claiming that the corpse was brought back across the Gobi to the homeland of the Mongols and buried in a secret grave.

But there is nothing certain about any of this. It was high summer. Bodies decay fast in August. Coupled with the need for secrecy, the return would need to be accomplished as quickly as possible. The cortège had 1,600 kilometres to cover, which for a cart travelling with care and attention would take some three weeks. The family might have drawn on Chinese expertise to preserve the body as much as possible, but the Mongols knew nothing of mummification. It would have been a hurried trip.

The Secret History says nothing about the funeral cortège or the burial, jumping straight over the year following the death to the great meeting on the Kherlen which confirmed Ogedei as Genghis's heir. It is inconceivable that such an emotional event as the transport and burial of their khan would somehow slip the minds of those who compiled *The Secret History*. The only possible explanation is that the whole matter was deliberately omitted. And the best explanation for such a taboo was firstly to preserve what had originally been a state secret, namely the death and progress of the cortège; and secondly to hide the knowledge of the burial site from all but the innermost circles.

This in its turn allowed legend to flourish. Soon, as with the death, folklore began to fill the information gap with stories, one of which was that the route of the cortège was marked by slaughter. The story was related by two historians, the Arabic writer Rashid al-Din, and Marco Polo. Rashid says bluntly: 'On the way they killed every living being they met.' Marco Polo's claim is indirect: 'when Mangou Kaan [Mönkhe Khan, Genghis's grandson] died, more than 20,000 persons, who chanced to meet the body on its way, were slain'.

Countless histories since, both popular and academic, apply this to Genghis and take it as gospel, without further comment. But it doesn't make sense. It is not in any of the Mongol or Chinese sources. Friar William of Rubruck, who was at Mönkhe's court in Karakorum in 1253–5, doesn't mention the story in his accurate and detailed account of his trip. Nor does Juvaini, who was in Karakorum at the same time as Friar William.

Look first at the foundation of the story. Both Rashid and Marco were writing fifty years after the event. Rashid, though he had access to Mongol sources, did not speak Mongolian; he relied on the help of his master, Ghazan (ruled 1295–1304, five generations removed from Genghis), and the ambassador from the Mongol court in

Beijing. And Marco did not attribute the murders specifically to Genghis's cortège, only to 'any emperor' and specifically to Mönkhe (who died fourteen years before Marco arrived in China; he did not see any imperial funeral). What he wrote of them was hearsay.

One justification for this alleged act was that it kept the secret of Genghis's death. But the argument is nonsensical. A secret was certainly to be kept, but it defies belief that killing people would preserve secrecy. Perhaps Chinese and Tanguts were dispensable. But what happened in Mongolia? Are we to assume that the guards killed their own people? On the steppe, everyone knows everyone else. On a clear day you can see for ever. Nothing would be more obvious than a cortège, and nothing would better advertise the fact that the cortège had something to hide than a mass of murders. Who would stay around to be caught? How could the guards guarantee to capture and kill every eyewitness? And the bodies: they could not be left to mystify and terrify the next passers-by. A royal cortège would not load itself with corpses.

The best way to preserve secrecy is to travel fast, travel small and not advertise the fact that you have something to hide.

The route of the cortège is unknown, of course. There is a clue in an incident related by the seventeenth-century historian Sagang Sechen, in which the wagon sinks up to its axles in mud, and a Mongol general sings to his holy lord, lion among men, born by the will of Eternal Heaven, about how everything he holds dear lies ahead of him. Palaces, queens, children, people, nobles, subjects, water, comrades-in-arms, place of birth – 'they are all there, my lord!' And lo – for this dirge, one of the most emotional of Mongol poems, is quasi-Biblical in its style – the Lord heard, and granted his blessing, and the groaning wagon moved, and the people rejoiced and accompanied the khan's body onwards to the great homeland.

Tradition holds that this incident happened, if it happened at all, in the Mona or Muna Mountains, today's Yin Mountains that hem the Yellow River's great bend north of the Ordos. To the west, between mountains and desert, is a low-lying area where marshes and meandering side-streams make a sort of mid-river delta, just the sort of ground in which a two-wheeled covered wagon might stick.

If it did, then the cortège would probably have been heading east, to the route covered so many times by Genghis in his campaigns against Jin. This eastern route, where the gravel plains of the Gobi give way to grassland, had become a sort of royal road. Today, part of it is crossed by the railway line that runs up to the Mongol capital, Ulaanbaatar, from the border crossing points of Erenhot (Erlian in Chinese) and Zamyn Uud ('Door of the Road').

A funeral cortège following this route would head almost due north for three days, until, on grassland now, it crossed the shallow and firm-bedded Kherlen to old Avraga. Nearby is a burial ground, so perhaps he lies here. But a more likely spot was ahead, upriver, in the Khentii, in a place for which many are still looking.

PART II
TRANSITION

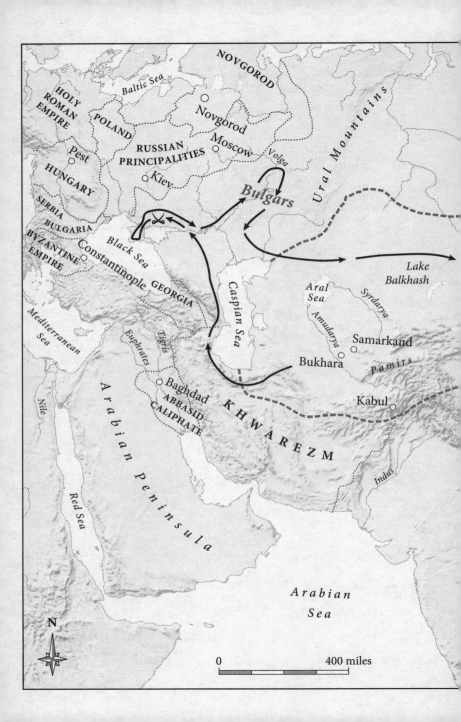

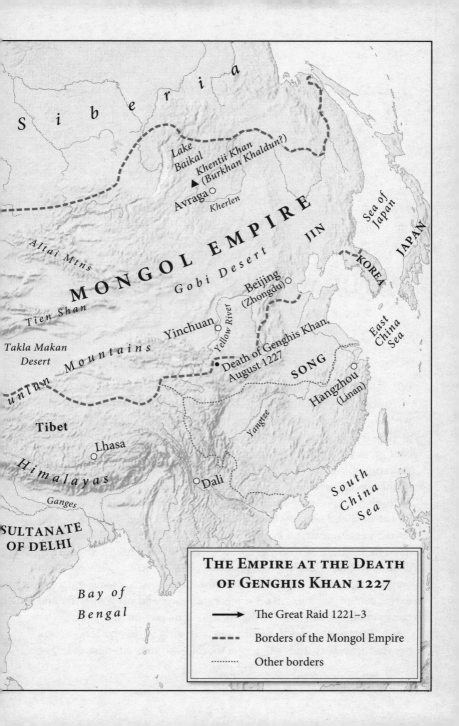

S i b e r i a

Lake
Baikal
Khentii Khan
(Burkhan Khaldun?)
▲
Avraga ○
Kherlen

MONGOL EMPIRE

JIN

*Sea of
Japan*

KOREA

JAPAN

Altai Mtns

Gobi Desert

Beijing
(Zhongdu) ○

Tien Shan

Yinchuan ○
Yellow River

*Takla Makan
Desert*

K u n l u n   M o u n t a i n s

● Death of Genghis Khan,
August 1227

SONG

*East
China
Sea*

Tibet

Lhasa ○

Hangzhou ○
(Linan)

Yangtze

H i m a l a y a s

Dali ○

*South
China
Sea*

Ganges

**SULTANATE
OF DELHI**

*Bay of
Bengal*

THE EMPIRE AT THE DEATH
OF GENGHIS KHAN 1227

→ The Great Raid 1221–3

▄▄▄ Borders of the Mongol Empire

⋯⋯⋯ Other borders

8

THE WOMAN WHO SAVED
THE EMPIRE

ONE THING YOU NOTICE IN MONGOLIA: THE WOMEN COMMAND attention. In the countryside, crones with walnut faces skewer you with direct, self-confident eyes, while outside tough, red-cheeked girls ride like master-horsemen. In Ulaanbaatar, the capital, you cannot walk across the main square without passing a beauty radiating self-assurance. For centuries Mongolia's nomadic, herding traditions ensured that women matched men in self-reliance. They rode, they ruled, they fought. In 1220, one of Genghis's daughters, whose husband had just been killed by an arrow, led the final assault on the Persian town of Nishapur. Widows of the well-off could take over their late husband's estates, which made some of them rich, powerful and fiercely independent. The world's greatest land empire, the very image of masculine dominance, owed much to extraordinary women, like Genghis's mother, and his first wife, and the daughter-in-law who is the focus of this section.

Her name was Sorkaktani, and she should be better known, because she was the most remarkable woman of her age. For twenty-five years, as a succession of storms threatened to destroy Genghis's creation, she piloted her family through to calmer waters. Reports by outsiders all concurred. 'Among the Tartars this lady is the most renowned, with the exception of the emperor's mother,' wrote one of the Pope's envoys, John of Plano Carpini. 'Extremely intelligent and able,' said Rashid al-Din, going on to praise her 'great ability, perfect wisdom and shrewdness'. 'All the princes marvelled at her power of administration,' said a Hebrew physician, Bar Hebraeus, and added a verse quotation: 'If I were to see among the race of women another woman like this, I should say that the race of women was far superior to men.'

Remarkable, too, in what she made of her four sons. One ruled Persia, one was a notorious rebel trying to impose himself from his base in Central Asia, and two became khans of the whole expanding empire. More than that – her second son, Kublai, was the one who gave modern China its identity. Genghis started the empire; Kublai brought it to its greatest extent; but without Sorkaktani to link the two, without her ambition, foresight, good sense, and a couple of interventions at crucial moments, Genghis's empire might have fallen apart.

And she was not even a Mongol. She was Kerait, the Turkish-speaking group that dominated central Mongolia when Genghis was born. The Kerait king, Toghril, blood-brother to Genghis's father, was Sorkaktani's uncle. Her father was Toghril's younger brother, Jakha, whose story reflects the complexities and dangers of shifting alliances among steppe tribes of Inner Asia. He was raised among the Tangut people of Western Xia, where he rose to the rank of commander – *gambu* in Tangut, which became part of his name, Jakha Gambu. When the Keraits were beaten, Genghis merged the tribes with marriages. Jakha had two daughters. The elder, Ibaqa, Genghis took as one of his five wives (he later handed her on to one of his generals, but allowed her to retain the status of queen). The younger one, Sorkaktani, then about twenty, he gave to his youngest son, Tolui, then twelve or thirteen. This was in 1203. The first of their four sons arrived six years later. At the time, no one would have guessed that the sons of Genghis's youngest would amount to anything much. Sorkaktani had to wait twenty-five years for the world to turn in her favour.

Her first lucky break came when Genghis died in 1227. Genghis had decreed that his third son, Ogedei, would be his heir as emperor, with all four sons exercising personal authority over their own areas, allocated as tradition demanded. Jochi, the eldest, was granted the most distant section, beyond the Aral Sea. But Jochi was dead by then,[1] so his estates were further divided between two of his sons. Central Asia, from the Aral Sea to Tibet, went to Chaghadai. Tolui, the youngest, as tradition demanded, inherited the lands of his father's 'hearth', which in this case meant the whole of Mongolia. This gave him a power-base that would eventually fall to Sorkaktani, but there was no reason yet for Sorkaktani to dream of glory for her sons, principally because Genghis's heir, Ogedei, took the reins of power with overwhelming authority.

He saw what Genghis had seen: that an empire needed a capital, a replacement for the old Mongol base of Avraga on the Kherlen River. For a clan, Avraga was a perfect HQ, near the safety offered by mountains, with a clear run over grasslands and desert to China, the source of trade and booty. Ogedei started his reign with a huge gathering in Avraga in 1228–9, where probably (possibly, perhaps) he sponsored the collection of the tales and information that went into *The Secret History*, but already Avraga was the past. For a nation and empire, the future lay further west, in the valley of the Orkhon River, where previous Turkish empires had ruled. Turks called it Khara Khorum, 'Black Boulder'. Genghis had chosen it as his new capital in 1220, but had done nothing about it. Ogedei fulfilled his father's dream, starting to turn Karakorum into a permanent settlement in 1235.

But first he needed sound government. In this his main guide was Genghis's Khitan adviser, Yelu Chucai. In 1229, Ogedei made him

---

[1] Having been passed over as heir, he had been ordered to join in the Great Raid but vanished into the steppes, 'hunting' or 'ill' – no one knew what. Anyway, he was out of favour with Genghis and died sometime in 1225–7.

the provisional head of the new Branch Secretariat – in effect, governor – for those parts of north China that had already been conquered, the first civilian official with such wide responsibilities.

What to do with this new estate? The place was devastated, on a scale hardly comprehensible today. Mongol princes had torn communities apart for slaves, the temples were crowded with escaped prisoners, deserters and refugees. Several at the new court suggested that the simplest solution, in these chaotic circumstances, was genocide. What use were farmers? Their work was pointless, they owned nothing of worth, and they were a source of opposition. They were of less value than cattle and horses. Let them be replaced by cattle and horses. Why not kill the lot and turn the land to pasture? It wouldn't take long for 10,000 warriors to slaughter 1,000 people each.

It was Yelu Chucai who stopped this lunatic talk. His life's work was to help Heaven along in its choice of rulers by transforming barbarity and ignorance into virtue and wisdom. A shattered north China was prime raw material. He sought to apply Confucius's rules for good government while at the same time promoting Buddhism to cultivate the mind, his ultimate goal being the creation of a society that transcended Confucianism, rather as idealistic Communists foresaw a society that would evolve through Socialism to perfect Communism.[2] His people, acting as scribes, interpreters, envoys, astrologers and tax experts, had proved increasingly vital in governing what had been won. He had been on hand in several cities to save libraries, treasures and scholars.

Now he seized the moment. Well aware that Mongols had no use for Chinese civilization unless it offered material gain, he pointed out that if the peasants prospered, they could be taxed and thus contribute to the economy. To this end, he drew up a plan for renewal and government such as China, let alone Mongolia, had never seen before. First, civil authority should be separated from the military, with its self-seeking and arbitrary brutalities. Jin would be divided into ten districts, each with its own tax-collection office, a land tax

[2] Igor de Rachewiltz, *Confucian Personalities*.

for peasants, a poll tax for city-dwellers, all to be paid in silk, silver or grain, all flowing to the government. The Daoist priesthood, puffed up in wealth and numbers by Genghis's personal tax exemptions, was corralled by taxes on temple businesses and by laws against further appropriations of Buddhist temples.

To all this, Mongol military leaders objected bitterly. But Chucai, with Ogedei's backing, held firm, and in 1231 his first taxes came in, right on budget, to the value of 10,000 ingots of silver. Ogedei made Chucai head of his government's Chinese department on the spot. And administration demanded educated people. In 1233, Chucai rescued from captivity scores of scholars and other notables. He set up a government publishing house and a college for the sons of Chinese and Mongolian officials, to build the next generation of scholars and administrators. He arranged for former Jin officials who had been enslaved to take qualifying examinations for the civil service: 4,000 entered; 1,000 regained their freedom.

Clearly, Ogedei was eager to pursue his father's vision. But he needed to build a better, more inspiring justification than conquest. His coronation in 1229 was a turning point. Genghis had laid the foundations for ever-wider empire, and Ogedei planned to build on that foundation, with a renewed advance westwards, an invasion of Korea, and the final conquest of north China. More than conquests, however, it was Ogedei who imposed *meaning* on them with a new ideology. It was he who decreed that Heaven had given the world to the Mongols. The idea – suggested by previous victories, proved by future ones – was already firmly in place when an ambassador from the Song court, Peng Daya, visited the Mongol court in 1232 and observed: 'Their constant expression is "Relying on the strength of Eternal Heaven and the Good Fortune of the Emperor".' The same formula would be used whenever Ogedei and his heirs wanted to assert their authority, in any of the languages and scripts used by them. It is used thirteen times in *The Secret History*; in a famous letter sent by Guyuk to Pope Innocent IV: 'By the strength of Heaven, from the going up of the sun to its going down, He has delivered all the lands to us'; and in the opening invocation on the slab-like gold or silver passports which allowed travellers and messengers to use the empire-wide pony express. A grand aim needed a grand title. Ogedei had declared himself not khan, but 'khagan', reviving an ancient Turkish term usually translated as 'Great Khan'. From then on, all the Mongol rulers were khagans, as was Genghis retroactively, with khan being applied to their juniors (a distinction lost in modern Mongolian, in which the medial 'g' has fallen from use). As de Rachewiltz puts it, all of this signalled 'the real transformation of a tribal federation into a conquering state with a new administration and an incredibly efficient system of communication, combined with a revitalized and much strengthened military organization'. In short, he argues, it was Ogedei who was 'the *real* founder of the Mongol empire'.

Now he had to turn his claim into reality. Top of the agenda were the unconquered bits of north China. The advance was in three wings, under the greatest of Mongol generals, Subedei; Ogedei himself; and Tolui. An army assaulted the formidable fortress of Tongguan, which blocked a ravine leading to the Yellow River almost 400 kilometres upstream from the Jin capital, Kaifeng. The attack failed. So, as Genghis had advised on his deathbed, the Mongols skirted the fortress to lay siege to Kaifeng. This was another epic siege, lasting a year, against a city of well over a million. The Mongols held their ground in the face of 'thunder-crash bombs', which could be heard 50 kilometres away, and which were lowered or dropped into the Mongol trenches, 'with the result that . . . the attacking soldiers were all blown to bits, not even a trace being left behind'. Starvation, plague, cannibalism and rebellion finally forced surrender. Again there was talk of mass executions; again Yelu Chucai's passionate protests averted them, leaving the starving inhabitants to scatter into the ruined countryside. The emperor, Aizong, fled south, determined to fight again, but as the Mongol grip tightened, his hopes died, and in February 1234 he hanged himself to avoid capture. Twenty-one years after Genghis's first invasion, all north China was in Mongol hands.

A few months into the siege, Tolui died. This was Sorkaktani's next stroke of good fortune, not that she would have seen it that way at the time. *The Secret History* tells of his death in a well-spun

A nineteenth-century reconstruction of an aristocrat's travelling tent, as described by the French monk William of Rubruck in 1246: 'I myself once measured a breadth of twenty feet between the wheel-tracks of a wagon, and . . . I have counted 22 oxen to one wagon.' These vast vehicles soon fell out of fashion, perhaps because Kublai's court was in China, which lacked Mongolia's oceanic grasslands.

account intended to dramatize the loyalty of a younger brother towards his elder, of a general towards his emperor. Ogedei, who had returned to Mongolia with Tolui, leaving the campaign in Subedei's hands, falls ill. Land and water spirits rage within him – probably the result of a lifetime of alcohol abuse. Shamans go into a huddle to divine the cause. After examining the entrails of slaughtered animals, they state that a sacrifice is needed. But no sooner have the shamans gathered captives, gold, silver, cattle and food for the offering than Ogedei becomes worse. A question arises:

could a member of the khan's family take on Ogedei's illness? Tolui
volunteers, for otherwise the people will be left orphans and the Jin
will rejoice. He has to drink an alcoholic potion of some kind. He
agrees: 'Shamans, cast your spells and make your incantations!'
What he does not know is that Ogedei is not simply suffering an
illness but death-pangs. Tolui drinks. The potion works fast. He just
has time to consign his family to Ogedei's care before words fail
him. 'I have said all I have to say,' he slurs. 'I have become drunk.'
On that he passes out, never to regain consciousness. The magic

works: he dies, Ogedei lives, for another ten years, eternally grateful to Tolui and his widow, Sorkaktani.

From 1235, Karakorum rose from the steppe. Mongolians had no experience of cities, so the architects and builders were Chinese. Earthen walls with four gates surrounded a small town, which included a palace with wooden floors, wooden pillars, a tiled roof and nearby cellars for the storage of treasures. Attached were private apartments, while in front stood a giant stone tortoise bearing an engraved pillar, like those that commonly guard Chinese temples – the very tortoise, perhaps, that still holds a lonely vigil beside Karakorum's replacement, the sixteenth-century monastery of Erdeni Zuu. Inside the palace a central aisle led to steps, at the top of which stood Ogedei's throne. Soon, one third of the town was taken up with government departments controlling sacrifices, shamans, merchants, the postal-relay system, treasuries and arsenals. But even when Muslim merchants and Chinese craftsmen began to crowd inside the walls, it wasn't much of a town. William of Rubruck, the French missionary who was there in 1254, said it was less fine than the town of St Denis north of Paris and that St Denis's basilica – the first Gothic cathedral, built in the mid-twelfth century and still a glory today – was worth ten of Karakorum's palace (a little unfair, considering that Christianity had a 1,000-year head start).

What it lacked in sophistication it made up in significance. It was a centre for *gers* by the hundred, wagons by the thousand and animals by the ten thousand. Rich Mongols, of which by now there were hundreds, had anything up to 200 ox-drawn wagons, which would be linked into huge trains of twenty or thirty, all strung together, lumbering slowly across the open steppe, driven by one woman in the lead wagon. No doubt a visitor would have seen one of those huge, four-wheeled, flatbed carts, 10 metres across, with axles like masts, drawn by twenty-two oxen, on which stood the imperial tent. No one knows how or where such a monstrosity was used, but it could in the 1230s have creaked its way back and forth between old Avraga and new Karakorum.

So began a new chapter for Sorkaktani, as Tolui's widow at the heart of an expanding empire. It was traditional in Mongol society for the widow of a wealthy man to administer her husband's estates (by which was meant people, tribes, clans and families, not lands) until her eldest son was of an age to do so. As it happened, her eldest, Mönkhe, was already twenty-three, but still Ogedei gave Sorkaktani enduring authority to handle Tolui's estates, with control over her family, an army of her own, a secretariat and the local population. In essence, Sorkaktani became the queen of Mongolia, though subject to her emperor.

Fate had made her independent, and she, approaching fifty, was shrewd and ambitious enough to keep it. When Ogedei proposed that she marry his son (and her nephew) Guyuk – an offer that would have linked the two main family lines – she courteously declined, saying that her prime responsibility was to her sons. She never did remarry, using her independence to earn herself an unrivalled reputation for wisdom and firmness over the next fifteen years.

Her good sense was apparent in the way she raised her four boys. She made sure they were well educated in traditional Mongol ways. But the empire was wide and had many faiths. She knew from her own experience – a Kerait and a Christian married to a Mongol shamanist – how important it was not to alienate allies and subjects. She even financed the building of mosques and madrassas – one being a madrassa in Bukhara, with 1,000 students – which, as Muslims noted, was a remarkable thing for a Christian queen to do. For her sons there were tutors in Buddhism, Nestorianism and Confucianism, and then wives who were chosen in Sorkaktani's own image, of different religions, but assertive, intelligent, undogmatic, and highly independent, who preserved the tolerance that had been one of Genghis's more surprising traits.

9

TERROR ON EUROPE'S EDGE

LIKE MANY A DICTATOR, OGEDEI SAW THE BENEFITS OF FOREIGN adventures. They give a sense of purpose, they unify, they guarantee income for the nation, leaders and ordinary soldiers. And in this case it would be fulfilling a destiny that he had just declared to be divinely ordained.

In 1235, Ogedei held a grand assembly and ordered the western conquests to continue under the great Subedei, now aged fifty, with over thirty years of campaigning behind him. It was he who had opened the way into Russia in 1221–3, he who should have the job of finishing off the Bulgars who had forced him into ignominious retreat. With Subedei rode a contingent of princes, among them Genghis's grandchildren: Batu (Jochi's son), Guyuk (Ogedei's), Mönkhe (Tolui's) and his own son, Uriyang-khadai.

There are no details at all of what was done to the Bulgars. Whatever it was, it did not take long. That, of course, was merely the beginning of something much bigger. In late 1237, the Mongols crossed the Volga. The Russian princes had learned nothing from the Battle of the Kalka River fourteen years before. Forests so dense that not even a serpent could penetrate, as one source put it, were no defence. The Mongols cut roads wide enough for three carts to pass abreast, and rolled forward with their siege engines. After one unidentified victory, the Mongols tallied the slain by cutting off the right ears of the dead, producing a harvest of (supposedly) 270,000 ears. Divided, cities tumbled like dominoes: Riazan, Moscow, Suzdal, Vladimir, Yaroslav, Tver. In early 1238, one Mongol army defeated Grand Duke Vladimir on the Siti River, while another headed for Novgorod.

Europe had warning enough of impending catastrophe. A Hungarian friar, Julian, made two journeys to Batu's camp in southern Russia in 1234–7, bringing back a letter from Batu to the Pope demanding instant capitulation: 'I know that you are a rich and powerful king . . . [but] it would be better for you personally if you submitted to me of your own volition.' In England, the chronicler Matthew Paris in St Albans recorded how 'the detestable people of Satan, to wit, an infinite number of Tatars . . . poured forth like Devils loosed from Hell, or Tartarus' – reflecting the enduring confusion in Europe between Tatars and 'Tartars'. The Mongol advance on Novgorod even had consequences for some English, namely the fishing folk in Norfolk. Every spring, the merchants of Novgorod sailed north down their section of the 'river-road' that linked the Baltic to Byzantium and went across the North Sea to Yarmouth to buy herrings. In 1238 they stayed at home to guard their city, leaving the herrings to glut the Yarmouth quays. No European leader could claim ignorance of the menace.

In the event, the spring thaw turned the flat lands around Novgorod to bogs, and the Mongols retired southwards for eighteen quiet months. In 1240, they turned instead on Kiev, the Russian capital, the mother-city of Slavs, the seat of Orthodoxy, with 400 churches gathered like a halo around the glory of St Sophia's Cathedral. As a Russian chronicler put it: 'Like dense clouds the Tatars [i.e. Mongols] pushed themselves forward towards Kiev, investing the city on all sides. The rattling of their innumerable carts, the bellowing of camels and cattle, the neighing of horses and the wild battle-cries were so overwhelming as to render inaudible conversation inside the city.' Kiev burned, its princes fled – to Moscow, which from that time grew as Kiev declined.

And now, at last, the grasslands of the Ukraine were open, with Hungary beyond. Well informed by spies and deserters, the Mongols knew what they faced – the countryside, the towns, the distances, the rivers, even the utter disarray of the opposition in Hungary and neighbouring Poland.

To secure Hungary, Poland would first be neutralized, over winter, when rivers were highways of ice and the lowlands like concrete. In early 1241, Lublin, Sandomir, and Krakow died in flames. In Krakow, so it was said, a watchman in the tower of the new Mariacki Church, the church of St Mary, had been sounding the alarm on his horn when a Mongol arrow pierced him through the throat. Today, a recording of the mournful bugle call known as the *hejna* sounds every hour from St Mary's, breaking off on the very note on which the watchman supposedly died. Tourists are told as fact that his death saved the city. Not so. On Palm Sunday, 24 March, according to local records, the Mongols set Krakow ablaze and 'dragged away an uncounted mass of people'.

On the River Oder, the citizens of Breslau set their own town on fire and retreated to an island in the river. From this quick and easy victory, the Mongols raced on 40 kilometres to Liegnitz (Legnica today, though historians still prefer the German form). Here, on the borders of the Holy Roman Empire, Duke Henry the Pious of Silesia confronted them, with an army of 100,000.[1] In this newly Christianized frontier country, Poles, Germans and Czechs made up a mixed bag of local worthies, Hospitallers, Templars, Teutonic Knights keen to defend their possessions on the Baltic, rough-and-ready units of German and Czech settlers, and even a contingent of Silesian goldminers all gathered in support of the duke. A Czech army of 50,000 under their king, Wenceslas, was en route to join them, but still a few days' march away as Henry headed south.

On 9 April, 10 kilometres outside Liegnitz, he met the Mongols. His forces were superior in number only. In every other respect – weapons, tactics, strategy, morale, ruthlessness – the Mongols

---

[1] As ever, we must bear in mind that all figures are highly unreliable.

utterly outclassed the knights, with their heavy armour, cumbersome horses and squabbling leaders. The Mongols performed their old trick, creating a smokescreen with burning reeds, milling about as if in confusion, then pretending to flee. The Polish cavalry galloped in pursuit, until suddenly the Mongols vanished and arrows zipped in from both sides. Duke Henry fled, fell fom his horse, tottered onwards in his shell of armour, was overtaken, stripped, beheaded and cast aside. The Mongols paraded his head on a spear around the walls of Liegnitz to terrorize the inhabitants. Something like 40,000 died – a disaster that scarred the soul of eastern Europe from that day on. King Wenceslas and his 50,000 Czechs, still a day's march away, turned for the safety of the Carpathians, leaving all southern Poland to the Mongols.

To the south, Hungary awaited her nemesis. This was a country in chaos. Hordes of Polovtsy, displaced from the Russian steppes by the Mongol assault, demanded residence. Hungarian barons, who would rather die than surrender their hard-won independence, were at odds with their king, Bela IV. Bela welcomed the Polovtsy as a potential private army; the barons hated them. The Mongols seized their chance. The southern army, now in Galicia, divided into three. Two columns cut across the Carpathians in a pincer movement, while Subedei raced down the centre, so that all three columns would meet up near the Danube. It took just three days for the advance guard to cover 280 kilometres, through enemy country covered in snow. In early April, the three columns snapped together on the Danube, ready to attack the Hungarian capital, Esztergom.

Bela had managed to raise an army at Pest, on the Danube's east bank, not yet linked to Buda opposite. The usual chance to submit had been offered, and rejected.[2] Batu and Subedei held back. They faced a strong army, backed by the Danube and a capital city, with its possible reinforcements. But Subedei was a genius, and part of his genius was that he fought only when certain of victory. So he withdrew his whole army towards the Tatra Mountains, a slow,

[2] Strangely, the Mongol envoy was the Hungarian-speaking Englishman Robert, first heard of as an interpreter with Muslim merchants in the Crimea; he will reappear shortly.

skirmishing retreat for six days, luring Bela away from the river and from help.

On 10 April, the Mongols backed across the River Sajo towards the gentle, vine-rich slopes of Tokaj, just up from the Sajo's confluence with the Tisza. The Hungarians settled opposite on a plain named Mohi, making a fort by chaining their wagons into a circle, confident in their superior numbers.

The Mongol generals saw the Hungarians 'crammed together and shut in as if in a pen' and knew what had to be done. Now, this was just one day after the Poles had been shattered at Liegnitz. Was this a coincidence? Surely not. The Mongols did not base victory on coincidences. It is fair to assume that the two armies knew all about each other, with messengers galloping across 450 kilometres of hostile territory – an achievement so astonishing that it beggars the imagination; yet so obvious and so routine for the Mongols that no one thought to record it; and so secret that no European sources mention it.

So that night Subedei knew there would be no reinforcements for his enemy and plenty for him if needed. He ordered troops back across the river, while a second contingent seized the only bridge with catapults and gunpowder, the first recorded use of this devastating weapon in Europe. The Mongols crossed by means of what became known in the First World War as a rolling barrage, with artillery lobbing shells just ahead of the advancing troops.

Ten kilometres downriver, Subedei himself led a second column over a pontoon of logs. By dawn both crossings were secure, and by 7 a.m. the Hungarians were driven back into their laager, now less of a defence than a trap. For the whole morning, arrows, rocks and fire took a terrible toll. At midday, the encircling Mongolians drew back, allowing an enticing gap through which the survivors fled, turning themselves from desperate defenders into easy game, stumbling across the spring bogs to ever more certain death. Some took refuge in a nearby church, only to perish when the flaming roof collapsed on them. Three archbishops, four bishops and two archdeacons died, and with them some 65,000 ordinary

Hungarians, Germans – even French, according to the abbot of Marienberg.[3]

Bela fled north, into mountain forests, then around in a circle that took him into Austria, and on south, through Croatia, where he found sanctuary on a succession of islands. In pursuit came Kadan, one of the heroes of Liegnitz, who thus brought Mongols to the shores of the Adriatic. Here he lost either track of or interest in his prey, and continued on southwards into Albania. After burning a few small towns, leaving 'nobody to piss against a wall' (as the cleric and chronicler Thomas of Split put it), he turned inland again. Bela went to ground on the island of Krk – Veglia, as its Venetian owners called it – to await better times.

Meanwhile, another Mongol contingent had galloped west, burning, destroying, raping and killing in a campaign of deliberate terror rivalling their actions in Muslim lands. Their rationale was exactly the same: these Christians, like the Muslims, had dared resist, and had therefore doomed themselves to the vengeance of Eternal Heaven. In the Danube port of Pest, taken in three days, they burned the Dominican monastery, slew the 10,000 seeking refuge within it, and 'heaped the bodies of the butchered multitudes on the river banks' in order to terrify those on the opposite bank. The author of this vivid scene, Thomas of Split, said that some Mongols 'skewered small children on their spears and carried them on their backs like fish on spits up and down the embankments'. For the summer of 1242, the Mongols briefly encouraged peasants to raise crops; but after the harvest the same peasants were slaughtered. There was no Chucai to suggest taxation rather than terror.

Beyond Hungary, of course, there was another world, as rich as China. Batu had ordered scouting raids into Austria. One of these penetrated into the Vienna Woods, almost within sight of the city, where they were chased off by Austrian troops, who caught up with them near Wiener Neustadt ('Vienna New Town'), 40 kilometres

---

[3] The abbot was writing in Vienna in 1242 (cf. Strakosch-Grassmann, pp. 191–3). Marienberg, his twelfth-century Benedictine abbey, was then in Austria, and is today's Monte Maria near Burgusio, in the Italian province of South Tyrol.

south of the capital. They captured eight of them, one of whom was found to be the interpreter Robert the Englishman, eager to co-operate to save himself from trial as a traitor. He failed, and ended in an unknown grave.

In just four months, the Mongols had overrun seven nations and routed the forces of Central Europe. All Christendom trembled. 'Hear, ye islands, and all ye people of Christianity, who profess our Lord's Cross, howl in ashes and sackcloth, in fasting tears and mourning.' So wrote the Landgrave of Thuringia to the Duke of Boulogne, urging united retaliation. But unity was not much in evidence. The Venetians, whose merchants had allied themselves to the Mongols in the Crimea, refused to send aid. Frederick, Holy Roman Emperor, took advantage of Bela's collapse to extort bits of western Hungary from him on his flight through Austria. Pope Gregory's main enemy was not the Mongols but the emperor, Frederick, who in despair begged Henry III of England for help, sending copies of his appeal all over Europe. Nobody took any notice. Proposals for crusades from both Pope Gregory and Frederick went unanswered.

So it is as certain as anything can be that western Europe would have fallen prey to the Mongols if they had followed up their dreadful successes in Hungary and Poland. But the 'if' is a big one. It seems likely that they would never have tried it. Hungary and its grasslands had been the goal, because the Hungarian plain looked like a good source of grass, the fuel needed to power the Mongolian cavalry. But once they arrived, they found they had a problem.

The average Mongolian horse needs about 4 hectares to feed itself year round.[4] An army of 150,000 men, with their 600,000 horses, needed some 24,000 square kilometres if they were to remain permanently. In Mongolia, no problem. But Hungary's Great Plain is a mere twentieth the size of Mongolia's grasslands. Subedei would have very quickly realized that Hungary was not a base to

---

[4] In the UK, experts recommend about 1–1.5 hectares per horse. But on the grass-lands of eastern Europe and Inner Asia, horses must endure harsh winters, which demand far more space.

expand from, or retreat into, or for raising reinforcements long term.

Of course, there is no telling what ideology might have dictated: demands for submission to the Pope and every king, perhaps, with Mongol hordes streaming towards Rome and Paris. But the Mongols also had a more persuasive reason to leave.

Ogedei had died the previous December. As we will see in a later chapter, disputes about the succession arose that put the fate of the whole empire in the balance. As Genghis's grandson, ruler of his own portion of the empire, with a vast army, Batu could play a decisive role. In June 1242 he pulled out of Europe and returned to his home on the Volga. When Bela emerged from his Adriatic island later that summer, he found a wilderness of burned towns, decomposing bodies, a population reduced to cannibalism, and not a Mongol in sight, leaving Europe stunned by its inexplicable salvation.

10

THE FOUNDATIONS SECURED

BACK IN MONGOLIA, OGEDEI HAD DRUNK AND HUNTED AND WASTED HIS way towards his grave. It was not that he was a bad man. He meant well, doing his best to win hearts and minds. But he allowed his administration to go to pieces – lavish gifts, expensive campaigns, ever higher taxes, and the consumption of far too much alcohol.

Chucai had tried to guide him, but Mongol colleagues saw Chucai's policies as a plot to fill the emperor's coffers at the expense of their own. Ogedei didn't help because, with this sudden influx of cash from Chucai's reforms, he became doubly profligate, demanding money both for his military campaigns and to invest in Muslim businessmen, who promised high returns. Chucai's work hit a dead end when Ogedei handed over tax collection in China to a Muslim 'tax farmer' called Abd el-Rahman. His cronies would buy the right to tax, with the result that they could impose whatever interest they wanted. They became the Mongols' loan-sharks, charging up to 100 per cent per annum (Ogedei considerately banned higher rates). Thus was started a vicious circle of scams. The Muslim businessmen would lend Ogedei's money at exorbitant rates of interest to the unfortunate peasants, who needed the loans to make good what had been lost in taxes. The result was predictable: people fled their homes to avoid the tax collectors and their strong-arm gangs. According to one estimate, 50 per cent of the population were either of no fixed abode or enslaved by Mongol officials.

From the mid-1230s, Ogedei drank himself steadily towards death. A special official was appointed by his staff to count the number of goblets he consumed, in a vain attempt to control his intake. The number went down, apparently, but only because he got himself a bigger goblet.

In December 1241 the emperor took part in the annual winter hunt, a huge event for which he had built a fence two days' journey in length to gather wild animals, mainly white-tailed deer and wolves. Then he started a night of heavy drinking, in the company of his favourite Muslim tax farmer, Abd el-Rahman. He died at dawn, on 11 December, aged fifty-five. *The Secret History* ends a review of Ogedei's reign with a self-assessment, almost certainly an addition to the text sanctioned, if not dictated, by Ogedei himself. His words were in the style of a shaman rendering respect to an ancestor, detailing his merits and sins as a way of deferring to the spirit of his mighty forebear, the nation's founder. Having been 'placed on the great throne', he had done four good things – attacked China, set up postal-relay stations, dug wells and imposed peace on his people – but there had also been four faults, three of which were an incident of forced marriages en masse, the secret execution of a faithful minister and the building of a wall to make a game reserve, all of which sound more like token crimes than real ones. The fourth and greatest was 'to let myself be vanquished by wine'. Perhaps that was why, as a form of self-punishment, he had himself buried not with his father on the Mongols' sacred mountain in northern Mongolia, but on his own private estate in Mongolia's far west.

Chucai himself died two years later, some say of a broken heart, aged fifty-four, after almost thirty years of devoted service to an impossible ideal.

Sorkaktani, already a power in the Mongol heartland, benefited from these upheavals, and learned from them. In 1236, two years after Ogedei finished the conquest of north China, she had asked for part of Hebei province as an 'appanage', a personal estate, on the grounds that her husband had conquered it. Owning land as opposed to people was a novelty in Mongolian culture, so Ogedei hesitated, but since – as Rashid al-Din wrote – he 'used to consult her on all affairs of state and would never disregard her advice', she got her way, acquiring a foundation for wealth and independence.

Travelling to Hebei, she and her son, twenty-one-year-old Kublai, would have seen the terrible destruction caused by the Mongol war machine: abandoned farms, overgrown fields, empty villages, refugees. A population of 40 million or so in the early thirteenth century, as recorded by the Jin, had dropped to about 10 million.[1] The figure is so astonishing that many scholars simply don't believe it. Perhaps households were broken up. Perhaps millions fled south. In any event, the social consequences of the war were catastrophic.

Sorkaktani's place in Hebei province, Zhengding, about 200 kilometres south-west of present-day Beijing, was less damaged than most areas, because it had been granted to a local warlord who had surrendered to Genghis. It was not a place many Mongolians would have bothered with. Famed for its Buddhist temples, pagodas and statues, then and now, it is on the western rim of the great North China Plain, where rich farmland gives way to low hills rolling between river valleys. Sorkaktani spotted a chance to build wealth. She would nurture her estates, woo her tenants by patronizing Buddhism and Daoism, and put the taxes to good use.

The same year, Kublai received an estate of his own from Ogedei, Xingzhou, 100 kilometres south of his mother's estate, a region of some 10,000 households. He was too young to be interested in good

---

[1] It was bad, but perhaps not quite that bad. The numbers, as gathered by the first Mongol census in 1234, derived from the number of households: 7.6 million dropping to 1.7 million. But what was the size of a household? Perhaps, with the disruption of war, individuals survived the destruction of their households. Perhaps a Mongol–Chinese household, swollen by refugees, was larger than a Jin–Chinese household. Perhaps north China was reduced by only – only! – 50 per cent.

government, and allowed local officials free rein, with predictable consequences: oppressive taxation, corruption, the flight of the fit and strong, and a dramatic decline in tax revenues. Shocked, Kublai ordered reforms. New officials were drafted, tax laws revised. People returned, teaching Kublai an important lesson about management.

Kublai had the sense to see that he had a lot to learn. Over the coming years, during which the empire almost tore itself apart, he hired a Brains Trust of half a dozen Chinese advisers, most of whom shared religious and intellectual interests and all of whom were prepared to work with their new overlords, offering guidance in finding their way among China's three great religious traditions – Buddhism, Daoism and Confucianism – and in the hope of moulding the Mongol leaders into good Chinese rulers. This was quite a remarkable step by Kublai, because it was conducted across a linguistic and cultural gulf. He did not speak much Chinese, and very few Chinese spoke Mongol. All communication was through interpreters.

Among the advisers, three were of particular significance.

The first was the Buddhist monk Haiyun, who had been famously clever as a child. On the question of happiness and sorrow, he said that at the age of seven, he had read Confucius and found him unhelpful. So he turned to Buddhism, and was ordained at the age of nine. When the Mongols seized Lanzhou, the capital of today's Gansu province, in 1219, Haiyun, now aged sixteen, was found wandering with his master, quite unconcerned amidst the devastation and looting. A Mongol general asked if they were not afraid of being killed by the troops. On the contrary, Haiyun replied calmly, they relied on the invaders for protection. Impressed, the commandant of north China, Mukhali, brought the pair to the attention of Genghis. The master died soon afterwards, and the pupil rose to become head of several temples, being further promoted by Yelu Chucai. When Kublai met Haiyun in Karakorum in 1242, he asked him which of the Three Teachings – Buddhism, Daoism, Confucianism – was the highest. Haiyun replied that Buddhism offered the best guidance for a prince wishing to promote virtue, relieve suffering, resist delusions, accept good advice, shun extravagance and distinguish right from wrong.

Haiyun introduced Kublai to another monk, Liu Bingzhong, a painter, calligrapher, poet, mathematician; the multi-talented product of the famous Daoist sect Complete Perfection, whose patriarch, Changchun, Genghis had summoned all the way to Afghanistan. Liu later converted to Buddhism, without losing interest in Daoism and Confucianism. While Haiyun returned to run his temple in Beijing, he remained on Kublai's staff, devoting his life 'to the ideal of modifying Mongol institutions according to Confucian principles'.[2]

The third adviser, Yao Shu, had joined Ogedei's staff in 1235, and was sent with Shigi on raids across the Song frontier, during which he too did his best to modify Mongol brutality. He later helped found a Confucian academy in Beijing. Resenting Mongol administration, he retreated to the country for ten years, until Kublai head-hunted him and invited him to Karakorum in 1251. He became tutor to Kublai's eight-year-old second son and intended heir, Jingim (Zhenjin in Chinese), and thus one of several Confucian scholars on hand to offer Kublai practical advice.

Kublai employed other nationalities as well, for he was keen to balance his past and future, local interests and imperial ones. For advice on government, he had his Chinese team. For military matters, he relied on Mongols. For translators and secretaries, Turks. It was a surprisingly large and varied group – some two dozen in all, a shadow cabinet carefully chosen for its political balance, almost as if Kublai was preparing himself for much more than local administration.

North of the Gobi, there was no agreed successor. Ogedei had designated a favourite grandson, Shiremun, as heir in a fit of pique at his son, Guyuk, but his widow, Toregene, took over the empire and very nearly ruled over its collapse. She ignored her husband's will and set about getting the throne for Guyuk. He was never going to be popular: in poor health, made worse by drink, moody,

[2] Hok-Lam Chan, 'Liu Ping-chung' in de Rachewiltz, *In the Service of the Khan* (see Bibliography).

suspicious and unsmiling. But Toregene was a determined lady. She won over most of the family with arguments and gifts. Jochi's son Batu, however, was not persuaded. He refused to come to a *khuriltai*, the great assembly of princes that would have to elect the next khan, claiming he was suffering from gout. Delays continued for five years, with Toregene constantly shoring up support for her son with intrigues and bribes.

The dispute threatened to tear the empire apart, with every prince making his own laws, changing the orders of Genghis himself. Genghis Khan's youngest brother, Temüge, now well into his seventies, even dared suggest that he, as elder statesman, should be nominated khan without even calling an assembly, a claim for which he would pay in due course. Chaos threatened, until Sorkaktani – who had scrupulously refrained from issuing edicts of her own – came out in support of Guyuk, giving Toregene a slight but significant majority among the princes. She at last arranged the assembly, which convened in the spring of 1245, with the gout-stricken Batu represented by his elder brother.

This *khuriltai* was the grandest imperial affair yet. As described by Juvaini, Karakorum became a stage for the display of new-found power and wealth. Nobles by the hundred gathered from every corner of the empire: most of Genghis's scattered descendants, sons and grandsons, cousins and nephews. They were joined over the course of several weeks by fawning leaders from north China, Korea, Russia, Hungary, Turkestan, Azerbaijan, Turkey, Georgia, Syria, even Baghdad, though it was as yet unconquered, arriving to create a satellite city of 2,000 tents. The Italian monk John of Plano Carpini, having just arrived, was busy gathering inside information from long-term residents who spoke Latin and French. The feasting and drinking went on for a week, during which the princes grudgingly offered the throne to Guyuk, who, after three routine refusals, accepted.

His coronation took place that August near Karakorum. Here the tributes from vassals and the Mongol elite arrived, in 500 cartloads of silks, velvet, brocade, gold, silver and furs, displayed in and around Guyuk's coronation *ord*, a huge tent-palace of yellow felt supported by gilded wooden columns. Guyuk was crowned on an ivory throne, inlaid with gold, made by a Russian goldsmith. It was Sorkaktani who oversaw a gigantic pay-off, the treasures being handed out to everyone, from grizzled companions of Genghis himself, down through commanders of 10,000, to platoon chiefs in charge of ten men, from sultans to humble officials, and all their dependants.

Together, Guyuk and Toregene wrung from the assembled princes a pledge that the throne would remain with Ogedei's line of descent; this in effect countermanded Genghis's own will, which specified that if Ogedei's descendants proved unfit to rule, the princes should choose from other descendants.[3] Sorkaktani made no attempt to push Mönkhe forward, for these were dangerous times. Genghis's ageing brother Temüge was put to death for having claimed the throne for himself. Genghis's *brother*! Executed! A few years earlier it would have been inconceivable.

Then scandal threatened to tear the family apart. Toregene had employed a Muslim woman called Fatima, who had been brought as a captive to Karakorum, where she set up trade managing the local prostitutes. Somehow she wormed her way into Toregene's household and became the queen's close friend and confidante, a sort of female Rasputin. Knowledge of the queen's secret views and court intrigues gave her far too much influence. Top people had to grovel their way into her good books, and resented her, praying for a come-uppance. It came soon after Guyuk succeeded, when his brother, Köten, fell ill. Someone suggested that Fatima must have bewitched him. Guyuk tried to reverse the damage. He prised her out of his mother's control, had her accused and tortured until she confessed, and then consigned her to a dreadful death, conferring upon her the upper-class honour of dying without shedding blood. As Juvaini describes, 'her upper and lower orifices were sewn up, and she was rolled up in a sheet of felt and thrown into the river.' Such a conflict between son and mother was no basis for sound rule.

What, meanwhile, of Batu? He was still advancing slowly across Central Asia with a small army. Guyuk suspected not submission,

---

[3] If *The Secret History* was written later, this would have to be seen as a spin injected by the actual successor, Mönkhe.

but an invasion. He mustered his own army and marched west-wards, intending a counter-invasion. All this took months, opening a window of opportunity for one of Sorkaktani's most crucial interventions – a difficult decision, fraught with danger. If she was discovered, all would be lost – her years of waiting, her careful net-working, her hopes for her sons. Recalling the ties of brotherhood between her late husband and Batu's father Jochi, she sent a secret message to Batu warning him of Guyuk's preparations for war. Batu prepared himself for action – unnecessarily, as it turned out, because in April 1248 the two armies were virtually squaring up along the shores of Lake Balkhash when Guyuk, always sick and now worn out by travel, died, possibly poisoned, possibly in a fight, but most probably from disease.

Batu, who was content with his own empire in southern Russia, had no interest in promoting himself as the new khan. And he owed Sorkaktani a favour. So he instantly turned his army into a princely assembly and proposed that Sorkaktani's eldest, Mönkhe, should succeed.

Back home, Guyuk's sons were too young to rule, while his widow was overwhelmed by events, closeting herself with shamans. Again, the empire lacked a leader. Local rulers looked after them-selves, wringing whatever they could out of their subjects, using the postal-relay system for their own ends. People remembered Genghis's words: that if Ogedei's descendants were unsuitable, then the new khan should be chosen from among the offspring of Genghis's other three sons. Two of them, Jochi (dead for over twenty years) and Chaghadai, had estates so distant that their heirs were out of contention. That left the children of Genghis's youngest, Tolui, and his widow, Sorkaktani – her four boys, Mönkhe, Kublai, Hulegu and Ariq, all names that dominate most of the rest of this book.

Now at last Sorkaktani went into battle on her own account. She was in her sixties, and it was her last chance. She had a lot going for her: her own power-base, money, respect, influence. The court was torn apart over the Fatima affair. And she had an advantage in that Guyuk's offspring were Genghis's great-grandchildren, whereas her own were his grandchildren, a generation closer to the great man.

Mönkhe, almost forty, was well qualified. He had led a Mongol army westwards into Europe, destroying the Hungarians at the Battle of Mohi. And his three younger brothers were also experienced generals. They would be vital when the empire resumed its god-given task of imposing Mongol rule on the world.

The dispute almost ended in 1250, when rivals came together at Batu's camp and heard Batu again demand that Mönkhe be elected. But Batu's camp was not a place for a proper assembly. In the summer of 1251 a second assembly, this one on the traditional site of Avraga, confirmed the choice. As if concluding a presidential election, Mönkhe was all generosity, appeasing and befriending his former opponents and their family. It worked, but not before one of the most destructive and disgraceful events of these violent times.

The scene is the princely assembly at Avraga. A falconer loses a favourite female camel. He sets out to find it, riding for two or three days here and there. He comes across an army. He notices a wagon full of weapons. He strikes up conversations, and discovers a plot to attack Mönkhe while everyone is feasting. Finding his camel, he gallops back and barges in on the new emperor with the news. A contingent of 3,000 investigates. They find that the rebel army belongs to Guyuk's son, Shiremun, once favoured as Ogedei's heir. The leaders are marched into Mönkhe's presence. After three days of interrogation, Mönkhe concludes they are traitors on the point of rebellion. More arrests follow, and confessions, and exilings, and executions: beheadings, tramplings, suicides. The purge, in late 1251 and early 1252, reached as far afield as Afghanistan and Iraq, all under the grim authority of Mönkhe's chief judge, Menggeser, who had served with Genghis's father, with Genghis and with Tolui. It was a terrible blood-letting, with perhaps 300 victims – not many by the standards of mass murders, but these were members of an elite in which everyone knew everyone else.

Now there was unity again, to seal which there would be a push outwards such as even this empire had never seen before. It would, of course, be a family affair, on a very grand scale. Hulegu would move west across the Islamic world to the Mediterranean. Mönkhe himself and Kublai would undertake the final conquest of the Chinese south, the kingdom of Song. A third advance, a minor one by comparison, would absorb Korea.

In early 1252, in the middle of her son's great purge, Sorkaktani, now seventy, died, and was buried in a Christian church way out west, in Zhangye, Gansu province. Later she became a cult figure, and is still remembered today. She died knowing that her ambitions had been accomplished. Tolui's line had taken over from Ogedei's. Her eldest was khan, his two brothers were top generals, the empire was secure, and Genghis's vision was once again in the process of fulfilment – changes that would in due course bring Kublai to the throne and form the foundations of modern China.

PART III
KUBLAI

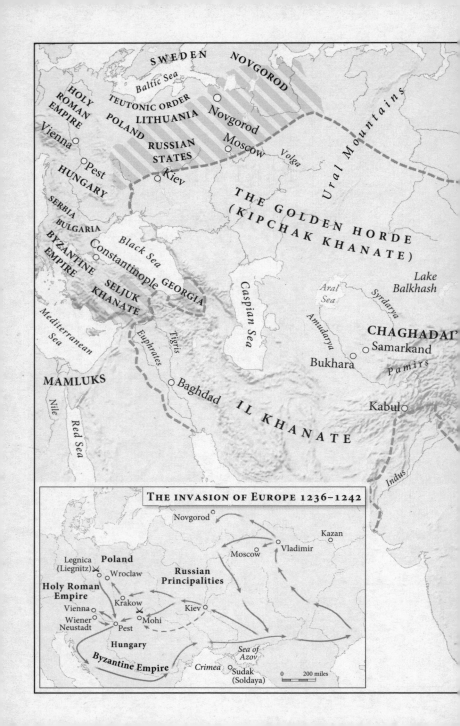

SWEDEN   NOVGOROD

Baltic Sea

HOLY
ROMAN
EMPIRE
Vienna ○

TEUTONIC ORDER
POLAND   LITHUANIA
                        ○ Novgorod
RUSSIAN   ○ Moscow
○ Pest   STATES   *Volga*

HUNGARY   ○ Kiev

Ural Mountains

SERBIA

BULGARIA

BYZANTINE
EMPIRE   *Black Sea*   GEORGIA
          ○ Constantinople

THE GOLDEN HORDE
(KIPCHAK KHANATE)

SELJUK
KHANATE

*Mediterranean
Sea*

Caspian Sea

*Aral
Sea*   *Syrdarya*   *Lake
Balkhash*

Amudarya   CHAGHADAI

Euphrates   *Tigris*

○ Samarkand
Bukhara ○   *Pamirs*

MAMLUKS

Nile   *Red Sea*

○ Baghdad   IL KHANATE

Kabul ○

Indus

THE INVASION OF EUROPE 1236–1242

Novgorod ○

Kazan ○

○ Vladimir
Moscow ○

Legnica
(Liegnitz) ✕   **Poland**
          ✕ Wroclaw
**Holy Roman
Empire**
Vienna ○   ✕ Krakow
Wiener ○   ✕ Mohi
Neustadt   ○ Pest
        Hungary
  Byzantine Empire

**Russian
Principalities**

○ Kiev

*Sea of
Azov*

Crimea   ○ Sudak
          (Soldaya)

0   200 miles

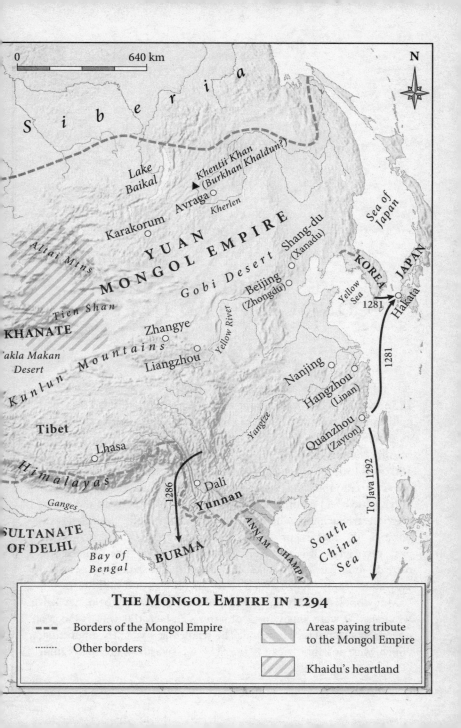

THE MONGOL EMPIRE IN 1294

- – – – Borders of the Mongol Empire
- .... Other borders
- Areas paying tribute to the Mongol Empire
- Khaidu's heartland

11

WESTWARDS AGAIN:
CONQUEST AND DEFEAT

PREPARING TO MOVE WESTWARDS TO SEIZE ALL ISLAM AND MORE. IN 1252, the Mongols knew what they were doing, because they had made a good start with Genghis over thirty years previously. Under its commander-in-chief, Hulegu, this was a formidable force, with fifteen commanders of 10,000-strong battalions, making some 100,000–150,000 men. Every man, as usual, had several horses, to provide remounts and meat. Among the best siege weapons that north China had to offer were 1,000 teams of experts in the use of traction trebuchets, which could lob rocks and 'thunder-crash' bombs 100 metres or more. Vanguards rode ahead to secure pastures. Herds of mares were gathered along the line of march to provide milk for *airag*. When the army finally struck westwards a year later, teams ranged ahead to repair bridges and build ferries.

Many books suggest that a Mongol advance was a storm, a whirl-wind, as if it were a new force of nature. In fact, this was as much a migration as a military invasion. The whole mass was self-supporting, which was possible because the way westwards was an irregular corridor of grass, right across to the Hungarian plain. Grass was fuel. As John Masson Smith has pointed out: 'The far-flung campaigns of the Mongols and the extraordinary extent of their empire were to a considerable degree the products of this great logistical boon.'[1]

What set this enterprise apart was that many of the men had their families along, and each family would also have had some thirty sheep on average. This was a nation on the move, occupiers and colonists, something over 250,000 people, with over a million horses and sheep, all widely dispersed to avoid overgrazing. Moving westwards a few kilometres a day, this was not so much a storm, more like a tide, a drifting horde some 12 kilometres across. Then think of the water needed, over 3 million gallons a day – easily supplied by a large river in flood, but what about when the grass runs out, the pastures dry up and rivers shrink? Eventually, the Mongols would discover that their reach had rather sharp ecological limits.

Other than fulfilling Heaven's command, Mönkhe had another motive for the invasion. There had been a rumour that a bunch of assassins were on their way from Persia. No one recorded finding the killers. But there was good reason to take the threat seriously, because these were not simply assassins, with a lower-case 'a'; they were the original Assassins, capitalized, a long-established and notorious menace in the Islamic world who gave their name to the very idea of murder for political and religious ends.

The story is rooted deep in Islamic sectarianism. From soon after the Prophet Mohammed's death, Sunnis, who based their teachings on the deeds and sayings of the Prophet and his successors, rivalled the Shi'ites, the Shi'at Ali (Party of Ali), who claimed that political authority derived from Mohammed's son-in-law Ali. The Shias in particular have spun off sect after sect, among them the Ismailis, who claimed that Ismail, the disinherited son of the Sixth Imam,

---

[1] 'Ayn Jalut: Mamluk Success or Mongol Failure?', *Harvard Journal of Asiatic Studies*, 44/2 (December 1984).

represented the true line of authority from Mohammed. Responding to Sunni oppression, the Ismailis formed a network of underground cells and a sub-sub-sect which revered a murdered Egyptian prince, Nizar. In the second half of the eleventh century, the Nizari offshoot of the Ismaili offshoot of the Shi'ites took over a formidable castle, Alamut, high up in the Elburz Mountains south of the Caspian.

Alamut was a fortress within a natural fortress, on a peak hundreds of feet above a single approach path, which itself could be entered only from either end of a narrow ravine. It was the perfect base from which the Nizari leader, Hasan, planned to impose a Nizari state. Other hilltop castles fell to Hasan, giving him an impregnable power-base from which to launch a malign campaign by extremists determined on murdering their way to dominance. The world soon knew Hasan's young fanatics as Assassins, because some Arabic-speakers referred to the Nizaris as *hashishiyya* – hashish-users. But it was not so. Hashish was widely known, not a Nizari secret. More likely the term was an insult applied to this despised and feared group. Hasan's victims mounted. Leaders across the Islamic world lived in terror. Terror spawned counter-terror. Nothing worked. The result: a live-and-let-live arrangement, with occasional assassinations and occasional unsuccessful reprisals. The Assassins were still there, in many different castles, when in 1219 the Mongols attacked neighbouring Khwarezm.

But the Assassins lacked sound leadership. The recent imam, Ala ad-Din, still only in his thirties, was driven crazy by isolation, drink and the uncritical obedience of all around him, with the notable exception of his teenage son, Rukn ad-Din. Terrified of his father's drunken moods, Rukn became convinced that the only hope of survival was to seize his inheritance. In November 1255, Ala went to a nearby valley, apparently to check on a flock of sheep. One night, an intruder severed his head with an axe. The probable murderer, who would presumably have implicated Rukn, was himself decapitated by an unidentified axeman before he could be questioned. Rukn ad-Din became the new and equally inadequate leader.

After much prevarication, Rukn submitted to the Mongols in

person without so much as a fight. Hulegu received him politely, for if he was treated well he would persuade others to give up and save the Mongols the trouble of attacking castle after castle. It worked: most Assassin castles, even Alamut, opened their gates.

Now that Rukn ad-Din had served his purpose, he would not be allowed to survive, for the Assassins had either resisted or been too slow to capitulate. Some 12,000 of the Nizari elite were killed. Rukn signed his own death warrant by requesting to present himself to Mönkhe in Karakorum. He was guided all the way across Central Asia to Mönkhe, who told him to go home and destroy his castles. On the way, the Mongol escorts took Rukn and his party aside, put his companions to the sword and kicked him to pulp – he was, after all, still a leader, which conferred upon him the honour of a blood-less death.

It was not quite the end of this strange sect. From 1103, the Assassins had an Arabic branch, fighting the Turks, the rulers of Egypt and the Crusaders (with whom on occasion they also collaborated). Their most redoubtable leader, Rashid al-Din Sinan, became known to Crusaders as 'The Old Man of the Mountain', a term later applied vaguely to any Assassin leader until their destruction. By 1273, the Syrian Assassins had been cowed by the sultan of Egypt, and assassinations finally ceased.

That was the end of the Assassins, but not of the Nizaris. In Persia, in the mid-nineteenth century, the Nizari imam was appointed governor of Qum, with the new title of Agha Khan, which became hereditary from then on. The Agha Khan led his troops and family into Afghanistan, allied himself to the British and settled in Bombay, where he remained for the next thirty years, rebuilding his wealth and raising racehorses. The present imam, the Harvard-educated Agha Khan IV, ministers to a scattered community of some 15 million Nizaris through the Aga Khan Foundation in Switzerland and his headquarters near Paris; a surprising outcome for a sect whose extreme violence led to their near extinction.

With that problem solved, the Mongols could turn to the rest of this part of the Islamic world, the Abbasid Caliphate, and its centre,

Baghdad, with which they had unfinished business, having tried and failed to take it in 1238.

In a sense, Hulegu had an easy target. The Abbasid Caliphate was already a spent force, divided against itself by innumerable sects and nationalities. Turks fought Persians, both fought Arabs. Syrians still resented the Abbasid conquest almost 500 years before, and yearned for a messiah to free them. To the east, the great Silk Road cities of Khwarezm – Bukhara, Samarkand, Urgench, Merv – were in ruins from the Mongol assault of 1219–22. At the centre, the royal line of Abbasids was debilitated by luxury. Rather like the Roman empire falling to the barbarians, as Philip Hitti says in his *History of the Arabs*, 'the sick man was already on his deathbed when the burglars burst open the doors'.

In September 1257, Hulegu, advancing 400 kilometres from the Elburz Mountains, sent a message to Baghdad telling the caliph, al-Musta'sim, to surrender and demolish the city's outer walls as a sign of good faith. The caliph was a lacklustre character whose predecessors had been puppets dancing in the hands of their Turkish masters, the Seljuks, on their long migration from Inner Asia to Turkey. He could only hope that this menace would pass, as the Seljuk menace had. He was after all the spiritual head of all Islam; God was surely on his side. 'O young man,' he blustered, 'do you not know that from the East to the Maghreb, all the worshippers of Allah, whether kings or beggars, are slaves to this court of mine?' Empty words, as it turned out. Not even a beggar, let alone a king, came to help him.

In November, the Mongol army, leaving their families and flocks behind, started their two-month advance on Baghdad from several hundred kilometres away. They came in three columns, from the north and east, while in the centre came Hulegu himself. Descending from the Iranian highlands along the Alwand River, he ordered his catapult teams to collect wagonloads of boulders as ammunition, since it was known that there were no stones around Baghdad. There was scant opposition. A Muslim force on low-lying ground near Ba'qubah, some 60 kilometres north-east of Baghdad, met with disaster when the Mongols opened irrigation channels, flooded them out, then moved in on the floundering foot-soldiers; 12,000 of them were killed as they tried to escape the muddy waters. Surrounding the city, the columns met at Ctesiphon, the long-abandoned ancient capital 30 kilometres south of Baghdad on the Tigris. They aimed to take the newer eastern section of the city, with its Abbasid palace, law college and 150-year-old walls, and then the two bridges that straddled the river on pontoons.

Messages had been exchanged, with no dent in the caliph's confidence. The House of Abbas had been in power for 500 years, he said, and was 'too firm to quake at every passing breeze'. Hulegu should turn back now, and maybe the caliph would overlook his offence. Hulegu laughed when he heard this. 'If Eternal Heaven is my friend, what do I have to fear from the caliph?'

By 22 January, Baghdad was surrounded. With the Tigris blocked upstream by pontoons and downstream by a battalion of horsemen, escape was impossible. The assault began a week later. Rocks from the Mongol catapults – giant machines called counterweight trebuchets, which will play a major role in a later campaign – knocked chunks off the walls, littering their bases with rubble. To gain better vantage points, the Mongols gathered the rubble and built towers on to which they hauled their catapults, the better to aim at the buildings inside. Under a steady rain of arrows that forced the inhabitants under cover, boulders smashed roofs and pots of flaming naphtha set houses on fire. By 3 February, Mongol forces had seized the eastern walls.

Panic reduced the caliph to mush. He sent envoys to sue for peace, among them the city's Catholicos, the leader of its Christians, in the hope of appealing through Hulegu's Nestorian wife, Toghus, a Kerait princess who was Toghril's granddaughter and cousin of Hulegu's mother Sorkaktani.[2] His appeal was partly successful. In messages shot into the city attached to arrows, Hulegu promised that the *qadis* (judges), scholars and religious leaders, including Nestorians, would all

---

[2] She had actually been married to Hulegu's father, Tolui, but the marriage was never consummated, Tolui being ten at the time. So she parted from him – yet ended up marrying an even younger husband, Tolui's son and in effect her stepson, Hulegu. There were no children, but he very much respected her guidance.

be safe if they ceased resisting. A second embassy sued for peace, and a third, to no effect. The caliph's vizier advised surrender.

The caliph wavered, while the city's morale collapsed. Thousands streamed out, hoping for mercy but, since there had been no surrender, all were killed, while those who remained hid in nooks and crannies. As another group of dignitaries were requesting amnesty, an arrow struck one of the Mongol commanders in the eye. Hulegu flew into a rage, had the dignitaries executed and ordered the city to be taken immediately.

On 10 February, the caliph led an entourage of 300 officials and relatives to Hulegu's camp to surrender. Hulegu greeted the caliph politely, and told him to order all the inhabitants to disarm and come out of the city, which they did; only to find themselves penned and slaughtered like sheep for having continued their resistance. Sources speak of 800,000 being killed. As ever, all figures should be treated with scepticism, but the Mongols, who were used to mass executions, were perfectly capable of such slaughter. No wonder Muslims today refer back to the fall of Baghdad as one of the greatest of crimes against their people and religion.

Three days later, the Mongols poured into the city and set almost all of it on fire. The Nestorians, however, were spared, and even profited, thanks to Hulegu's wife, Toghus. She was renowned both for her wisdom and her stout defence of her faith, the outward sign of which was the tent-church she transported wherever she went. So when she interceded for the Christians of Baghdad, Hulegu listened. While Baghdad burned around them, they found sanctuary with their patriarch in a Christian church.

To crown his victory, Hulegu chose to conduct an exercise in humiliation. Taking over the caliph's Octagon Palace, he threw a banquet to which he invited his prisoner.

'You are the host, we are your guests,' he taunted. 'Bring whatever you have that is suitable for us.'

The caliph, quivering with fear, volunteered to unlock his treasure rooms, and the attendants brought out 2,000 suits of clothes, 10,000 dinars in cash, jewel-encrusted bowls, and gems galore, all of which Hulegu shared among his commanders.

Then he turned on the caliph. Now, he said, 'tell my servants where your *buried* treasures are'.

There was indeed a buried treasure, as perhaps Hulegu already knew: a pool full of gold ingots, which were dug out and distributed, as were the harem of 700 women and the 1,000 servants.

Next day, all the possessions from the rest of the palace – royal art treasures collected over 525 years – were stacked in piles outside the gates. Some of the booty was sent back to Mönkhe in Mongolia. The rest, according to Rashid al-Din, joined loot from Alamut, other Assassins' castles, Georgia, Armenia and Iran, all of it being taken to a fortress on Shahi Island in Lake Urmia, the salt lake in Iran's north-western corner. Supposedly, it was buried on the island with Hulegu himself in 1265.[3]

At last, the city foul with the stench of the dead, Hulegu ordered a halt to the killing and pillaging.

There was only one more set of executions: the caliph himself and his remaining entourage, killed in a nearby village. Only the youngest son was spared. He was married off to a Mongol woman, by whom he had two sons. That was the end of the Abbasid line, the first time in history that all Islam had been left without a religious head.

Now came the peace. Bodies were buried, markets restored, officials appointed, reconstruction begun, the rest of the country assaulted. Most towns opened their gates. Some did not, with the usual consequences: in Wasit, 15 kilometres to the south-east of Baghdad, according to one source 40,000 died. The whole region was Hulegu's.

As creator and head of a new dynasty, yet still deferring to his brother Mönkhe in Mongolia, Hulegu named himself the Il-Khan, the 'subservient' or 'obedient' khan, and it was as the Il-Khanate that Mongol rule in the world of Islam would be known until its end seventy-seven years later.

---

[3] It is not an island now, because the lake has shrunk. The grave and its treasure – if they exist – have never been found.

After the fall of Baghdad, Hulegu ruled from Afghanistan to the Persian Gulf.

Beyond lay Syria, Egypt and who knew what else.

Syria was a land divided, its coast being a medley of Crusader states, with an Arab dynasty ruling Aleppo and Damascus inland. The Christians quickly allied themselves to Hulegu, seeing his anti-Muslim campaign as an extension of their own crusades. Hulegu was as brutal as always to Muslims and, for the sake of his ageing Christian wife, magnanimous to his Christian allies. One petty emir ruling in Diyarbakir, in today's south-east Turkey, made the mistake of crucifying a Christian priest travelling with a Mongol passport. As a curtain-raiser to the campaign westwards, the Mongols took his stronghold, captured him and subjected him to a death by a thousand cuts, slicing his flesh away and cramming the bits into his mouth, then cutting off his head, which became a sort of talisman as the campaign proper gathered pace. It moved across the Euphrates, bringing a six-day massacre to Aleppo in January 1260, the lands being granted to the Crusader king, Bohemund VI. Homs and Hama capitulated. Damascus was abandoned by its sultan, who fled to Egypt. Ked-bukha – one of the greatest generals, who was not a Mongol but a Naiman – personally beheaded its governor. Christians rejoiced, bells rang, wine flowed and a mosque was restored to Christian worship. Six centuries of Muslim domination seemed over. Then the Mongols turned southwards, to Nablus, whose garrison was exterminated for resisting, all the while making use of the good pastures on the Syrian borderlands.

Now, at last, for Egypt. The Muslim leaders of Egypt were Turkish former-slaves-turned-rulers, the Mamluks (*mamluk*, 'owned'), who had murdered their way to power only nine years before. There would be no surrender from them.

At this point, news arrived of an event in Mongolia that changed everything. In August 1259 Mönkhe had died, in circumstances which will emerge in Chapter 14. A princely assembly was pending. Hulegu returned to his new home, Persia, with two thirds of his invasion force, leaving Ked-bukha in command of the remaining 20,000 men.

The current Egyptian sultan, Qutuz, now did something that seemed foolish, but – since Qutuz had once been a Mongol captive and knew what he was doing – turned out to be extremely smart. When Hulegu sent envoys demanding surrender, Qutuz cut off their heads. To the Mongols, nothing could have been better designed to guarantee invasion.

Qutuz's action could have been a deliberate provocation, because he could well have known that he had a window of opportunity to beat a Mongol force reduced by Hulegu's departure, and on the very edge of sustainability. In Syria, in May, the main rivers drop, the pastures wither. The Mongol horses could eat and drink only because two thirds of them had left for home. The Mongols were shortly to learn a fundamental truth about campaigning in these parts, a truth stated by John Masson Smith: 'Any forces that were small enough to be concentrated amid adequate pasture and water were not large enough to take on the Mamluks.' A wiser leader might have thought twice. But faced with the murder of their envoys, the Mongols had no option but to fight, which was (perhaps) exactly what Qutuz wanted.

In July 1260, a force of some 15,000–20,000 men, about equal to or a little less than that of the Mongols (no one knows the numbers for sure), left Egypt for Palestine. This was a very different type of army than that of the Mongols. With Egypt's limited pasture, the average Mamluk had just one horse, well cared for, bigger and stronger than the little Mongol horses. The Mamluks depended on weaponry, not manoeuvrability: top-quality bows, arrows by the million, lances, javelins, swords, axes, maces and daggers. In addition, the Mamluks were selected for their physical excellence, whereas the Mongols were ordinary citizen-soldiers, superb only as long as they could choose battle on their own terms.

This time, they could not. The place was called Ain Jalut, the Spring of Goliath, because here, where the Jezreel Valley ends up against the curve of the barren Gilboa Hills, David supposedly slung his fatal stone. No good account of the battle survives, but according to probably the most reliable one,[4] Qutuz arrived after a

---

[4] An oral report by Sarim al-Din, assessed in Peter Thorau: 'The Battle of Ayn Jalut: a Re-examination', in *Crusade and Settlement*; see Bibliography.

50-kilometre march from Acre early on the morning of 3 September 1260, choosing the site for its wooded ridges and good water supply. Behind him were the Gilboa Hills and the rising sun. He scattered troops into the nearby hills and under trees, and arrayed the rest of them at the bottom of the hills. The Mongols came around the hills from Jordan, to meet the Mamluks as they advanced slowly, making a terrifying noise with their kettle-drums. Too late, the Mongols, blinded by the sun, discovered that they had been outmanoeuvred. With reinforcements streaming from Gilboa's side-valleys, the Mamluk cavalry, fresh and well-armoured, closed around the depleted and weakened Mongols. Two Mamluk leaders who had joined the Mongols defected, reducing the Mongol forces even more.

The Mongols died almost to a man. According to one account, Ked-bukha was magnificent to the end, spurring on his men until his horse was brought down, he himself caught and taken before Qutuz. He refused to bow, proclaiming how proud he was to be the khan's servant. 'I am not like you, the murderer of my master!' – his last words before they cut off his head.

It was here in today's West Bank that the Mongol war machine finally ran out of steam in the west. They were not invincible after all. The Mongols would mount several later attacks on Syria, but could never hold it because, once away from good pastures, they had no natural advantage. Genghis's dream of world conquest had reached its limits first in northern India, then in Hungary, and now in the Middle East.

But in China there were worlds still to conquer.

12

THE TAKING OF YUNNAN

AT THE OTHER END OF EURASIA, KUBLAI WAS FRONT-MAN FOR HIS
brother Mönkhe. With his Chinese advisers, he was well qualified
when in 1252 he asked his brother for an extension of his responsibilities in north China. There was a good strategic reason for such a
request – to ensure supplies for occupation troops. He had his eye
on the rich farmlands along the Yellow River and its tributaries, in
today's Shaanxi and Henan provinces, roughly between the ancient
capital of Xian and the newer and recently conquered one of
Kaifeng. Mönkhe gave him two areas, one on the Wei River, an
irregular blob almost half the size of England running from the Wei
Valley southwards to the Song border, and another in Henan.
Following Yelu Chucai's advice, his mother's shrewd practices and
Mönkhe's imperial strategy, he allowed the peasants to work, taxed
them fairly and also established 'military farms' – colonies dedicated
to supplying the troops with food. It worked. He had his power-
base, and was now looking south, towards the Song empire of
southern China, which was a very much greater challenge than the
world of Islam.

Since its foundation almost 300 years before, Song China had become the world's greatest power. Though cut almost in half when the Jurchen from Manchuria seized the north in 1126, southern Song was everything that Mongolia wasn't. Seventy million people in hundreds of cities – fifty-eight of them with over 100,000 inhabitants – crowded into China's ancient heartland, the fertile plain of the river the Chinese call the Chiang and Europeans know as the Yangtze. Both a blessing and a curse, its waters irrigated and sometimes flooded its paddy fields. It was also the region's major highway, navigable for 2,700 kilometres, linking a dozen of the biggest cities. What a contrast with Mongolia, which had not a single navigable river, scarcely 1 per cent of Song's population, and just two little towns.

Mere numbers give no clue to Song's real strengths: its cultural depth, economic drive and political unity. Song dominated all its neighbours, Tanguts and Tibetans in the west, Nanzhao (Yunnan as it became) and two Vietnams (as in 1954–75, but with different names) in the south. True, north China was lost to its Jurchen conquerors, but the southern Song preserved the old culture, ruling from their new capital, Hangzhou (Linan as it was then). Song had experienced a renaissance, fuelled by new methods of rice-growing. More and better food, population growth, trade, new industries (like cotton), people on the move in search of self-improvement, the spread of education, more civil servants – all these changes interacted to bring about the boom. The growth of wealth funded the arts, gardening, fashion, ceramics and architecture. Industries flourished – coal-mining, metallurgy, paper-making. Song porcelain became one of China's glories. For artistry, wealth, inventiveness, venerability, for the quantity and quality of practically any cultural and social trait you care to measure, southern Song was unrivalled. Islam was a novelty in turmoil, Europe a backwater. India? Southeast Asia? Japan? Africa? Nothing comparable.

With the inland frontiers blocked by 'barbarian' kingdoms, Song turned seawards. The Yangtze, its tributaries and their canals formed 50,000 kilometres of river highways, along which merchant ships sailed to a coastline dotted with ports that were bases for ships with refined sail-systems designed to take advantage of the regular monsoon winds. Quanzhou was the greatest, known to foreign merchants by its Arabic name, Zaytun, which means 'olive tree' in Arabic but actually derives from its avenues of *citong* (coral trees). Six-masted seagoing junks, with 1,000 people aboard, were made safe with watertight compartments, a feature not seen in Europe until the nineteenth century. A Song captain set his course with a compass, an invention taken over from geomancers almost two centuries before it came to Europe. Foreign trade spread Song coins from Japan to India. Chinese ceramics were exported to the Philippines, Borneo and beyond.

The examination system for recruiting civil servants, already well established, was enlarged, giving new power to the 20,000 'mandarins' and their 200,000–300,000 employees. Laws curbed the rich and helped the poor. State officials were paid well enough to limit corruption. The state, its income secured by taxes and by monopolies on salt and mining, looked after its people as never before, building orphanages, hospitals, canals, cemeteries, reserve granaries, even funding village schools. Taxes were reformed to win the cooperation of the peasant-farmers. To the state, the revenues from taxation were immense, and carefully recorded. In the late twelfth century, Song revenues from maritime customs duty alone amounted to 65 billion coins, handled in cumbersome strings of 1,000. Soon after the year 1000, Song had started printing bank-notes – an experiment that led to inflation and was abandoned.

Printing was a defining trait of Chinese society in general and Song in particular. Money and books were printed with wood-blocks, from images cut in reverse. It was this technique that underpinned the explosion in records and reading matter that had started in the eighth century in China, Japan and Korea.[1] The output of printed books was phenomenal. Soon after the Song came

[1] The immense labour of carving each page in reverse inspired the next logical step – printing with movable type, an idea independently conceived and perfected by Johann Gutenberg in Germany 400 years later. In China (and Korea, where it was actually employed in 1234) it was a dead end, firstly because wood-block printing was cheap and efficient; and secondly because a typesetter needed several thousand characters. It was quicker to carve than typeset.

to power, the whole Buddhist canon was published – 260,000 pages in two-page blocks. There were vast official text collections and encyclopedias with up to 1,000 chapters. A fashion for collections inspired inventories of anything and everything. Scientific treatises and monographs appeared, some with print runs in the millions. From these intellectual interests sprang many brilliant men and at least one genius, Shen Gua, a sort of eleventh-century precursor to da Vinci and Darwin, who recognized the nature of fossils, theorized that mountains had once been seabeds, improved astronomical instruments, pioneered advances in mathematics, described how compasses worked, wrote on pharmacology, and took a shrewd interest in politics, history and literature.

Song's capital, present-day Hangzhou, was the world's most populous city, with 1.5 million people, more than the whole population of Mongolia. A century of imperial spending had turned it into a boom city and one of the world's finest ports. Its setting – the Eye of Heaven Mountains, the West Lake – was as beautiful as its palaces.

How could the Mongols dare to dream of victory over this one city, let alone the fifty-seven other cities of 100,000 inhabitants or more, let alone the 70 million peasants and the rich lands of the Yangtze Basin?

Well, they had to. It was their destiny, ordained by Heaven.

Obviously, a frontal assault on Song, across the busy, broad and well-defended Yangtze, would risk failure. The Mongols were not in the business of failure. Mönkhe needed something that would give him an edge. It so happened that to the south-west of Song, outside its borders, was a statelet that could, if taken, act as a base from which to open a second front.

Kublai was to be in charge, and about time too. He was thirty-six and had never yet been given responsibility for anything but his own estates. A first campaign, an untried leader: Mönkhe was careful to give Kublai the best of help, in the form of one of his most experienced generals, Uriyang-khadai, the fifty-year-old son of the legendary Subedei, conqueror of half Asia and much of Russia.

Their target was a long way away, and very hard to get to. It was the core of what had, for 250 years until around AD 900, been a great kingdom, Nanzhao, now reduced to a rump centred on its capital, Dali, after which it had become known. Dali, which controlled the road, and thus the trade, between India (through what is now Burma) and Vietnam, was a knot of forested mountains and competing tribes, notoriously difficult to get into, let alone control.

For a region and a culture few Westerners have ever heard of, this was no mean place. Dali's Bai people, a Tibetan-Burmese tribe, had emerged as the dominant group in 937, and retained a sturdy independence for three centuries under its royal family, the Duans, who ruled an area about the size of Texas. To the north, Sichuan province is notoriously wet, so the Chinese dubbed Dali and its surrounding area Yun-nan, 'South of the Clouds'. Dali was a sort of Inner Asian cross between Afghanistan and Switzerland, its tribal rivalries held in check by rulers made rich by trade, and at peace with the Chinese, who had learned enough to leave the place to its tribes, its mountains, its glorious lake and its charming climate. Today, Dali still thrives on its ancient roots: the Bais in their bright, wrap-around shirts and top-heavy headdresses, stone houses decorated with wood carvings lining cobbled streets, artists at work on the local marble.

Dali itself was not much of a challenge. Three centuries of peace had made it complacent. It had no army to speak of. The main problem was to get there across Song. That would mean gathering in territory newly conquered from the Tanguts, and then slicing southwards for 1,000 kilometres along Song's western borders.

Mustering in the semi-desert of the Ordos from the late summer of 1252, Kublai's force took a year to gather itself. It must have been all cavalry, because it would have to cross many rivers and valleys. In the autumn of 1253, this great force headed south-west for 350 kilometres along the Yellow River to the Tao, then south across the foothills of the Tibetan plateau into what is today northern Sichuan. This was a pretty remote area, even for the Mongols, but it had been invaded (conquered would be too strong a word) by Ogedei's second son, Köten, in 1239. That autumn, Kublai camped on the high, bleak grasslands of today's Aba Autonomous Region, with no trouble apparently from the locals, the notoriously wild Golok tribesmen.

There would be no need for destruction if Dali capitulated. That was the ideal outcome. The *Yuan Shi*, the official history of the Yuan dynasty, tells of how Kublai's Chinese advisers had managed to talk sense into his barbarian soul. One evening, Yao Shu told a story of how a Song general, Cao Bin, had captured the great city of Nanjing without killing 'so much as a single person; the markets did not alter their openings, and it was as if the proper overlord had returned'. Next morning, as Kublai was mounting up, he leaned over to Yao Shu and said: 'What you told me yesterday about Cao Bin not killing people, that is something I can do.'

It was not that simple. Following normal practice, Kublai sent three envoys ahead offering Dali the chance to capitulate. Dali's leading minister, Gao, the power behind the Duan ruler, executed them. This foolish and provocative act guaranteed an all-out assault – the very crime that had led Genghis to invade Muslim lands in 1219.

Kublai divided his forces into three. One wing rode eastwards, off the high grasslands, down on to the Sichuan Basin, by today's Chengdu, replenishing supplies in the newly harvested fields of Dujiangyan, where dams and artificial islands dating back some 1,500 years controlled the Min River. Kublai himself headed south over the grasslands, meeting up with the first column, perhaps three days later. Meanwhile, Uriyang-khadai took a difficult route some 150 kilometres further west, deep into the mountains of western Sichuan, cutting across valleys and ridges to the main road between Dali and Tibet. This would give a fast two-day run to Dali when the time came. Gao massed his forces on the Yangtze, whose upper reaches formed a valley a day's march over a ridge to the east of the city. But the river was no obstacle to the Mongols. They had crossed dozens on their way south. The crossing was made at night, in silence. Led by a general named Bayan, of whom more later, the Mongols appeared at dawn on Gao's flank, attacked, inflicted terrible damage and forced a rapid retreat back to Dali.

With Uriyang-khadai galloping in along the lakeside from the north, Dali was now at Kublai's mercy. At this point, given the opposition, you might think that all-out slaughter would follow. But, as Genghis had shown, urbicide had to have a strategic reason: to encourage other cities to surrender. It saves time and trouble when cities surrender and subjects are grateful for their survival. Here, there were no other cities to be conquered. Kublai, learning from both Cao Bin and his grandfather, ordered restraint.

Everything fell into place quite easily with the city's surrender in January 1254. The leading minister and his underlings who had executed the envoys were themselves executed, but that was all. The king, a puppet before, remained a puppet, pampered into subservience. Mongol troops remained, gradually inter-marrying with locals.

Uriyang-khadai went on to 'pacify' tribes further south and east, penetrating today's north Vietnam, taking Hanoi in 1257, then retreating rather hastily in the face of tropical heat, malaria and some spirited resistance. This is easily said, but it was an immense operation. Yunnan to Hanoi is 1,000 kilometres. In four years the Mongols had marched all the way round Song's western frontiers, meeting hardly any resistance. Kublai now had all the information he needed to plan the next phase of the war against the south.

Although Yunnan was too remote to be a base for the invasion, Kublai's campaign changed the course of the region's history, and China's. After twenty years of nothing much, in 1273 Yunnan's first high-level administrator arrived. Sayyid Ajall was a Turkmen who had survived Genghis's assault on Bukhara in 1220 because his grandfather had surrendered at the head of 1,000 horse-men. The nine-year-old boy, raised in Mongolia and China, went on to make a distinguished career in various government posts, ending in Yunnan. With the help of his sons, it was he who brought Yunnan fully into the empire, which eventually made it part of China today.

13

IN XANADU

WITH YUNNAN UNDER HIS CONTROL, AND WONDERING HOW TO TAKE on the rest of China, Kublai was poised between two worlds – Mongolia and China, grassland and farmland, steppe and city, nature-worshippers and ancestor-worshippers – and he needed both. The Mongol elite provided his traditional backing and his cavalry; the Chinese elite provided his bureaucracy, his record-keepers, his tax-gatherers, his infantry. He could not keep the Chinese on side from a mobile HQ of tents and wagons; he could not retain the trust of Mongols from a Chinese city. He needed a new sort of base from which to rule this growing part of his brother's empire, a capital of his own that was both Chinese and Mongol.

Mönkhe understood the problem and told him to go ahead. In 1256, his Chinese advisers set out to find a suitable site. There was not a huge range of choices if he was to be within reach of Beijing, yet also on grasslands, in traditional Mongol territory.

The grasslands of Inner Mongolia are surprisingly close to Beijing on the map, a mere 250 kilometres, but a world away in practice, even today. It's a seven-hour drive, which takes you on a steep, slow climb through the hills where the Great Wall runs, and on to

Zhangjiakou. The city once marked the frontier, which is why Mongols (and foreign explorers) called it Kalgan, from the Mongolian for 'gateway'. Now it is thoroughly Chinese, part of China's northward thrust into its frontier province, Inner Mongolia. Herders object at their peril.

Beyond, though, up on the Mongolian plateau, near today's Duolun,[1] there are still rolling grasslands and gentle hills that would delight Kublai's soul. This was a land rich with associations, for it was Genghis's campsite on his way south to Beijing and on his way back from its conquest. Under Kublai's senior minister, Liu Bingzhong, the Golden Lotus Advisory Group – as his Brains Trust was called – identified the site. It was originally called Lung Gang (Dragon Ridge), so Liu and his team first had to cast a spell to evict the dragon and raise a magical iron pennant to prevent its return. A lake in the middle of the plain had to be drained and filled in before work could start. There was nothing much around to build with – hardly a tree, no stone quarries. It all had to be started from scratch, with teams of pack animals, wagon trains and riverboats carting timber, stone and marble from dozens, even hundreds of kilometres away.

Kublai was wary of calling his new HQ a capital, perhaps preferring not to challenge the 'true' imperial capital, Karakorum. For the three years it took to build, and for four years thereafter, the city was known as Kaiping, being renamed Upper Capital (Shang-du) only in 1263, as opposed to Da-Du, the Great Capital (Beijing), or Dai-Du as it was in Mongol.

English-speakers know it as Xanadu, because that's how Samuel Taylor Coleridge spells it in his dreamy, drug-induced poem that begins:

> In Xanadu did Kubla Khan
> A stately pleasure dome decree,
> Where Alph the sacred river ran
> Through caverns measureless to man
> Down to a sunless sea.

[1] Dolon Nur, Seven Lakes, as it is in Mongolian.

So famous is the poem, so weird the imagery and so widespread the name that many assume the place is no more real than Camelot. Not only was it real – it still is.[2]

Xanadu has changed over the years. The first time I visited, in 1996, it was a glorious wilderness: no fence, no gate and no charge. The sky was pure Mongolian blue, the breeze gentle, and the only sound a cuckoo. Waving grasses and pretty meadow flowers rose and fell gently over the billows made by eroded, overgrown walls. The ground was strewn with rubble. I gathered a few bits, awed by what I was touching – *Oh my God, the dust of Xanadu!* The base of Kublai's main palace, the Pavilion of Great Peace, was still there, an earthen mound about 50 metres long standing some 6 metres high above the grass. Paths made by wandering tourists wound to the top. The front was an almost sheer earth face, punctuated by a line of holes, left by timbers used to strengthen the rammed earth. A platform of earth had survived 700 years of fierce summer downpours and rock-cracking winter frosts, yet of the building itself there was not a trace. As for the rest of the site, it was a blur of ridges and grass. I couldn't make much sense of it.

A few years later, in 2004, there was a new tourist camp of Mongolian *gers*, a fence, a rickety gate, a small entry fee, and a little museum, beside which was a glass cabinet containing an immense block of white marble, 2 metres high. It was part of a pillar, its four sides brilliantly carved bas-reliefs of intertwining dragons and peonies, symbols of both war and peace. I tried the door. To my astonishment, it opened. Feeling as privileged as a prince and guilty as a schoolboy, I ran my fingers over marble that might have been touched by Marco Polo and Kublai himself. It was proof of the magnificence of the place, and the skill of Kublai's Chinese artists, not to mention the labour involved, for the closest source of marble was the famous marble mines of Quyang in Hebei province, 400 kilometres away.[3]

---

[2] Check it out on Google Earth, 42°21'37"N, 116°11'06"E.
[3] For those who doubt Marco's veracity, the find confirms his words: 'There is at this place a very fine marble palace', though which palace exactly remains obscure.

In 2008 I came again, this time with Xanadu's greatest archaeological expert, Wei Jian, professor at Renmin University, Beijing. It was he who had unearthed the marble column. Now it had vanished into storage. The gate had been replaced by a grand, Stonehenge-style trilithon, its supports inspired by the marble pillar. It was flanked by a huge stone bas-relief of armies and courtiers crowding in on a massive Kublai, sitting knees akimbo on his throne. An incised plaque provided a brief biography, in Mongol, Chinese and – in anticipation of mass tourism – English. But Xanadu is too far from Beijing for many tourists, and Duolun is not yet big enough to attract them. The tourist camp stood forlorn and abandoned. With Wei's help, the site itself at last came into focus.

The original city had three sections, all squares, nested inside each other in the style of other Chinese imperial cities. The outer wall made the biggest square of just over 2 kilometres a side, 9 kilometres in all. Brickwork about 6 metres high sloped back at a 15-degree angle to a flat top, paved, easy to patrol. Every 400 metres a U-shaped bastion stuck out, but there were no guard towers. The wall was built to assert status, not to withstand an assault, for there were no more enemies anywhere near. The outer sector was in the shape of a set-square, in the northern part of which was a park of gently undulating grasslands, where deer nibbled meadow-grass, wandering through glades of trees, drinking from streams and fountains. This was Kublai's Arcadia, an artificial version of the Mongolian grasslands, where he could pot a deer with his bow and send falcons skimming in pursuit of songbirds. In the south-east corner of the big walled square was a smaller one, the Imperial City, containing the mud-brick or board houses for workmen, craftsmen and officials, and several temples, all laid out in a grid of streets. And inside this, a moat containing a third walled square, the Inner or Forbidden or Palace City (the names vary), containing forty-three royal residences and meeting halls with Chinese-style, curled-up eaves and glazed tiles. Various pavilions – of Crystal, Auspiciousness, Wisdom, Clarity, Fragrance and Controlling Heaven – were overshadowed by the royal palace itself, the Pavilion of Great Peace.

Yuan poets, Marco Polo's descriptions and modern archaeologists (principally Wei Jian himself) allow you to imagine the scene as you approach from the south, as Marco Polo did when he arrived in China in 1275.

On your right, you pass a hill, with an *ovoo*, or shrine, on top. Pale in the distance, the horizon is a wave of gently sloping hills, some of them sharpened with more *ovoos*. Directly ahead, on the open plain, stands a straight wall, 8 metres high, blocking everything beyond except for a mass of roofs, bright with blue, green and red tiles, with one roof standing proud above the others. There are bastions, corner towers, a main gate. In the words of one poet, Yuan Jue:

> These gate towers of Heaven reach into the great void,
> Yet city walls are low enough to welcome distant hills.[4]

Across the grassland run many tracks, crowded with bullock carts, camels and yaks, arriving full or departing empty, for it takes some 500 carts a day to supply the 120,000 inhabitants who serve Kublai's growing court. In the distance, you might glimpse a patch of white – not sheep, but the emperor's white horses, by the thousand. The tracks converge to make what another poet, Yang Yunfu, called 'the broad imperial road' leading to the city through a mass of round felt tents, horses, traders and food stalls.

> While clouds cover the Main Street sun,
> Winds blow clear the North Gate sky.
> A thousand gutters turn white snow to ice,
> And ten thousand cook stoves raise blue smoke.

Beyond is the main entry, an arch as high as the wall, fringed by bulwarks, topped by a guardhouse with banners waving in the breeze, and a huge wooden door. Street-traders offer textiles, food and drink. You and your horsemen clatter across a moat, then on over paving stones through the entry, a tunnel of 24 metres (you can

[4] This and the next quote are from *Miscellaneous Songs on the Upper Capital*, with thanks to Richard John Lynn (see Bibliography).

still pace it today, as I did). A road leads straight through a line of mud-brick houses for 600 metres to a second wall, a second gate. That's the Imperial City, where the emperor, his family and his retainers live in wooden houses tiled in the traditional bright blues, greens and yellows you saw from the plain, their eaves ending in circular tiles in the form of dragons, birds and animal heads. And there, stretched out on a brick-faced platform, stands the ornate two-storey building with the roof you saw from afar: Kublai's palace, the Imperial Pavilion of Great Peace.

The palace stood on top of the 50-metre-long platform of rammed earth, with two wings on either side embracing a courtyard, and access from below by wooden staircases. Yes, wood, because no stones have been found nearby, which means the whole palace was made of wood, like a temple, except for its tiled roof. Wei's words recalled its glory: 'We think it had over 220 rooms. It was a place of celebration. For instance we know they had races around the palace, with the winner being awarded a prize by the emperor. And at the full moon there were parties here, because the moon is round, perfect, harmonious, bright like Kublai's dynasty.'

Much has been revealed by Wei's work. But much is still uncertain. That marble pillar, for example, which Wei found not far from the Imperial Pavilion. Perhaps it was part of the Crystal Palace, so called because it had glass windows. Perhaps it was part of a 'marble wall', which Rashid al-Din mentions, but which, if it ever existed, has vanished, along with much of Xanadu's stonework. Wei even threw out the suggestion that the Imperial Palace of Great Peace has been attached to the wrong building. Only more detailed work will solve these mysteries.

And somewhere in the parkland in the city's northern section was the extraordinary structure which is the only reality in Coleridge's surreal poem. There was no sacred river called Alph (though there is a river called the Shangdian, 'Lightning'), no caverns measureless to man (this is rolling grassland, after all), no incense-trees, and the Pacific (450 kilometres away) is no less sunny than any other sea.

But there was a stately pleasure dome, and we can track the

references from dome to Coleridge. His source, which he had been reading when he fell into an opium-induced sleep, was a seventeenth-century book of travels by Samuel Purchas quoting Marco Polo's eyewitness account, available in English since 1579. Marco describes what he calls the Cane Palace in detail:

> In the middle place of that park thus surrounded with a wall, where there is a most beautiful grove, the great Kaan has made for his dwelling a great palace or loggia which is all of canes, upon beautiful pillars gilded and varnished, and on top of each pillar is a great dragon all gilded which winds the tail round the pillar and holds up the ceiling with the head . . . it is all gilded inside and out and worked and painted with beasts and with birds very cunningly worked. The roof of this palace is also all of canes gilded and varnished so well and so thickly that no water can hurt it.

It stood in the summer months, when Kublai was in residence, and was placed in storage the rest of the time.

By 'cane' Marco meant bamboo, a word that did not yet exist in any European language. Bamboo does not grow in north China, but it does in Yunnan, which Kublai himself had conquered in 1253, three years before he started work on Xanadu. Bamboo is superb for building with – lightweight, many times stronger than oak, easy to cut, long-lasting. A bamboo palace would neatly show off Kublai's new acquisition to steppe-dwelling northerners.

What shape and size was this 'great palace or loggia'? Marco does not mention a dome, but that's what it had to be. Bamboo is a tree, and like all trees it tapers. Placed side by side, thin ends together, bamboo stems fall naturally into a circle. Marco gives the dimensions of the poles – 15 paces in length, 3–4 'hands' in width. These, he says, were split lengthwise and overlapped to form long, semicircular tiles. A computerized reconstruction suggests there were 840 of them.[5] With just a single, uniform item, Kublai had

---

[5] Thanks to Tom Man and Ben Godber for the CGI. Details are in my *Xanadu*. The results are in the colour section of this book.

the elements of a circular roof some 30 metres across. Columns, decorated with dragons, supported the domed roof. Such a structure would act as an aerofoil, like the wing of a plane, with tremendous lift – 24 tonnes in a gale – counteracted, as Marco says, by 200 silken cords and nails of some sort (probably wooden) through the bamboo tiles. The whole structure was sealed against rain with lacquer, in the Chinese style.

This is an informed guess, leaving many problems that will be solved only if the Cane Palace could be built for real. But assuming this virtual reconstruction is correct, the palace's purpose becomes clear. It was a symbolic centre-point for royal occasions. Xanadu was made to bridge two worlds, Mongolia and China. But the city itself was more Chinese than Mongol, because Mongolians had no tradition of building cities. I believe that Kublai wanted a symbol of his commitment to both cultures. On the one hand, the materials and building skills were thoroughly Chinese; on the other, it has the look of a Mongolian tent, a *ger*. It was round, with something like a smoke-hole, and crucially it was temporary, standing only for the summer months; solid as a Chinese building, but movable as a Mongolian tent.

It seems that Kublai's Cane Palace, the original Pleasure Dome, could have served a unique purpose, which made it the most original creation of its time.

The emerging capital, half Mongol and half Chinese in conception, was still too Chinese for traditional Mongols. Back in Karakorum, there were those who were jealous of Kublai's success and muttered that he was getting above himself, too ambitious by half, dreaming of his own empire by rivalling the true capital. And far too rich. Could he perhaps be taking for himself some of the tax receipts that should by rights be coming to Karakorum? Mönkhe heard the talk, and wondered if there was any truth in it. In 1257, he sent two tax inspectors to audit Kublai's officials. They found fault, listed 142 breaches of regulations, accused Chinese officials, even had some executed, and, with Mönkhe's authority, took over the collection of all taxes in Kublai's estates. What could Kublai do? He might have objected, fought back, rebelled. Instead, wisely, he conciliated, appealing to Mönkhe brother to brother. It worked. The two embraced in tears, Kublai all contrition, innocence and loyalty, Mönkhe offering forgiveness and renewed trust.

The fact was that the two brothers needed each other. Kublai depended on Mönkhe's support, and Mönkhe wanted Kublai to solve a problem, created by Genghis himself thirty years previously. He had been so impressed by the aged Daoist monk Changchun, the one summoned from China all the way to Afghanistan, that he had granted Changchun's sect freedom from taxation. Daoists, once the junior religion, had revelled in their new-found wealth and status. Wealth being a wonderful source of inspiration, Daoist sects had multiplied. There were now eighty-one of them, according to one account, with ascetics at one end of the scale and at the other fortune-tellers who were hardly more than hooligans, happy to rip paintings and statues from Buddhist temples.

Buddhists objected, equally violently. They were much strengthened by an influx of priests from Tibet, for reasons that will become clear in Chapter 16. By 1258, the Buddhists were keen to have their revenge on the Daoists. The row had to stop because otherwise there would be no stability in north China, and no secure base from which to undertake the much more important matter of the invasion of Song. Kublai was the key.

In early 1258 Kublai convened a conference of Daoist and Buddhist leaders to knock their heads together. To Xanadu came 300 Buddhists and 200 Daoists, held apart by the presence of 200 court officials and Confucian scholars. Kublai was in the chair.

The Daoist case rested on two documents, both of which claimed that Laozi (Lao-tsu), the Daoist sage, had undergone eighty-one incarnations, in one of which he was known as the Buddha. Therefore, they contended, Buddhism was actually a sort of sub-Daoism. It was an insulting idea, made worse by the Dao agenda, summarized in their catchphrase *hua-hu* ('Convert the barbarians!'). What they did not appreciate was that Kublai was already in the process of becoming a Buddhist, having been inducted by his mentor, a young Tibetan priest known as Phags-pa, about whom we will hear a lot later.

In fact, he did not need to bring his prejudice to bear. The Daoists were not used to debate and came over as charlatans. Phags-pa cross-questioned the senior Daoist on the authenticity of their main 'Convert the barbarians' text, with its claim that their founder, Laozi, had died in India, not China. Why did Sima Jian, the great first-century historian, not mention this interesting claim or the document asserting it? Obviously (he concluded) because Laozi actually died in China and the document was a forgery. The Daoists, lacking both references and arguments, were left looking foolish. Kublai offered them one last chance. He challenged them to call upon ghosts and demons, and prove their magical powers by performing supernatural feats. Naturally, they demonstrated no powers at all.

Kublai delivered his judgement. Buddhism was in, Daoism out. Seventeen leading Daoists were singled out for ritual humiliation, having their heads shaved; all copies of the fraudulent texts were to be destroyed; and 237 temples restored to the Buddhists. But he was wise enough not to be vindictive, for he knew he could not afford to alienate Dao's many adherents. There would be no executions, merely a return to the status quo earlier in the century, before Changchun's sudden elevation thirty-one years before.

The debate sealed Kublai's return to favour. He had imposed peace with firm executive action, displaying intelligence and moderation. Everyone approved, and he was all set for his next big tasks: the creation of Beijing as the seat of his government, and then the invasion of the south.

14

KUBLAI EMERGES

LIKE MANY DICTATORS, MÖNKHE RELIED ON FOREIGN CONQUEST TO pre-empt dissent at home, bring in a flow of booty and provide employment for the elite. Not that anyone would have put it in those terms, because those motives were hidden by the overwhelming truth, as the Mongols now saw it, that they had unfinished business with the world at large. Three of Sorkaktani's sons – Mönkhe, Kublai and Hulegu – were now all dictators, all eager for further expansion. Persia and southern Russia were secure; so now for the rest of China; and then the rest of the world.

The task ahead was formidable, but less formidable than it had been before the conquest of north China. The Mongols had battle-hardened armies based in Xanadu and Yunnan, north China and ex-Western Xia. The Song armies were unwilling mercenaries led by scholar-officials. And the Mongols knew what they had to do, because they had done it before in north China: take a city or two, seize Chinese infantry and siege engines, and make themselves into a juggernaut. True, the climate was subtropical in summer, the land-scape tortuous, the distances immense and diseases rife. Who would bet on success?

At least Mönkhe had a good HQ. Set up thirty years before by Genghis himself, Kaicheng lay some 200 kilometres south of the Yellow River, near the head of the Qing Shui River, in the forested foothills of the Liupan Mountains, where Genghis had spent the summer of 1227 before he succumbed to the disease that killed him. It was a good site, because it was out in the open, yet within a day's gallop of the Liupan's secret valley, with its steep forests, fertile soils and medicinal plants. It lay just 70 kilometres from the Song border.

Mönkhe knew well enough the immensity of the task. His plan was to start big, by cutting his opponent in half. Three columns would converge on the Yangtze at Wuchang (now part of the mega-city of Wuhan), the key to the lower Yangtze and thus to the capital, Hangzhou. One of the columns would be Kublai's, advancing from Xanadu south for 1,400 kilometres. Actually, Kublai's involvement was in doubt for a time because he was suffering from gout, the disease that would afflict him all his life. When Mönkhe suggested he be replaced by one of Genghis's nephews, he was indignant. 'My gout is better,' he protested. 'How is it fitting that my elder brother should go on a campaign and I should remain idle at home?' In Wuchang, Kublai would meet up with the two other columns: a second led by Uriyang-khadai, arriving from Yunnan (almost 1,500 kilometres away), and a third from Kaicheng. Mönkhe himself would lead an advance into the centre of this region, striking south-west for 650 kilometres, taking Chengdu in the heart of Sichuan, finally turning south-east (for 250 kilometres) to Chongqing, the river port that was the link between the Yangtze's downriver trade and the overland route to Tibet.

Mönkhe arranged for the correct rituals to ensure Heaven's backing – honouring his grandfather's spirit at his grave-site, scattering milk from his herd of white mares – then headed south, across the Gobi, through what had once been Western Xia and was now imperial land, to Kaicheng. The summer of 1257 he spent in the Liupan Mountains, gathering his forces. The following spring, his army took Chengdu and moved on through Sichuan's mists, so thick, it is said, that dogs bark when they see the sun.

Progress was slow. It was early 1259 before he reached

Chongqing. To take it, he first had to seize a formidable fortress 60 kilometres to the north. Set on a sheer 400-metre-high ridge, it dominated three rivers which flowed together before joining the Yangtze. This operation brought Mönkhe to a dead halt. Weeks turned to months, spring to summer. The heat built up. Disease struck. Several thousand of his men died.

In August, escaping the heat in the nearby hills and drinking far too much wine, he went down with something very serious – probably cholera. His bowels turned to water, cramp wracked him, and he was dead in ten days.

All action should have ceased as Mongol leaders refocused their attention on the succession. First came the rituals of burial, which took at least a month, perhaps two: the preparation of the body for travel, the 1,800-kilometre, month-long return to Karakorum, four consecutive days of mourning, then the final 500-kilometre procession eastwards over the grasslands, into the Mongols' original heartland, up the Kherlen River, and thus at last to the sacred mountain of Burkhan Khaldun, the burial place of Genghis and his son Tolui. The site itself was of course secret, with horses trampling the graves and saplings and coarse grass slowly covering the spot. There are many theories, but, as we shall see, where exactly Genghis, Tolui, Ogedei, Mönkhe and later emperors lie is still a mystery (to be addressed in Chapter 24).

Next on the agenda would be the great assembly of the princes and the clan leaders, the *khuriltai*, that would elect the next khan. But winter was coming on. The election would take place the following spring, allowing time for claimants to ensure they had the backing they needed.

And what meanwhile of Kublai? He had been about to cross the river now known as the Huai, 250 kilometres into Song territory, when news came of Mönkhe's death. He had been on the road for weeks, had covered 1,000 kilometres, and had another 400 – perhaps ten days' march – to go to reach his rendezvous. There was a Song troop ahead. Scouts were bound to hear of his brother's death and spread the news, and inject new heart into the Song opposition.

So he had a decision to make: to sit about doing nothing and allow the Song time to mount a counter-offensive; to retreat, and abandon conquered territory; or to act. He knew from experience what was right. He talked the matter over with his No. 2, Batur. The same age as Kublai, Batur came from an eminent military family, being the grandson of Genghis's great general Mukhali. Between them the decision was made: they would pretend the news was merely gossip designed to spread fear and despondency, and would carry on with the invasion. 'We have come hither with an army like ants or locusts,' Kublai said, according to Rashid al-Din. 'How can we turn back, our task undone?'

His advance continued, to the universe of water that was the Yangtze, meandering lazily across rice-rich plains, more inland sea than river, a barrier over 10 kilometres wide. Having crossed it, he laid siege to Wuchang, to be joined some three weeks later by Uriyang-khadai's 20,000-strong force from Yunnan. They'd had a hard time, taking fortresses on the mountain passes, losing 5,000 men to disease. The town would surely have surrendered but, in early October, Song contingents, released from fighting Mönkhe by his death, arrived to fight Kublai.

Kublai faced a tricky decision: to continue the siege of Wuchang, or return to Mongolia to engage with the business of the succession. Increasingly, imperial strategy was being trumped by affairs back home. In December, Kublai decided he could hesitate no longer. But which to choose: finish the job, or pull back?

The Song commander, Jia Sidao, a wily diplomat who undoubtedly knew of the pressures on his adversary, tried to nudge him into withdrawal. Jia, one of the most famous and controversial men of his age, has an important role to play in Kublai's story. His grandfather and father had been men of medium-grade military rank, nothing exceptional, but good enough to put a silver spoon in Jia's young mouth. In his home town, the Song capital of Hangzhou, he had been one of the *jeunesse dorée*, with a penchant for pretty girls, drinking and gambling. He was also lucky. His sister had been chosen as an imperial concubine; she became the emperor's favourite, bearing him a daughter, his only surviving child, and rising to the high rank of Precious Consort in the harem. In 1236, the emperor had fallen ill and a senior official was going to suggest pensioning him off. Jia heard of the plot, told his sister, who told the emperor, who acted to save his throne. Good jobs followed, and by the time he was forty Jia was powerful and rich. He dabbled in art and antiques. He had a glorious estate in the hills overlooking the West Lake, where he threw parties for guests by the thousand. With time and wealth enough, he was able to indulge a very strange hobby: he loved to set crickets fighting each other. Indeed, he became such an expert in crickets and their aggressive ways that he wrote a handbook on the raising and training of champion crickets. He also had literary pretensions. His rivals (of course) called him arrogant and frivolous, and muttered about the way he siphoned off state cash to buy art treasures for his mansion, the Garden of Clustered Fragrances. In 1259, when he was forty-six, he was appointed Chancellor of the Empire with responsibility for upgrading Song's shaky finances and armed forces. He thus found himself in charge of the defence of Wuchang.

He opted for diplomacy, proposing to pay an annual tribute in exchange for the Mongols agreeing that the Yangtze be the new frontier between the states. Kublai would have none of it. After all, he was already into Song territory. Yet he was in no position to continue the invasion, not just because of Jia's opposition, but because something rather ominous was afoot back home.

As Kublai learned in a message from his worried wife, his younger brother Ariq Böke – Ariq 'the Strong' – master of the empire's nomadic heartland, was raising troops, presumably because he wanted to be khan. Could Kublai possibly return? If Kublai needed a further reason, he had it two days later when messengers came from Ariq himself, bringing nothing but innocuous greetings and enquiries about Kublai's health. Kublai asked what their master was doing with the troops he had raised. Disconcerted, they wriggled. 'We slaves know nothing. Assuredly it is a lie.' Kublai smelt treachery. Politics now trumped empire-building. He abandoned the siege of Wuchang and headed back to Mongolia.

It was the end of the invasion for the time being. Jia soon

recaptured what had been taken. Song would remain unconquered for another twenty years. Kublai found all his attention focused on a dispute that would rapidly escalate into civil war.

As 1259 turned to 1260, ploy was followed by counter-ploy, with messages being carried back and forth across the steppes and the Gobi at full gallop, and the two would-be emperors dicing for advantage as if they and their supporters were pieces on a vast chess-board. In the spring, Ariq, newly arrived in his summer quarters in the Altai Mountains in Mongolia's west, declared himself khan. Kublai was incensed. This was outright rebellion, not so much against Kublai, but against the tradition of the khan being elected by the princes. The leading ones – Hulegu and Jochi's son Berke, now ruler of the Golden Horde[1] in southern Russia – were not even in Mongolia, and were anyway bitter rivals over both territory and religion. Berke had converted to Islam the better to rule his Muslim subjects; Hulegu had been killing Muslims by the thousand.

Ariq's bravado backfired. Princes and generals who had not responded to his call rallied to Kublai. To save the empire, there was one thing to be done: he had to declare himself khan, with as much validity as possible. This could not happen with *total* validity, because that would take a full assembly in Karakorum, which he was not yet ready to hold. So in early May 1260, those who backed Kublai were called to Xanadu for the ceremony.

He was, as ever, between two worlds. His roots were in the grass-lands, yet he had Chinese estates. Here he was in a Chinese-style city built on the grasslands, about to declare himself emperor – of what exactly? A Mongolian empire? A Chinese empire? Quickly, he saw that in order to rule, Chinese traditions had to trump Mongolian ones. He proclaimed his virtues, in the style of a Chinese emperor: he would rule with goodness and love, lower taxes, feed the hungry, revere the ancestors. He did not summon Mongolian shamans to

[1] Golden because Genghis's family was the 'Golden Clan', and Horde because the Mongolian *ord* (or *ordon*, in an alternative form) meant a palace, which back then was a tent used as a palace. Originally, the Golden Horde was the gold-decorated palace-tent at the heart of Batu's (Berke's brother's) camp.

examine the scorched and cracked shoulder-bones of sheep. Instead, he called upon a Chinese adept who knew how to cast the *I Ching* (*Yi Jing* in pinyin), the *Book of Changes*, the 2,000-year-old oracle that holds a unique place in Chinese culture. The reading produced a hexagram, the Qian, representing primal power, the power of Heaven. One of its attributes is a word with many positive meanings. The dictionary lists some: the first, chief, principal, fundamental, basic substance. It has an aura of associations, suggesting whatever is sublime, original and great. It hints at the powers behind the origin of the universe.[2] No name could have better appealed to Chinese sensibilities, which is why, incidentally, it is also the name of today's Chinese unit of currency. When the time came, the word would be the perfect name for Kublai's dynasty: the Yuan.

On 5 May 1260, Kublai took the plunge. The assembled princes begged him three times to accept the throne, which as tradition dictated he declined twice. The third time, he graciously accepted. The princes swore their oaths of allegiance and proclaimed him the new emperor – not yet of the Yuan dynasty, but of the Great Mongol Nation as founded by his grandfather.

Now the empire had two Great Khans – a khan and an anti-khan. Which would turn out to be which?

Through that summer, the two sides did more jockeying, each tit-for-tat move raising the stakes. Ariq returned to Karakorum to assert his rule from there. Kublai tried to put his own man in charge of his uncle Chaghadai's realm, only to hear that the 100-strong mission had all been caught by Ariq, who made his own candidate khan of Chaghadai's lands and then executed all of Kublai's envoys.

Kublai closed down the frontier, starving Karakorum of the supplies which until then had been imported from China. He could do this because his cousin, Khadan, controlled Western Xia and the Uighur regions further west. As winter came on, Kublai recruited more troops, bought 10,000 extra horses, ordered 6,000 tonnes of rice – a year's supply – then led his well-supplied army northwards. The next autumn produced a showdown in the grasslands of eastern

[2] Stephen Karcher, *Total I Ching: Myths for Change*.

Mongolia. Two battles ended inconclusively, with great loss of life on both sides. But Ariq had no resources left. He pulled back into the forests and mountains of Siberia and then, abandoned by allies, fled to Chaghadai's realm, whose isolated capital, Almalik, became a place of 'dearth and famine'. Kublai occupied Karakorum for the winter. In the spring, Ariq found his support draining away, symbolized for his aides when a whirlwind tore his audience tent from its 1,000 pegs, smashed its support post and injured many of those inside. To his ministers, it was an omen of coming defeat.

At which moment – early 1262 – he was saved by rebellion against Kublai back home. The trouble came from Shandong, the heart of north China, a rich coastal area near the mouth of the Yellow River. The local warlord, Li Tan, was the son-in-law of one of Kublai's top officials and had helped Mönkhe fight the Song. Kublai thought he was a staunch ally and backed him with injections of cash. It seemed a good bet, because Li's son was at court, in effect a hostage. But Li, in control of the local salt and copper industries, was more interested in feathering his own nest than keeping in with Kublai. He decided that he, as a Chinese, had a better future with the Song than with the Mongols. He arranged for his son to slip away from Kublai's court, then turned his army loose on local Mongols, seized warehouses, and was clearly intent on establishing his own breakaway kingdom. It took several months to crush him – literally, for his punishment was to be sewn into a sack and trampled to death by horses, the traditional fate reserved by Mongolians for those of princely rank. Only then was Kublai free to turn back to the business of dealing with Ariq.

The winter of 1263 was a harsh one for an army to be trapped in Central Asia. Ariq was short of food and weapons and friends. Men and horses starved. Allies – even some of his family – defected. The following year, he accepted the inevitable and came begging for peace, brother submitting to brother. As Rashid describes it, the meeting was full of emotion. Ariq approaches Kublai's huge palace-tent in the traditional manner, raising the flap that covers the door and letting it hang over his shoulder, awaiting the call to enter. Summoned inside, he stands among the secretaries, like a naughty schoolboy. The two brothers stare at each other. Kublai softens. Tears come to the eyes of both men. Kublai beckons.

'Dear brother,' he says, 'in this strife and contention were we in the right or you?'

Ariq is not quite ready to admit the fault is all his: 'We were then and you are today,' he says. It is almost good enough for Kublai. He assigns Ariq a place among the princes.

But he is not free. The following day, there is an examination to establish how things had come to this pass. There follows much finger-pointing as commanders dispute who had influenced Ariq the most. These are difficult matters, because Kublai wishes to establish guilt, yet find cause not to execute his own brother.

In the end, ten of Ariq's associates are put to death, with Ariq and his top general being spared, though still under arrest. What to do about Ariq? Who would rid the khan of his troublesome brother? Not, it seemed, Eternal Heaven, for Ariq was not yet fifty, and in fine fettle, a constant reminder that Kublai's claim to the throne was not unchallenged.

Then, suddenly, out of the blue, in unexplained circumstances, as Rashid baldly states, Ariq 'was taken ill and died'. Was he murdered? Some suspected so at the time and others have claimed so since. It was certainly a wonderfully convenient solution to an intractable problem.

And then Heaven, or at least fate, stepped in again. Hulegu in Persia, Berke of the Golden Horde in southern Russia, and Alghu, the restored khan of Chaghadai's realm, all died within a few months of Ariq's death. As a result of Ariq's opposition, what a waste the last five years had been. The great task of invading China had been put on hold, the stability of Mongol rule across all Eurasia threatened, the Mongol heartland divided against its Chinese territories, the rulers of the three western khanates set at each other's throats. Now, at a stroke, all was resolved. Never mind that his coronation had not been strictly legal: Kublai was now head of the family business, in direct command of Mongolia, north China, much of Central Asia and some of Song, and overlord of his subsidiary khans in Persia and southern Russia.

And there was so much more to be conquered. It was time to look south again, for without the rest of China there would be no world rule.

15

A NEW CAPITAL

BEIJING WAS NO ONE'S FIRST CHOICE AS A CAPITAL – TOO FAR NORTH, NO good rivers – until the Mongols' predecessors, the Jin, invaded from Manchuria in 1122. With the Song ruling southern China from Hangzhou, it was the northerners from outside the Chinese heartland who made Beijing a capital, and drew Genghis's attention.

The city that the Mongols seized and devastated in 1215 was small by modern standards, a square of 3.5 kilometres per side standing south-west of today's Tiananmen Square. In 1260, it had still not recovered from the destruction meted out by Genghis's army. No doubt the sights and sounds of medieval Beijing would have returned to its alleyways: travelling barbers twanging their tuning forks to signal their arrival, soft-drink sellers clanging their copper bowls, the day- and night-watchmen sounding their bells, street vendors yelling everywhere. But the walls and the burned-out palaces were still in ruins.

Kublai had several options. He might have ignored Beijing and ruled from Xanadu. But if he did that he would declare himself forever an outsider. Seeing the benefits of governing from a Chinese base, he might have chosen to revive an ancient seat of government, like Kaifeng or Xian. But Beijing had a major advantage: of the many possibilities for a Chinese capital in the north, it was the closest to Xanadu and to Mongolia. In 1264, only eight years after building Xanadu, Kublai decided to make Beijing his main capital. He would abandon Karakorum and commute between his two bases, spending summers in Xanadu and winters in Beijing, which was his way of straddling his two worlds. That's why Beijing is China's capital today. Mongol traditionalists never forgave him, and some today still regard him as a traitor.

How best to handle this dilapidated piece of real estate? Incoming dynasties have often made their mark by total demolition and reconstruction (as the Ming would do to Mongol Beijing). But the ancient alleyways, as Kublai's advisers pointed out, were seething with resentment. Kublai decided on an entirely new capital.

Just north and east of the Jin capital was a perfect site, where run-off from the Western Hills fed Beihai (the North Lake), which for thirty years before the Mongols arrived had been a playground for the wealthy. The 35-hectare lake had been created by the Song 300 years before, and then in the twelfth century chosen by the Jin emperor as the site of his summer palace, with a second retreat on top of today's Jade Island, the city's highest point (now crowned by the seventeenth-century White Dagoba, Beijing's equivalent of the Eiffel Tower). The imperial buildings had been ransacked when Genghis assaulted Beijing, but the lake was still at the centre of the abandoned and overgrown park. This would be the heart of the new city.

It would be thoroughly Chinese, starting virtually from scratch. After fifty years of neglect, imagine the lake choked with silt and plants, summerhouses decaying around its edges, and here and there smallholdings where farmers had dared colonize the once-royal parkland. With saplings and bushes cleared, an imperial camp sprang up: a royal area of several grand *gers*, lesser establishments for princes and officials, hundreds more for contingents of guards, grooms, wagoners, armourers, metalworkers, carpenters and other workers by the thousand, including, of course, architects.

Overall authority for the design was borne by Liu Bingzhong, the architect of Xanadu. But among his team of architects was one of particular significance, who is not mentioned in the official Chinese sources, for he was an Arab named something like Ikhtiyar or Igder al-Din (a rough re-transliteration from the Chinese version of his name). That we know of him at all is due to a Chinese scholar, Chen Yuan, who in the 1930s came across a copy of an inscription dedicated to Ikhtiyar's son, Mohammad-shah. Ikhtiyar had, presumably, proved his worth in Persia after the Mongol conquest a generation before, for he was summoned to head a department in the Ministry of Works and become an expert in town planning. In his old age, he was selected to mastermind Kublai's grand new scheme. As the inscription says, 'The services of Ikhtiyar al-Din were highly appreciated, but he was beginning to feel the weight of his advancing years.'

Yet in the official Yuan history, Ikhtiyar's name is omitted, his three Chinese junior colleagues alone being mentioned. Possibly this was deliberate racism. Kublai, like his grandfather, was happy to engage talent wherever he found it, but his Chinese officials might not have been. An Arab employed by Mongols showing Chinese how to build a Chinese city! It looks as if the official historians simply wrote Ikhtiyar out of the story, until Chen Yuan rediscovered him.

Kublai founded his new capital with a temple honouring his ancestors in Confucian traditions, thus showing himself to be both a good Mongol and a good Chinese. The temple's eight chambers commemorated great-grandparents; Genghis himself; and Genghis's sons. Genghis also acquired a Chinese 'temple name': Taizu (Grand or Highest or Earliest Ancestor), a title for dynastic founders. It was Kublai, therefore, who gave Genghis his Chinese credentials and thus founded the widespread belief amongst Chinese today that Genghis was 'really' Chinese.

All of which explains why Beihai Park, once a playground for emperors and princes outside the old walls, is today a playground for everyone, right at the heart of the city. For this, Beijingers, picknicking on its banks and paddling its rowing boats, owe Kublai some gratitude. It was he who turned it into an Arcadia that is now a tourist pleasureground, he who first built a bridge across to Jade Island and landscaped its slopes with rare trees, winding staircases, temples and pavilions.

The city would have the three-in-one form of previous Chinese capitals, notably Changan (today's Xian), the Tang capital in the seventh to tenth centuries – palace, inner city and outer city nestling inside each other. In its day, Changan/Xian had been the greatest city in the world. This was the mantle of power and glory to which Kublai now laid claim, creating the city known as Da-du (Great Capital), or informally by its Mongol-Turkic name, Khan-balikh, the Khan's City (or Cambaluc, as Marco Polo spelled it).

In August 1267, several thousand workers started to build ramparts over the hills and along the three winding rivers. They used earth, not stone, digging out a moat for the raw material. The 382 smallholders who had moved into the area were thrown out, with compensation. After a year, rammed-earth walls 10 metres thick at the bottom rose for 10 metres, tapering to a 3-metre walkway at the top, making a rectangle measuring 28 kilometres all the way around, punctuated by eleven gates. Inside, a second wall rose to conceal the Imperial City, and inside that a third wall, within which in due course would lie the palace and its attendant buildings.

From March 1271, 28,000 workers began to build the Imperial City's infrastructure, setting out a network of right-angled roads, Manhattan-style, each block the property of a top family, complete with its grand house. At the heart, off-centre, just to the right of Beihai Lake, was the palace, which was ready enough in 1274 for Kublai to have his first audience in the main hall, though work continued for the rest of his reign. The palace and its gardens were surrounded by 10-metre walls that linked eight fortresses. Beneath the trees – rarities carried in from distant parts by elephants – grazed deer and gazelle, overlooked by walkways, which were gently slanted so that the rain drained away before it could soak aristocratic feet. The palace, with a roof of red, yellow, green and blue tiles, was a single storey, with a vast central hall where 6,000 dinner guests dined beneath animal frescoes set off by gold and silver decorations.

Eventually, when all China fell to the Mongols, this would become the capital of the whole united nation, and so it has remained. The heart of today's Beijing, the Forbidden City, was built right over Kublai's creation – destroyed after the end of Mongol rule – its entrance facing south, like the door of any Mongolian tent. The 800 palaces and halls, the 9,000 rooms, the entrance from Tiananmen Square – all these are where they are because Kublai chose to place his palace there.

Kublai now had a theatre in which to stage epic displays of power. Autocrats have always known that power and display go together. Underneath the different rites lie fundamental similarities, asserting the stability of the state, its power over the individual, the importance of the power structure, the legitimacy of the ruler, and the ruler's superhuman qualities, connecting him (or occasionally her) with the divine. One piece of theatre that crops up in several societies is the ceremonial hunt, which symbolized the benefits of collective action.

Kublai, smart enough to see the advantages of ritual but with no experience in their form, had teams of advisers to guide him. There were precedents galore, notably an immense three-volume corpus of imperial rituals recorded half a millennium before during the Tang dynasty (618–906), when China was unified, rich and stable.[1] Tang scholars believed these rituals originated in remote antiquity, some 2,000 years BC, and were then modified by the introduction of Confucian, Buddhist and Daoist practices. The 150 rituals, the symbolic essence of government, combined cosmology and ethics in rules for sacrifices to the gods of heaven and earth, of the five directions, of the harvest, sun, moon, stars, sacred peaks, seas and great rivers; to ancestors; to Confucius. There were rites for the sovereign for receiving and entertaining envoys, for victories, for the marriage of dignitaries, for investitures, for coming-of-age ceremonies, for bad harvests, for illness and for mourning, and variations of all these, depending on whether they were conducted by

[1] David McMullen, *Bureaucrats and Cosmology: The Ritual Code of T'ang China*, in Cannadine and Price (see Bibliography).

the emperor or a proxy, and for every rank of official from the emperor down to those of the Ninth Grade.[2] Rules specified the tents, the musical instruments, the position of participants, and the words of prayers for any and every occasion. The rituals had their own huge and complex bureaucracy, with four departments – for sacrifices, imperial banquets, the imperial family and ceremonies for foreigners – and a Board of Rites within the Department of Affairs of State. These demanded hundreds of specialists; but all the 17,000 scholar-officials of all the other departments were expected to have intimate knowledge of particular rituals in their own areas of expertise. This immense, vastly expensive and horribly cumbersome apparatus was considered absolutely vital to the workings of the state. If Kublai wanted to be taken seriously as a Chinese ruler, this was what he had to take on board.

So, in late middle age, Kublai displayed and regimented for all he was worth, which was more than any ruler on earth at the time and, by Heaven, he knew how to use his wealth to raise himself from man to monarch, from monarch to demi-god.

His power base at court, through which his influence spread over China and beyond, was his *keshig* – his 12,000-strong court of family, officials and officers, all of whom had at least three different sets of clothing, each a less lavish match for Kublai's own costumes, one for each of the three main state occasions: the khan's birthday at the end of September, New Year's Day and the annual spring hunt.[3]

Take New Year's Day. This was a festival designed to emphasize both Chinese and Mongol credentials. Kublai's court ceremony mixed simple old private rituals with Chinese court festivities to create a celebration of gargantuan proportions. Marco Polo describes it. Thousands dressed in white, all in due order behind the royal family, overflow from the Great Hall into surrounding areas,

[2] The Central Secretariat (civil service) had nine ranks or grades, each divided into Senior and Junior, making eighteen levels that assigned status and determined preference, deference, salary and other perquisites.
[3] The number of these occasions rose in the sources with the passage of time, often to four, sometimes to twelve or thirteen (*trois* and *treize/tres* being easily interchanged in versions of Marco Polo's *Travels*).

40,000 of them, though we must always remember his habit of tossing out suspiciously large round numbers. A high official of some kind – top shaman, Buddhist priest or senior chamberlain, Marco is not sure – calls out 'Bow and adore!' and the whole assembly touches forehead to floor, four times, in a mass kowtow. A song follows, then a prayer from the minister: 'Great Heaven that extends over all! Earth which is under Heaven's guidance! We invoke you and beseech you to heap blessings on the Emperor and the Empress! Grant that they may live ten thousand, a hundred thousand years!' Then each minister goes to the altar and swings a censer over a tablet inscribed with Kublai's name. Officials offer presents of gold, silver and jewellery, many of them in eighty-one examples, being the doubly auspicious number of nine times nine. Treasures are displayed in coffers mounted on richly adorned elephants and camels.

Then comes the feast. Kublai, with his chief wife, Chabui, on his left, sits at the high table, which is literally high, placed on a platform. On his right, on a level about half a metre lower, are the princes and their wives. To one side is a huge buffet table, decorated with animal carvings. The centrepiece is a golden wine-bowl the size of a barrel with four dispensers, from which servants draw wine into golden jugs. Down the hall range ranks of small tables, several hundred of them, flanked by carpets on which sit the guards and their officers. To one side of the dais is an orchestra, its leader keeping a close eye on the emperor.

Polo mentions an odd element in this scene, something that recalls Kublai's nomad roots. Even today, when entering a *ger*, you must take care to step right over the threshold, the bottom bit of the doorframe, without touching it. If you kick the threshold by mistake, it is a bad omen; on purpose, it's an insult. So at each door stand two immense guards armed with staves, who watch for infringements, with orders to humiliate those who infringe, stripping them of their finery or giving them some nominal blows with a stave. Once everyone is seated, the banquet begins, with those at tables being served by butlers. The khan's butlers 'have the mouth and nose muffled with fine napkins of silk and gold, so that no breath or odour from their persons should taint the dish or the goblet presented to the Lord.'

The Lord graciously receives a cup from a butler. The orchestra proclaims the significance of the moment. The cupbearers and the foodbearers kneel. The Lord drinks. When he deigns to accept food, same thing. These observances punctuate the feast, until the end, when the dishes are removed and it's time for entertainment, a cabaret provided by actors, jugglers, acrobats and conjurors.

Kublai's new Beijing was the centre of hunting on an industrial scale, the countryside out to 500 kilometres – forty days' journey, as Marco says – in every direction being dedicated to the business of supplying the court and controlled by a 14,000-strong army of huntsmen. All large game was the emperor's: boar, deer, bear, elk, wild asses, wildcats of various species. For his own hunt, Kublai had a zoo of hunting cats, cheetahs and tigers specially trained to catch and kill larger prey. Eagles, too, were trained and deployed by Kazakhs to hunt not just hare and foxes, but deer, wild goats, boar, even wolves.

Marco Polo tells us all about the spring hunt, which was of such staggering size and opulence that it is easy to forget its underlying purpose. Hidden beneath Chinese wealth lie Mongol roots, the old idea of disparate clans united under one leader. The palaces and much of Beijing empty into wagons by the hundred, on to horses by the thousand. For Kublai himself, four elephants are harnessed together, carrying an enormous howdah, a room made of wood, lined on the inside with gold leaf and dressed outside with lion-skins. A dozen senior aides ride beside him in attendance. There are 2,000 dog-handlers and 10,000 falconers, so Marco says, each with his bird (though the figures are to impress rather than to be exact).

The emperor makes stately progress on his elephants, say 20 kilometres a day, arriving every evening at a campsite that is a tent-city. Along the way, birds of many species scatter and soar from their new nests. 'Sire! Look out for cranes!' exclaims a high official, and the emperor releases a gerfalcon. Sometimes dogs are used, huge mastiff-like creatures trained by handlers known as 'wolf-men'. And, in Marco's words, 'as the Lord rides a-fowling over the plains, you will see these big hounds coming tearing up, one pack after a bear, another pack after a stag, or some other beast.'

A nineteenth-century illustration of Kublai's howdah. Originally, this seems to have been a travelling HQ in war. This version acted as a hunting lodge. In Marco's words, 'The Emperor himself is carried upon four elephants in a fine chamber made of timber, lined inside with plates of gold, and outside with lions' skins.

After a week, Kublai's elephants bear him into the camp that will be the court's HQ for the next three months. It is a traditional spot, chosen for its broad expanses and wealth of game. Falconers and hawkers, with their hooded birds on their wrists and bird-whistles at the ready, scatter for several kilometres in all directions. His three tents are ready – a huge one which can hold a whole court of 1,000 people, sleeping quarters and a smaller audience chamber. All are weather-proofed with tiger-skins and lined with ermine and sable, the most valuable of Siberian furs. Spread out all around are the tents of the royal family, Kublai's senior wife, Chabui, the three sub-sidiary wives, the princes, the girls from the Ongirat (the Mongolian clan that traditionally supplied Genghis's family with mates) brought in for the harem, and the tents of the senior ministers, the attendants, the falconers, grooms, cooks, dog-handlers, household staff, secretaries, all with their families, and all of course protected by contingents of soldiers.

Meanwhile, the business of the court continues, with conferences and audiences and messengers coming and going and ambassadors from abroad. So it continues until mid-May, when the immense operation reverses itself, bringing emperor and entourage back to the capital, where, as the summer begins to build, preparations start for the three-week haul to Xanadu.

This was another equally immense operation. It involved scores of carriages and hundreds of retainers shepherding the emperor on his elephants like some travelling hive tending a queen bee. The 400 kilometres were divided up by twenty walled and gated towns, each staffed year round, ready for the 24 hours in spring and autumn when the imperial train came through. Most of these way-stations have vanished, but four are still visible, in the form of low ridges and faint squares. One of them, Huanzhou, is clear enough on Google Earth (42.15 N, 115.58 E). It's a smaller version of Xanadu, which lies 20 kilometres away – living evidence of the distance covered in a day by Kublai's entourage and of the cost involved. Twenty small towns, each in use for just two days a year. All because the emperor needed to commute between his two worlds, Mongolia and China, the Old and the New.

16

EMBRACING TIBET, AND BUDDHISM

UNHAPPILY FOR THOSE WHO WISH IT WERE NOT SO, TIBET IS PART OF China: threatened, dominated, invaded, colonized, occupied and developed out of any possibility of regaining its independence. Or gaining it, as China officially says, arguing that Tibet was part of China since China became China. When was that exactly? It depends how far back you wish to go and what you mean by 'China'. But one answer lies 750 years ago, when the Mongols took control of Tibet and made it part of their empire.

Up until the early thirteenth century, China had no claims on Tibet. The opposite: Tibet had at one time ruled half of present-day China. Many accounts say that Chinese, or rather Mongolian, involvement with Tibet started with Genghis's coronation in 1206, which was enough to inspire Tibet to tender voluntary submission. Not so, as Luciano Petech states in the most authoritative recent analysis.[1]

To understand the development of the link between Tibet

---

[1] In Rossabi (ed.), *China among Equals* (see Bibliography).

and Kublai's China demands backtracking some twenty years.

The first step was taken in 1239, by Ogedei's second son, Köten, who, after campaigning in Sichuan, settled on the Tibetan borderlands not far from present-day Wuwei. He invaded the next year, damaged a monastery and killed 500 men. A Mongol general, a Tangut named Dorta, was keen to proclaim Mongol authority by carrying the abbot away with him, but the abbot pointed him towards his superior, the sixty-two-year-old head of the Saskya monastery (Sakya, as it is today), the other side of Lhasa, not far from the Nepalese border. The death of Ogedei briefly delayed things, but in 1244, a rather pressing invitation arrived for Saskya Pandita[2] from Köten. 'I need to have a master to tell me which path I should take. I have decided to have you. Please come in total disregard of road hardships.' If he made excuses, troops would be sent to fetch him. With little choice in the matter, the lama started a journey of 1,700 kilometres from Saskya to Wuwei, across some of the toughest landscapes on earth, accompanied by two nephews, aged nine and seven. He arrived at Köten's base in 1246, only to find the Mongol absent, attending the election of Guyuk as the new emperor. On Köten's return, the two agreed that the lama would act as the Mongol agent in Tibet. The lama wrote to various Tibetan leaders suggesting they cooperate: 'There is only one way out, which is to submit to the Mongols.' To seal the pact, the lama's seven-year-old nephew was married to Köten's daughter. As Petech says, by this agreement 'Köten laid the foundations of Mongol influence in Tibet', the influence that one day China would inherit.

Now three deaths occurred in quick succession: the new emperor Guyuk, Köten and the senior lama. The next emperor, Mönkhe, eager to assert his rights in the area, sent troops into Tibet, with attendant destruction. He and several princes assumed the patronage of a number of Tibetan sects. One of the princes was Kublai, who thus found himself competing for influence in Tibet with, among others, his brothers Mönkhe, Hulegu and Ariq.

---

[2] That was his title, by which he is usually known. His name was Günga Gyaicain, and he is still revered as one of the supreme Buddhist scholars.

Kublai now made a small gesture of immense significance. He was still a prince, still under the thumb of his brother Mönkhe, but with ambitions to extend his rule in north China. Kublai had already realized that he needed to balance his Chinese Confucian and Daoist advisers with a strong Buddhist one, and by happy chance one of the late Saskya lama's two nephews was at a loose end in Köten's HQ. His name was something that looks totally unpronounceable to Westerners, Blo-gros rGyal-mtshan, but he would shortly acquire a title, Phags-pa[3] (Noble Guru), which is how he is known. The boy was a genius, and even as a teenager became hugely influential. Kublai invited the eighteen-year-old Phags-pa to court. It suited them both. The boy was grateful to have a sponsor in a chaotic world; for Kublai, this young priest could be the key to Tibet and to a religion that could offer many political advantages.

In 1258, Kublai, about to declare himself emperor, found in his new faith a rather better justification for conquest than he had inherited from his grandfather. Genghis's heirs believed that the world had been given to them by Heaven. Genghis himself had moved beyond conquest to government, with a script, laws and a bureaucracy. Kublai, inheriting an empire that he planned to expand to infinity, needed much more: he had to legitimize his rule not only to Mongols and Chinese, but also to any other culture that would become part of the empire in years to come. Phags-pa revealed that Buddhism could give him what he wanted, offering something that did not exist in Chinese religions, or Islam, or Christianity. It was the concept of the 'universal emperor', the *chakravartin-raja*, who ruled over all and 'turned the wheel of the Law'. Here was an ideology that justified world conquest and world rule.

Phags-pa sealed his position when, in 1258, he took part in the debate in Xanadu set up by Kublai between Buddhists and Daoists, coming down, of course, firmly on the Buddhist side. This left him in a strong position when Kublai had himself declared khan in 1260. In 1261, Kublai gave Phags-pa – at the age of just twenty-six – the

---

[3] The 's' is silent now. Back then, it was sounded. At a conference in China in 2012, a Tibetologist scolded me for pronouncing it. Transcribing Tibetan is a minefield.

title of State Preceptor and made him the supreme head of the Buddhist clergy in his Chinese domains.

Kublai set out his new policy in a decree known as the Pearl Document. 'Although it is necessary to act in accord with the Law of Genghis Khan, which embodies all the best qualities of this world,' he had 'perceived that the path of Buddha Shakya Muni is the true one'. Therefore he appointed Phags-pa head of the 'entire confraternity of clerics', who were exempted from military service, taxes and postal-relay services.

This was revolutionary, since it specified the union of church and state, of secular and ecclesiastical. From now on, Mongol rule would be based on these so-called Two Principles, embodied in the Teacher (Phags-pa and his successors) and the Khan (Kublai and his heirs). This new ideology was re-expressed in a document known as *The White History*. 'If there is no spiritual power,' it said, 'then creatures will fall into hell, and if there is no royal power, then the state is ruined.' Kublai, with the support of his 'sagacious friend', would become head of both church (Buddhist, of course) and state, the fount of worldly welfare and spiritual salvation.

There was a problem: who was the true head of state – the Buddhist emperor of China or his Tibetan mentor? The question provoked a long discussion in Xanadu. Phags-pa made his precocious case: 'You ought to pray to the lama in person, and heed what the lama says.' No, said Kublai, that was not suitable. It was Kublai's wife who found a middle way, at the same time in effect granting Tibet autonomy within the growing empire. In a small assembly, the lama could sit 'in the middle' – that is, exercise authority. In a large assembly, 'to avoid disobedience, let the Khan sit in the middle. Let him act in affairs of Tibet according to what the lama blesses. Let the Khan issue no orders without having declared them to the lama. But in other affairs, large and small, let him not conform to the lama's words.' Both agreed, and Phags-pa initiated Kublai into the rites of the highest deity of Lamaism, Hevajra, whose cult centred on Phags-pa's own Saskya monastery.

And that opened the way to a world of spirits, in particular to a terrifying, black-faced, six-armed, skull-covered guardian-deity named Mahakala, revered by millions across Asia as the 'Great Black One'. He is sometimes a manifestation of Shiva, the Destroyer, sometimes one of Shiva's attendants. Like most Buddhist gods, he varies from culture to culture. In any event, it's better to have him onside. Kublai adopted him as a 'tutelary deity', in the words of the eminent Mongolian historian Shagdaryn Bira. Kublai could 'pretend to have acquired all his mysterious powers in the cause of ruling his empire. Thus the Mongolian khan could enjoy not only the favour of Tengri, but also the favour of the powerful Tantric god.' You can see him today portrayed in a shrine in the only Yuan-dynasty building left in Beijing, the White Pagoda (built by a Nepalese architect, Aniga, in the 1270s to commemorate Kublai's commitment to Buddhism).

Did Kublai really believe the religion he had taken on? I don't think so. It was too neat, too carefully considered, too political. He displayed none of the fire of the new convert, no fundamentalist drive to impose his beliefs on his people or on foreigners. There was too much of his mother's shrewdness in him for that. What he needed was a strengthened Buddhist church to balance the demands of Daoists, Nestorian Christians and Confucians. Later, when two European merchants, the Polo brothers, turned up in Xanadu, the same agenda would lead him to suggest that they should go home, contact the Pope, and bring him some Catholic priests. Instead they brought him one of their sons, the young Marco Polo, with totally unforeseen consequences which will emerge later.

Soon after his 'conversion', Kublai sent Phags-pa home as abbot of the Saskya monastery, along with his younger brother. Most of Tibet being far beyond Mongol reach, they were supposed to establish Kublai's sway over the whole country – 'control without conquest', as Igor de Rachewiltz puts it in his biography of Phags-pa.[4]

This was not so easy. Locals objected, apparently seeing in Phags-pa not so much a brilliant young mind as a turncoat who had adopted Mongol clothes and manners. The whole project almost

[4] *In the Service of the Khan* (see Bibliography).

foundered when his brother died in 1267, aged twenty-nine. Kublai sent an army from Qinghai, which cowed the opposition and established a Pacification Bureau that would run the country as a secular authority. Politically, Phags-pa was sidelined, spending the next few years engaged on a task which we shall get to in a moment. By 1269, Tibet was an integral part of Kublai's empire, where it remained for the next eighty years, until the Mongol empire fell apart.

Meanwhile, Kublai had had a startling cultural insight. He had identified a problem that sprang from the nature of Mongol achievements, and from his own ambition; and he wanted Phags-pa to provide the solution.

As we've seen, Kublai grew up in two worlds, Mongol and Chinese. He spoke Mongol, but struggled with Chinese. His problem was this: how to make written records that spanned these two worlds, and others yet to come?

Mongolian had a fine vertical script introduced on Genghis's orders from his new vassals, the Uighurs. It was an alphabetical script, which means it could represent most sounds in most languages fairly well. Chinese script, though beautiful and expressive, is infinitely more complex, and has tremendous cultural momentum after over 3,000 years of use. For Kublai to try to impose Uighur script on China would have been impossible; it was equally impossible to use Chinese script to write Mongolian. Kublai's officials had to rely on translations. It was a tedious and cumbersome business.

As his reign went on, problems multiplied. Genghis had conquered the Tanguts, who had their own Chinese-like script. Then there was the script of the Khitan, the Manchurian people who had been the Mongols' predecessor dynasty in north China. And Sanskrit, the language towards which his new subjects in Tibet looked as the fount and origin of their religion. And Tibetan itself, of course, already some 600 years old. Not to forget Korea, which the Mongols had already attacked once in 1216, and to which Kublai would soon return. And what of those languages of people under the control of Kublai's brother Hulegu, principally Persian? And if things went as he hoped, if all south China fell to the Mongols, they would be in contact with Burmese, Vietnamese, Japanese, and who knew what other cultures, all with their own languages and scripts. A bureaucratic nightmare loomed.

Once Kublai saw the problem, he saw a solution. China was in a sense unified by its script, which linked diverse dialects; Kublai wanted a script that would unify the world. The thought occurred to him when Xanadu was ready and Ariq's rebellion had been crushed; Kublai was already thinking about a new capital in what is now Beijing and planning the long-delayed invasion of southern China. He needed to consolidate, to ensure the most efficient management possible as a basis for expansion. It was here that young Phags-pa came into his own. In 1267, Kublai told him to invent a new script, a script in which any language under Heaven could be written.

Phags-pa, fluent in Tibetan, Mongolian and Chinese, and probably with a good knowledge of Uighur and Sanskrit as well, analysed their phonetical demands and modified his own Tibetan script into a sort of International Phonetic Alphabet of some sixty signs, most representing individual vowels and consonants, but including some common syllables. Tibetan reads from left to right, but Phags-pa designed his script to be read vertically, in deference to the Uighur system introduced by the great Genghis. The letters are mostly made of straight lines and right angles, hence its name in Mongolian: square script. For representing Mongolian and other languages, it is certainly a big advance on Chinese: Genghis in Chinese transliterates as *chéng jí sī*;[5] in Phags-pa's script it is *jing gis*.

After two years of work, it was done. Kublai was delighted, and raised Phags-pa from State Preceptor to Imperial Preceptor, with income to match. He ordered that all official documentation be recorded in the new 'State Script' and set up schools to teach it. It was used on seals and the paiza, which gave authority to high officials to demand goods and service from civilians. 'By the power

[5] 成吉思

of Eternal Heaven, by the protection of the Great Blessedness [of Genghis]', ran the text on one of them. 'Whoever has no reverence [for this] shall be guilty and die.'

That was the high point of Phags-pa's international influence. He returned again to Tibet shortly afterwards as head of the Saskya monastery and sect, which exercised an uneasy sway over the other Buddhist sects. Suddenly, in 1280, he died. He was only forty-five, and there were suspicions he had been poisoned. The Tibetan civil administrator was suspected. There was no proof, but Kublai had the man executed anyway.

The script looked good on seals, stone slabs, coins, even porcelain. You still see it today on Mongolian banknotes and the occasional statue. If you visit China's prime tourist attraction, the Great Wall at Juyong (just short of Badaling), you will see an ancient arch, Cloud Terrace (Yun Tai), built in 1342 as a gateway through the pass. Its flagstone floor, now glassed in, is scarred with parallel tracks from an infinity of wagon wheels, making it look like an abandoned railway tunnel. Under the arch are five flat surfaces carved with intertwining bas-reliefs of warrior kings, buddhas, elephants, dragons, snakes and plants, all framing a Buddhist text in six languages: Sanskrit, Tibetan, Mongol, Tangut, Chinese – and Kublai's answer to this Babel, Mongol and Sanskrit versions in Phags-pa's script.

But for routine records it never really took hold. Despite a special academy set up to study and teach the script, Kublai's officials stonewalled as bureaucrats always do with orders they don't like: they said yes, and did nothing. Their resistance had nothing to do with the quality of Phags-pa's script. The problem lay in human nature. Learning a script, however easy, is a demanding business, and traditional scripts are incredibly tenacious. Trying to overcome the cultural inertia of his Chinese officials was like trying to row an iceberg. It just wasn't going to happen.

In a sense it didn't matter. Kublai's involvement in Tibet had already done more for his empire than a new script would ever achieve. By bringing Phags-pa on board, he added a vast new territory to his domains, and established a precedent for

The two scripts used in Kublai's empire:

The Uighur script introduced by Genghis Khan on a *paiza* (*paizi* in pinyin), or safe-conduct pass (right), and on an imperial seal (below). Both begin with the words 'By the power of Eternal Heaven . . .' The script is still in use today in Inner Mongolia.

On a Yuan coin (right), the script devised by the Tibetan monk Phags-pa records four words: *tay (1)*, *wen (2)*, *thung (3)*, *baw (4)*. They record the Chinese of Kublai's time. In today's pinyin, they transliterate as *dà yuán tōng bǎo*, literally 'Great Yuan authorized treasure', i.e. 'currency of the Great Yuan'.

Sino-Tibetan relations from then on. In the late sixteenth century, when the Mongol tribes were constantly vying for supremacy, a Buddhist cleric being cultivated by the dominant khan of the day, Altan, declared Altan to be the reincarnation of Kublai; in return, Altan granted him the title Dalai Lama (*dalai* being Mongolian for 'sea', a traditional symbol of power). Thereafter, it was the Dalai Lama who ruled in Tibet, and remained ruling until 1959, when Mao invaded, ten years after his Communists had seized power. Initially he had promised minorities their own governments, but soon reversed that position. He sent troops into Tibet on the grounds that its independence was an illusion based on China's weakness, and that the Communists were merely restoring the status quo as established by Kublai.

As far as Mongols were concerned, it was Mongolia that conquered China, Mongolia that occupied Tibet, Mongolia that established a Mongol empire. Fortunately for China, Kublai decided to establish a Chinese dynasty, making his grandfather its posthumous founder, thus turning history upside down.

In Chinese eyes, Genghis and Kublai and all their conquests were actually Chinese.

And so therefore is Tibet.

17

THE CONQUEST OF
THE SOUTH

SOME THINGS ARE NON-NEGOTIABLE. FOR KUBLAI, CONQUEST OF
Song was one of them. He had tried once, and failed. Like his grandfather, Kublai was not to be put off by failure. He returned to the
task in 1268, after crushing Li Tan's rebellion. It was a formidable
challenge. Song was all rivers and cities, exactly what Mongolia and
most of north China wasn't. Cities were the prizes, because that was
where the rich lived and the powerful administered – there were no
castles such as the European and Japanese nobility had. As a result,
cities were tough nuts, well supplied with explosives, many of them
on rivers, the better to trade and feed themselves. The Mongols
needed not only even better ways to take cities, but also something
new – a navy of river boats, which would have to be started from
scratch.

The key was the mighty Yangtze, beyond whose lower reaches
lay the capital, Hangzhou. Any advance therefore had to be by river.
The Yangtze flows from west to east, while Kublai's armies would

be invading from the north. But right in the middle of the Mongol–Song border a major tributary, the Han, ran southwards, making a river-road straight down to the lower Yangtze – and Hangzhou.

There was just one problem. The Han had its own key, in the form of the town of Xiangyang,[1] which lies on the Han at the junction of two other rivers, 250 kilometres north of the Yangtze. Today, Xiangyang and its sister-city across the river, Fancheng, form the super-city of Xiangfan. In Kublai's day, Xiangyang was a moated fortress-city and a major trade crossroads, with a population of 200,000 people, linked to Fancheng by a pontoon bridge. Xiangyang would have to be eliminated by any army heading south by river.

This was common knowledge on both sides, because the city had been a prime target twice before – in a Jin assault in 1206–7 and in Ogedei's 1235–41 campaign. It had not fallen either time, but surrendered in 1236 to the Mongols, who held it only briefly, before returning north. So Xiangyang was used to taking punishment and had been busy rebuilding its defences. It had 6 kilometres of solid stone walls, some 6–7 metres high, set in a rough square just over a kilometre across; three of the six gates gave directly on to the river, which was a highroad for supplies and communication half a kilometre wide when it was in flood, and far too deep to wade; in winter, when the water was low, it became a maze of frozen channels and sandbars; and the moat, fed from the river, was 90 metres across; all of which meant that attackers could not get close enough either to assault the walls with ladders and towers or to undermine them.

This chapter is largely about the solution to this problem, which when solved led on to Kublai's greatest achievement: the creation of a unified China and the establishment of borders that are largely still in place today. The evidence is patchy, but still good enough to

---

[1] Xiangyang has been through all sorts of different versions and spellings – Saianfu in Marco Polo, Sayan-fu in Rashid, Hsiang-yang in more recent but pre-pinyin times.

conclude that modern China owes its existence to the device that broke the siege of Xiangyang – a device such as China had never seen before.

It began with Mongols approaching the city in early 1268, under the command of the young and famous Aju – famous because military glory was in the family. He was the son of Uriyang-khadai, who had won Yunnan for Kublai ten years before, and the grandson of the legendary Subedei, who had masterminded Genghis's and Mönkhe's western campaigns. Almost as soon as he started his advance, Aju found he needed help, in the form of infantry – and boats, a novelty for the Mongols, built by a Song defector named Liu Zheng. Kublai complied, giving Aju the amphibious force he needed for an advance by river and by land.

Aju and his army would not have found much in the way of loot to sustain them, because in preparation for a siege city rulers customarily ordered a scorched-earth policy, clearing the surrounding countryside of anything that might help the enemy: high buildings, trees, stones, metals, tiles, vegetables, straw, animals, grain. Much of this went into the city,[2] where there was work to be done: stores to be gathered, civilians trained as militiamen, women organized in cooking gangs, itinerant entertainers expelled as potential spies, fire brigades equipped with water jars, double and triple crossbows made ready, trebuchets checked.

Trebuchets are a major theme in this chapter. The backbone of Chinese siege technology was the 'traction trebuchet', a frame about 4 metres high on which pivoted an 11–12-metre pole, with a sling on one end and ropes on the other. A small rock or incendiary device was loaded in the sling, a team hauled on the other end, the sling whipped round and released the missile. The whole operation took no more than 15 seconds. For lobbing rocks over walls, the traction trebuchet was standard technology. Any army would muster scores, sometimes hundreds of teams, working in relays. They needed their own food, armour and horses. Before a siege, defenders gathered

[2] Details from a military handbook, *The Essentials of Military Preparedness* [*Wu-pei ji-yao*], dated about 1830, but the practices it quotes are ancient ones.

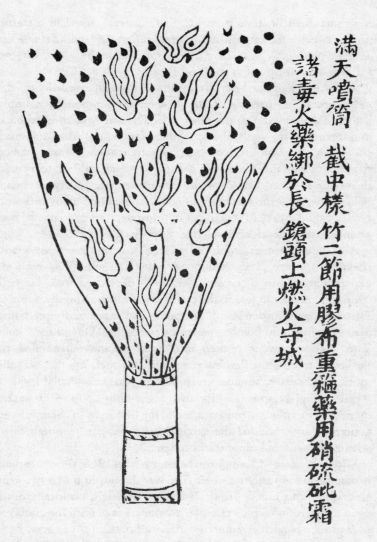

満天噴筒　截中樣竹二節用膠布重裹藥用硝硫砒霜

諸毒火藥綁於長鎗頭上燃火守城

This precursor to the cannon, acquired by the Mongols from the Chinese, was both a biological weapon and a shotgun. Its bamboo barrel fired a combination of poison and shards of porcelain. Its label (top right) reads 'sky-filling spurting tube'.

huge quantities of stone from surrounding areas, for their own use and to deprive the opposition of ammunition. Defending trebuchet teams would work in relative safety from inside the walls, with an artillery-spotter up above to direct them.

Trebuchets had one huge disadvantage, though, especially for the defenders. If they used rocks, the cheapest ammunition, they simply supplied ammunition to the other side. The same rocks arced back and forth over the walls, shattering heads, breaking arms, smashing roofs, on occasion in such numbers that the missiles crashed together in mid-air. Whether in defence or attack, 100 devices could deliver up to 12,000 rocks per hour, hour after hour, day after day. Where would all the ammunition come from? How many men and horses would it take to find it, cut it, transport it? The challenge was an incentive to develop more effective projectiles.

All Chinese armies employed experts in explosive devices and chemical warfare. The techniques, based on some 700 years of experimentation by alchemists, had been developed from the first use of gunpowder in war in the early tenth century. Rapidly, a whole range of gunpowder-based weapons had appeared: exploding arrows, mines, and bombs thrown by trebuchets. One of these consisted of gunpowder packed into bamboo and surrounded by broken porcelain, the first known use of shrapnel. Another was the much more deadly 'thunder-crash bomb', which detonated inside a metal casing, blasting to bits anything within about 400 square metres. The exploding poison devices, the first steps in chemical and germ warfare, included the original dirty weapon, a bomb filled with excrement and poisonous beetles.

When the siege of Xiangyang began early in 1268, these weapons brought Aju's advance to a halt. The war developed into a five-year epic, a sort of Chinese Trojan War. Unfortunately, no local Homer spun the siege into epic verses, so details are few, until the climax.

A proper blockade required yet more boats, 500 of them, built under the supervision of Kublai's admiral, Liu Zheng. The construction took months. Through the summer, the Mongols erected fortifications downriver on either bank to bombard Song boats ferrying in supplies. As winter came on again, Aju extended the siege across the river to include Fancheng. An attempt by the Chinese to break out ended in disaster for them: hundreds were captured and beheaded. After that, the Chinese sat tight, with enough supplies reaching them to survive. In spring 1269, Kublai sent in another 20,000 troops to strengthen the besiegers. In August, after eighteen months of action and inaction, 3,000 Song boats came up the Han to attack the new Mongol fortifications and were repulsed with the loss of 2,000 men and fifty boats. Kublai's commanders requested another 70,000 troops and more boats. The Chinese defenders, reassured by secret-service officers smuggling in orders, cash and letters sealed inside balls of wax, were equally determined to resist.

What could break the stalemate? As a Mongol general told Kublai, the army needed better artillery. The Mongols already had artillery of many kinds – mangonels, trebuchets, arrow-firing ballistas – having acquired the technology and specialist troops after the siege of Beijing in 1215. The problems were Xiangyang's moat and stone walls. The Mongol–Chinese artillery simply didn't have the range or the power.

Kublai, hearing of the problem, also saw the solution: a siege engine such as China had never seen before. He knew that the empire's best siege-engine designers were in Persia, 6,000 kilometres away, because he had seen reports of the siege of Baghdad by his brother Hulegu in 1258. Hulegu had catapults that breached walls. Traction trebuchets could not do that. Hulegu's machines were of a different order.

They were counterweight trebuchets, the heavy artillery of their day, in which men pulling on ropes were replaced by a box filled with ballast (usually rocks), the advantage being that the weight could be enormous, the throwing arm lengthened, the missile heavier, the sling extended, the range increased and accuracy improved.

The counterweight trebuchet had emerged in the Middle East in the twelfth century, spreading to Europe soon after crusading armies came across them in about 1200. Information flowed both ways, the machines developing in both Europe and the Islamic world into specialized devices that not only destroyed walls but seized imaginations, influenced strategy and made stars of their engineers (who therefore had a good reason never to record their secrets). By the end of the fifteenth century, they were gone, blown away by gunpowder. They were only wood, after all.

Today there is an international subculture of 'treb' enthusiasts who have worked out the secrets of these giant machines. Combining theoretical science, history and practicality, they are keenly, many obsessively and some eccentrically dedicated to the business of hurling huge loads as far as possible without the use of explosives. In the 1990s, a 30-tonne trebuchet threw half a dozen cars, sixty pianos and many dead pigs, earning a good deal of notoriety. Websites speak of plans for Thor, with a 100-foot arm and a 25-tonne counterweight, which will supposedly toss Buicks as the war god tossed thunderbolts. At the time of writing, Thor was still a dream.

I can understand the passions they arouse. On a visit to Caerphilly Castle, South Wales, I got to use one. There is beauty in what happens when this pent-up energy is released, because it involves only natural elements – wood, iron, rock, rope, gravity – carefully managed. A jerk on the trigger frees the arm. The counterweight drops, the arm rises, the sling follows with its missile. The only sounds are soft, like a giant exhalation: a whisper from the greased axle, the swish of the sling. It's all in slow motion, rather graceful. Away the missile flies, in this case landing harmlessly in a field. Then the great beast resettles with little sounds of satisfaction – sighs from the counterweight swinging back and forth, the clunk of heavy stones rearranging themselves inside, the slap of the empty sling against the waving lever-arm.

So we know what Kublai was after. He knew it was possible. It was just a question of joining the dots. Nothing could have better shown the advantages of having an empire all run by one family, bound together by a network of transcontinental communications. Off went Kublai's letter by pony express. Five weeks later and 6,000 kilometres away, his message was in Tabriz, northern Persia, HQ of his nephew Abaqa, Persia's ruler since the death of his father, Hulegu, in 1265. Abaqa had on hand several engineers who had built the counterweight trebuchets used in many sieges: Baghdad, Aleppo, Damascus, Syria's crusader castles. He could spare two of them, Ismail and Ala al-Din. In late 1271, the two arrived with their families at Xanadu and were given an official residence for the winter. The following spring, after demonstrating the principles to the emperor, the two men – plus Ismail's son, whom he was training to follow in his footsteps – found themselves in the battle zone, staring at Xiangyang's solid walls, the moat, the broad river and Fancheng, Xiangyang's sibling city across the river.

Ismail's machine, probably built on site, must have weighed 40 tonnes and towered almost 20 metres high. There were many variables, like the exact weight of the counterweight in wet and dry weather, the effect of temperature on the grease used on wooden axles in wooden bearings, the right timber to use for the lever-arm, the shape of the 100-kilo missiles, which were hacked from a local quarry.

The Mongol general Ariq Khaya decided on an indirect approach by assaulting Fancheng. After destroying the pontoon bridge to prevent supplies being carried across, Ismail would have fine-tuned his device like an artilleryman, with ranging shots. Then, as Ariq Khaya's biography in the *Yuan Shi* says, Ismail's *hui-hui pao* (Muslim catapult) 'breached the walls . . . [since] the reinforcements from Xiangyang no longer reached the fortress, it was captured'.

That created a situation the Mongols had often faced. To force Xiangyang to surrender, Fancheng had to die, very publicly. Some 3,000 soldiers and an estimated 7,000 others had their throats cut like cattle, the bodies being piled up in a mound to make sure that the massacre was visible from Xiangyang.

But there was no surrender. So Ismail turned his siege engine on Xiangyang, dismantling it, floating it across the river, reassembling it within range of Xiangyang, 'at the south-east corner of the city', according to the *Yuan Shi*. Ismail, a master of his art, now knew his machine's abilities very precisely. The missile, we are told, weighed 150 catties, which is just short of 100 kilos. The result was astonishing. In the words of Ariq Khaya's biography, 'The first shot hit the watch-tower. The noise shook the whole city like a clap of thunder, and everything inside the city was in utter confusion.'

There then followed a debate about whether to follow through with an assault, which would, of course, end with another pile of bodies, but with rather less strategic purpose. Ariq Khaya had his own ideas. He went in person to the foot of the wall and called for the city's leader, Lü Wenhuan. 'You have held the city with an isolated army for many years,' he shouted (presumably through an interpreter). 'But now the approaches are cut off even from the birds of the air. My master the emperor greatly admires your loyalty and if you surrender he will give you an honourable post and a generous reward. You may be sure of this, and we certainly shall not kill you.'

Lü, 'suspicious as a fox', hesitated briefly, finally believed the assurances, and surrendered the city on 17 March 1273. Ariq Khaya was as good as his word. Lü instantly made himself a traitor in Song eyes and accepted high office on Kublai's side. He would prove a valuable asset in the coming campaign.

It is hard to overstate the significance of this victory.[3] Not only did it open the way militarily to Song's heartland, but it began to destroy the workings of Song government. In Hangzhou, the prime minister, Jia Sidao – Kublai's old adversary, the rich politician who liked crickets and their pugnacious ways – had kept the truth from the Song emperor, so the news of Xiangyang's fall struck the court like a ball from a Muslim catapult.

A grateful Kublai rewarded both catapult experts. Ala al-Din became an overseer, a top local official, serving the Yuan for the next thirty years. Ismail was given some 9 kilos of silver, about ten years' income for an artisan. He had no time to enjoy it, because a year later he fell ill and died. His work, though, lived on. His position

---

[3] This was one of the most famous sieges in Chinese history, so famous that Marco Polo heard its story and loved to tell it. The trouble was that by the time he came to dictate his adventures, he had apparently told the story so many times he had written major roles for himself, his father and his uncle, who, he says, supervised the construction of the trebuchet. If you wish to be generous, this is a flagrant bit of self-promotion. Let's be frank: it's a lie, because Marco did not reach Kublai Khan's court until 1275, two years after the great siege was over.

and expertise were inherited by his son, Abu-Bakr, beginning a line of succession that would continue almost until the end of the Yuan dynasty.

In Hangzhou, panic took hold. Suddenly, top people woke up to the threat to their comfortable and civilized ways, their literate discourses, their picnics by the West Lake, their time-honoured rituals, their glorious works of art. It was unthinkable – never before in China's history had barbarians threatened the southern heartland.

And then catastrophe upon catastrophe. Without warning, the Emperor Duzong died, at only thirty-four. Next, the Mountain of Heavenly Visage, the beautiful volcanic range a day's ride west of Hangzhou, shook itself and released devastating landslides and flood waters. It was a dire omen, because in Chinese a landslide and an imperial death are different meanings of the same character, *bēng* 崩. Disasters were linking up, like tears in old silk, and there was no one to patch Song's tattered fabric. Heaven was withdrawing its mandate to rule. An age approached its end.

For this vast and vital campaign, Kublai wanted to leave no room for error. He retained Aju, the victor of the Xiangyang siege, but placed him under his dynamic and widely experienced statesman-general, Bayan. He was from a legendary family. His great-grandfather, grandfather and great-uncle had been the three who, sixty years before, had spared the life of Genghis's enemy, Targutai, and been rewarded by Genghis for their loyalty. Bayan's father had been with Hulegu in 1256 and died in action. Bayan had joined Kublai as one of his top civilian administrators. He had a reputation for calmness under pressure and for brilliance (he had learned Chinese). At the age of only thirty-four, he found himself with the task of taking one more giant step towards world conquest.

The advance down the Yangtze was to be an immense operation. The army that Bayan and Aju gathered around Xiangyang in summer 1274 numbered about 200,000 infantrymen, over half of them northern Chinese, backed by a river fleet of 800 newly built warships and another 5,000 smaller boats for transport, carrying 70,000 sailors, 14 per boat. This was a flexible, amphibious, multinational force. It needed to be, because the Song still had 700,000 men at their disposal and 1,000 warships on the Yangtze.

Victory would come. But, as Kublai had seen in the Yunnan campaign, military victory had to be matched by victory of another sort, over the hearts and minds of ordinary people. If the conquest of Song was to last, it would take good government; and that meant minimizing the suffering of civilians.

Bayan's first task in the autumn of 1274 was to get his army down the Han River to the Yangtze, a distance of about 250 kilometres. But the Han was blocked by 100,000 men camped around two fortresses which were linked by a cross-river chain. To avoid another siege, Bayan ordered his troops to bypass this section of river, carrying the boats overland on bamboo poles. By spring 1275, Bayan and Aju had led their force out of the Han Valley into the flood plains of the Yangtze, approaching the three cities that form today's Wuhan and the great fortress of Yang-lo downstream.

Avoiding a frontal assault, Bayan sent Aju to establish a bridge-head across the river, which somehow – we have no details – became a key to breaking through the Song fleet. Yang-lo's commander fled, the shattered Song fleet sailed away downriver, and the fortress surrendered. Progress was much aided by the ex-commander of Xiangyang, Lü Wenhuan, who had also been the boss of many downriver garrisons. A word from him and commanders surrendered, allowing the Mongol army to advance steadily.

In Hangzhou, Bayan's reputation grew with every victory. They called him 'Hundred Eyes', because that's what his name sounds like in Chinese (bǎi yǎn). Jia's reputation, by contrast, sank daily as the court officials and ordinary people reviled him for his love of luxury, his accumulated treasures, his wasteful parties. In an attempt to regain his authority, he decided to take command of the army himself. That February, he led a force over 100,000-strong out of the city, a vast throng 40 kilometres long heading westwards to intercept Bayan's progress down the Yangtze. Suddenly, the capital was bare of troops, and more were needed.

At this point, the emperor's widow, the formidable Dowager Xie, became her people's inspiration. With an odd-looking dark skin and a cataract in one eye, she had been a reassuring force for years, generous, restrained, never ambitious to extend her authority beyond the palace. Now she spoke out, urging ordinary people to join the war effort. It worked. By March 1275, all over the country, men streamed to arms, as many as 200,000 of them.

A month and 250 kilometres later, Jia was in today's Anhui province, deploying his army near Tongling, aiming to block the river. Easier said than done: the river is 2.6 kilometres wide here. Still, at Tongling, a midstream island could act as a keystone. Joined by 2,500 warships, many from the bruising defeat at Yang-lo fortress, others from Hangzhou, Jia awaited Bayan's arrival.

Bayan's navy, though, carried well-tried contingents of every armed service – the Mongol cavalry (also scouting sideways and ahead), the Chinese infantry, a good supply of turncoat Song commanders, and terrific artillerymen, including Ismail's 'Xiangyang catapult', shepherded by barges. No details of the battle survive, only the results. Artillerymen set up the giant trebuchet. Stones rained on to boats, cavalry attacked on shore, infantry were landed on the island, and Jia's demoralized forces scattered, leaving 2,000 boats in Mongol hands. Jia fled, humiliated and doomed. Dowager Xie stripped him of office and banished him to Zhangzhou, on the coast 800 kilometres south. But there was no escape. When approaching their destination, his guards killed him.

Bayan, meanwhile, continued his victorious progress downriver. Wuwei, Hexian and Nanjing all surrendered, inspiring half a dozen other leaders to bring their towns into the Mongol camp, and in two cases to commit suicide (the first of many, as we shall see). In Nanjing, Bayan recalled Kublai's long-term agenda: to govern for ever. For four months he paused, setting up a local government for his thirty city conquests and his 2 million new subjects. From here, he opened negotiations with the Song court, only to have three of his envoys murdered by locals before they entered Hangzhou.

Now it was summer. The Mongol and northern Chinese wilted in the sticky heat. Bayan was all for pressing on, but was forced to delay because Kublai was faced with another rebellion at home – the subject of Chapter 19 – and wanted the benefit of Bayan's advice. The delay left Aju to fight off a renewed challenge from the Song and mop up other cities, notably Yangzhou and its nearby river port Zhenjiang. Here, in another great battle, the Song blocked the river with unwieldy seagoing warships all chained together, which, when the little Mongol ships set a few ablaze, acted as a giant fuse that destroyed the lot: another military catastrophe, 10,000 dead, another 10,000 captives. Now the Mongol forces were within 225 kilometres of the Yangtze's mouth, with Hangzhou lying round the nose of the Shanghai peninsula. Overland, it was also 225 kilometres. One last push would do it.

Back in the field in September, Bayan planned his final assault, a three-pronged attack by sea and by land. He would lead the central prong, following the Grand Canal. The main naval and land forces made fast progress. But Bayan's corps hit a problem, in the form of unexpected and dogged resistance from the ancient and prosperous town of Changzhou, newly reinforced by 5,000 Song soldiers. Bayan gave them a chance to surrender, firing a message wrapped around arrows, warning of the dire consequences of resistance: 'You should reconsider your position promptly, so as not to regret things later.' They did not reconsider, and once again the Mongols committed urbicide. Some 10,000 people died, many of them gathered up to form a vast mound of earth-covered bodies.

The capital gave way to panic and paranoia. Soldiers mutinied, deserters fled. The Empress Dowager tried to delay the inevitable, with a self-deprecating plea for mass support. The impending peril 'is entirely, I regret, due to the insubstantiality of Our moral virtue'. People should recall over 300 years of moral and charitable rule, and come to engage the enemy. They did, by the ten thousand, but there was no leadership, and the motley militias merely added to the confusion and panic.

For six weeks, Dowager Xie sent out envoy after envoy, seeking some sort of settlement, offering tribute and a share of the country. Bayan, settling in around Hangzhou, demanded total capitulation, offering his assurance that surrender would buy peace for the people and security for the royal family. Some in court advised fighting to the last man, others wanted to abandon the capital altogether, but Dowager Xie saw there was no choice. Hangzhou was all but surrounded, and weakening daily as soldiers and civilians fled south.

The end, at least in this area, came quickly. The prime minister, Chen Yizhong, scuttled for safety. On 26 January 1276 the Empress Dowager sent a note to Bayan in his HQ 20 kilometres north of the city, acknowledging Kublai's overlordship: 'I respectfully bow a hundred times to Your Majesty, the Benevolent, Brilliant, Spiritual and Martial Emperor of the Great Yuan.' A week later, the city's prefect, representing the court, handed over the Song dynastic seal and a memorandum stating the boy-emperor's willingness to give up his title to Kublai and hand over all his territories. Bayan made a triumphal entry into the city, with his commanders and contingents in full array. Hundreds of pretty courtesans trembled at the thought of what might happen to them, and 100 of them drowned themselves to avoid finding out. Finally, on 21 February, came the formal ceremony of submission, when the five-year-old Emperor Xian[4] himself led his officials into Bayan's presence and bowed in obeisance towards the north, the direction in which Kublai resided.

Bayan was as good as his word, and Kublai's. In Beijing in 1215, the Mongols had gone on an orgy of destruction and killing. This time, there was a peaceful handover, a strict ban on unauthorized troops entering the city, the safety of the royal family guaranteed, the royal mausoleum protected, no attempt made to upset the currency, or even the style of dress. Mongol–Chinese officers made inventories before removing the treasures for transport northwards. Militias were disbanded, regulars incorporated into Bayan's armies. Officials, of course, were all replaced with Mongols, northern Chinese and several Song turncoats, but in other respects, as Bayan reported proudly to Kublai, 'the market places of the nine thoroughfares were not moved and the splendours of a whole era remained as of old'. An edict from Kublai told everyone to continue

---

[4] All the Song emperors had the family name Zhao. They also had temple names, which confuses non-specialists. Xian was his given name.

their lives as normal; officials would not be punished; famous sites would be protected; widows, orphans and the poor would be assisted from public funds.

On 26 February, the first of two great entourages left Hangzhou for Beijing – 300 officials, 3,000 wagons of booty. A month later, Bayan handed Hangzhou over to subordinates and headed north with a second entourage, the royal family: the boy ex-emperor, his mother, the princesses, the concubines, the relatives, with the ailing Dowager Xie following when she was fit enough to travel.

Three months later, in June, this immense throng arrived in Xanadu, to be welcomed by Kublai, whose joy was such that he had no praise high enough for Bayan. He conferred upon him twenty sets of 'garments of a single colour' – to receive just one being a high honour – and reconfirmed him as co-director of the Ministry of Military Affairs. 'Hundred Eyes' was the empire's hero.

The Empress Dowager and her grandson, ex-emperor Xian, were then settled in Beijing, where they were given tax-free property. Kublai's wife Chabui took a personal interest in their well-being. The old lady lived out her life with a small official stipend and attendants, and died six years later. Her grandson was sent off to Tibet, where he became a Buddhist monk. In 1323, the Yuan dynasty's ninth emperor ordered him to commit suicide, perhaps – according to rumour – as an example of 'literary inquisition' imposed because the emperor took offence at something in Xian's poetry.

And so, officially, the Song dynasty ended not in a bang of destruction, but in an extended whimper.

But there was another end, of despair and suffering and heartbreak. In the words of Richard Davis, it made 'a drama of unthinkable intensity'.[5] Its prologue came just before the final capitulation, when the Song court sent southwards the two remaining young princes, Shi (aged four) and Bing (three), brothers of the young ex-emperor Xian. With them went a spirit very different from that which

[5] Richard Davis, *Wind Against the Mountain* (see Bibliography).

marked the ceremonies of capitulation – a spirit of outraged resistance to alien domination.

As the princes fled, the Mongols advanced and death filled the air – not just imposed death to crush outposts of resistance, but self-selected death, whether in action or by suicide. Richard Davis, in his evocation of this terrible time, lists 110 named, prominent male suicides – prominent, certainly, but not of the highest rank. There were many hundreds of others at lower levels of government, and many thousands of ordinary people of both sexes and all classes. To take one extreme example: in January 1276, Ariq Khaya met stiff resistance from Changsha (then Tanzhou), 750 kilometres inland in Hunan province. Resistance was, of course, useless. The town's leader, Li Fu, made careful arrangements for the mass suicide of his family and household. All made themselves drunk; all were put to the sword by Lu Fu's assistant, who then killed his wife and slit his own throat. Others died in similar ways. All around the town, so the official history of the Song dynasty says, people 'annihilated their entire family. No wells in the city were empty of human corpses, while strangled bodies hung in dense clusters from trees.' The Xiang River became thick with the dead. Was this an exaggeration? Possibly; but when the town fell Ariq Khaya saw there was no need for further punishment, because the city had in effect committed suicide.

Meanwhile, the two small princes and their entourage had been taken south, picking up recruits to the loyalist cause, for they had with them immense amounts of cash. They had then taken to ships, hopping from port to port down the coast, heading for Vietnam – an army of 200,000 carried by a navy of 1,000 ships. There was a terrible storm. One of the princes, Shi, died on an island not far from Vietnam. By now, the Mongols had overtaken them on land. With the remaining prince, Bing, the fleet slowly backtracked along the coast to the bay where the Pearl River broadens out west of Hong Kong. Here a dense cluster of islands offered protection.

You cannot get much further south than this. But all was not lost. They found a good island base from which to stage a comeback. To the north were shallows that seemed to exclude enemy warships. At the southern end hills fell sharply into the sea, from which the island took its name: Yaishan, Cliff Hill. It was here, in the summer of 1278, that the six-year-old Bing and his loyal followers – including his stepmother the Dowager Consort, his real mother, and chief counsellor Lu Xiufu – made their stand, with many of their followers in warships, many others ashore, racing to throw together simple houses and fortifications.

The Mongol forces were 80 kilometres upriver, in the city that used to be called Canton and is now Guangzhou. In late February 1279 the Song navy's 1,000 ships prepared for battle, the sides of their vessels covered with mud-encrusted matting against flaming arrows and incendiary bombs, protected with staves to ward off fire-ships and well stocked with food and water. With the young prince on the flagship, the fleet was, according to one account, chained together in preparation for an imminent onslaught.

The Mongols, with only some 300 ships, approached from down-river and round the coast. With their inferior numbers, they were in no hurry to attack. Their commander sent a message giving the Song a chance to surrender. No deal. Now the Mongols discovered they had the advantage of mobility over their chained and anchored enemy. They set a blockade between the Song vessels and the shore, cutting off their water supply, and settled down to wait for the moment to strike. For two weeks they sat there, while the Song ran out of water.

Then, on the rainy morning of 9 March, one half of the fleet rode the outgoing tide into the flanks of the demoralized and weakened Song; and six hours later the other half struck from the other direction with the rising tide.

The result was a catastrophe for the Song. Accounts speak of the sea turned red by blood, and of 100,000 dead. Scholars say the real figure was horrific enough – perhaps 30,000–40,000. The only witness who recorded the details was the loyalist Wen Tianxiang, who was a hostage in one of the Mongol ships. He later captured in verse the horrors he had seen:

Human corpses are scattered like fibres of hemp.
Foul smelling waves pound my heart to bits.

When they saw what was happening, many – hundreds, perhaps thousands – committed suicide by leaping into the water with weights attached to them. One among them was Li Xiufu, the adviser to the boy emperor. On his back when he jumped he bore the little prince, the last of his line, the thirteenth generation of Song rulers, still in his gown of royal yellow, with the imperial golden seals strapped around his waist.

18

BURNED BY THE RISING SUN

HUNTING THE SONG LOYALISTS TAUGHT KUBLAI AND HIS COMMANDERS something new: seafaring. In 1274, having seen his warships sail down the Yangtze and then fight at sea, Kublai looked outwards across the ocean, to Japan.

Officially, Japan had had remarkably little to do with China for 400 years, despite the fact that long before it had taken from China the roots of much of its culture. The two had no running disputes, no cause for war; indeed the opposite, because there were long-established private trading contacts. Gold, lacquerware, swords and timber flowed in from Japan, in exchange for silk, porcelain, perfumes and copper coins. None of this reflected official policy. But it was happening under Song rule. Strategists in Xanadu foresaw the Japanese sending aid to Song. Better take them out, the sooner the better.

It seemed perfectly possible. Japan's emperor was a figurehead ruling rival warlords and samurai warriors more interested in chivalry than national defence. There was no large field army and no navy at all. Kublai had well-tried armies, commanders with un-rivalled experience, a powerful new navy, and a springboard in the form of his vassal, Korea, whose southern coast is a mere 200 kilometres from Japan.

The Mongols had first invaded Korea in 1231 as part of Ogedei's drive to expand Mongol rule. At that time, Korea had proved a tough nut, in the hands of generals who had kept the Mongols at bay, much helped by their naval skills, which allowed them to hole up on an offshore island and in effect thumb their noses at the Mongol cavalry. In response, the Mongols turned to arson, slaughter and theft, all on a vast scale. In their 1254 invasion, they had taken some 200,000 captives and devastated much of the country. In 1258, the king and his officials staged a counter-coup and sued for peace, the crown prince himself travelling to China to submit – directly to Kublai, as it happened, because Mönkhe was campaigning far away to the west. It all worked out nicely: both the Korean king and Mönkhe died, and Kublai was left with a new vassal. In 1259, a joint Korean–Mongol force re-established the king, Wonjong, in the old capital, Kaesong, and blotted up what remained of the military opposition. Kublai gave a daughter to Wonjong's son in marriage, so that eventually his grandson would inherit the throne. Kublai was not loved, but he was the power behind the throne. Now he needed ships; and ships rolled from Korea's shipyards, first for the conquest of Song, and then to transport a Mongol–Chinese army across to Japan.

Kublai had a justification for war. He sent a demand, carried by Korean envoys, that the king of this 'little country' submit instantly. It caused outrage mixed with terror. After six months, the government ordered the envoys to leave with no answer at all. Nothing more was heard from Kublai for three years, his forces being engaged in the conquest of Song. It was not until September 1271 that another Korean envoy arrived, officially bearing a request to submit, unofficially warning the Japanese to prepare for an attack. Again, there was no official reply, but now vassals were ordered back to their fiefs, and constables and stewards set about strengthening the thirty decrepit coastal castles.

So when in 1272 a Mongol ambassador landed, demanding that his letters be forwarded to the emperor at once, Japanese martial

In a Japanese view, Mongolian soldiers wear all-embracing
cloaks of chainmail.

spirit had revived. The shogun, a feisty twenty-two-year-old called Tokimune, sent him packing – a gross insult to Kublai, and nothing less than an invitation to invade.

Kublai was soon ready. In 1273, Xiangyang fell, releasing reserves for action elsewhere; Korea was at last at peace; and there were ships enough in Korean and Song harbours for the assault. In the autumn of 1274, some 300 warships and 400–500 smaller craft, with crews of 15,000 and a fighting force of up to 40,000, depending on which source you believe, left Masan on the south Korean coast to cross the 50 kilometres of sea to the islands of Tsushima, the historic stepping-stone from the mainland to Japan.

On the shore, locals put up a spectacular but hopeless defence, which became the stuff of legend, full of Japanese chivalry and Mongol barbarism, of lone warriors issuing dignified challenges, of poisoned Mongol arrows flying like raindrops in spring, of the sea made crimson by blood, of the governor's honourable suicide. Stories tell of 6,000 dead and the Mongols carrying 1,000 heads back to their ships to embark for the next stepping-stone, Iki, 50 kilometres away, which met a similar end.

On Kyushu's coast, warlords gathered their forces in castles and behind walls, pennants fluttering. Four days after the assault on Iki, the Mongol fleet anchored in the bay dominated by the town that was then called Hakata, now Fukuoka. Two headlands, reaching westwards as if to welcome ships from all mainland Asia, made this the natural invasion point. Unopposed at sea, Kublai's forces made easy landings on the beaches. There the Japanese waited. As one Japanese account put it, the grandson of the Japanese general fired whistling arrows as the signal for action to start, 'but the Mongols all laughed. Incessantly beating their drums and gongs, they drove the Japanese horses leaping mad with fear. Their mounts uncontrollable, none thought about facing the Mongols.' Not for long: chivalric tradition dictated that Japanese warriors could not skulk like cowards behind walls, but should meet the enemy head on.

Among them that day was a young warrior named Takezaki Suenaga, from Higo province, a *gokenin* (a direct vassal of the shogun, the military ruler) who later acquired enough wealth to commission a series of paintings that were then pasted together to form two scrolls illustrating this and the later invasion of 1281. The scrolls were probably created some twelve years after the Mongol defeat to record Suenaga's role in the battle. The Invasion Scrolls passed through various hands, being dismantled, re-assembled and added to, but still providing a vivid portrayal of the invasion.[1]

The section of the scroll depicting the 1274 invasion shows the young Suenaga, aged twenty-nine, sporting a trim moustache and goatee beard, advancing through pines with five followers. They carry very long bows (by Mongol standards), which they wield with great skill, firing at the gallop, quivers on their backs, protected from head to toe by armour of overlapping metal plates.

Suenaga is a headstrong character, eager for action. A picture shows him thrown from his wounded horse, which spouts blood, while a Mongol shell explodes nearby. This shell has been the source of controversy. Though some scholars think the image is an eighteenth-century addition to increase the drama, others believe the content is authentic. Could it be that both ideas are correct? As we have seen, the Mongols had long known about explosives, having acquired them after they seized Beijing in 1215. So this could well have been Japan's first experience of explosive weapons, delivered, presumably, by half a dozen men working a traction trebuchet on a ship's prow.

Suenaga, like any good samurai, is obsessed with individual glory, and not at all concerned at the lack of centralized command. Others acted in the same way. But individual bravery was not enough. The disjointed defence allowed some Mongols to break out and penetrate far enough inland to burn the nearby town of Hakata.

As the day died, the Japanese took refuge away from the beach, barricading themselves into the local capital, Daizafu, 16 kilometres inland. Could the Mongols have dislodged them? We will never know, because a storm was brewing. Chinese–Mongol–Korean captains urged their troops back to the ships to ride out the bad

[1] The story forms part of an extraordinary book by Thomas Conlan, *In Little Need of Divine Intervention* (see Bibliography).

weather at sea. The next day would surely allow another landing, another breakthrough, and victory.

But in the worsening weather, a flotilla of 300 Japanese open boats crept up the coast towards the Mongol fleet, some bearing a dozen soldiers with bows and swords, some loaded with dry hay to act as fuel for fires. These little ships infiltrated the ranks of their massive targets, moving in close beneath the overarching hulls. As the wind picked up, many of Kublai's ships were already on fire, and the Japanese rowers headed for the bays and beaches they knew so well.

The dawn revealed sights both dire (for Mongols) and uplifting (for Japanese). Ships scattered by wind, hulks smouldering, the flotsam of a broken army left behind as the survivors limped for safety to Korea. Korean records claim that 13,000 were drowned.

Kublai did not take defeat to heart. It had all been due to the weather, nothing to do with Japanese elan. Next time, surely the Mongols' natural superiority would tell.

Neither the Hojo shogun, Tokimune, nor the emperor in Kyoto had any doubts about the explanation for what had happened. As a Japanese courtier noted in his diary, the storm 'must have arisen as a result of the protection of the gods. Most wonderful! We should praise the gods without ceasing.'

But what of the future? The gods would only help those who helped themselves. Tokimune ordered Kyushu's coastal provinces to build a wall, which was an original idea, for as a nation the Japanese had not previously built many military installations. The project did something to give Japan's rival provincial rulers a common purpose, a stronger sense of nationhood.

The spirit of resistance hardened. When more envoys came from Kublai in May 1275, they were taken to Kamakura and executed five months later.[2] The shogun might as well have slapped Kublai's face. Court and civil leaders economized, so that national wealth could be poured into defences – the wall and small, easily

---

[2] The tomb of their unlucky leader, Du Shizong, is in a temple in Fujisawa, close to Kamakura.

manoeuvrable boats that would run rings round the mighty Korean warships. Since the enemy would surely try to land in undefended spots, there would be a secondary line of defence, with troops guarding the coasts north and south.

Next time – and undoubtedly there would be a next time – the Japanese would be ready.

19

CHALLENGE FROM THE HEARTLAND

AS A GLANCE AT THE MAP TELLS YOU, CHINA TODAY STRETCHES HALFWAY across Asia. Its western limits are almost on the same longitude as India's western edge. This is surprising, because it is far beyond the traditional Chinese heartland as defined by its old northern limits, the Great Wall. The Wall ends deep in Central Asia; but today's border is as far again beyond. How come China is so big?

The reason for China's size, remember, is because Genghis and Kublai made it so. But this leads on to another problem: Kublai's empire nominally stretched way beyond today's borders. This suggests that the question should be entirely flipped: how come China is so *small*? Why does it not reach even further into Central Asia?

The answer is that Kublai was limited by the amount of force he could bring to bear on his independent-minded relatives. One reason for this was that they had ready access to horses, which made them as hard to catch as quicksilver. There was nothing much to be done about the more distant parts of the empire – the Il-Khanate in

Persia, the Golden Horde of southern Russia – but Central Asia, though far from China's heartland, was on Mongolia's doorstep. In one sense, all of Kazakhstan and a good deal of the other 'stans' to the south were part of Genghis's inheritance and therefore part of Kublai's, and so might well have remained in the Chinese sphere. But in this direction Kublai reached his limit. He was now constrained by distance and by his troops' inability to pin down his mercurial relatives.

This takes us into a murky backwater of history – the rivalry between Kublai and a distant cousin – but it is important because the outcome explains much about the shape of China today. The opposition dictated how far Kublai could go. That he went no further presented an idea of China that endured through a time of retreat under the successor dynasty, the Manchus, when these remote regions were ruled again by Mongols as semi-independent Manchu vassals. It re-emerged in the eighteenth century as the 'New Kingdom' – Xinjiang – when the Manchus regained control, extending the borders once again to the limits defined by Kublai.

This vast and varied region, from the deserts of Uzbekistan and the grasslands of southern Kazakhstan into the heights of the Tien Shan and the wastes of western China, had no political unity, and exported nothing but trouble. In part this was because it was increasingly Islamic, even in Kublai's day; and in part because neither local rulers nor Chinese emperors could win total control.

It was in Central Asia that Kublai's real threat lay, because it came from his own family, from the descendants of Genghis's chosen heir, Ogedei, whose line had been pushed aside by Tolui's powerful widow in favour of her children. The relative in question was Khaidu, Ogedei's grandson. This is his story. It is a peculiar one, in that it played out over Khaidu's rather long life, and over a good deal of Kublai's. For some forty years, the two ill-matched contestants engaged in a sort of long-distance boxing match, Khaidu the lightweight throwing punches from Inner Asia, occasionally attracting the gaze of his heavyweight opponent, who always had other claims to his attention.

There was never a hope of Khaidu actually winning, but his

successes highlight another theme, common to many great-power rulers: conquest (if it can be managed at all) is simple, however hard-fought; administration is complicated. Conquest unites subordinates in a great adventure; administration allows free play to character, ambition and the formation of rival groups. Things fall apart, especially at the edges, which in this case was an area some 3,000 kilometres from headquarters. It took as long for an official to reach Khaidu as it took an English official to reach America in the 1780s. By the time he got there, after a four-month journey, who knew what might have happened in the meantime?

Born in about 1235, Khaidu had been too young to be caught up in the purges unleashed by Mönkhe against Ogedei's line in 1251, but old enough to be given his own estate when Mönkhe made peace with the survivors the following year. At sixteen, Khaidu was master of a territory some 2,000 kilometres to the west of Karakorum, a land running down from the Tien Shan into desert, but divided by the lush valley of the Ili River, one of the main routes linking China and the west. This, Asia's geographical dead centre, was his base, where he grew to manhood, far from the ever-more-Chinese world of Kublai. Here he started empire-building on his own account.

The story does not come easily, because it means making sense of obscure events, teasing significance from odd references in shadowy sources about petty squabbles. Marco Polo faced the same problem, which he solved, as he often did, by riding roughshod over history and going for a good yarn. In this case it was not a bad idea, because the gossip he picked up captures something essential about Khaidu and the nature of his rebellion.

Marco remembered Khaidu because of his daughter, Kutulun, another one of those formidable women who stamp their mark on Mongolia's history. Kutulun was famous not for her political skills but for her fighting ability and independent spirit. 'This damsel was very beautiful,' Marco begins, as if opening a fairy tale,[1] 'but also so

---

[1] Marco calls her Aijaruc, Ay Yoruk in Uighur, meaning Moonlight. Perhaps it was her nickname.

strong and brave that in all her father's realm there was no man who could outdo her in feats of strength . . . so tall and muscular, so stout and shapely withal, that she was almost like a giantess.' Khaidu doted on his Amazonian daughter and wanted to give her in marriage, but she always refused her suitors, saying she would only marry a man who could beat her in a wrestling match. Her rule was that a challenger had to put up 100 horses. After 100 bouts and 100 wins, Kutulun had 10,000 horses. Now, as in all good fairy tales, a noble prince appears, the son of a rich and powerful king, both father and son suspiciously anonymous. So confident is the prince that he puts up 1,000 horses. Khaidu, eager for a wealthy son-in-law, begs her to lose the fight on purpose. Never, she says. He'll have to beat me fair and square. Everyone gathers to watch. They wrestle without either gaining an advantage, until suddenly Kutulun throws her opponent. Shamed, he departs, leaving his 1,000 horses behind. Her father swallows his anger at the loss of a good match and proudly takes her on campaigns. She proves a great warrior, sometimes dashing into the enemy ranks to seize some man 'as deftly as a hawk pounces on a bird, and carry him to her father'.

Are we to believe this? Well, she existed – Rashid al-Din mentions her briefly. What is convincing is the light the story throws on Khaidu, the admirer of traditional pastoral-nomadic virtues – pride, bravery, strength, fighting spirit, independence. He was no lover of scholars or artists. As Morris Rossabi says, a man with such attitudes would naturally come into conflict with Kublai.

By the early 1260s, the empire was no longer unified, but a great family estate being fought over by descendants. In Central Asia, three Mongol powers battled to increase their own shares: the Golden Horde in today's southern Russia, the Il-Khans in Persia, and Chaghadai's heirs in between the Aral Sea and western China.[2] Into this free-for-all Khaidu was now elbowing himself, making space in the borderlands between Chaghadai's lands, the Golden

---

[2] Actually, there were three and a half powers: there was also a White Horde, who were Golden Horde relatives often acting semi-independently. Just to add to the confusion, the White Horde is known as the Blue Horde in Russia.

Horde and Kublai's China. All, of course, acknowledged that they were family, created by Genghis. Each claimed he was best suited to wear Genghis's mantle. Everything was under strain, pulled by forces over which successive claimants had little control. In the west, Islam drew Mongol rulers; some resisted, some converted, the converts looking to an old enemy, Egypt, for support. In the centre were some who held to traditional nomadic virtues, despising the very cities and cultures they relied upon for their incomes. In the east, Kublai ruled, the nominal overlord to some, to others a traitor for choosing to be so Chinese.

Khaidu – intelligent, competent and cunning, in Rashid's account – moved steadily into rebellion. In his twenties, he supported Ariq in opposition to Kublai and refused Kublai's summons to his coronation in 1264. Soon after, all three Central Asian Mongol leaders died – Hulegu in Persia, Alghu in Chaghadai's territory and Berke in the Golden Horde – leaving a power vacuum across all Central Asia. Khaidu grabbed more land, reaching west towards Persia and east into present-day China, relying on the Golden Horde's new ruler as an ally. Kublai tried to bring order to his squabbling family by sending a representative, Barakh, who managed to seize control of Chaghadai's estate. Barakh and Khaidu fought on the banks of the Syrdarya. Khaidu won a great victory, and then proposed peace in the name of Genghis.

In 1269, there was a peace conference in Talas (today's Taraz, on the border of Kazakhstan and Kyrgyzstan), to which the new rulers of all three established Inner Asian Mongol 'nations' came, with Khaidu making a fourth. Three of them – the Golden Horde leaders having no interest in this local matter – divided the whole disputed region between them, with Barakh and Khaidu, the dominant participants, somehow agreeing to share the trade from Samarkand and Bukhara. The two confirmed their treaty with the great oath that made them *anda* – blood-brothers – and by 'drinking gold', as the saying went, which meant exchanging golden cups and toasting each other.

A theme emerges from these events. Barakh, originally sent by Kublai, and the upstart Khaidu were operating as independent monarchs. No one checked back with their nominal overlord, Kublai, except, according to an unsourced quotation in the *Yuan Shi*, to send a rather rude message: 'The old customs of our dynasty are not those of the Han laws.' In other words, they were declaring themselves independent of Kublai, because he had turned from the ways of Genghis.

It quickly emerged that the peace conference was a sham. No one trusted anyone else. Everyone prepared for more fighting. The Golden Horde ruler, Mönkhe Temur, stayed out of it, leaving the other three to scrap, in a vicious round of assaults, alliances and deceptions from which, in late summer 1271, Khaidu emerged as khan of a state 2,500 kilometres across, overlapping today's southern Kazakhstan, most of Uzbekistan, and almost all of Kyrgyzstan. This area had no name; Marco Polo refers to it as 'Great Turkey', others call it Turkestan. Roughly speaking, it ran from the River Amudarya in the west into Xinjiang in the east, from Lake Balkhash in the north down to the Tien Shan – 1.25 million square kilometres in all, which is the size of France, Germany and Italy combined.

This was no mean achievement. Khaidu had proved himself smart enough to exploit his opponents' weaknesses and Kublai's move into the Chinese heartland. He was a commander in the tradition of Genghis himself, tough, austere – he didn't touch alcohol – tolerant of religions other than his own shamanism, and also careful to look after his economy. Through an efficient chancellor, he introduced his own currency (coins with a high silver content have been found in a dozen cities). He is even credited with building Andijan, which in the 1280s became a crossroads for trade in the rich Ferghana Valley. Traditionalist he may have been, but he also took after Genghis in his awareness of the need for administrative skills. He created regiments of cavalry, with a decimal command structure traditional among Mongol armies. In this way, he was able to incorporate many, and often rival, Mongol and Turkish tribes. The horsemen were reinforced by infantry and 'naphtha-throwers' – teams expert in the use of trebuchets and other siege engines. How strong were his armies? The sources toss around the figure of 100,000, probably an exaggeration, and anyway rather fewer than the armies mustered by Persia, the Golden Horde and Kublai's China. What they lacked in quantity they made up for in quality. They were terrific at raids: quick advances, hard strikes, quick retreats.

But economic revival did not last long, and dreams of wider empire were soon shattered. The same year as Khaidu's coronation, Kublai tried to bring him to heel. He sent a delegation of six princes led by his fourth son, Nomukhan, to Almalikh, well inside Khaidu's territory, with the aim of persuading him to come to court in Xanadu or Beijing. Khaidu took no notice, keeping his army out of harm's way, securing his western borders. Nomukhan did not have enough horses or troops to mount an offensive. Time passed. Nomukhan built up a court and turned himself into yet another independent warlord, until captured by one of the many restive cousins and sent off to the Golden Horde, where he languished for ten years until his release. Kublai, totally involved in the war against Song, simply gave up trying to control Khaidu's distant realm.

All this was good news for Khaidu. After re-occupying Almalikh, he was free to deal with constant cross-border raids from Persia and several uprisings from disenchanted members of Chaghadai's family. Sitting squarely over the old Silk Routes, he presided over a shaky revival, building an arc of allies all around the fringes of the empire, reaching out southwards into Tibet and eastwards to Manchuria. For forty years – until the final showdown, as we will see in Chapter 22 – his ambition was to be the true heir of his grandfather Ogedei, Genghis's appointed successor. In the end he failed, but he had a lasting impact: he kept Kublai roughly within the borders that define China's north-western limits today.

20

WHAT KUBLAI DID FOR
CHINA

KUBLAI HAD INHERITED ASTONISHING MANAGERIAL SKILLS. HE WAS NO
intellectual genius, but he had talents that made him one of the
greatest CEOs of all time. He was a good judge of character (with
one notorious exception) and had the knack of hiring people who
were smarter than he was. Like his grandfather, he was happy to
employ anyone with talent. His advisers formed an international
team. Muslim traders were headhunted to become financial administrators. He employed sixty-six Uighur Turks, twenty-one of whom
were resident commissioners or local officials running Chinese
districts, while several others tutored princes of the royal family.
Also like his grandfather Genghis, he could spot organizational
problems, totally unprecedented ones caused by the novelty of
unfolding events, and then, out of the blue, devise solutions that
actually worked. Genghis had taken tribes, broken their structure
and forged a nation, then started to forge an empire. Kublai took the
process further. His task was primarily conquest, then government,
for which his people were doubly unprepared, firstly because they

had had no government before Genghis and secondly because no previous non-Chinese conquerors had taken on all China, north and south. There is no precedent in history of such small numbers successfully taking on so much and so many.

Kublai's main fault was that he could not be content. How could he be, if he was to be true to his grandfather's mission, to set the bounds of empire wider still and wider, until all the world acknowledged Mongol supremacy?

At home, by comparison, he was a rock. That, too, was a consequence of his mission. Having seen that China was the key to imperial rule, he needed China to be stable and prosperous, for that would be his foundation for world rule ordained by Heaven. From this astonishing ambition came something just as remarkable: not a grim dictatorship, but a revival of much that had vanished from Chinese society during the turmoil of the previous century. For a brief moment, about two decades, all of China underwent something of a renaissance. Kublai, as a foreigner, would never be truly accepted; but he was indisputably the boss, and it is arguable that the changes he brought improved the lot of his new subjects. There is no way of assessing public opinion, but from the lack of uprisings we can assume many felt that unity with peace under the Mongols was better than a nation divided between Jin and Song.

This judgement conflicts sharply with commonly held opinions about Mongol rule – which is often seen as nothing but a catalogue of abuses – along the following lines.

Almost all the top positions were held by Mongols. They lorded it over the population as the new landowners, the new elite, the new aristocracy. A new class system brought new humiliations: Mongols at the top; in second place, those from the Muslim lands – Persians, Arabs, Uighurs, Turks – who knew about business and trade; then the 40 million northern Chinese, along with other fringe minorities, like Tatars, Khitans and Koreans; and finally, at the bottom of the heap, the new subjects, the 70 million southern Chinese, who at a stroke turned from a people who were heirs to the richest and most sophisticated culture on earth to subjects and servants. Many were actually enslaved, and a slave trade sprang up. The Chinese were banned from carrying weapons, hunting, military training, raising horses, praying in groups, holding fairs. If a Mongol murdered, he was exiled; a Chinese murderer was executed. The examination system, by which scholar-officials acquired office, was no more. In the ten grades into which Mongols categorized their Chinese subjects, Confucian scholars ranked ninth, below prostitutes, above only the lowest of the low, the beggars.

All this is true. But it is not the whole truth. The scholars, aristocrats and officials represented only a tiny part of Chinese society. Most people were peasant-farmers and ordinary town-dwellers. With such a vast population, with such teeming cities, with such a thin upper crust of Mongols, no reforms permeated from top to bottom. For ordinary people, the routines of everyday life hardly changed. Or actually improved.

Stability depended on more than the raw exercise of power. Kublai was the most powerful man of his day, one of the most powerful of all time, yet, as his actions showed, he knew that his authority was only in part top down, flowing from him through the court and his army of officials to the masses. It was also bottom up. Ordinary people had to feel happy and secure, or unrest would fester and spread from below. North China was sick enough as it was, recovering from the half-century of warfare initiated by Genghis back in 1211; the south was seething from his own campaign of conquest; all needed healing.

The foundation of stability was the vast mass of peasant-farmers, on whom all depended for food. To look after their interests, Kublai set up a new Office for the Stimulation of Agriculture, with eight officials and a team of experts who organized aid, built fifty-eight granaries that could store almost 9,000 tonnes of grain, arranged tax remissions, and banned Mongols from grazing their wandering herds on farmland. Fifty-household local councils helped with production, irrigation, even schools – an idea that proved too revolutionary to work, but which did at least show that the emperor was no mere barbarian nomad. Taxes now flowed not directly to the landowner, who in the north was probably a Mongol, but to the government, which then divided the revenue between itself and the landowner. The peasant-farmer still paid, but at least Kublai tried to curb abuses. He also insisted that forced labour, which remained vital for large-scale public projects like canals and the postal system, was rather less forced than previously.

Let's look at how he ruled in more detail. He had a good start, under the aegis of Genghis's Khitan adviser, the great Yelu Chucai, who successfully set up a decent working bureaucracy, despite opposition from some dyed-in-the-wool factions. But, as we have seen, Kublai faced a much vaster problem: namely how to combine steppe-land with town and farmland, nomadism with settled cultures, the few with the many. He was not ready simply to abandon the one (from which he derived his core values) and adopt the other. Besides, he also had to take into account Muslims, a vital component in that his brother ruled a good chunk of Islam and Muslims were important as governors, tax-gatherers, financial advisers and business partners. His response was to make it up as he went along, sometimes finding solutions in the practices of previous dynasties, sometimes devising his own. Over thirty years, he created a form of government that owed much to China, but was also uniquely complex and cosmopolitan.

He had one supreme advantage: he was not bound by precedent. Previous emperors had governed through several executive agencies. Kublai saw that this would be a recipe for disaster. He had just one, the Central Secretariat, with him at the top, ranging down through chief councillors (usually two or three, occasionally up to five), privy councillors, assistants, some 200 officials and hundreds of clerical staff, in eighteen levels, the status of each minutely defined in terms of precedence, title, salary and perks.[1]

The Secretariat controlled six ministries: Personnel, Revenues, Rites, War, Punishments and Works, each of which had dozens of departments. The Ministry of Works, for instance, had fifty-three of them. Checking up on all ministries and their departments was a Censorate, a sort of National Audit Office, with three national headquarters.

[1] This section is mostly based on Mote, *Imperial China 900–1800* (see Bibliography).

Entirely separate from the civil administration was the Bureau of Military Affairs. This was established by Kublai in 1263, after Li Tan's rebellion, as the guarantor of his power. It was hard-core Mongol territory, top secret, staffed by Mongols, with all Chinese excluded to prevent them knowing anything of the army's strength, dispositions or armaments. It controlled all the armed forces, the appointment of officers, the training of Chinese and Central Asian units, the records, and all its own auditing procedures. This was perhaps Kublai's greatest stroke of administrative genius – to create a huge and enduring establishment loyal not to him personally, but to the state.

Then there was the court. Specialized staff took care of the rituals, protocol, kitchens, granaries, warehouses, clothing and special food. Teams of artisans supplied gold, silver, porcelain, gems, textiles. There were departments for the hunting facilities and the stud farms. This was a universe unto itself of servants, managers, entertainment specialists, historians, translators, interpreters, astronomers, doctors, librarians, shrine-keepers, musicians and architects.

Other institutions were not under the direct control of any of the above. Three academies were devoted to Mongol studies (speaking Mongolian being an asset for ambitious civil servants), and a Muslim Bureau of Western Astronomy – set up by a Syriac Christian named Isa (Jesus) – gave Muslims their own research facilities. The Commission for Tibetan and Buddhist Affairs, Phags-pa's private empire, acted as a sort of Tibetan government-at-a-distance, supervising the Pacification Bureau in Tibet and the ever-growing Buddhist interests across China: temples, monasteries, properties.

It was the Bureau of Military Affairs' job to handle the transition in China from conquest to a permanent military administration. This involved a big change, and would store up trouble for the future. Under Genghis, the Mongol system had drawn every family into its military machine. Families had to be supported, first with booty, then, as territory fell, with land. But few Mongols had the ambition or talent to administer farms. Many were absentee landlords. The system tended to collapse of its own accord, leaving the estates ruined and their people destitute. Mongol landowners sold up and found themselves cast adrift, with no skills, no education, no place back in their homeland, yet still supposedly part of an elite. They were the empire's equivalent of poor whites in the American South. Later, this would be part of the sickness that ate at the soul of Kublai's heirs.

The provinces were another of Kublai's creations. As the tide of Mongol conquest flowed outwards, newly conquered regions were given their own mini-versions of the Central Secretariat, and these remained as branches of government in China's eleven provinces, which then acquired branches of all the other departments. They were not provincial governments – Kublai wanted his officials governed from the centre, to avoid local empire-building – but they formed the essence of the provincial system set up in succession by the Qing and then by the Communists in 1949. Today, the provinces of Yunnan, Shaanxi, Sichuan and Gansu all owe their existence to Kublai.

As in effect CEO of Mongolia Inc., Kublai was committed to keeping the wheels of commerce rolling. Craftsmen were favoured with rations of food, clothing and salt, and were exempted from forced labour. Merchants had previously been seen as parasites; now they were encouraged. Trade, mainly with Muslim lands, boomed.

In some ways, Kublai was the ideal patron of the arts. He had no pretensions to being an expert in art, but he knew it was tremendously important, and since he wished to appeal to all his subjects, he encouraged artists without worrying about their race or creed. He was thus, almost by default, a force for change. The Nepalese metalworker and architect Aniga, designer of the White Pagoda, became head of all artisans nationwide, ending up with a mansion and rich wife found for him by Kublai's wife Chabui.

Take ceramics, for which China had been famous, with ten main kilns in the north and fourteen in the south. The war had largely destroyed ceramic production in the north, but southern kilns continued to fill wagons rolling into the great southern port of Quanzhou, the place Marco Polo calls by its Arabic name, Zaytun, then onwards by ship to South-east Asia, India and the world of Islam, half of which, remember, was ruled by Mongols, who quickly adopted the refined tastes of their subjects. Indeed, Quanzhou, from which most goods were exported, was under the thumb of Persian merchants. With Kublai standing back, the southern kilns could focus on exports, and on experiments to give their customers what they wanted, namely, quality. As a result, Yuan potters developed, as one expert, Margaret Medley, puts it, 'the fine white porcelains, hard, vitrified and translucent, that we now automatically associate with the name of China'. There was more. In the Middle East cobalt, an extraordinarily rare metallic element, had long been used to give a blue tinge to statuettes and necklace beads. Yuan potters acquired it and made 'cobalt blue' ceramics famous, along with the white wares of Fujian and the grey-green celadons of Zhejiang, for any one of which modern collectors pay vast sums. Exports boomed, and taxes – on kilns, craftsmen and production – rolled into Kublai's coffers.

Working in groups to make use of their wealth, merchants became bankers, lending at exorbitant rates of interest. They and Kublai's government were partners: laws forced merchants to convert their metal coins into paper currency on entry, which gave the government a reserve in metals, which was used to support loans at around 10 per cent annual interest back to the merchant groups, who became, in effect, government-sanctioned loan sharks. From trade, everyone profited. Even the peasants? No doubt Kublai, with a financial adviser at his shoulder, would have argued that merchant wealth translated into government wealth, which financed public works and allowed tax relief to the needy. If peasants chose to get into debt with a loan shark, that was their fault.

Kublai's big economic success was to extend the use of paper money. Paper money is a great invention, for practical reasons, as the Chinese had discovered almost 300 years before when the Song unified the country and revolutionized it with a booming economy. Unification, wealth and stability opened the way to a single currency based on copper coins – those cumbersome strings of 1,000 coins. Since rich merchants did not like handling such a weight of cash, local governments issued certificates of deposit – so-called 'flying money' – that could be redeemed in other cities. The elements had been in place for centuries, principally paper (AD 105 is the traditional date of its invention), which came to be made from the beaten inner bark of mulberry trees, and printing with carved wood blocks (eighth century, from Japan). In 1023, the state printed the first banknotes, introducing two previously unknown problems: inflation and counterfeiting.

Kublai, with the right advice, had both difficulties under control in an economy of which a modern finance minister would be proud. Four economic pillars – national unity, internal stability, high confidence, good growth – allowed for a far more effective system of paper money than the Song had had. He tried three systems, one backed by reserves of silk, the other two by silver, of different purities, the last of which became universal, to the astonishment and admiration of Marco Polo. It was the oddest notion, that a whole society should place value on the solidified slurry made from the under-bark of mulberry trees. Why the system worked was a total mystery to him.

It worked firstly because stability preserved confidence in the currency; secondly because Kublai allowed a free exchange with silver on demand; thirdly, he did not print too much cash, thereby avoiding significant inflation. It is a neat trick, which later dynasties (and many modern governments) failed to match. Soon after Yuan rule ended in 1368, paper money fell out of use for 400 years.

Another element in Kublai's revolution was a new legal system.[2] Since he had come from Mongolia, all China's preceding codes, with legal traditions dating back 2,000 years, were suddenly null and void. Genghis's legal system, a list of statutes recorded by his adopted relative, Shigi, did not have the sophistication for a vast and complex society like China's. Advisers quickly began afresh, combining elements of the two systems. How they did it exactly is not known, because the texts have survived only in bits. Day-to-day justice depended, as it always had for over 700 years, on the Five Punishments: death by strangulation or decapitation; exile

[2] This section is based on Paul Heng-chao Ch'en, *Chinese Legal Tradition under the Mongols* (see Bibliography).

for life to three distances – 1,000, 1,250 or 1,500 kilometres – depending on the seriousness of the crime; penal servitude up to three years; beating with a heavy stick, from 60 to 100 blows; and beating with a light stick, from 10 to 50 blows. For the most serious crime – treachery – Kublai revived a seldom-used precedent: death by slow slicing, from which comes the sadistic notion of 'death by a thousand cuts', the punishment meted out to the unfortunate emir of Diyarbakir. Not a thousand, actually, but eight initially – face, hands (2), feet (2), breast, stomach and head – to be increased in stages – 24, 36, 120 – depending on the pain to be inflicted.

This sounds grim, but in fact the Yuan code was noted for its leniency. The Song code had listed 293 offences punishable by death. The Yuan had only 135, which, as one scholar notes, 'contradicts the common notion that the Mongolian rulers employed very harsh punishments against criminal offenders'. Indeed, the successor dynasty, the Ming, pushed the number back up again. Moreover, the actual number of executions was remarkably low. Between 1260 and 1307, 2,743 criminals were executed (though nine years are missing from the dynastic records). An average of seventy-two executions per year out of a population of 100 million is about one fifth of China's current rate.[3]

In other respects, too, Kublai favoured leniency. Criminals received the equivalent of control orders. For first-time robbery with violence, a criminal was punished, and in addition tattooed on the right arm with the words 'robbery or theft once'; he was ordered to register with local authorities wherever he went; and to serve as an auxiliary policeman for five years – a combination of punishment and community service, of discrimination and surveillance that reinforced the bonds of society.

How come the world's most powerful man and the head of a regime noted for its iron control ruled an administration of such relative leniency? Partly because Kublai's dictatorship was not, like

---

[3] In 2009, the Dui Hua Foundation, a San Francisco-based non-profit humanitarian organization, estimated that 5,000 people were executed in China, 'far more than all other nations combined', though the precise number of executions is a state secret.

modern ones, all-embracing, all-intrusive; and partly because his people did as they were told, and Kublai knew harshness was counter-productive. In 1287, hearing that some 190 people had been condemned to death, Kublai ordered reprieves. 'Prisoners are not a mere flock of sheep . . . It is proper that they be instead enslaved and assigned to pan gold with a sieve.'[4] There speaks a man who knew how to get the best from his assets.

Here's an odd thing. The Mongols loved the theatre. They loved it mainly because it was a total novelty, and they were seduced by Chinese dramatic traditions. The Chinese had been watching dance-shows, musicals, recitations, story-tellings, pageants and variety shows for centuries, with a boom in drama under the Song. Kublai made sure his people had theatre, lots of it. But he didn't want just the old stuff. He wanted new writing, designed to appeal to the Mongols and his very international court. That meant it would have to be easy to follow, because Kublai himself did not speak very good Chinese. This caused something of a revolution among the Song literati. Traditionally, they had contradictory attitudes towards the theatre. They loved it for its entertainment value, but plays were written in common language, actors were held in low regard and actresses were considered whores. In brief, from any point of view other than their own, Song literati were appalling snobs. No one thought of plays as literature; no one thought of preserving them. As a result, very little survives from pre-Yuan times.

All this changed under Kublai. At court, there were two bureaus responsible for music and acting, which performed court rituals and popular performances. The customer called the tune and, by comparison with his subjects, the customer had simple tastes. As one of the first translators of Yuan drama, Henry Hart, put it in slightly non-PC terms in 1936: 'Nurtured on the windswept deserts, exulting in battle and rapine . . . they preferred drama written and acted in the everyday language of common people.'

---

[4] Paul Heng-chao Ch'en, p. 46; quoted by Rossabi, *Khubilai Khan*, p. 130 (see Bibliography).

It was this demand that reinvigorated Chinese drama. A new breed of playwrights emerged, many of them scholars frustrated by the ending of the examination system, eager to supplement their meagre incomes, to win recognition and to find an outlet for their literary skills. They created, as one historian of Chinese drama, Chung-wen Shih, has written, a 'body of works qualitatively and quantitatively unequalled before or after in the Chinese theatre, and making Yuan drama one of the most brilliant genres in Chinese literary history'. This rich field has one disadvantage for the historian. The authors were still embarrassed to have their names associated with their products, so very little is known about them. Fortunately, one playwright, Zhong Su-cheng, gathered biographical notes about Yuan writers in *A Register of Ghosts*, its very title a comment on the invisibility of its subjects. Of the 152 listed, 111 are dramatists.

Thousands of plays must have been written, of which some 700 are known by name and 150 have survived. They are of a type known as 'variety plays', or 'mixed entertainment' – what we would call musicals, except that with the involvement of fine writers they are much more than musicals. They examine contemporary concerns: oppression, injustice, corruption, struggles with authority. They do so in their own terms, of course. The plays do not display the internal agonies and destructive passions common in Western drama from Shakespeare onwards. Some flee the real world, like *The Romance of the Western Chamber*, which derives from a story first written down around 800. A student rescues a beautiful girl from rebels; he woos her; her fierce mother objects; a clever maid helps them; the mother is won round; happy ending. Rewritten several times, the story has remained popular ever since. Others have more bite. They could not be set in the present, for fear of giving offence to the empire's officials. They try to do what drama should do, which is to make current concerns timeless and, if possible, seize the literary high ground.

Let Guan Hanqing (Kuan Han-ch'ing) stand for all, because he was the most prolific of Yuan playwrights. Practically everything about his life is vague. Born around 1240, he died very old in the late 1320s. He wrote sixty-three or sixty-four musical plays (the authorship of one is disputed), of which fourteen or eighteen (another dispute) survive. Heroines were his forte, exemplified in his best play, *The Injustice to Dou E*. She's a simple village girl, a young widow of eighteen. A coarse suitor wrongly accuses her of murder. She is dragged into court and beaten by a corrupt magistrate. When she refuses to confess, he threatens to beat her mother-in-law. To save her, Dou E makes a false confession and is condemned to death. On the eve of her execution, she makes three wishes, one of which is that the area should suffer three years of drought. After her death, all her wishes come true, proving that Heaven has heard her prayers. The drought attracts the attention of her father, a high official, who reopens the case. Dou E reappears as a ghost to accuse her accusers. Justice is done, the universe re-balanced. But it's more than a good story, in ways that escaped Kublai's court. Dou E is a symbol of the suffering nation. When she is abused – as the Mongols abused China – the laws of Heaven are overturned, corruption and stupidity rule. But virtue cannot for ever be despised. Her death spurs Heaven to action, returning justice to an unjust world – great themes that ensured the play's survival in several later versions, including one performed by the Peking Opera today.

21

KAMIKAZE

AFTER THE CONQUEST OF THE SOUTH, KUBLAI COULD TURN AGAIN ON Japan. He was now sixty-five, and time was snapping at his heels. But it was more than his age that drove him. He acted like a man obsessed, with the need to fulfil his grandfather's ambitions for world conquest and the need to punish this 'little country' for its temerity in resisting him.

Accounts of this campaign have, until recently, been dominated by the Japanese point of view, because they were the victors and history belongs more to winners than losers. The story has been often told: how the mighty Mongol–Chinese fleet was about to crush the hapless, outmoded Japanese samurai when the Heavens themselves came to the aid of the Japanese by unleashing a typhoon that swept Kublai's fleet to oblivion. Soon thereafter, the Japanese called the storm the Divine Wind, the *kamikaze* (*kami* also having the sense of *god*, *spirit* and *superior*), referring to it as proof that Japan was under the protection of Heaven. This suited the ruling elite, whose power depended in part on faith in their ability to perform the correct religious rituals. It was to evoke the idea of heavenly protection that the suicide pilots of the Second World War were called *kamikazes*: they were a new divine wind that would ensure protection against foreign invasion. It was a comforting idea. Yet research since 2001 has revealed the notion of the storm-as-rescuer to be a myth. After almost 800 years, it turns out that the Japanese were far more capable than they themselves believed. It was not the Divine Wind that saved them, but Mongol incompetence and Japanese fighting strength.

There was a bad smell about this operation from the beginning. Kublai was out of touch with reality. He seemed to believe that the mere decision to attack would inevitably lead to victory, as if will alone decided military matters. He made impossible demands, ignored logistical problems, and – crucially – took no account of the weather.

To guarantee success, Kublai needed a bigger fleet than before to carry more land forces; for that he needed the compliance of Korea, his unwilling vassal. But Korea had borne the brunt of the 1274 debacle. Her grain had been commandeered, her young men drafted as shipbuilders and warriors, leaving only the old and very young to till the fields. There was no harvest, and no manpower to rebuild the fleet. For five years, Kublai had to send food aid to keep Korea alive. Still it would not be enough. Ships would also have to come from the south, the former Song empire, and its reluctant inhabitants.

It would be simple, of course, if only Japan would acknowledge Kublai's overlordship. In 1279 yet another embassy arrived in Japan, with instructions to be extremely polite, to avoid the fate of their predecessors. Unfortunately, they arrived just at the moment rumours were spreading fear across the land. A local beauty had vanished in mysterious circumstances, supposedly abducted by a band of Mongol spies who had made a base on an uninhabited rocky islet. A Japanese force had invaded to rescue her. The Mongol chief had dragged her to a cliff top and threatened to kill her, but she had cast herself into the sea and swum to shore, while all the Japanese were murdered by the Mongol spies. She alone survived to tell this dramatic tale, so the story went. True or not, the Kamakura government believed that the three-man delegation from Kublai was part of the same plot. The three were beheaded, and resolve strengthened. Foot-soldiers and cavalry massed on Kyushu. The barrier around Hakata Bay grew longer and higher. Japan braced itself for an assault that was now seen as inevitable.

And Kublai ordered that the fleet should be ready to invade in little more than a year. It would be the biggest fleet ever to set sail, and would remain the biggest for over 700 years, until exceeded by the Allied invasion of Normandy on D-Day, 6 June 1944. It would have a Korean as admiral of the fleet and a turncoat Chinese, Fan Wenhu, as commander of land forces. Their force numbered about 140,000. The plan was for two fleets, 900 ships from Korea and 3,500 from Quanzhou in Fujian, to link up at the island of Iki, 30 kilometres off the Japanese coast, and then invade the mainland together.

That was the plan. It was highly optimistic: 4,400 ships is a vast fleet, especially if they were warships, as accounts usually suggest. In fact, a little long division shows that this invasion was very unlike the Spanish Armada, which consisted of 130 massive warships carrying 27,000 men, about 200 per ship. Kublai's fleet was more comparable to the D-Day force: some 5,000 vessels, 156,000 men, 31 per vessel, most of which were landing craft. So except for a few massive warships, mainly from Korea, what we are dealing with here is a fleet of small ships. Portsmouth to Normandy is a mere 170 kilometres, a six-hour crossing by engine-driven ships. Kublai would be relying on wind power and oars to cover for the 900-strong Korean fleet 200 kilometres and for the 3,500 much smaller vessels from the south a forbidding 1,400 kilometres. Even with a good wind in the right direction, it would take them six days to reach the rendezvous.

Obviously, Kublai and his commanders aimed to get the conquest over before the typhoon season started in August. But any experienced sailor would have known that it was crazy to rely on a tight schedule. Kublai, the supreme commander, knew a lot about warfare in large, open spaces on land, but he had never been to sea, let alone seen what a typhoon could do. Blinded by desperation and isolated by power, he was taking a fearful risk, and there was no one to tell him the truth.

*

Things went wrong from the start. The Korean fleet reached Iki, as planned, around the end of May, and waited, and waited. The southern fleet in Quanzhou could not even leave on time. A commander fell ill and had to be replaced. Food rotted in the heat. Epidemics spread. After departure, contrary winds drove many ships into ports along the coast.

Eventually, on 10 June, the commander of the Korean fleet occupied Iki anyway, then, after waiting another two weeks, crossed the small gap to an island in the middle of the bay.

Meanwhile, the southern fleet, now a month behind schedule, went straight for the mainland, anchoring off the low-lying little island of Takashima in Imari Bay, 50 kilometres south of Hakata, intending to march north to meet the others on land.

But the assault never gained momentum. Both fleets found it hard to make landings. Every likely site for 20 kilometres round the bay of Hakata was blocked by the new wall. The Japanese also took the fight out from the shore, rowing nimble little skiffs out at night to cut cables, sneak aboard, cut throats and start fires. True, from the larger ships siege bows acted like artillery, firing massive arrows that could splinter a Japanese dinghy. But the traction trebuchets which might have been effective inshore against land forces were useless when trying to hit moving targets from moving decks. Kublai's generals bickered in three languages and most of their troops – the Chinese and Koreans – had no heart to fight for their new Mongol masters. The Japanese, with a unified command, years of preparation and on home territory, had well-fortified positions from which to stave off assaults and mount counter-attacks.

From the Mongol point of view, the Japanese were everywhere, in huge numbers, galloping back and forth wherever a landing was threatened. One Yuan source later claimed there were 102,000 of them. But Mongol and Chinese officials were recording a catastrophic defeat and had every reason to exaggerate the strength of the opposition. Current estimates suggest a force in the order of 20,000 – enough to hold back the Mongols, Chinese and Koreans, whose huge superiority in numbers was negated by the difficulty of mounting a joint sea-and-land operation so far from home and by being hopelessly scattered. For almost two months, 23 June to 14 August, the two sides skirmished, with no conclusion.

On 15 August, nature intervened. The first typhoon of the season approached, earlier than usual. There's no telling just how ferocious this particular one was. To sailors in small boats, it wouldn't have made much difference.

The warships would have been built for storms, but not the 3,500 twenty- or thirty-man landing craft that came from the south. The Korean sailors knew what was coming. To avoid their being dashed on the rocks, their admiral ordered his fleet out to sea. Those who could boarded in order not to be stranded ashore. Many were still clambering aboard or struggling through the shallows when the storm struck. No one recorded the details – the waves, the shredded sails, the broken oars, the smashed ships, the armoured men tossed to their deaths – but some 15,000 of the northern force and 50,000 of the southerners died at sea, while hundreds of others perished at Japanese hands, or were overwhelmed in the small boats that had remained near the rocky shore.

It was a catastrophe never matched in scale on a single day at sea before or since, and never on land either until the atom bomb destroyed Hiroshima, killing 75,000 at a single blow, in 1945.

The flagship, bearing the admiral, Fan Wenhu, and a general, Chang Xi, was wrecked on one of the many offshore islands, Taka. The two mustered other survivors, a couple of thousand strong, who raided locals for food and repaired one of the wrecks, in which the admiral limped home. He lived to fight another day, though he was reduced in rank. The other survivors were mopped up by Japanese. Three were allowed to return, to tell Kublai of the fate of his great armada and its all-conquering army. As for the rest, thousands were killed on the beaches, thousands drowned, thousands were enslaved, while the ships turned to driftwood or vanished into the belly of the ocean. A Korean account of the scene on one rocky foreshore gives a sense of the disaster: 'The bodies of men and broken timbers of the vessels were heaped together in a solid mass so that a person could walk across from one point to another.'[1]

No wonder the Japanese soon saw it as an intervention by the gods even greater than that in 1274, and the idea of divine protection was entrenched from then on. Both court and military authorities prayed assiduously to keep foreigners at bay. Temples and shrines flourished. Not that prayer was the only defence, for the wall was maintained and manned constantly for the next thirty years, as a result of which some of it has lasted pretty well to the present day. The idea of divine intervention became rooted in Japanese culture. Few questioned the conclusion: that Japan had been saved by a divinely ordained typhoon.

Yet there is growing evidence that this was not so, that the real salvation was down to the Japanese themselves. It is there in Suenaga's story, as recorded in the Invasion Scrolls, for he fought on both occasions. He talks his way on to a small boat to carry the fight to the enemy. He boards a Mongol ship and takes two heads. He's brave, eager to take a risk, but well in control of himself. He's one among many. There's a terrific sense of common purpose. And it works. Amidst the usual chaos of war, all these uncoordinated actions by individuals are enough to hold back the enemy and keep them out in the bay. Crucially, there is no mention of the typhoon at all. Success is all down to the Japanese. Suenaga shows respect to the gods with prayers, but there is no hint in the account or the pictures that Heaven actually intervenes during or after the action. As Thomas Conlan puts it in his fine study of the invasion, 'The warriors of Japan were capable of fighting the Mongols to a standstill.' Suenaga and his fellow-fighters were, in the words of Conlan's title, 'In little need of divine intervention'.

Further support for this argument comes from marine archaeologists. Their inspiration was a remarkable man named Torao Mozai, who is worth a brief diversion. He was named Torao (meaning 'male tiger') after the day on which he was born in 1914. He joined the navy, but contracted TB in 1939, which probably saved his life, because he spent the war convalescing. Later he got a doctorate in

[1] From Delgado, *Khubilai Khan's Lost Fleet* (see Bibliography).

engineering and taught at Tokyo University until 1979. After his retirement at the age of sixty-four, 'Tiger' Mozai started a new career researching Kublai's lost fleet. In Hakata Bay, fishermen had found a few stone anchor-stocks, but these might have come from one of any number of uncounted wrecks. In 1980, he decided to focus on Takashima, the pretty, pine-covered island where the southern fleet had anchored. Mozai was interested in the bay. He adapted a sonar probe used for finding fish, learned to dive (at sixty-five!), built up a small team of divers and began to find interesting objects on the seabed: spearheads, nails, pots, but no 'smoking gun' proving that they came from the Mongol fleet. Then, in 1981, a farmer called Kuniichi Mukae brought him the proof. Seven years before, Mukae had been digging for clams when his spade struck something hard – a little square of solid bronze with writing engraved on it in the script devised by Kublai's Tibetan mentor, Phags-pa. An archaeologist, Takashi Okazaki of Kyushu University, told Mozai what it said: 'Commander of 1,000'. It was the official seal of one of Kublai's senior officers.

Inspired, Mozai established a research institute, the Kyushu and Okinawa Society for Underwater Archaeology, and continued work. From layers of mud and sand, he and his team dug up swords, spear-heads, stone hand-mills for grinding rice, more anchor-stocks, and round explosive catapult balls, proof that the Mongols had cata-pults on board, indirect proof that Suenaga and his friends had indeed been bombarded with thunder-crash bombs in 1274. In 1984, the ageing Mozai handed over to one of Japan's very few marine archaeologists, Kenzo Hayashida, who in 1994 discovered three massive wood-and-stone anchors in one of the island's bays. Carbon-dating showed the trees from which the anchors were made had been cut in 1224, plus or minus 90 years, which nicely covered the time when the fleet was built and sailed.

Other finds led his team out 150 metres into 15 metres of water, where, in October 2001, feeling their way into a metre of sea-floor gloop, they found 168 objects – bits of pottery, oven bricks, a bronze mirror, belt-fittings and at last, in July 2002, the remains of a large vessel, a scattering of ship's timbers, all swirled together as if by a blender. The pots were Chinese, and they came from the long-established kilns at Yixing in Jiangsu – enough to convince Hayashida that these were the remnants of Kublai's southern force.

Work continues, but – as he explained to me when he showed me round his laboratory in 2005 – some conclusions are clear. The ship was about 70 metres long, dwarfing anything else in the world at the time. European sailing ships would not approach anything of this size until the nineteenth century. Only as the age of steam approached did the last Western sailing ships exceed Chinese and Korean men-o'-war.[2]

But size is not everything. What really matters in ocean-going vessels is construction. And here, it seems, Kublai's naval architects were so rushed that they cut corners. Randall Sasaki, of Texas A&M University, College Station, who has made a study of the 500 or so timber fragments, was surprised to see that the nail holes were very close together, many of them grouped as if the builders were following an old design with old materials. 'This suggests the timbers were recycled,' he says. 'Also, some of the timbers were of poor quality.'

There's more, from Hayashida: 'So far, we have found no evidence of sea-going, V-shaped keels.'

These two pieces of evidence, combined with the catastrophic loss of even large vessels that should have been able to ride out a typhoon, suggest a startling but logical conclusion: in response to Kublai's demands for mass building at high speed, his naval craftsmen improvised. They took any ships available, seaworthy or not. The good ones they put into service, the poor ones they refashioned with the same material. Except for the new ones built by the Koreans – none of which has yet been found at Takashima – the vast proportion of Kublai's fleet were keel-less river boats, utterly unsuited to the high seas. Kublai's ambitions led inexorably to a massive failure of quality control. Overseers may have said that orders had been fulfilled, that the boats were all ready. No one told

---

[2] Kublai's ships were dwarfed by the 145-metre leviathans built by the Ming emperor Zhu Di to sail the world in the early fifteenth century.

Kublai that if things got rough, these boats would be death-traps. With his insane ambitions and his lack of naval knowledge, he had in effect scuppered his own fleet before it set out.

22

A MURDER, AND A
SECRET GRAVE

THERE'S NOTHING LIKE A MURDER TO REVEAL HIDDEN EMOTIONS. There's nothing like an assassination to reveal a government's faults.

This story shows the failing heart of Kublai's administration. He had created a monster with a prodigious appetite for men, materials and money, and it had to be kept fed. One man seemed to have the secret, and for Kublai that was a good enough reason to ignore the hatred that spread like a plague around his power-obsessed and deeply repellent minister. For twenty years he allowed disaster to brew, until it cooked up a melodrama more sensational than fiction, involving a suicidal fanatic, a mad monk, a farcical plot and the murder of the man himself. Marco Polo jumped on the story. But he didn't know the half of it.

The villain of the piece was Ahmad, an Uzbek, as we would now call him, from Banakat, near Tashkent. The town was taken by Genghis in 1220. Ahmad's mother seems to have been captured, because as a boy Ahmad was in the entourage of Chabui when she married Kublai, then a prince of twenty-four. He graduated to

Kublai's household, helping with finances and military expenditures, a background from which arose, in the words of his biographer, Herbert Franke, a 'relentless craving for total control over government finances'.

When Kublai was enthroned in 1261, Ahmad became responsible for requisitioning provisions for the court. He rose fast. The next year he had two jobs, a senior position in the Secretariat and a role as a transport commissioner. He hated to be supervised, always a bad sign in an administrator, and asked to be made directly answerable to Kublai himself. His bid failed, and Kublai gave his son and heir, Jingim (Zhenjin in another spelling), jurisdiction over the Secretariat. It was the start of Ahmad's long-running feud with Jingim.

Ahmad's job was to increase government income, and he was never short of ever more ingenious ideas for taxation. In 1266, he struck gold as head of a new Office for Regulating State Expenditure. By improving records, he managed to enrol some 600,000 new tax-paying households, increasing the empire's tax base from 1.4 million households to almost 2 million.

Kublai loved the result, and Ahmad prospered with a portfolio of jobs. His growing power was matched by his arrogance, and his arrogance by his unpopularity. But he didn't care. Most foreign officials were unpopular, as Marco Polo recorded: 'All Cathayans [northern Chinese] detested the Great Kaan's rule because he set over them governors who were Tartars, Saracens, or Christians who were attached to his household and devoted to his service.'

Disputes continued, over Ahmad's attempt to establish another council to outflank the Secretariat, and about his objections to the new auditing office, the Censorate. 'Why should we have a Censorate?' he said. 'There's no reason as long as the money and grain come in!' In 1270 he got his council – the Department of State Affairs – the fourth of the great pillars of government, along with the Secretariat, Military Affairs and the Censorate. And in addition he became director of Political Affairs. In Kublai's eyes he had the magic touch and could do no wrong. By 1272, he was Kublai's top financial official. All complaints – there were several attempts to

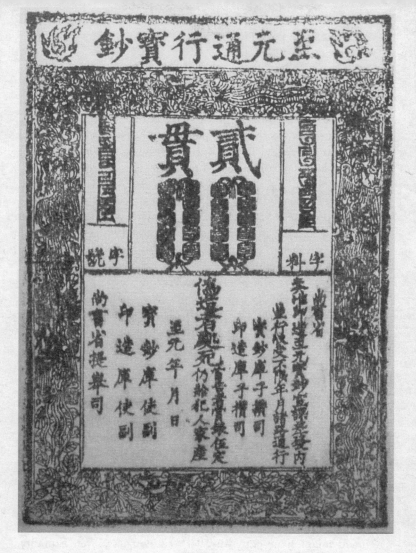

A 1287 banknote is headed 'High Yuan Trade Office Treasury Note' in Chinese (running right to left), with a similar statement (immediately below, left) in Phags-pa script, running vertically. Two oval 'strings' of 'cash' show the number of coins represented by the note, in this case 2,000. Since each 'string' weighed about five kilograms, this so-called 'flying money' had great practical advantages. The bottom panel, in Chinese, Tangut and Manchu, warns that 'counterfeiters will be executed'. Mongol is not represented, either in language or in Uighur script, which suggests that traditional Mongol lands were of little importance to Kublai's economy.

impeach him – were sidelined by Kublai, because nothing was allowed to get in the way of mobilizing resources to fight the Song.

When victory seemed assured, Ahmad was part of the team summoned to advise on how best to exploit the new conquest. One point at issue was whether Song paper currency should be replaced by the Yuan currency. Bayan, the much-lionized commander of southern forces, had promised Kublai's newly acquired Song subjects there would be no change. Half Kublai's advisers agreed, arguing that such a change would undermine credibility. The others disagreed, probably on the say-so of Ahmad, who saw profit in making the exchange. Kublai's casting vote went with Ahmad. The unfortunate southerners were offered a derisory exchange rate: one Yuan note for 50 Song ones.

Now Ahmad was almost supreme, having raised himself above the government's checks and balances and made himself into a Middle Eastern vizier. He declared state monopolies on salt, medicinal herbs, copper tools and the sale of iron, which enabled him to manipulate their prices, to his own advantage. He made a son governor of the southern capital, Hangzhou. He set up transport bureaus in each of the eleven provinces, nominating Muslims to head five of them, a slap in the face for his Chinese colleagues. He had rivals demoted, exiled or imprisoned. Many died or were executed, or simply vanished. One senior military officer named Zui Pin, a distinguished veteran of the Song campaign and now a senior provincial official, complained that Ahmad had set up 200 unnecessary government offices and appointed some 700 friends and relatives to posts across the empire. Ahmad had his revenge, accusing Zui Pin and two colleagues of stealing grain and making unauthorized bronze seals. All three were executed in 1280.

Ahmad might have got away with ruthlessness, even brutality. Corruption was another matter. He was eternally, fatally acquisitive, proposing through his associates that a property here, a jewel there, or a beautiful horse for his stud would oil the way to this or that appointment. He had a particular eye for women. All told, according to the Persian historian Rashid al-Din, he acquired 40 wives, 400 concubines and 3,758 horses, camels, oxen, sheep and donkeys.

Still Kublai remained in thrall to Ahmad's financial acumen, drive, self-confidence and plausibility. In the spring of 1282, the emperor promoted him to the rank of Left Chancellor, leaving only the Right Chancellor above him in the official government hierarchy. The dreadful possibility arose that if he was not stopped he and Kublai would end up running the empire together.

Ahmad had one enemy who was not so easy to handle. Kublai's son and heir, Jingim, absolutely loathed him, one reason being that the prince had been an admirer of Zui Pin and sent officers to save him from execution, only to be told they had arrived too late. In Ahmad's presence Jingim tended to lose his temper. Once he punched Ahmad in the mouth. When Kublai asked what the matter was, Ahmad muttered through clenched teeth that he had fallen off his horse. Ahmad tried to gain control by proposing a high court of justice that would have authority over all the princes. This was too much even for Kublai. He issued a mild rebuke, saying that he had never heard of anyone trying to censure the imperial clan.

Now, at last, a plot was hatched. There were two conspirators, both highly unstable characters. The driving force was Wang Zhu, a hard military man who had acquired a big brass club as a murder weapon. His accomplice was a shady Buddhist monk named Gao, who claimed to be a magician. The two had met on a campaign, when Gao cast spells that hadn't worked, then killed a man and used the corpse to fake his own suicide. He was now on the run.

Kublai was in Xanadu, as usual in spring. Beijing was left to Ahmad. The plotters seized their chance, as the official history relates, though in four different and often contradictory versions, which conflict again with Rashid al-Din and Marco Polo. This is my attempt to make sense of the story.

The two plotters hatched a lunatic scheme, involving a crowd of 100 or so, who would turn up at the city gates purporting to be the entourage accompanying Jingim, the heir apparent, who had suddenly decided to return to Beijing for a religious ceremony. It would be night-time, too dark for a quick check of who these people were. The idea was that Ahmad, galvanized by the approach of the one man he feared other than the emperor himself, would lead the way out to greet them, and that would be the moment to strike.

On 26 April, the two put their complicated scheme into effect. They sent two Tibetan monks to the city council to announce the 'news' and give orders to buy the right equipment for the ceremony. The council members were puzzled. They checked with the guards: no, no orders had been received. So where exactly was the heir apparent? The monks looked embarrassed and could not answer. Suspecting foul play, the commander of the guard arrested the monks and set out guards.

Next Wang Zhu put his back-up plan into action, sending a forged letter as if from the heir apparent to the vice-commissioner of the Department of Military Affairs, Bolod, telling him, in effect, to go 'to my residence for further orders'. That worked. With the main guards out of the way at Jingim's palace, Wang Zhu hurried off to Ahmad, urging him to get all his Secretariat colleagues together to greet the 'prince'. That worked too, but only just. Ahmad sent out a small advance guard to meet the mock-prince and Wang's rent-a-crowd of horsemen, a meeting that took place some 5 kilometres out of town. The guards, of course, saw at once that the whole thing was a scam. The rebels had no alternative: they killed the guards and proceeded.

At about 10 p.m. they gained entry to one of the city's north gates and made their way to the west door of the prince's palace.

Here they struck a problem. The guards were ready, and highly suspicious. Where were the prince's usual outriders, they asked. 'We beg first to see these two men, then we will open the gates.'

A pause.

The rebels backed off, worked their way around the palace in the darkness, and tried again, this time at the south door. There had been no time to rush a message across town to warn the guards. The gates opened. Guards arrived minutes afterwards, but were pre-empted by another forged note from the 'prince' demanding troops as an escort, which, astonishingly, were supplied.

Now Ahmad and his entourage came out. All the new strangers

dismounted, leaving the lone shadowy figure of the mock-prince on his horse. The figure called out to Ahmad. Ahmad stepped forward. Wang and a few followers were right behind him. They led him further forward, then away into the shadows, out of sight. Wang drew from his sleeve his brass club, with which he struck Ahmad a single fatal blow.

Ahmad's No. 2 was called next, and was killed in the same way.

Now Ahmad's retainers realized something was amiss and yelled for help. All was sudden chaos, with guards and rebels mixed up in the dark. Gao, the counterfeit prince, galloped off into the night, arrows flew, and the crowd scattered, leaving Wang begging to be arrested, certain that his noble act would be recognized.

No such luck. The monk Gao was found two days later. On 1 May, both were condemned to death, along with the commander of the city guard.

Before the axe fell, Wang cried out 'I, Wang Zhu, now die for having rid the world of a pest! Another day someone will certainly write my story!' The three were beheaded and quartered, while Ahmad was given an official burial.

It was the new commander of the Beijing guard who brought the news personally to Kublai, covering some 500 kilometres in a non-stop gallop, changing horses along the post-road. It took him two days to reach the emperor. Kublai at once ordered his vice-commissioner for Military Affairs, Bolod, to investigate.

Ten days later, Bolod was back with the truth about Ahmad's corruption. Kublai, appalled at his own role in Ahmad's rise, flew into a rage and turned everything upside down: 'Wang Zhu was perfectly right to kill him!' He ordered the arrest of all Ahmad's clan members and associates, right across the empire. Everything he had done was undone, everything he owned was seized. His harem was disbanded, his stolen property returned, his slaves freed, his herds broken up, his remaining appointees – 581 of them – dismissed. That autumn, his four sons were executed. Kublai ordered his tomb to be opened, his corpse to be beheaded in full public view and then his remains to be thrown outside Beijing's main north gate to be consumed by dogs.

*

Kublai was old and failing. His empire had reached its limits, yet he was desperate to extend it further. He even planned to re-invade Japan, until other disastrous foreign adventures – Burma (Myanmar as it now is), Vietnam and Java – showed the idea to be impossible.

After his conquest of Yunnan, Burma became a neighbour, and a target. The Burmese king, Narathihipate, ruled a once-prosperous Buddhist realm, whose capital, Pagan, gloried in 5,000 temples. When Kublai demanded submission, the king – arbitrary, brutal, known as King Dog's Dung to his unhappy people – executed the envoys, which of course invited invasion. Marco Polo reported what happened when, in 1273, Mongol archers turned 200 Burmese war-elephants into pincushions: 'They plunged into the wood and rushed this way and that, dashing their castles against the trees . . . destroying everything that was on them.' The Mongols captured twelve of them and marched them home as gifts for Kublai. Victory was not followed up by conquest. That would have to wait. But when it came, in 1286, shattering a kingdom already half shattered by regicide, conquest imposed nothing more than occasional tribute, never enough to repay the cost of imposing it.

The two states that comprised today's Vietnam – Annam in the north, Champa in the south – also owed allegiance, in Kublai's view. A seaborne invasion against Champa ended in humiliation, for the Vietnamese proved very good at guerrilla war. Kublai's response was a joint land and sea assault on the north, intending to seize the south. That inspired outraged resistance, with peasants tattooing their arms 'Death to the Mongols!', under a charismatic leader, Tran Hung Dao. He ordered scorched-earth withdrawals inland and used a tactic that had beaten the Chinese 300 years before. In March 1288, his army allowed Mongol ships up the Bach Dang river to Haiphong, then placed sharpened stakes just beneath the surface, pointing upstream. The Mongol ships, retreating downriver, were impaled, torn open and sunk. A catastrophe for Kublai, and one of Vietnam's greatest victories, still recalled today, because the remains of the stakes were found in 1988 and are now a tourist attraction, the Bach Dang Stake Yard.

Java was no near neighbour, but it – or rather its eastern end, Singhasari – was a light of wealth and stability that drew Kublai like a moth to a flame. In 1289, an envoy arrived demanding submission. His answer was humiliating expulsion. Kublai, as Heaven ordained, prepared a 1,000-strong fleet, and invaded in 1292. The young king, Vijaya, tempted the Mongols inland with promises of tribute, then turned on them and chased them into a hasty retreat, with many losses and no gains – except to Vijaya's kingdom, which, as Majapahit, grew to include most of Indonesia.

The world's most powerful man seemed unwilling to acknowledge that dreams must die, ambitions fade, the body age, and that the best he could hope for was an empire within the borders he had set for it. His demons were depression, drink and food. In 1281, his favourite wife, Chabui, his chief companion and adviser for forty-one years, died. Then there came the scandal of Ahmad's murder, bringing with it the sudden proof of his declining abilities and poor judgement. Still, at least his succession was secured, in the form of Jingim, now in the prime of life at thirty-eight. He had been the intended heir since the death of an elder brother in childhood. After Ahmad's murder, he came into his own, and Kublai rallied enough to take another wife, Nambui, a distant cousin of Chabui's. He was still fit enough to face life: at the age of almost seventy, he managed to make her pregnant. Having borne a son, she began to act as his go-between, protecting him from overwork. Then tragedy struck again. In 1285, Jingim fell ill from some unspecified disease and died.

There was still a remnant of the old Kublai left, enough for one last effort. All this time, Khaidu had been active, often almost forgotten amidst the business of administration and foreign adventuring. But he had been busy building support all around the fringes of the empire, reaching out southwards into Tibet and eastwards to Manchuria.

Kublai was faced with the grim prospect that all the northern reaches of his empire, a great arc of steppe-land from Xinjiang, across his original Mongolian homeland and into Manchuria, would fall away to become the pastoral-nomadic empire to which the rebels aspired. Kublai sent Bayan – general, Grand Councillor, conqueror of the Song campaign – to occupy Karakorum, while he himself led another army to reclaim Manchuria.

Marco describes Kublai directing impossibly large forces from his miniature fortress borne by four elephants. Kettle-drums boom, arrows fall like rain, the battle sounds like thunder, Kublai wins, the rebel commander is captured and executed. Khaidu pulled back westwards, remaining de facto khan of Inner Asia for three more years, until, after several more battles, he died, after forty-five years of campaigning.

Personal losses, rebellion, defeat abroad: it was all too much. Kublai turned to food and drink. At court banquets, he gorged on boiled mutton, breast of lamb, eggs, saffron-seasoned vegetables in pancakes, sugary tea and of course *airag*, the Mongolian drink of choice. It was the drink in particular that undermined him. As activity declined, as his powers waned, he put on weight, ballooning year by year into extreme obesity. He must have known it would kill him, but he didn't care. Now well into his eightieth year, he was hardly able to function except through his wife Nambui.

He knew where he wanted to be buried: back in the land of his birth, in the heartland of the Mongol people, where the last of the Siberian mountain ranges, the Khentii, begin to give way to grass-lands. This was where his grandfather, who had started it all, was born, and this was where he was buried.

On 28 January 1294, New Year's Day by the lunar calendar, Kublai was too ill to attend the usual ceremonies. No dressing in white, no great reception to receive tributes and praise from visiting vassals, no reviewing the parade of richly caparisoned elephants and white horses, no presiding over the banquet in the Great Hall. Everyone must have known the end was near. A messenger was sent galloping off to the only man who might be able to lift the emperor's spirits: Bayan, awaiting his next assignment in Datong, 300 kilo-metres away. But there was nothing Bayan could do, except promise eternal loyalty. Kublai knew his end was approaching and asked that Bayan be one of the three executors of his will. He weakened steadily, and on 18 February he died.

A few days later, the funeral cortège was ready. Considering Kublai's wealth and the money he had been spending on his campaigns, it would have seemed quite austere. Still, there would have been hundreds: members of the family and government who were fit enough for the journey, plus guards, drovers, grooms, cooks, household servants, spare horses, carts for the women, carts for the tents, camels carrying all the paraphernalia suitable for a royal procession that would be on the road for three weeks and 1,000 kilometres. Somewhere quite near the front, behind a guard, would have come Kublai's hearse, a wagon bearing a tent concealing a large coffin, well sealed and packed with spices and other preservatives. Covering perhaps 50 kilometres a day, the line would have wound over ridges and valleys up on to the Mongolian plateau, then out over the Gobi's dusty wastes, until at last the gravel gave way to grassy hills and the forested foothills of the Khentii.

Imagine: a line of fur-clad men, led by a masked shaman with a drum and rattle, pass through a cordon of guards. Several in the procession shoulder poles that carry a simple coffin draped in blue and yellow silk. They wind up through slender firs, emerging on to open ground, with a view over a snow-covered valley, a frozen river and hills marching away into the distance. A second group has been up here for some time, tending fires to melt the iron-hard earth. Others have dug with iron spades to make a grave. There is a reverent deposition, prayers, an invocation by the shaman. The earth is replaced, horses led back and forth to disguise the work, guards set in place to keep away all but family members.

No one knows where this scene, or something like it, took place, because the burial was as secret as Genghis's had been. Kublai was beside his father, Tolui, his brother Mönkhe and his grandfather Genghis, all of them part of the landscape from which they and their empire had sprung.

PART IV
AFTERMATH

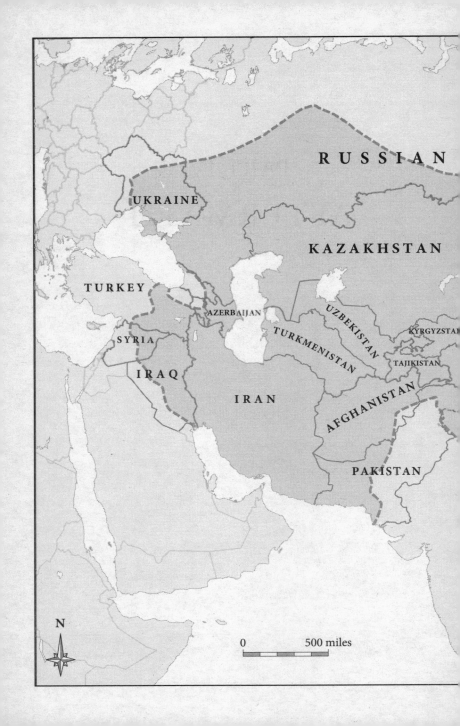

RUSSIAN

UKRAINE

KAZAKHSTAN

TURKEY

AZERBAIJAN

UZBEKISTAN

KYRGYZSTAN

SYRIA

TURKMENISTAN

TAJIKISTAN

IRAQ

IRAN

AFGHANISTAN

PAKISTAN

N

0   500 miles

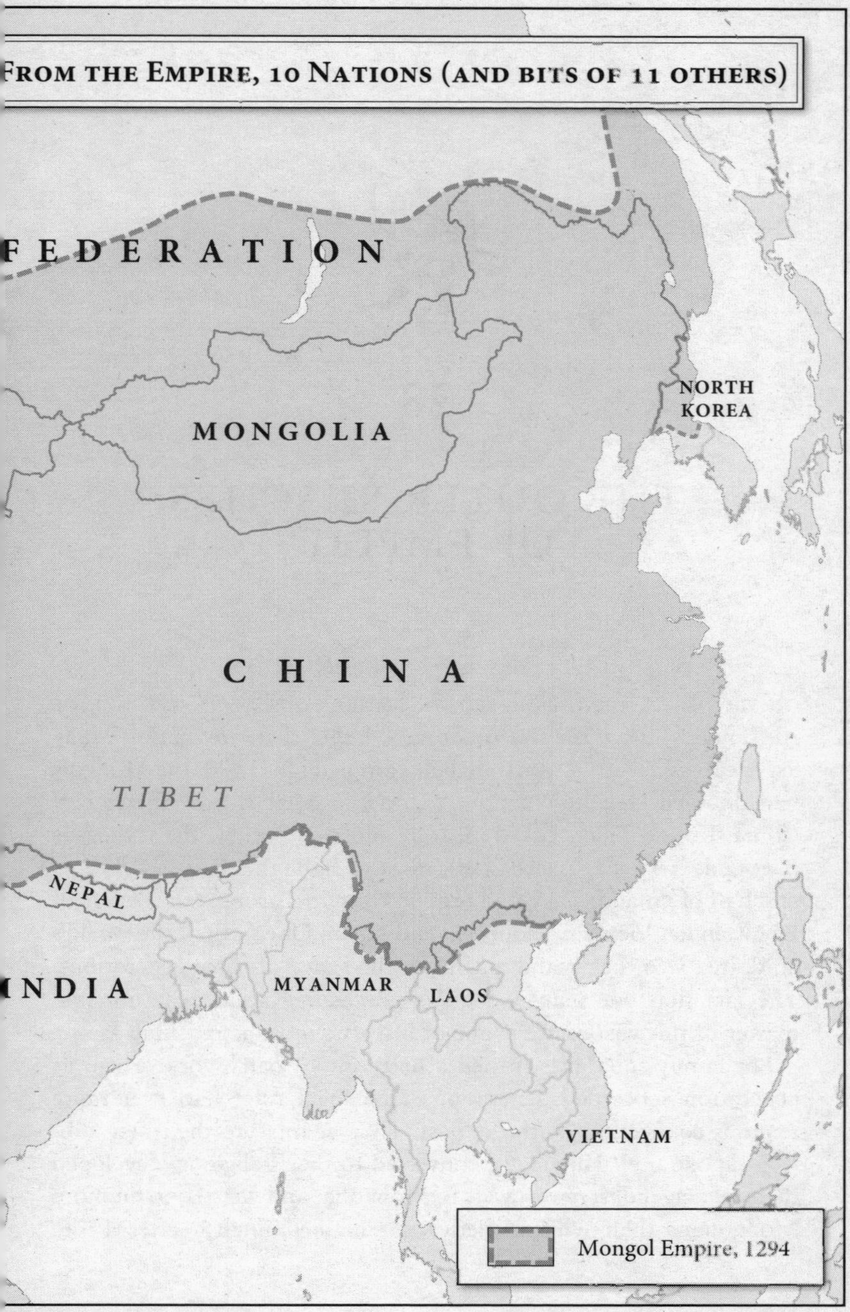

FROM THE EMPIRE, 10 NATIONS (AND BITS OF 11 OTHERS)
FEDERATION
MONGOLIA
NORTH KOREA
CHINA
TIBET
NEPAL
INDIA
MYANMAR
LAOS
VIETNAM
Mongol Empire, 1294

23

THE OUTER REACHES
OF EMPIRE

ON HIS DEATH, GENGHIS RULED AN EMPIRE FOUR TIMES THE SIZE OF Alexander's, twice the size of Rome's, larger than any nation today except Russia. And it was only half complete. By 1300, the Mongols had doubled Genghis's conquests, adding what is now the rest of China, Korea, Tibet, Pakistan, Iran, most of Turkey, the Caucasus (Georgia, Armenia, Azerbaijan), most of habitable Russia, Ukraine and half of Poland. They had probed western Europe, the borders of Egypt, India, Vietnam, Indonesia and Japan. One sixth of the world's land area was theirs; and all this in the space of three generations. The fact that one man, Genghis's grandson Kublai, was nominal master of this vast estate is one of history's most astonishing facts.

But family squabbles turned a unity into a patchwork. Then, as generation succeeded generation, each local ruler had ever more tenuous connections with the past. They adapted to their new subjects, spoke their languages, converted to their religions, developed their own agendas, never went to Mongolia, and were soon no more Mongolians than white Americans remained English after 1776.

Their history, though technically the tail end of the Mongol empire, is really a collection of local histories: China, Persia, Central Asia, Russia, all looking back to Genghis to buttress their claims, all with the vaguest of borders, all seeking alliances with each other, yet ready to fight. A detailed history of them all would be like describing three-dimensional chess. Such a huge and varied entity could never hold together.

In China, Kublai had done what the Romans did for northern Europe: roads, canals, trade, efficient taxation, a postal-relay system unrivalled for efficiency until the coming of the telegraph. Paper money underpinned the economy. Yelu Chucai would have been gratified.

But the Mongols never truly belonged. Though some of Kublai's successors could speak Chinese, not one of them learned to write it well. They despised and feared their subjects, forbade them to bear arms, excluded them from their own government and employed foreigners to administer them. Mongol rule depended on power, upheld with ever stricter laws and ever fiercer punishments, which inspired ever more resistance. Generals rivalled each other, and demoralized troops defected to rebels. Many top Mongolians fawned on courtly fashion, took the royal coin, and forgot the simplicity and toughness of their nation's founder. Others back on the grasslands remembered; and mutual suspicions grew.

Rot spread from both top and bottom. Kublai's heir, the peaceable, cautious Temur Oljeitu, died without an heir, and factions formed. Royal clan rivalled clan for influence, for the tensions between the steppe-loving Mongolian elite and those dominated by the Chinese bureaucracy were never resolved. There were intrigues and assassinations, including one emperor, the twenty-year-old Yingzong (his Chinese temple name). In 1328, a two-month civil war ended in executions. In 1331, plague ravaged parts of China, perhaps the beginning of the Black Death that would soon spread to Europe. Famine followed. People fled their villages. The Yellow River broke its banks, drowning uncounted thousands and setting a new course to the sea. The economy collapsed into hyperinflation.

Quite possibly, no government could have survived such terrible afflictions. But the fact was that the Mongol emperors and their administrators were not up to the job. As Genghis had said, if ever the Mongols forgot their tough, nomad roots, they would no longer deserve to govern. To summarize the great French historian of Asia, René Grousset: softened by a bloated court, cut off from the real world by favourites and mistresses, these descendants of the most redoubtable and terrible conqueror known to history dwindled away into feebleness, ineptitude and tearful vacillation. They died young, killed by alcohol and soft living. Of Kublai's eleven heirs – if you count Yingzong, who lasted just two months before being murdered – the average age at death was thirty.

From the 1340s, society began to divide against itself. Gangs turned to banditry, local leaders organized self-protection forces. Secret societies spoke of dire omens and coming catastrophes. In the plague-ravaged, flood-torn lowlands, rebels known as Red Turbans ripped at the empire's decaying flanks, eventually merging with another seditious group, the White Lotus Society. Two rival Red Turban leaders proclaimed their own dynasties. A White Lotus leader, who called himself the Prince of Radiance, promised a Buddhist uprising and the resurrection of the Song, hoping to recruit some 200,000 who were being forced to re-route 160 kilometres of the Yellow River. His scheme was discovered, and he was executed. His chief of staff kept the dream alive, with his own capital, coinage and bureaucracy; but his warlord generals were more eager to pillage their own estates than to cooperate in campaigns. One rebel group actually sacked Xanadu.[1]

It seemed obvious that Heaven was withdrawing its mandate to rule. The prophecies of doom were self-fulfilling. Looting drove people to flee, creating refugees who, for protection, followed bandit leaders, took up arms and became looters themselves. Attempts by central government to send in troops failed, and rebels gained in confidence. By the 1350s, the whole fabric of society was

---

[1] I once photographed the results, a collection of beheaded stone statues that had been dug up in the 1990s and have now been taken into storage.

CLOUD TERRACE: IMPERIAL SCRIPTS SET IN STONE

In Juyongguan pass (near the Great Wall at Badaling) is Yun Tai – Cloud Terrace – built under the last Mongol emperor in 1342. In the arch's roof are carvings which include the empire's main scripts – Sanskrit, Tibetan, Uighur, Western Xia, Chinese – and the one devised by the Tibetan Phags-pa to replace all the others. It never did.

Above: *Cloud Terrace was originally a base for three pagodas, destroyed when the Mongols fled from China in 1368. A replacement temple burned down in 1702.*

Above: *The paving stones still have the ruts made by wagons 700 years ago.*

Above: *The six scripts all record the same Buddhist incantation.*

XANADU

Kublai's first capital, which became Shang-du, his 'Upper Capital', or Xanadu in its common English spelling. At its centre stands the base of the royal palace. The low, grass-covered mounds are scattered with rubble, which included the marble pillar (**bottom left**).

Above: *Xanadu's three square sections – outer, inner and royal – show it to be thoroughly Chinese in design. The section nearest the camera was a field for hunting.*

Above: *The base of the palace where Kublai received Marco Polo.*

Left: *Incised in marble, dragons and peonies symbolize both war and peace.*

Above: *A reconstruction of Kublai's 'cane palace' in Xanadu suggests that it symbolized the union of his two worlds, China and Mongolia. Made of bamboo from southern China and decorated in the Chinese style, it was round and easily dismantled, like a Mongolian ger.*

Below: *In the only authentic portrait of him, an ageing, overweight Kublai is swathed in ermine, as befits the world's most powerful monarch. Beside him is his favourite wife, Chabui.*

EMBRACING BUDDHISM

Kublai was an adopted Buddhist; perhaps he believed; certainly he saw the political advantages. Buddhism offered three of them: it countered the influence of the two great rivals, Confucianism and Daoism; it strengthened his grandfather's ideology with the concept of a 'universal ruler'; and it summoned to his aid at least one powerful spiritual entity.

The White Pagoda, Beijing's only surviving 13th-century building, remains a base for worship, as it was when Kublai ordered its construction.

Below: *The statue of the White Pagoda's Nepalese architect, Aniga, recalls Kublai's readiness to employ international talent.*

Above: *The terrifying, six-armed and multi-skulled Buddhist deity Mahakala. Better for Kublai to have him onside, especially during the invasion of southern China in the 1270s.*

Above: *Tiles in the White Pagoda proclaim the temple's Buddhist roots.*

CATASTROPHE IN JAPAN

Nothing revealed the limits of Kublai's imperial reach more than his failures to take Japan. Two great armadas, in 1274 and 1281, were both destroyed by storms. Japanese rulers ascribed salvation to the gods, and called the typhoon the *kamikaze*, the divine wind. Probably they would have won anyway. Japanese fighting spirit would have made lasting conquest impossible.

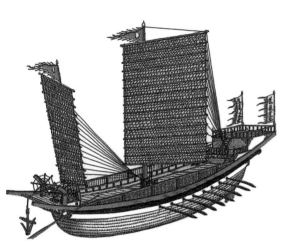

Left: *Kublai's Chinese-Korean navy was a formidable force. The second invasion had 4,400 ships, mostly small landing craft, with a core of warships like this one. But Kublai's demands forced short-cuts in construction. This produced ships unable to withstand the typhoon that, in 1281, sent the fleet to its doom.*

Below: *A portrait of the Japanese warrior Suenaga shows him almost killed by an exploding ceramic shell (inset) during the 1274 invasion. Later, he took some Mongolian heads, which he presented to his commander (**below right**).*

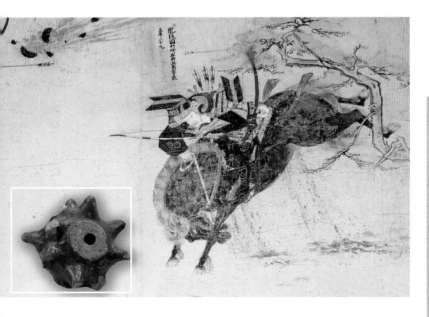

Above: *After 1274, the Japanese built a defensive wall around Hakata Bay, which the Mongol-Chinese-Korean invaders could not take before the typhoon hit.*

Above right: *Today the wall is partly rebuilt as a memorial to the event that preserved Japan's independence.*

Above: *A beautifully decorated Mongol-Chinese war helmet.*

Above: *Kenzo Hayashida, marine archaeologist, shows the bronze seal of an army commander (as it says in Chinese in Phags-pa's script), proof that Kublai's navy lay on the ocean floor.*

How the News Went West

This 1459 map by Fra Mauro of Venice (with north at the bottom) was one of the first to take Marco Polo seriously, and bring the wealth of China to European attention. Cathay – a corruption of 'Khitan' – was a common term for north China. Here it is spelled 'Chataio'. The great city in the middle is Beijing – labelled 'chabalek', which is Marco's Khanbalik, the Khan's City. The Lugou Bridge (now usually known as the Marco Polo Bridge) heads away top right (i.e. south-east). Xanadu (Shang-du in Chinese) – 'Sandu' – is near the bottom (i.e. north).

unravelling, with a dozen areas of rebellion spreading turmoil across much of eastern China. Three main Red Turban groups, all controlling sections of the Yangtze, rivalled each other for the crown.

One of these was led by Zhu Yuanzhang, the Yuan's nemesis and the most extraordinary man of the age, whose odd, craggy features – large nose, big ears, bushy eyebrows and a prominent bulge on his skull – compelled attention and made him seem 'awesome and profound'.[2] He was a child of his times. His grandfather had been with the Song forces when they were shattered by the Mongol fleet in 1279. As a boy, he was given to a temple and became a monk, begging his way around, seeing the grim conditions, understanding the people and their ways. He had lived through the famine of 1344, when the ground cracked, 'the farming people were like ants frantically twirling in a hot pan', and he survived on grass and tree bark. Then came the plague. In his part of Anhui province, ten villages died, 'a scene of chilling desolation'.

In 1351, the rebellion started, as 'poor farming folk . . . in their short coats and straw sandals, wearing their red headbands and carrying red banners, shouldering their bamboo staves and their hoes, with long spears and axes, killed the officials, occupied the cities, opened granaries to distribute the stored grain, battered down jails and freed prisoners, set up their own names and titles – they sounded the death knell of the Yuan dynasty'. The following year, Zhu, aged twenty-four, joined in and quickly rose through the ranks. Then he set out on his own, gathering an army of 20,000–30,000. He built a team of scholarly advisers, winning a reputation for brilliance, idealism, discipline and vision. From destitute villager to monk, to field captain and successful general – his rise was almost as astonishing as Genghis's. Towns fell to him, among them Nanjing, a bastion of Yuan power. That gave him control of the Yangtze Valley, the heart of the old Song empire, thus in effect reversing much of Kublai's conquest. Victories and his growing military skills won talented followers. In Mote's words, 'a motley

[2] These details are from Wu Han's biography of Zhu, translated in Mote's *Imperial China*, pp. 541–8.

array of amateur commanders had become professional generals equal to any in Chinese history'. Zhu began to see himself as an emperor-in-waiting. After disposing of his greatest Red Turban rival in 1363, he astutely spun his image away from the rebel group, with their reputation as warlords, and chose a new dynastic title: Ming ('radiance').

Now he turned to his main task, which was to throw out the Mongols without alienating those who might defect to him. He issued a proclamation, which in summary ran:

> True, Mongol rule was legitimate. Within the four seas and beyond there are none who have not submitted to it. How could this be the consequence of human powers? It was in truth bestowed by Heaven. When they took over, their ruler was enlightened and their officials good. But thereafter, the officials abandoned and destroyed the norms of conduct. The people's hearts turned against them. Now Heaven despises them. The time has come for change.

Intelligence, high ideals and good management paid off. On 9 September 1368, Zhu's general, Xu Da, arrived at Beijing. The last Mongol emperor, Toghon Temur, saw the game was up and fled with his family, household and a few guards. Five days later, Xu Da took the city, with very little resistance. The Yuan dynasty ended, and the Ming started, with Zhu as its Taizu, or Grand Progenitor.

With Toghun went some 60,000 of the Mongol elite, leaving up to 400,000 Mongols to fall into the vengeful arms of the Ming. The survivors settled briefly in Xanadu, before being chased out by the Ming and retreating on northwards. In a lonely outpost in today's Inner Mongolia, Toghun died, of shock and despair at the enormity of his loss.[3]

Back on the grasslands, the survivors never accepted their

---

[3] If there is any truth in the long lament ascribed to him by the Mongol prince Sagang, writing 300 years later. 'My most variously adorned Daidu [Beijing]!' he begins. 'My glorious, cool summer retreat, Xanadu! Its yellowing plains, the source of pleasures for my divine ancestors! My errors are to blame for the loss of my empire!'

expulsion. For almost 200 years, khans of the so-called Northern Yuan went on claiming they were the 'true' rulers of China, because they 'knew' the truth: that the Ming emperor had captured Toghun's queen, who was pregnant. Since her son would be killed if his paternity were known, she prayed for a miracle. Marvellous to relate, Heaven extended her pregnancy to twelve months and the boy was accepted by the new Ming emperor as his own. So the 'truth' was that the Ming emperors were really Mongols. It was all nonsense, but for centuries, as Mongolia sank back into civil war and anarchy, petty khans called themselves 'Emperors of the Great Yuan' until the last one surrendered to the up-and-coming Manchus in 1635.

To understand the Mongol sub-empire in Russia, the Golden Horde, we must go back to before Genghis's death. His first-born, Jochi, had been a problem. He was, probably, a 'Merkit bastard', his mother having been held captive by the Merkits until rescued by Genghis. Accepted by Genghis, he had overseen the conquest of Siberian forest tribes, and also fought in China and the Islamic world. But his possible illegitimacy rankled, his brothers distrusted him and his father doubted his abilities. The two grew apart. Yet his inheritance would have been vast: all the land westwards from Lake Balkhash over the Urals, across Russia to the Danube; and from the Caspian northwards to Moscow, and beyond. 'Would have been', because he died in 1225, and his huge inheritance fell to Batu, the second of his fourteen sons.

So eleven years later it was Batu, serving Ogedei, who was the supposed mastermind behind the renewed assault on Russia. He was no military genius, made some major errors and was widely reviled – not, however, by Mönkhe, who, with Batu's support and much intrigue, became khan of khans. Batu therefore became Mönkhe's and then Kublai's man in the far west, in effect emperor of the *ulus* later called the Golden Horde.

It's worth recalling the size his estate. It covered most of today's Kazahkstan, almost half of Russia, and all of Ukraine and Belarus – almost as big as the United States or China, making his realm in size a western equivalent to Kublai's own Yuan empire. A great deal of it was steppe, ideal for nomads, unfortunately for the local tribes, who were driven out or enslaved. Batu and his thirteen brothers divided the depopulated steppe into vertical strips and migrated between summer and winter pastures, in epic commutes. William of Rubruck, who came via Batu's son Sartaq in 1253 on his way to Mongolia, wrote: 'His camp struck us as extremely large, since he has six wives, and his eldest son, who is with him, two or three; and to each woman belong a large dwelling and possibly two hundred wagons.'

As the mention of the 'dwelling' suggests, the Mongols of the Golden Horde also built. Batu had founded a capital, Sarai, when he left Hungary in June 1242. A century later, Sarai was a substantial city of walled enclosures and earth-brick houses.[4] When the Moroccan traveller and writer ibn Battuta went there in the 1330s, he recorded thirteen mosques and a dozen different cultures, with each ethnic group having its own quarter.[5]

Jochi's line also had other rights and possessions in the Middle East and China, for neither Persia nor China were handed out to Genghis's heirs as unified fiefs until Mönkhe allotted China to Kublai and Iran to Hulegu in 1251. But all of this was liable to change. For instance, Mönkhe gave the Caucasus to Batu's brother Berke, and when Hulegu advanced westwards to complete the conquest of Islam he encroached on Batu's domains. Every campaign opened a fresh dispute. Berke became the first Mongol to convert to Islam and condemned his cousin's destruction of Baghdad, a split that intensified when Batu died and Berke inherited the whole vast estate. A Muslim now ruled the west, while a traditional Mongol ruled Persia, with an undefined frontier between them. War was virtually certain.

In 1262, a year after the Egyptian army had mauled the Mongols

---

[4] Now reconstructed as a film set near its original site, 100 kilometres north of Astrakhan on the lower Volga.
[5] This is known as Old Sarai, because in the mid-fourteenth century it was superseded by another Sarai – 'New' Sarai – which lasted for fifty years until sacked by Timur (Tamburlaine).

at Ayn Jalut, Berke invaded Persia, stalled – and then, of all things, allied himself with Egypt before his death in 1265. That alliance brought Chaghadai's *ulus* into action, making a brief three-way civil war. From then on, the Golden Horde was in a permanent state of war with the Il-Khans in Persia, Chaghadai's realm, and at times Khaidu, while on occasion reaching out to Kublai for support (a link that brought an admixture of Buddhism to the Horde).

Then there was Russia. Batu required all Russian rulers to 'go to the Horde' and obtain permission to rule. A few even went all the way to Mongolia for confirmation. Russians recall the two centuries of rule by the Golden Horde as the 'Tartar [or Tatar] Yoke'. In fact, it was less of a yoke, more of an accommodation, achieved in 1251 when Alexander Nevsky, Prince of Novgorod, decided to fight the Lithuanians, the Germans and the Swedes, and submit to the Mongols. With occasional uprisings and feuds, the Russians and Mongols cooperated. 'Scratch a Russian,' runs a common proverb, 'and you find a Tartar.' Russian cities had Mongol supervisors. Russian nobles lived in the Horde's capital, Sarai; many of them took Mongol wives; some became officers in the Mongol army; there was even a Russian unit in Beijing.

Actually, the Mongols in the west were now virtually ex-Mongols. By the late fourteenth century, the khans were divided against each other, west (roughly today's Ukraine and southern Russia) versus east (the east being most of today's Kazakhstan), princes of the Right Hand versus those of the Left, Golden Horde versus Blue (or White), each having its own history of rivalries and alliances, and its own subdivisions into tribes, clans and nationalities. When the Horde broke into half a dozen separate khanates in the fifteenth century, local leaders still claimed Genghis as an ancestor and went on doing so for another two centuries

Why did they last so long, when other Mongol sub-empires collapsed after less than a century? The answer seems to be that in all other cases the Mongols were interfused with their subject populations. They were, to use David Morgan's word, *contaminated* by them. Not so the Golden Horde, whose people remained semi-nomadic, preserving their lifestyle and army apart from the Russians from whom they drew their wealth, until in 1783 a resurgent Russia under Catherine the Great annexed the Crimea and its Tartar – more correctly, Tatar – remnants.

In Persia, Mongol rule sucked blood from stones. The Il-Khans (subordinate khans), as they called themselves, enslaved, plundered and taxed to the limit, exacting a land tax, tithes, a poll tax and a tax on all commercial transactions, including prostitution. Beyond the ravaged countryside and its bitter peasantry, trade favoured the cities, allowing the Mongols to amass enough wealth to keep a precarious hold, even as they lost contact with their roots.

Oppressive rule started with Hulegu himself, who remained a shamanist, if anything, because his funeral in 1265 included human sacrifices. Three heirs favoured Buddhism, until a great-grandson turned Muslim and razed all Buddhist buildings (though two rock-cut Buddhist cave systems survive). Eastern Christian sects also flourished, principally Nestorians, so much so that for a brief moment it seemed to a few that Persia – perhaps all Islam – would adopt Christianity, thanks to the Mongols.

This is how it happened.

In 1286, the new Il-Khan, Arghun, found himself needing support against Egyptians and other Muslims, and came up with an extraordinary idea. He wanted to approach Europe to suggest another crusade, Christians and Mongols together. Considering the horror caused in Europe by the Mongol advance only forty years before, this sounds totally bizarre; but there had been some co-operation between Mongols and Christian crusaders twenty years earlier. In exchange for Europe's help, Arghun offered to deliver Jerusalem to them. To set the scheme in motion, he needed a sophis-ticated, well-travelled, multilingual envoy, and it happened that there was just the man on hand, thanks to Kublai.

His name was Rabban Sauma, an Önggüd – a Turkish group living in western China who had converted to Nestorianism. Sauma, together with a young protégé called Markos, had gained Kublai's support to make a pilgrimage to Jerusalem, a decision that launched them on a remarkable journey across the whole of Eurasia. Sauma knew Turkish,

Chinese and probably Mongol from childhood. Now he knew Persian as well.

Arghun gave Sauma letters to the Pope, the Byzantine emperor, and the French and English kings. In 1287, he and three companions left for the Black Sea, where they took a ship to Constantinople, where he met the Emperor Andronicus, and then to Naples and Rome, only to discover that the old Pope was dead and a new one not yet chosen. He was greeted instead by cardinals, who did not seem to realize their guest was a heretic. On the matter of a crusade, they could not commit in the absence of a new Pope. So he travelled on to Paris, where France's ambitious teenage king, Philip the Fair, gave him a great reception and a comfortable house. Sauma put his case. Philip seemed to be impressed. If Mongols were ready to help retake Jerusalem, what could Christians do but respond? In fact, he was eager to make a display of strength for reasons of his own – to gain control over English domains in France, to assert French claims to Flanders, to keep the Vatican from siphoning off funds from French church properties.

Assuming Philip was now a fully paid-up member of the Mongol–European Alliance, Sauma moved on to Edward I of England, who fortunately was in his French colony, Aquitaine. Sauma reached Bordeaux in October 1287 and was at once invited to see the king. After presenting Arghun's gifts of jewels and silk, he put forward the idea of a crusade. Edward loved it. He himself had vowed to take up the Cross that spring. It fitted his plans precisely. Sauma surely believed he had two thirds of his task done.

Everything now depended on Rome, for without the Pope there could be no crusade. Still, however, there was no Pope. Winter was closing in. Sauma headed south, to the mildness of Genoa, a garden paradise as he called it, where he could eat grapes year round. After three months of growing frustration came the news: *Habemus papam*, Jerome of Ascoli, enthroned as Nicholas IV on 1 March 1288.

An invitation followed, and an audience, with a fine speech from Sauma, the delivery of Arghun's gifts and a generous response from Nicholas. Sauma celebrated Mass and received communion from the Pope himself, before a huge crowd, on Palm Sunday, with further celebrations on Passover (Maundy Thursday), Good Friday, Holy Saturday and Easter Day.

Finally, it was time to leave. Nicholas handed Sauma a few assorted relics and a letter for Arghun, which at last came to the point. Jesus had given authority to Peter, and thus to all succeeding Popes. Arghun should recognize the true faith. As for a crusade, well, let Arghun convert, accept papal authority, and God would give him the strength to seize Jerusalem and become a champion of Christianity. In brief: no deal.

Back in Persia, Arghun was sidetracked by challenges from the Golden Horde and rebellious Muslims. He died in 1291, along with his dreams of further conquests. By then, it was too late anyway. That same year the Egyptian Mamluks took Acre, the last Christian outpost in the Middle East, and the crusading era came to an end.

What if Nicholas had backed the alliance? The papacy, France, England and the Mongols would have fought in defence of the crusaders holding their castles in Syria, possibly with some strange consequences. Islam pushed out of the Middle East. Jerusalem delivered to the Pope, under an English–French–Italian–Mongol administration. Arghun a Christian convert. Christianity taking a leap into Central Asia. And all because Kublai had decided that Sauma had a role to play in his plans, and because his great-nephew was ruling Persia.

Meanwhile, the Persian coffers were empty. The population had been squeezed dry. For the Il-Khans, failure to drive the Egyptian Mamluks out of Syria in 1304 marked the end of expansion, with Egypt and the Mediterranean forever beyond reach. In 1307 a Mongol embassy reached Edward II in England, but it was the last effort at self-promotion.

Mongol rule ended not in violence, but in nothing but impotence. The last Il-Khan, Abu Sa'id, succeeded in 1316 aged only eleven, and ruled for nineteen peaceful years before Mongol rule expired. As Morgan puts it, 'Abu Sa'id, despite unremitting effort, left no son by any of his numerous wives.' There was no one to take power. Rivals sponsored implausible rulers, warlords grabbed themselves petty kingdoms, and the Il-Khans simply vanished, leaving chaos, until the arrival of the next would-be Genghis, Timur, better known to English-speakers as Tamburlaine, two generations later.

In Central Asia, Chaghadai's estate – his *ulus*, or country – was really no country at all, never being a single entity, neither in terms of geography nor government. It was basically the old Khara Khitai empire, blotted up by Genghis in 1218, plus a bit more to the west – a vague expanse running from the Aral Sea across to central Xinjiang. It included much of today's Uzbekistan, Tajikistan, Kyrgyzstan, northern Afghanistan, south-east Kazakhstan and a good deal of the deserts of north-west China. That's over 2 million square kilometres, about the size of western Europe, though it's hard to tell, because at either end were two of the most desolate places on earth, the Kyzyl Kum and Takla Makan deserts. Its unmapped borders – with Kublai's China, Persia, the Golden Horde and India – shifted with the ebb and flow of inter-family rivalries.

Across its centre ran important trade routes, linking great cities – Samarkand, Bukhara, Kashgar – but there was no established capital, no traditional administration to inherit, no cohesion, and in terms of history no clear storyline. Khans came and went, at the whim of the successive overlords – Mönkhe, Kublai and subsequent Great Khans. Initially, the administration of the cities was in the hands of a Muslim named Mahmud, known as Yalavach ('the Messenger') and his son Masud Beg, but both also served in China and both were briefly expelled by local khans. The rulers remained nomads, sometimes happy to plunder their own Turkish subjects and their cities for cash. Some became Muslims, some Buddhist, and some neither. They built hardly anything. The few records are by outsiders. In the east, Khaidu was carving out his own *ulus*, now allying himself with Chaghadai's successors, now fighting with them.[6] It's not that *nothing* is known. But to list who did what, when and to whom would be fruitless for all but specialists, because it led

---

[6] From about 1270, he dominated a good part of Chaghadai's *ulus* and their histories overlap.

nowhere. No theme or personality emerges to compel our attention. Constrained by rival Mongol empires east and west, Chaghadai's heirs looked south to Afghanistan and India, invading them several times, but even these adventures left no lasting mark.

The Chaghadai *ulus* died as it lived, in obscurity, in the 1340s. Ravaged by the Black Death, it was divided between rival emirs and khans who were not of Chaghadai's line. Happily for historians, this mess was the raw material from which Timur would mould a proper empire, complete with a court, buildings, scholarship and bloody victories, thus briefly assuming the mantle of Genghis Khan in a way that Genghis's son Chaghadai had not.

Across the former empire, there remained the memories of a golden age, of the glory that had been, of the giants who had lived in those days. And the magic lasted, drifting across Eurasia and down the centuries. Every ruler wanted his handful of Genghis's magic dust. Long after Russian victory over the Golden Horde in 1480, members of the Golden Kin commanded noble status, right into the nineteenth century. The dreadful Timur claimed to be a Genghisid, though he wasn't. He justified himself as a sort of reincarnation of Genghis – modest roots, heavenly favours, brutal conquests and so on. It was this false claim that explains why Timur's descendant, Babur, called himself 'Mughal' when he seized power in India in the early sixteenth century, establishing a dynasty that ended when the British shuffled the last Mughal off the throne in 1857. His name, by the way, was Bahadur, a distant echo of the Mongol *baatar*, hero, the second element in Mongolia's capital Ulaanbaatar (Red Hero). Even today, we remember: a 'mogul', originally a wealthy Indian, then a wealthy Anglo-Indian, is now a tycoon.

And so, against a slow but steady dissipation, the wisps of the great explosion preserved the evidence of their origins. Genghis remained a monster to his victims. In his heartland, though, his reputation, like the ember of a supernova, burned sharp and bright, and still does, with implications for the future which we will get to later.

24

GRAVE-HUNTING ON THE SACRED MOUNTAIN

GENGHIS'S TOMB IS LIKE THE LOCH NESS MONSTER: THE MORE YOU look, the more it isn't there. The only certainty is that very little is certain. It is said by many that 'they' know the real location, and have always known. In the 1970s, the nation's most eminent academic, Professor Byambin Rinchen, told Igor de Rachewiltz 'that the area had been positively identified before 1970'. The historian Badamdash told me: 'The grave is in the foothills of Burkhan Khaldun. It is a state secret.' But what is the nature of this state secret? Who are 'they'?

I went to see one of Mongolia's most respected historians, Dalai, who lived in one of the grim apartment blocks that arose in Ulaanbaatar after the Second World War. He was in his seventies, but looked older, an image of ageless wisdom. History, his life's work, was written on his lined face, sounded through his powerful bass voice, was apparent in shelf upon shelf of books in old Mongol, Cyrillic Mongol, Chinese, Russian, Japanese, Korean and English. There was Owen Lattimore's *Mongol Journeys* – Lattimore, doyen of Mongolists and an inspiration to me in my student days. I asked to look at it. The dedication startled me: 'To Dalai. In token of 10 years of friendship. Owen.'

He pointed to a dusty corner: 'I have Lattimore's camera. He left it here in case he should return. And his projector. And a suit of his clothes.' Lattimore died in 1989, at the age of eighty-nine, and had not been in Mongolia since the 1970s. The camera, projector and suit had been sitting there for some thirty years, awaiting a collection that never came.

When I asked about the grave, Dalai said, 'Many people are now searching for Genghis's grave. But I have never tried to find it. My heart would not let me. I recall Genghis's orders: "Don't touch my burial ground!" Since then, no one has touched it. It is a holy place, and should not be touched.'

Does the grave exist? Does the secret knowledge of the burial site exist? To neither of these questions is there an answer. Perhaps only those who know it know that they know it. Perhaps they just think they know it. Perhaps they are certain they don't know it. Perhaps, in the terms famously defined by Donald Rumsfeld, the grave is a known unknown.

Actually, the search is not just for one grave but for a whole necropolis, a Mongolian Valley of the Kings, where Genghis's family and heirs, including Kublai, lie buried. Tomb-raiders assume the khans must be accompanied by wives, concubines, slaves, horses and Eternal Heaven knows what else of gold, jewellery, costumes and weapons.

It is a matter of huge potential significance. If the grave exists, and if it were ever found, it would create a frenzy in archaeology, scholarship, cashflow and – since China claims Genghis as its own – international relations. Occasional efforts are made by the Mongolian government to assert control over the search; a hard task, since regulation would mean spending money and limiting tourism. And the tensions are wound ever tighter by those who argue that the search itself is a sacrilege, that what was intended to be secret should remain secret, and that anyway foreigners should be excluded from something so intimately connected with the nation's roots. And all these passions swirl around a site the very existence of which, let alone its position, is a mystery.

The *Yuan Shi*, the history of the Yuan dynasty, records how imperial burials were made. When the retinue reached the place of burial, 'the earth removed to dig the pit was made into lumps which were disposed in order. Once the coffin had been lowered, [the pit] was filled and covered in the order [of the lumps]. If there was earth in excess, it was carried to other places far away.' A European observer, Friar John of Plano Carpini, who visited Karakorum in the 1240s, wrote, 'They fill up the pit . . . and place over it the grass as it was before, so that the place should be impossible to find afterwards.'

If this was the case with Genghis, where did it happen?

The *Yuan Shi* seems to offer help by saying that the site was in the 'Qi Lian Gu' (起輦谷), which sounds promising, since *gŭ* means 'valley'. Many attempts have been made to see this as the transcription of a Mongolian name, with no success. In fact, the phrase means only 'raise imperial carriage [or hearse] valley', i.e. the valley where the emperor's funeral carriage was raised for burial.[1]

The only near-contemporary record is infuriatingly vague. In 1232 and 1235–6 – within a decade of Genghis's death – the Song court sent two embassies to Genghis's successor. The two ambassadors, Peng Daya and Xuting, claimed they saw where the conqueror was buried. 'Mongolian graves have no tumuli,' Peng reported. 'Horses are allowed to trample the area until it is as flat as its surroundings. Only at Temujin's grave-site have posts [or arrows] been erected in a circle of 30 *li* and horsemen set on guard.' His colleague added: 'I saw that Temujin's grave was to one side of the River Lu-gou (濾溝), surrounded by mountains and rivers. According to tradition, Temujin was born here and for that reason was also buried here, but I do not know whether this is true.'

The two eyewitness accounts raise many questions. Did they actually see the enclosure and the guards? How did they know the dimensions? Was the circle 30 *li* (15 kilometres) across or in

[1] Pelliot analysed all this in his *Notes on Marco Polo*, Vol. 1, pp. 330 ff (see Bibliography).

circumference? How do a 15-kilometre circle and trampling horses and a river fit with a mountain burial? And, most tantalizing of all, what was the Lu-gou River? Some major rivers had Chinese as well as Mongol names, and this was one of several versions of the Chinese name for the Kherlen. But Genghis was born on the Onon, not the Kherlen; and anyway, Xuting himself admits to uncertainty.

My guess is that these two diplomats asked to see Genghis's grave, without realizing that they were asking for something that could not possibly be granted. The site of the grave was to be kept secret, closely guarded until such a time as no one would be able to identify its position. On the other hand, it would be bad form to deny such officials their request outright. So they ride for a few days to the Khentii Mountains. They are taken roughly to the right area, get the name of the river wrong, pick up some distorted information – official disinformation, perhaps – see a few distant horsemen and are told that to enter the sacred site is taboo; not that there would be anything to see anyway, because it was all trodden flat and covered with saplings.

Soon even soft information like this began to slip away into hearsay and rumour. Marco Polo, writing fifty years later, said that 'all the great kings descended from the line of Genghis Khan are taken for burial to a great mountain called Altai'. The same name crops up again almost four centuries later in Sagang's *History*. He writes that the corpse was buried 'between the shady side of the Altai and the sunny side of the Khentii mountains'. Both descriptions are so vague as to be almost useless.

It is hardly possible to doubt that the burial is somewhere in his homeland, in what is today the mountainous Khentii province. Many sources mention Burkhan Khaldun as the site of what is called the Great Forbidden Precinct (Mongolian: *khorig*, a prohibition or prohibited area, often a burial place). There were many *khorigs*, but the 'Great' one was where Genghis and many of his descendants were buried. The Persian historian Rashid al-Din says that when Kublai's heir, his grandson Temur, became khan he put his brother Kamala in charge of 'the great *ghoruq* [*khorig*] of Chingiz-Khan, which they call Burkhan-Qaldun and where the great *ordos* [palace-tents] of Chingiz-Khan are still situated . . . There are four great *ordos* and five others, nine in all, and no one is admitted to them. They have made portraits of them there and constantly burn perfumes and incense. Kamala too has built himself a temple there.' In due course, nine tents would become eight, which became a travelling shrine, the Eight White Tents, drifting back and forth across Mongol lands until finally settling south of Ordos City in Inner Mongolia, where they were transformed into today's Genghis Khan Mausoleum.

So almost a century after Genghis's death, his burial ground was marked with tents, a temple and much ceremony. It was all private, but it should have left some traces – presumably on Burkhan Khaldun itself.

This raises a question: which mountain is Burkhan Khaldun? Most Mongolians think they know – it is the mountain in the Khentii range known as Khentii Khan. So sure are they that they have been worshipping on the mountain for some 300 years. It doesn't matter to them that the grave itself remains secret because they commune with his spirit.

But that leaves researchers with a problem. Though almost everyone assumes that Burkhan Khaldun is today's Khentii Khan, no source confirms it. And there are things about the idea that just don't fit. The closer you look, the more problematical it becomes. We will see some of the problems close up, on the mountain itself. But there are also problems in the sources, in particular *The Secret History*. It leaves no doubt as to the importance of the mountain. It is mentioned in reverential tones dozens of times. Yet in one incident, when young Genghis escapes from the Merkit, he rides off from his campsite and hides on Burkhan Khaldun, which the Merkit circle in an attempt to catch him before heading home with his young wife. But, if this is Khentii Khan, he couldn't have done it. The distances are too great, the landscape too rugged. Either the incident is fictionalized, or we should be dealing with a different mountain. One possible theory is that every clan had its own Burkhan Khaldun – except that none has been identified. We are left with a paradox: Burkhan Khaldun must be Khentii Khan; but it can't be. If this is disinformation on the part of Genghis's entourage, it is supremely successful.

Another problem is what, if anything, the grave might have contained. Again the evidence is not much help. Juvaini, who began writing his history at the new Mongol capital of Karakorum only twenty-five years after Genghis's death, says that upon his election by the Mongol princes Genghis's son and successor, Ogedei, ordered that 'from moonlike virgins, delightful of aspect and fair of character, sweet in their beauty and beautiful in their glances . . . they should select 40 maidens . . . to be decked out with jewels, ornaments and fine robes, clad in precious garments and dispatched together with choice horses to join his spirit'.

Human sacrifices for Genghis? It is not totally impossible, because it was an ancient custom in China and across Central Asia that ordinary soldiers, servants, wives, concubines and animals were killed to accompany the ruler in the afterlife. It was certainly said that before the arrival of Buddhism Mongol khans were buried with concubines, along with other possessions.

But the evidence is shifty, even in China. These practices had never been universally observed, and as centuries passed the living were increasingly replaced by replicas. No Mongol tomb containing sacrificial victims has ever been found. And Juvaini does not claim that the forty moonlike maidens were actually buried with the khan, which would have meant digging up the grave, with all the risks to security that would have involved.

Finally, the idea of a grave filled with riches does not fit comfortably with the image that Genghis liked to present. He had accepted the guidance of his top adviser, Yelu Chucai, and adopted the guise of a simple sage. In the words of his 1219 memorandum carved on to a stela (and quoted in full on page 73): 'Heaven has wearied of the sentiments of arrogance and luxury . . . I return to simplicity. I have the same rags and the same food as the cowherd or the groom.' Given the need for secrecy, would his heirs have ignored his implied will and given him a lavish burial? More likely, surely, that they kept it quick and simple.

Clearly the first task for grave-hunters is to check out Khentii

Khan. It's a daunting prospect for outsiders. The mountain (2,362 metres) is actually the western part of a 12-kilometre ridge with two peaks (the second, Asragt, being slightly higher, 2,452 metres). Our needle, always assuming it exists and is in this area, could be any-where on the southern slopes of this haystack: an area of something like 100 square kilometres of forested ridges, peaty plateaus, steep-sided valleys and bare uplands, all trackless, hard to get to, hard to leave. The nearest town, Möngönmört, is 70 kilometres from the mountain.

The first outsider to explore the mountain was an Englishman, C. W. Campbell, a long-time British resident in China, who travelled from Beijing to Urga, as Mongolia's capital was known then. This was in 1902–3, when all Mongolia was under Chinese rule. Having arrived in Urga he backtracked to visit a gold mine in Khentii, and then carried on for another two days to climb Khentii Khan, 'the holiest of the many holy mountains in Mongolia'. His account touches on most of the themes that dominate later explorations, my own included.

The first thing he emphasizes is the mountain's popularity as a pilgrim route and object of veneration. It was visited every year by the *amban*, the Mongol prince who acted as Chinese viceroy in Mongolia. He came 'with a retinue of magnitude, to make oblation to the great nature-spirits, and Mongols and Chinese alike make pilgrimages from great distances to enlist their favour'.

Campbell made his climb in September, describing typically tough conditions:

Our camping-place (4500 feet) was strewn with the remains of fires, mutton bones, skeletons of camels, felled logs, and broken carts, relics of the yearly visits of the Urga Amban. I rode up the mountain, through a thick forest of pine, larch, and cedar . . . as we emerged on the exposed ridge above a strong nor'wester drove [the temperature] down to 17° (–8°C) and the crests of the higher hills were veiled with snow. In half an hour we reached the main altar where the Amban worships [possibly the site of 'Kamala's temple'] . . . The summit was reached without difficulty, except for the wind. The pilgrimages of centuries have marked recognizable paths, and Mongols ride the whole way up over tree-roots and fallen trunks. The slope was forested, but the broad uneven crest was blown bare of trees, and its surface was a mass of large loose stones of irregular shapes. When approaching the mountain, I observed from a distance of 6 miles a rounded boss on the summit . . . I clambered over this, and found it to be an oval tumulus, 250 yards long east and west, and 200 yards north and south, of the same loose stones which cover the mountain.

I had no doubt that it was a human creation. There are two large stone *obos* on the crest of the tumulus, and on one of them there were the remains of a bronze censer. From a fragment of a Manchu inscription on this, which I copied, M. Dolbejev, of the Russian Consulate at Urga, read the date of the twelfth year of Chien-lung (AD 1748).

This is a remarkable tumulus, probably the largest in Mongolia. I am unable to believe that it is merely a prayer cairn, and it is a conjecture . . . which I think is entitled to attention, that we have here the veritable tomb of Jinghis.

Note the main elements: the relatively easy climb, the shrines on the ascent and at the top, and the great mound of stones on the summit. He missed one feature: a platform which seems to be scattered with what later researchers took for graves. He must have crossed it, but these collections of rock attracted no comment.

Given that few foreigners went to Mongolia before it became the world's second Communist state in 1924; that it was then pretty much closed off until the next revolution of 1990; and that conditions are horrendous – iced over in winter, boggy in summer – it is not surprising that so little work was done on the subject of Genghis's grave until recently.

First off the mark post-war was an East German, Johannes Schubert, of Leipzig's Karl Marx University,[2] who explored the

[2] The Mongol–East German connection has an odd origin. In the 1920s, when newly independent and Communist Mongolia started to look outwards, the government sent fifty children to be educated in Berlin. Back home, these children became a little elite, with great influence. After the Second World War, when East Germany became part of the Communist world, the link came into its own.

mountain in a week-long expedition with Mongolia's pre-eminent archaeologist, Khorlogiin Perlee. He described it in an account that confirms just how hard it is to get to and how tough the journey can be. This was in 1961, but it sounds like something out of the Middle Ages.

Schubert started from Möngönmört, as expeditions must, with four local Mongols and a caravan of thirteen horses winding their way single file through the willow bushes, crossing and recrossing the Kherlen – a tough journey for a man approaching his sixty-fifth birthday. On the mountain, dense forest gave way to the overgrown terrace described by Campbell – *ovoos*, two big, three-legged iron cauldrons, a bronze container and remnants (Schubert guessed) of the temple built by Kamala.

Higher up, as the trees became thinner, they came out on to a flat place 'scattered with holes, which are filled up with boulders and between which grow scanty mosses'. (Please note these holes; they will play a significant role later.) And finally, on top, they came upon a field of 200–300 *ovoos*, with a main one where bits of armour, arrow-points and various lamaistic objects had been laid. Undoubtedly, Schubert concluded, this was the historic Burkhan Khaldun; and somewhere on these slopes must be Genghis's tomb.

But it was all guesswork. The search demanded high-tech archaeology, which became available only when, in 1990, the fall of Communism opened the country to outsiders.

The Japanese were the first to seize the opportunity, with the Three Rivers Project of 1990–3, named after the rivers that rise in Genghis's ancestral homeland – Kherlen, Onon and Tuul. Since the backer of the four-year enterprise, the newspaper *Yomiuri Shimbun*, wanted to recoup its investment in terms of publicity, there was no shortage of hype. According to the introduction of the report written by an eminent Japanese archaeologist, Namio Egami, the project's stated purpose – to find Genghis's tomb – was 'so significant it may mark the beginning of a new history of the world'. It was an immense undertaking, with almost fifty members, ground-penetrating radar, superb cameras, global-positioning devices, many cars and a helicopter.

First call, of course, was Khentii Khan. Approaching from below, the team rediscovered the ruins of the temple which may or may not have been built by Kamala; then, landing by helicopter on the top for an hour, they recorded the existence of the 200–300 cairns described by Schubert (not that anyone on the expedition seems to have read his account). They found no trace of any ancient tomb up there, or indeed anywhere else. No one ventured down from the top or up from the bottom, so no one saw the 'holes' described by Schubert on the middle level of the mountain. The project went on to find an astonishing range of graves and implements at other sites, without turning up a hint of anything from the early thirteenth century.

The huge expenditure could hardly be justified by reporting hundreds of minor Turkish graves and offering detailed descriptions of the countryside as observed by satellites, aerial cameras and radar. The Three Rivers team needed to produce 'underground relics' that were 'treasures of the world'. Luckily, two areas proved potentially rewarding. One was Avraga, the pre-Genghis capital, an important site, which the Three Rivers report glorifies with a bald and totally unsupported conclusion: 'It is almost certain that Genghis Khan's tomb is in this area.' The second possible source of 'treasure' is truly a wonder – a stone wall enclosing a section of a ridge in the neighbouring hills. It is known locally as the Almsgiver's Wall, and is almost certainly nothing to do with Genghis, because ceramics found there are Liao, the dynasty overwhelmed by the Jin in 1125, some forty years before Genghis's birth. Yet the Three Rivers report blithely says that, from geographical observations and interviews (neither detailed), 'it appears that Genghis Khan was buried somewhere in [the Almsgiver's Wall]'. Two different sites claimed for the grave with equal vigour, no new evidence at all for the burial – despite its many important findings, in terms of pure Genghis research the Three Rivers Project achieved remarkably little.

Seven years later came the most determined and perhaps the most well-publicized grave-hunter: Maury Kravitz, a financier from Chicago. Kravitz, who had one of the world's greatest libraries on the subject of Genghis, raised $5.5 million, set up an advisory board and signed a contract with the Institute of Geography for exclusive rights to search for the grave. With reservations. He was banned from excavating on Khentii Khan.

The place he chose to excavate was the Almsgiver's Wall, which we have to take into consideration because Kravitz and others were so eager to connect it to Genghis. It is, after all, an easy 130 kilometres from Avraga, 30 kilometres from Genghis's probable birthplace near Binder, 90 kilometres from Khentii Khan, just on the frontier between mountain hideaways and rich grasslands.

It is a beautiful site, up a side-valley just off the plain that sweeps northwards from Avraga into the Mongol heartland. A teetering mass of frost-torn boulders rises above slopes loosely scattered with firs. A natural tower of rock dominates the lower slopes, like a steeple. It is known as Genghis's Tethering Post, as are several other such outcrops in the region. Most likely, they were created by the collapse of ice caps tens of thousands of years ago. Typically, they are on mountain tops, though this one is unusual in being on a lower slope.

The site's main feature is the wall, 3 kilometres in length, which runs for 500 metres across the bottom of the slope and then in a rough semicircle uphill and along the ridge at the top, incorporating some of the giant boulders. It is an impressive example of dry-stone walling, 3 or 4 metres high, sheer on the outside, leaning back a few degrees for solidity against a sloping bank of lesser stones, making a bulwark roughly triangular in cross-section. The stones forming the outside edge are roughly dressed. Some could have been lifted by one man, most could be managed by two or three, but a few would have needed a team. It must have taken a small army to build, and surely had nothing to do with the Mongols. They did not do stone walls, at least not on any scale, as the excavations in Avraga show.

What on earth was it for? It is not a fortress, for there are no gates, towers or defensive features, and attackers would have no trouble climbing in. It could hardly have been a town wall. Anyway, it's on a hillside, mostly too steep for houses. According to one bizarre suggestion, it might have been a game reserve; but a wall backed on the inside by a slope of rubble would hardly keep in an aged cow.

But it proved a terrific site for Kravitz and his team, with several extraordinary finds.

One was a skeleton dressed in the rusty remains of iron armour. A small pot stood close to the left shoulder. There were no other grave-goods to help with identification. With more time, it would have been possible to date the bones. As it was, the 'soldier' was replaced under a wooden covering, which was sealed under an iron roof, with a sign claiming that this was a 'Mongol 13th-century grave'.

Nearby was a series of odd shapes made with stones, each formed of four curving lines about 4 metres long, compiled of stones averaging about 3–5 kilos. The lines of stones bent through 90 degrees, and came together at both ends in small stony heaps. Alongside one set of stones was a skull – that of a woman aged about twenty-five – and four small bones placed in two pairs at an acute angle. Of the few scholars who know of these finds, most explain them as underfloor heating. But that makes no sense. There is no sign of a source of heat, and the shapes are on a steep slope, and there is no evidence of any building, like foundations, or roof tiles, or post-holes. And what of the skull and the strange little bones? It is all a total mystery.

Soon after, the fact that Genghis was on the agenda brought Kravitz's dig to a sudden end. Top people became incensed that foreigners were meddling in Mongolia's most sacred places, even though there was no proof that the Almsgiver's Wall was sacred to the Mongols, certainly not Genghis. Kravitz's team got their march-ing orders, as the press reported with some glee. They never returned. Kravitz himself was too overweight, unfit and old to mount another expedition. He died in 2012.

I visited the site in 2009 and found it decaying, though largely untouched. I was with the old geographer Bazargur and his nephew, Badraa, both of whom had worked with Kravitz's team. Wading through thick grass, our boots releasing the sharp scent of worm-wood, we came to the main house. It was as if Kravitz's people had made a panic-stricken exit the day before, not seven years previously. Photographs were still pinned to the wall, a half-rolled map on a table.

I walked, scrambled and climbed around the wall. It's impressive, but we shouldn't get too carried away. This is no Stonehenge. At a very rough estimate, it consists of something like 50,000 tonnes of rock, which 500 men could build in a summer. Nor is it of top quality. The rubble on the inside does more than support; it pushes, so that in many places the whole wall has fallen. Like walls around many cemeteries all over the world, this one seemed to be a statement: 'Ordinary folk keep out!'

As for any connection with Genghis, there's nothing for and lots against. Besides being Liao – pre-Mongol – it doesn't fit with anything in history or tradition. Genghis's burial was done secretly. The Almsgiver's Wall is about as public a place as you could imagine. Nor does it fit with a 15-kilometre fence, or with a herd of horses galloping over a newly made grave. Its purpose remains a mystery.

It seemed to me that the only way forward was to get more closely acquainted with Burkhan Khaldun, by which I mean Khentii Khan, the peak officially designated the focal point of the cult of Genghis.

From a distance Khentii Khan seems quite accessible: not too high, only 200 kilometres from Ulaanbaatar, a day's run by car. But the 30-kilometre approach road is over permafrost, which melts in spring, turning the track to mud. In summer, rain regularly makes it impassable. In 1992 the area was finally declared a National Park and nature left to take its course. The mountains crowd in, forcing the track to cross the Kherlen over a heavy-duty wooden bridge, built for government officials to make their occasional visits to the sacred slopes. Mountains rise only to about 2,500 metres, poking bare crests above the forest like the pates of tonsured monks. This is the domain of deer, moose, bear and wolf, the same species that inhabit the Siberian taiga stretching away northwards. The track to the mountain leads through bogs, over a steep ridge and across the shallow, stony Kherlen.

Among recent visitors, the most helpful to me was the great Mongolist Igor de Rachewiltz, in the Department of Pacific and Asian History at the Australian National University, Canberra. He climbed the mountain in 1997, an experience he described in two unpublished papers. His team of ten people had three vehicles, with several horses hired in Möngönmört following on behind. 'A horrible ride,' he wrote to me later. 'We got bogged several times and spent hours extricating ourselves.' As they set up camp at the lower *ovoo*, a feast was prepared, while a shaman did his stuff – 'with dancing, chanting, drumming, trance, the lot'. At the end of the feast, 'we were informed by the shaman that the spirit of Genghis Khan had granted permission for all of us to climb the mountain in order to revere him'. It took 20 minutes to reach the first plateau, where Igor, like Schubert, found fragments of what he, like others, assumed had been Kamala's temple.

The next level seemed far more interesting than in Schubert's description, because it really looked to Igor like a vast burial ground: 'a flat, bare area a few hundred metres wide, the ground clearly pock-marked by ancient excavations, i.e. by holes dug and then refilled with earth, stone and debris'. Igor's intriguing conclusion was that it seemed 'plausible, and indeed most likely [that] here, on the south and southeastern side of the mountain . . . the Mongol emperors lie buried'.

My first attempt to reach the site in 2002 was a near disaster, with many errors, but it provided an important insight. My guide, a former tank commander named Tumen, was not as fit as he might have been and had never been on the mountain, so the decisions were mine, unfortunately. By now, reader, the details of the approach will be familiar to you: bogs, mud, willow bushes, ruts. But it was all new to me. For reasons too embarrassing to list, I insisted that we leave the car and driver, got us lost and wandered into the wrong valley, stumbling for hours through clouds of flies and over firs felled by a forest fire. We camped in untouched wilderness, cooking noodles over a reluctant fire of damp deer-dung. It was hell. By nightfall I had realized my error.

But the next morning, as we retraced our steps, I saw something that was merely strange at the time, but would prove to be significant. In low-lying ground, where the willow bushes gave way to coarse grass, I stumbled on a collection of stones, all roughly fist-sized, forming an irregular blob about 1.5 metres across. Perhaps someone had been buried down here. But it seemed an odd place for a grave, away from the mountain, in the middle of a boggy slope, where no one had any reason to come; and an odd shape too, even assuming the effects of centuries of weather. The stones were suspiciously clear of grass. Wouldn't a grave be overgrown? It seemed to me that they had more likely been washed together by some natural process. I took a picture, and put the puzzle to the back of my mind.

Suddenly, now that the mist had cleared and we were away from the obscuring foothills, I saw our unmistakable and unclouded goal. Khentii Khan was a grey shoulder of rock rising clear above its surrounding forests, jutting out like a flexed muscle. In the right conditions, we would have been well on our way. But the conditions were not right. The western sky was being swallowed by a dark-purple cloud-bank, flowing towards us with throaty rumbles. Erdene, the driver, and his car had vanished, and we didn't have mobiles since there was no service in this remote spot. The storm drove us into a rain-battered tent.

Next morning, Erdene found us, after a series of typical Mongol adventures. He had fled the storm, got stuck, fallen asleep in his seat, been rescued by poachers who needed a lift back to their own vehicle, which was in a bog and had to be towed, and finally returned under pure blue skies to find us, bringing a freshly cooked marmot.

This time, we stuck to the right track. Forty minutes later, the valley closed in, the track rose through trees and we reached its end. Beneath firs stood the enormous *ovoo* of tree-trunks mentioned by Schubert and Igor, littered with tangles of blue silk and flags. We were on a pilgrim route marked by shrines, a sort of Mongolian Stations of the Cross. A 20-minute climb through cool, sweet-smelling firs brought us to a flat area of mossy hummocks. In among the slender firs was another *ovoo* of fir-trunks, in front of which stood two enormous metal pots for sacrificial offerings and an altar, also of tree-trunks, covered with empty bottles and saucers for incense. This was obviously the spot where a building had once stood. A temple, presumably.

I looked around for evidence. Right at the edge of the flat area, where footsteps had worn into the soft earth, were bits of tile. With a rush of excitement, I picked up a couple – two bits of grey-brown pottery, coarsely made, unglazed. The tiny impressions on the inner surface suggested the tiles had been moulded or dried on some sort of sacking – typical of Chinese-style roof tiles. They would reveal when the temple was built, if they could be dated.

Kamala's temple? If so, surely those who built it would not have got the wrong place, and Genghis's tomb would be somewhere close. But it made no sense. If Kamala had genuinely wished to respect Genghis's wishes, he would have kept the grave secret; in which case, would he really have drawn attention to it by setting workmen to dig the place flat, cutting trees, importing clay, making a kiln, baking tiles and ensuring regular observances?

Again the path rose steeply through firs, twisting upwards over roots. It is not a hard climb, which is as it should be for a sacred mountain. The whole point of a sacred mountain is that it should be accessible – not too easy, of course, but not forbidding either. For anyone prepared to make the long approach with horses and a tent, Khentii Khan is no harder than a Pyrenean stage on the pilgrim route to Santiago de Compostela, though without the cheer of a pilgrim hostel.

After climbing for another half-hour, we emerged on to the second plateau, where a cool wind blew between stunted evergreens. Ahead and above loomed the bald shoulder of the summit. All around were the features mentioned by Igor – scores, perhaps hundreds, of irregular collections of stones, some of them just the right size for graves. There were also a few little *ovoos*, where pilgrims had thrown together loose rocks in passing. My mind had been set on graves by Igor's words: 'Ancient excavations . . . holes dug and then refilled . . . the Mongol emperors lie buried.'

Except that I could not believe it.

The suspicion had been planted in my mind by the 'grave' I had seen the day before, down in the boggy and trackless lowlands. It had seemed to me then that the features were probably natural. I felt the suspicion harden. The piles of rock were the same in both places:

some roughly circular, but irregular as puddles, and of no standard size, ranging from 1 metre to 3 or 4 metres across. If the feature down below was not a grave, neither were the ones on the mountain.

Later research supported the idea.[3] This is a region of permafrost, in which only the top few feet of ground thaw in the summer. Soil of this type has a life of its own, because freezing soil expands, as ice does, in winter and contracts again in summer, with results that depend on the type of rock and soil, and the slope, and the amount of surface water. Natural forces act on the raw materials in strange and complex ways. From gravels, stones and rocks, periglacial environments produce a wonderful variety of polygons, circles, rings and mounds that look artificial, as if nature has indulged in Zen gardening on a massive scale (indeed, some of the first scientists in the Arctic thought they really were artificial). I became almost certain that the 'graves' on Khentii Khan are 'stony earth circles', made as frosts and slight differences in temperature and expansion push rocks into similarly sized groups. Wind and rain scoop away debris, leaving rock 'puddles' that look very much like rough graves.

Was this a place for a khan to be buried in a secret grave? I couldn't see it. It did not fit with grassland flattened by galloping horses and an overgrowth of forest. This plateau was hard for horses to reach en masse, and with the scantiest of tree-covering, and on a highway to the summit – as public a place as you could get within 1,000 square kilometres.

Above, the high altar of this natural cathedral was suddenly lost in a cloud-bank, its edge rolling ominously downhill. Further research, on both the platform and the summit, had to wait.

My next chance came in 2009, with four adventure tourists. After the now familiar approach up and down steep slopes, over streams and the Kherlen, and in and out of peat bogs, I was back on the platform with the 'stony circles', if that's what they were. I needed evidence, which meant opening up a 'grave' or two. To anyone who

[3] My main source for these paragraphs is Peter Williams and Michael Smith, *The Frozen Earth: Fundamentals of Geocryology* (see Bibliography).

saw these as graves, the idea would have been appalling, sacrilegious. But I had no qualms. It was obvious that every 'circle' was part of a stream of stones and small boulders moving downhill immeasurably slowly, and every stream a part of the process of erosion that had been going on for millennia.

It took only a few minutes to unpack a couple of corpse-sized rock-puddles and to find, less than half a metre down, nothing but peat. After taking pictures, I set off again over rock and grass for the summit.

An hour later, I was on a long, gentle approach to the tumulus described by Campbell, the *ovoo* of Schubert. It is indeed a dome so regular that it looks artificial. On its top was one large pimple and many smaller ones. A faint trail over the pink-tinged rocks led diagonally up the right-hand end. Beneath angry clouds, I climbed to the top, emerging by the large pimple. It was in fact an extremely solid and well-built *ovoo*, consisting of a dry-stone wall in a circle some 5 metres across and a metre high. Inside the low wall was a pile of stones from which rose a pole topped by a silver war-helmet and black horse-tails – replicas of Genghis's war-standard – together with several bows, all swathed and padded in fluttering lengths of blue silk: Genghis-worship and Buddhism, interwined.

The conditions were not good. From ragged cloud came salvoes of thunder and bursts of rain, driven by a bitter wind. My flock of tourists were scattered, and unfit, or aged. One had got lost completely, being found only much later, so time was short. I glanced round, saw 100 – or 200, I don't know how many – smaller *ovoos* (made over the last century, apparently, for Campbell saw only two), took hurried pictures in a grim light, and left.

Later, back in the tranquillity of home, I turned at last to the matter of the tumulus, the giant *ovoo*, the cairn. Could it possibly be Genghis's tomb? Let's see what would be involved. The dome of granite rocks is about 250 by 200 by 30 metres – that's a total weight of about 630,000 tonnes. With granite available all around in manageable chunks, the cairn could be built in a year by 2,000 men, if they had several hundred oxen to drag the rocks to the site in wagons. But wait. In Mongolia you can't work outside in winter, which reduces the working year to five months. And the workforce and oxen need food, herds, tents, pastures and horses, all presumably down in the valley below. We must imagine lines of men and animals trooping up and down the mountain daily, perhaps with a core of them staying up near the summit.

So yes, for a great power it would have been technically feasible. The cairn is about 360,000 cubic metres, which makes it a mere baby compared with the tomb of China's First Emperor outside Lintong, near Xian (five times the volume), or with the Great Pyramid of Giza (over twice the volume). But these are not fair comparisons. Both Egypt and China could draw on vast populations for slave-labourers in the tens of thousands, working over flat landscapes, with time to spare. The Great Pyramid took perhaps twenty years to build, with a workforce of 100,000. In the First Emperor's case, it took 40,000 men four years to collect the earth for his tomb-mound.[4]

It would have been possible for Genghis's heir, Ogedei, to set up a tent-city for a thousand or two, ferry in food in wagons by the hundred, and order them to spend a few years at the task. But the idea is totally at odds with both tradition and the sources. Mongols did not build mounds for royal graves, and the sources speak only of a secret grave in the Forbidden Precinct. It is hardly conceivable that such a vast project would have left no traces in official histories, or the earth, or literature, or folklore.

The clinching argument is a geological one. Go back 13,000 years. The mountain is covered by ice, the last of three glacial advances that have gripped Mongolia over the past 50,000 years. The previous two advances have ground the mountain lower, smoothing its slopes, leaving a core of granite sticking up from the summit, 100 metres across at its base, with buttresses rising to a high point of 50 metres. The volume of the column is much the same as the cairn today, but in a different form. The icy shell begins to melt, breaking the granite pinnacle into boulders, stones and pebbles. As it collapses, spilling ice and water on every side, it drops

[4] My own rough calculation in *The Terracotta Army*.

the rocky detritus to form a neat dome, much as it is today, except that winter ice and summer rains continue to eat away at the cairn, breaking the rocks and carrying them downhill in slow-motion streams. The rocks out on the plateau, the rocks down on the mountainside below, the rocks forming the 'graves' – they all come from the same source, the bare and broken mountain top.

Men could have built it up. But they didn't. Ice broke it down.

Obviously, if the cairn on top was natural, the grave wasn't up there. And, when I eventually had my two roof tiles dated, they suggested that the worship of this mountain developed much later. In May 2013, one of them was subjected to a process known as thermoluminescence analysis, which roughly identifies the date at which the tile was fired. Doreen Stoneham of Oxford Authentication reported that it was roughly 450 years old, with a large area of error. 'The most likely age lies in an envelope of 300 to 600 years, i.e. AD 1400–1700.' In short, too late to be anything to do with Kamala, who built his temple around 1300.

Which merely adds another possibility to the mystery. This mountain had been the focus of veneration for centuries. For how long, and why? It was (and remains) a predominantly Buddhist veneration. Buddhism spread from Tibet into Mongolia from the late sixteenth century onwards. Following Tibetan practice, top-level priests were designated 'incarnate lamas' or 'living Buddhas', deities who appear in the flesh for the benefit of humans. In the mid-seventeenth century, Mongolian Buddhism came to be dominated by a line of senior Mongolian 'incarnate lamas', the first being Zanabazar, a prince's son who was enthroned as an incarnation at the age of four in 1639. In about 1700, Zanabazar's mobile monastery of tents formed the heart of what became Ulaanbaatar. But for about fifty years previously, the tent-monastery had moved from place to place, often in the Khentii Mountains. Zanabazar would naturally have honoured Khentii Khan. So perhaps the temple was Zanabazar's. Perhaps, if Khentii Khan and Burkhan Khaldun are one and the same, it was the coming of Buddhism that inspired the change of the mountain's name to Khentii Khan, allowing the term Burkhan Khaldun to slip away into folklore and history.

The mystery of Genghis's tomb remains, which should be no great surprise. If, as masters of half Eurasia, the khan's family wished their hero's grave to be kept secret, chances are they could arrange it.[5]

[5] The latest search for the grave was carried out in 2009–12 by Albert Lin, at the University of California, San Diego. Lin, supported by *National Geographic*, used remote-sensing technology – satellite imagery, ground-penetrating radar, magnetometry and electro-magnetometry, 3D data visualization – and 'crowd-sourcing', which meant 112,000 volunteers searching 95,000 pictures online to identify likely grave-sites. The project found much of interest, but as this book went to press had published nothing on the subject of Genghis's tomb.

25

WHAT THE MONGOLS
DID FOR US

IN MARCH 2003 AN EXTRAORDINARY ARTICLE APPEARED IN THE
American Journal of Human Genetics. A group of twenty-three
geneticists working in Oxford University had been studying the
DNA from some 2,000 men across Eurasia. To their surprise, they
found a pattern common to several dozen of their sample men,
irrespective of where they came from. The same genetic pattern,
with slight local variations, ran through sixteen population groups
scattered across the whole territory, from the Caspian to the Pacific.
If the proportion of men with this pattern (8 per cent of the sixteen
groups) is extrapolated across the entire population of that area, the
startling conclusion is that 16 million men are in effect part of one
vast family.

How are we to explain this? The data came from a study of
Y-chromosomes, which men possess and women do not. Each man
has a pattern on his Y-chromosome that is his unique signature, but
the signatures have similarities which allow geneticists to spot
family relationships, which can be traced back through time and

space, pinpointing their 'most recent common ancestor'. Working with thirty-four generations and allowing thirty years for a generation, the team placed the common ancestor about 1,000 years ago, in Mongolia.

This suggested a startling hypothesis: that one man living in Mongolia in the ninth to twelfth centuries had scattered his genetic material across half of Eurasia, with the result that it is now shared by one in 200 of all men living today.

Chris Tyler-Smith, then at Oxford's Department of Biochemistry, described what happened next:

'We knew there was something extraordinary in the data as soon as Tatiana [Zerjal, the DPhil student doing the analysis] drew the first network. The star-cluster stood out because of the high frequency, large numbers of neighbours, and distribution in many populations. We had never seen such a thing before. You can tell at a glance it represents a single extended family.

'Tatiana immediately said: "Genghis Khan!"

'At first it seemed like a joke, but as we accumulated more data and did the calculations to determine the most likely time and place of origin, this turned out to be the best explanation.'

Proof came when the researchers placed the sixteen selected groups on a map of Genghis's empire. The two made a perfect fit. Actually, one group, the Hazaras of Afghanistan, lay just outside the borders – but that fitted too, because Genghis was in Afghanistan for a year or so in 1223–4 before retreating back to Central Asia.

Quite possibly the common ancestor of these 16 million males was not directly related to Genghis. But in any event, it was Genghis who was responsible for scattering this genetic signature across northern China and Central Asia between 1209 and his death in 1227. Beautiful women were part of the booty in warfare, and it was a leader's right to be given them by subordinate officers. In theory, all booty belonged to Genghis, who was a stickler for asserting his right and then displaying his generosity by allocating the booty, in this case the women. Whoever possessed this gene, he or they (for it may have been a set of brothers or cousins), must have been travelling with the army across Eurasia, fathering children along the way. Let us say that our man produces two sons. The consequences of doubling the number of male descendants every generation for over thirty generations are so dramatic that the calculation escapes from the real world before its conclusion. After five generations – by about 1350 – one man has a trivial 320 male descendants; but another five generations later, in 1450–1500, he has 10,000; after twenty generations he has 10 *million*; and after thirty, impossible billions.

To find 16 million descendants today, then, is perfectly possible. It is tempting to credit our man with terrific reproductive capacity – Genghis himself, perhaps, as numerous news stories proclaimed. In fact, these particular genes do not influence either looks or behaviour; all they do is determine sex. So there must have been some other factor at work to ensure the spread of the gene. As the authors state, it can only be sheer political power with a vast geographical reach. 'Our findings demonstrate a novel form of selection in human populations on the basis of social prestige.' Sociologists and gossip columnists know about the sexual success of alpha males, but this is the first time it has been seen in action in evolutionary terms. Genghis may not have spread the gene himself; but he certainly created the conditions for it.

The paper caused quite a stir at the time. Its findings have since been replicated by Russian scientists[1] and inspired much related research, attracting some 250 citations in other scientific papers. A word of warning, though. The original conclusion was that Genghis provided the *means* of spreading the gene. But Genghis is such a force in history that the message has become distorted. The title of the Russian paper says the star-cluster is 'attributed to Genghis Khan's descendants', as if he were the common ancestor. Same thing with many websites: 'Genghis Khan a Prolific Lover' (*National Geographic*), '1 in 200 men direct descendants of Genghis Khan' (*Discover*).

---

[1] S. Abilev et al., 'The Y-chromosome C3* star-cluster attributed to Genghis Khan's descendants is present at high frequency in the Kerey clan from Kazakhstan', *Human Biology*, February 2012; 84 (1):79–89.

It's not Genghis's own DNA that explains matters. It's the behaviour of his people. It is fashionable to seek a genetic explanation of behaviour. Here, though, it's the other way around. It's the behaviour that lies behind the genetics, behaviour unleashed by the world-changing character that emerged on the Mongolian grasslands some eight and a half centuries ago.

Given that empires change civilizations, what other effects of Genghis's empire remain today?

Rather fewer than you might think. Size matters, but it is not everything.

In Europe, the Romans left vast amounts of hardware – roads, buildings, aqueducts, stadia – but they also rewrote Europe's software: language, art, literature, law, almost every aspect of culture you can think of, affecting the inner and outer lives of all its many peoples.

The Mongols left – well, not much. True, they lasted for only a fraction of the time of the Romans: 150 years against over 1,000. But length of time does not equate with cultural impact. Alexander flashed across the skies of history like a comet, but he left a lasting light. The British were in India for 200 years and the cultures are still interfused. Why? Because the Romans, the Greeks and the British had something to say, quite apart from their military successes. The Mongols didn't. Yes, Yuan China was famed for its ceramics, art, drama, poetry and much else, as was Persia. But this was creativity *despite* Mongol rule, not because of it; and it was not Mongol culture, but Chinese and Persian. Where there were no locals to create, as in the Golden Horde, very little of value was created. As Thomas Allsen puts it, 'they were, in sum, agents not donors'.[2]

Compare them with those other great conquerors, the Arabs. There are interesting parallels between the Arabs of the sixth century and the Mongols of the twelfth: a mass of feuding tribes, wealthy neighbours, access to major religions, great leaders,

---

[2] *Culture and Conquest in Mongol Eurasia*, p.191 (see Bibliography).

explosions outwards in a series of epic and successful conquests. But with very different consequences. Islam is with us still, in strength and great cultural depth; not so Mongolian religion – Tengrism – or its culture.

The main difference lies in their ideologies. Islam expanded in conjunction with the new religion, while the Mongols were inspired by conquest alone, with religion coming along behind to act as a justification. In Islam, faith bred conquests; for the Mongols, conquests bred faith.

It might have worked. But Tengrism – the notion that heaven gave the world to the Mongols – has a serious deficiency. It totally lacks any ethical and moral content. Tengri was not presented as the creator of the universe, or as humanity's ultimate judge. No Mongol would tremble at the possibility of standing before Tengri to account for his or her actions in life. Nor did the concept offer anything to oppressed subjects. Genghis created unity by destroying the upper segments of Mongol tribal organization, and channelling loyalty to himself and his Golden Clan. This was not a religion well suited to the long-term government of other cultures. Tengrism did not seek converts.

What a difference from Islam, which claims, like Christianity, to offer guidance for all mankind, victors and conquered alike, creating the *umma*, a community of believers. In theory, no one is excluded from Islam on the basis of ethnicity or social background. Iranians, Turks, Malaysians, Indonesians, Chinese, converts of many races and cultures – all form part of the *umma*.

If Mongols wished to govern their urbanized subjects long-term, they really had no option but to adapt – as in China, where Kublai brought in Buddhism to justify the idea of world rule – or adopt the religion of their subjects, most notably Islam. In the Golden Horde, despite keeping a distance between themselves and Russian culture, some Mongols converted to Russian Orthodoxy. If they had stayed in Hungary, they would probably have become Catholics.

The result of this difference was Muslim intolerance and Mongol tolerance, of a sort. Muslims dismiss other religions, since they are by definition untrue, while asserting the truth of their own. The Mongols, on the other hand, were happy to allow any set of beliefs as long as those who professed them acknowledged the Mongols as world-rulers, in waiting if not yet in practice. Their brutality in the Muslim world was not anti-Muslim – it was just anti those who disputed Mongol rule. The khans favoured religions entirely indiscriminately, depending on political need. For instance, Kublai asked the Polos to bring Christian priests, not because he wanted to turn Christian but because he wanted to counterbalance the bitter rivalry between Buddhists and Daoists.

With the same pragmatism, the Mongols did not insist on dogma, other than the supremacy of Genghis. There were no subtleties to be explained, no great truths to be proclaimed, other than Genghis's divinely ordained rule. For this we should be grateful. Imagine what horrors the Mongols might have let loose if they had been set on killing all those who refused to accept their beliefs. As it was, all they demanded was compliance. That's why they left hardly a physical or intellectual trace: no buildings, no philosophies, no universities, no moral guidance, no literature for the subject peoples.

Yet there are wisps of evidence, like the remnants of a supernova that recall the great explosion. It was an explosion of people: at first Mongol armies, then the non-Mongol troops blotted up by the Mongols, and finally, as if in a series of reverberations, massive transfers of captives. For almost two centuries, Eurasia became a sort of ethnic blender, mixing people and peoples as never before. Each campaign was like a slow-motion explosion, scattering, obliterating and transferring tribes, ethnicities and populations. The Tanguts were almost annihilated; Chinese were taken west, Muslims and Tibetans east. Kazakhs and Uzbeks emerged for the first time, with consequences for the future Soviet Union and for today's Central Asia.

At its highest levels, the empire became a United Nations of intellectuals, administrators, soldiers and artisans of twenty-two nationalities, cultures and religions other than Mongols and

Chinese.[3] Traditionally, the Mongols, like all the other nomadic groups, had captured, adopted, married and enslaved captives, but this was something new. As warriors and herders, they had been generalists who could turn their hand to anything; now, to run an empire, they needed specialists by the thousand. It all goes back to Genghis. Remember the Naiman scribe Tatar-tonga and his Uighur script? The Khitan administrator Yelu Chucai? Another example: after the conquest of Khwarezm, Genghis chose the Muslims Mahmud Yalavach and his son Masud Beg to help administer north China because they 'were adept in the laws and customs of cities', as *The Secret History* says. Genghis's heirs followed suit. The friar William of Rubruck (in north-eastern France), newly arrived at Mönkhe's court in Karakorum, met a French goldsmith called William (Guillaume) Boucher, who had been captured in Hungary. He had devised a bizarre silver 'tree', which is worth a small digression. It consisted of four pipes, from each of which came a different drink – wine, mare's milk, mead and rice wine. The pipes, which had snakes (or perhaps dragons) twined around them, sprang from model lions. The whole thing was capped by an angel holding a trumpet in its articulated hand and arm. It must have been life-size, because underneath was hidden a man who, when the right moment came, blew into a tube leading to the angel, which would raise the trumpet to its lips and emit a blast, at which waiters offstage would pump their individual drinks into the four pipes. The idea possibly came from devices worked by water and compressed air in European and Byzantine courts, but one thing is certain: it was totally, eccentrically un-Mongol, a statement of a new multicultural identity. An early fourteenth-century Chinese writer, Cheng Zhu-fu, gloried in Mongol internationalism: 'Our Dynasty, with

[3] Thomas Allsen, 'Ever Closer Encounters' (see Bibliography). He lists Italians, French, Flemings, Greeks, Germans, Scandinavians, Hungarians, Russians, Qipchaqs, Alans, Armenians, Georgians, Nestorians, Jews, Muslims, Ongguts, Khitans, Jürchens, Uighurs, Tibetans, Tanguts and Koreans. Specialists included administrators, clerics, merchants, shipwrights, musicians, goldsmiths, armourers, cooks, textile workers, scribes, translators, carpetmakers, architects, artists, stonemasons, printers, engineers and, of course, uncountable numbers of soldiers and servants.

supernatural military power, and benevolent leniency, has brought order to the Four Seas. Loyal, virtuous, brave and talented men from a multitude of places and myriad countries all willingly enter the emperor's service.'

As the Persian author Rashid al-Din put it in his *Collected Chronicles*, 'Today, thanks to God and in consequence of him, the extremities of the inhabited earth are under the dominion of the house of Chinggis Qan and philosophers, astronomers, scholars and historians from North and South China, India, Kashmir, Tibet, [the lands] of the Uighurs, other Turkic tribes, the Arabs and Franks, [all] belonging to [different] religions and sects, are united in large numbers in the service of majestic heaven.'

Rashid and his work are perfect expressions of Mongol internationalism. Born Jewish, he converted to Islam, rose in the service of the Il-Khans and was commissioned to write a history by Ghazan (1294–1304), a fifth-generation descendant of Genghis. He then extended it to cover the whole known world and its civilizations. Researching what became the first world history, he interviewed a huge range of scholars – Chinese, Kashmiri, Uighur, Mongolian, Hebrew, Arabic, Tibetan and European – to produce three atlas-sized volumes in both Arabic and Persian. Working with a team of researchers and co-writers, Rashid used written sources as well as his informants, including a collection of books and scrolls concerning early Mongol history that were concealed from outsiders by their royal owners and have now vanished. He was author and general editor of a project that combined the work of government ministry, university department and publishing house. One of his colleagues, an influential Yuan scholar-administrator named Bolad, had his own sub-committee of researchers. The project made Rashid rich: he supposedly received a million dinars from Ghazan's successor (about 5 per cent of the government's annual revenue) and became a patron of many artists. But the *Chronicles* was not his life's work. Besides being a top Il-Khan minister, he created what was in effect his own university in Tabriz, wrote several volumes on Islamic theology and an instruction manual on agriculture that reveals a detailed knowledge of Chinese techniques for raising, among other things, fruit trees, cereals, vegetables, mulberries and silkworms.

To finish Rashid's story: genius, power, wealth and hard work do not guarantee peace and happiness. He was accused by a jealous rival of being part of a plot to kill the khan, Oljeitu. He said he had done nothing but prescribe a medicine to help cure the khan. This was taken as an admission of guilt. He was beheaded and his head 'carried about the town for several days with cries of "This is the head of the Jew who abused the name of God!"'[4]

Amidst the flow of information and people, doctors were particularly in demand. Chinese medical works were translated into Persian and Arabic.[5] As William of Rubruck says of the northern Chinese doctors he saw at Karakorum: 'Their physicians are very well versed in the efficacy of herbs and can diagnose shrewdly with the pulse. But they do not employ urine samples, not knowing anything about urine.' They appealed because they had more complex systems and a longer tradition, not that they were better, since all medical treatments were, by modern standards, hopeless. They favoured mercury, for instance, because it was supposedly an elixir of life, despite the fact that it kills you.

Astronomers, too, were much admired, because they were, in today's terms, astrologers, credited with being able to predict the future. That was one reason why Genghis admired Yelu Chucai – 'on the eve of each military operation, [the emperor], without fail, ordered his excellency to foretell its good or bad fortune.' Several famous Chinese astronomers went, or were taken, from China to Iran, because Hulegu 'was infatuated with astronomy' – or rather astrology. When he crushed the Assassins, from their stronghold of Alamut emerged the greatest scholar of the age, Nasir al-Din Tusi, who had been captured by the Assassins. Inspired by him, Hulegu built an observatory at Maragheh, near Tabriz. With a library of 40,000 books, 100 students and astronomers from both China and Byzantium, it remained in operation for some fifty years. Its major

[4] Boyle, *Successors*, p. 5 (see Rashid al-Din in Bibliography).
[5] For further details, see Allsen, *Culture and Conquest*.

achievement was to merge the calendars of all the main cultures of the day and region: Greek, Arab, Jewish, Christian, Persian and Chinese. Kublai did something similar in Beijing, where a Muslim observatory ran for almost a century.

But what, in the end, was the lasting cultural impact of all these exchanges? Once again, not much. The potential was huge, the cross-fertilization enormously stimulating, the technical achievements astonishing; yet there were no fundamental advances to be credited to specifically Mongol influence. Despite the accuracy of the observations in astronomy in both the Il-Khanate and China, no Copernicus came forward to explain the movements of the planets, no Galileo presented Kublai with a telescope. Despite a wealth of opportunity, no great leap forward followed.

But the exchange of people did achieve one huge leap backwards. Consider for a moment the marmots of Mongolia. These creatures, common on the Central Asian grasslands, are charming to look at and make an excellent stew, but are generally better avoided because they are favoured by fleas, which can harbour a virulent bacillus that kills both fleas and marmots. In the right circumstances, when marmots are few, the fleas may spread to other species – rabbits, rats and eventually humans. Once in the bloodstream, the bacillus causes a reaction that has a fatality rate of 90 per cent or over. It strikes the lungs, the blood and finally the lymph glands. These glands, unable to drain off the poison, balloon into hard, dark, nut-sized swellings known as 'buboes', to which the affliction owes its name – the bubonic plague, better known as the Black Death.

Sometime in the 1340s, the marmots of Mongolia suffered a decline. The bacillus, *Yersinia pestis*, sought other hosts and found them conveniently commuting along the pony-express routes created by the Mongols in their explosive conquests over the preceding 150 years. A few years later, the fleas and their nasty little parasites reached the Crimea. There the local Mongols were besieging the ancient port of Feodosiya, which Italian merchants from Genoa had taken over in the previous century as a 'factory', or trading station, renaming it Kaffa. Stricken by the plague, the

Mongols withdrew, with a parting shot. In December 1347 they catapulted the plague-ridden bodies of their own dead over the walls to infest the Italians. The next ship heading back to the Mediterranean carried the plague, in its rats, in its flea-ridden materials and in its crew. From Italy and southern France the plague spread north at an average rate of 15 kilometres a week, visiting upon Europe its greatest catastrophe ever. In three years something like 25 million people died, perhaps more. A papal inquiry put the figure at 40 million. This represented a third of Europe's population. In some places the death toll may have topped 60 per cent. The devastation was almost universal, and the effects scarred cities, cultures and minds for generations.

Given the potential, given the exchange of skills and information, what more might have been achieved? One thing, certainly, would have transformed our world in astonishing ways.

The question is this: why didn't the Mongols invent printing with movable type, as Gutenberg did a century and a half later? Kublai almost had it in his hands, for he had access to most of the elements that inspired Gutenberg: need, the right script, technical ability.

There was certainly no shortage of books or paper or printing. China had had paper since the second century AD. There were books by the million, and had been for 500 years. The eastern method of printing was to cut text or a picture in reverse into wood, and this block, when covered with ink, was used to print on paper. The technology was basic, effective and technically easy, but with fundamental inefficiencies. It took days to make a block, pages could be printed only one at a time, and the information could be used only in that form: the block. Every new page demanded a new block. Discarded blocks of out-of-print books clogged the yards of printing-works until they became firewood.

The solution was obvious. If each character had its own block, you could make up any text you liked, and re-use the characters after printing. No need to carve every page, no need for the millions of discarded blocks. China had the know-how. The invention of printing with movable type is attributed to a certain Bi Sheng

(Pi Sheng) in the eleventh century. His idea was to cut his characters in wet clay, in reverse, and bake them. To print, he selected his characters, put them in a frame, inked them, and took a rubbing with cloth or paper. The technique worked, the technology improved. The first people to use movable metal type were the Koreans, in a fifty-volume *Prescribed Ritual Texts of the Past and Present*, printed in 1234. The Mongols had first invaded Korea in 1216, with much back-and-forth over the next fifty years. It was Kublai who finally made Korea a vassal of the Mongol empire in 1270. Which means that possibly Kublai personally, certainly his scientific advisers, knew about printing with movable metal type.

They also knew the problems of doing this with Chinese. It was even more trouble than block-printing. The business of choosing the correct character from at least 8,000 offered no advantage in design and not much in speed. Besides, it was an implied threat to two ancient skills, calligraphy and block-carving. True, there were those who remained intrigued by the idea. In 1297, Wang Zhen, a magistrate from Dongping in Shandong province, made 30,000 wooden characters set out in two revolving round tables, which gave easier access to the type.[6] Later, Chinese governments produced some astonishing publications with movable type – like a 1726 encyclopaedia of 5,000 volumes that used 250,000 characters – but for day-to-day use this method of printing remained no more than a technological oddity.

Yet Kublai had the answer, right there, in front of his face. It existed in the form of the alphabetical script adopted from the Uighurs on his grandfather's instigation. It existed again in the alphabetical script devised by Phags-pa. The genius of the alphabet, any alphabet, is that it is based on a few dozen symbols, which roughly represent the whole range of linguistic sounds. Its fuzziness and simplicity gives it a massive advantage over scripts based on syllables (which is why Chinese keypads are in pinyin, the Latinized form of their script).

So Kublai had at his disposal several of the major elements that in

---

[6] There's a model of it in the Gutenberg Museum, Mainz.

Gutenberg's hands almost two centuries later helped the Renaissance on its way. Out went scribes and their beautiful, slow ways; in came the printing press and a slew of advances, all feeding on each other: mass markets, universal literacy, cheap books, and scholars exchanging information and standing on each other's shoulders. In 1454, Gutenberg and his team perfected a whole new technology and printed 180 copies of his famous 42-line Bible. By 1500, 250 printing operations across Europe were producing 2,000 titles – over 200,000 books – per year. In 1518–25, Germany alone printed a million books each year – and one third of them were by Martin Luther, whose anti-papal 95 *Theses* kickstarted the Reformation and who has therefore, with some justification, been blamed and praised for causing the greatest split in the Christian church. From the Renaissance and the Reformation sprang a new Europe, a Europe that seized the world, dominated trade, founded nations, discovered new lands – precisely what Genghis and Kublai intended for their empire.

It could have happened. Kublai and his extremely bright advisers might have taken the next steps, which were to turn Phags-pa's script into metal type, set it in frames and start printing. There was even a good financial reason to do this. Kublai could have printed vast amounts of paper money, with complex designs and several colours to prevent counterfeiting.

Why didn't it happen?

Several vital elements were missing. One was the right sort of paper. In China, paper was soft and absorbent as toilet paper, ideal for scribes working with brushes and for block-printing. In Europe, scribes working with quills needed a much firmer, non-absorbent surface, which was the sort of paper Gutenberg needed to produce crisp, tiny lettering. Secondly, China did not have olives or grapes that needed to be squashed with heavy-duty presses, the devices that Gutenberg adapted to make the printing press. And thirdly, someone would have needed to come up with Gutenberg's astonishing invention, the hand-mould, which could produce several hundred new lead types per day. This device, which now exists only in museums, was fundamental in printing for the next 500 years.

These are technical problems, which Kublai's people might have solved if they had set their minds to the task. But there is a final, and perhaps fundamentally crucial, reason why there was no Yuan printing revolution. The purpose of printing is the transmission of information, and it seems that the Mongols had no information they wished to transmit; in fact, the opposite – they had a lot of information they wanted to keep secret. Deep down, what Kublai had created was Mongolia Inc., a vast corporate entity dedicated to creating wealth and power for itself, with no end goal save its own eternal survival. There was no great truth to be promulgated, no great literature to be captured in book form and made public. All the Mongols could do was to oversee – encourage is too strong a word – the transmission of the art and literature of their subjects, principally the Chinese and Persians and Arabs. In the end, they had nothing much to say on their own account.

Yet, of course, their conquests changed the world. Of all the changes that flowed from the empire, the most intriguing is their role in the event that changed that world yet again: Europe's rediscovery of America. By joining dots, a trail can be made connecting Genghis to Columbus.

The first big dot is Marco Polo. His father and uncle had preceded him, but they would never have written up their experience. It was Marco and his *Travels* that form the starting point of a very extended process. He left China in 1291, taking four years to reach Venice. Kublai died in 1294. Marco's book was written in 1299.

Sixty-nine years later, the Mongols were thrown out of China and foreigners were left dealing with the Ming for the next 250 years – a dynasty that was the very opposite of the Yuan: shut off, introverted, utterly convinced that foreigners had nothing to offer. Across Central Asia, ex-Mongol sub-empires collapsed and vanished. Islam divided east from west. Old links broke, memories faded, few could testify to the truth of Marco's book, and more doubted it. For two generations, the *Travels* became a book of unbelievable marvels, its factual basis lying in a semi-fossilized state.

Its resurrection as a guide to the real world was due to two factors. The first was the revival of learning in the first half of the fifteenth century. The church kickstarted the process, because Rome had an urgent desire to unite a Christendom long divided into west and east, Roman and Orthodox. In 1439–43 a General Council in Florence brought hundreds of scholars together, including an astrologer and physician named Paolo dal Pozzo Toscanelli. Also at the conference was one of the most brilliant men of his age, Nicholas of Cusa, who owned a copy of Marco's book. A few years later, he became a mentor to a Portuguese cleric named Fernão Martins, a future canon of Lisbon and adviser to Portugal's King Afonso V, just at the time that Portugal's explorers were seeking sea routes to the east. Note the dots in our trail: a freemasonry of scholars, an interest in Marco Polo's story, links with an expansionist Portugal.

At virtually the same time, 130 years after Marco's death, the door to the Silk Road network of transcontinental routes to the east was slammed and locked. The Turks, who had been moving west from Central Asia for 1,000 years, seized Constantinople. All the lands that had once owed allegiance of some sort to the Great Khan – where once a virgin carrying gold, or at least a man with the right credentials, could be helped from camp to camp and city to city in safety – fell to the Muslims.

So Europe's merchants turned to the sea routes, along which flowed silks, precious stones and spices, brought by Chinese junks to Malaysia and Arab ships to India and the Middle East. But this was a galling arrangement. Eastern pepper, for instance, underwent a fiftyfold increase in price on its journey to Europe's kitchens. Obviously the thing to do was for European merchants to fetch these goods themselves, and cut out the middlemen. Hence the race in the late fifteenth century to discover and sail round southern Africa; and hence Columbus's big idea – to reach the East by sailing round the world the other way, westwards, to contact the land of the Great Khan, as described by Marco.

It all depended on Marco's reliability. Some were beginning to take him seriously. One was a monk named Mauro, who would any-way have been familiar with Marco's reputation for truthfulness, since both were Venetians. In 1459, at the request of Afonso V,

Mauro completed a world map that was the first to include details from Marco: the Yangtze and the Yellow River, many cities with a host of names familiar from Marco's book, even the first mention of Japan in a western map.

Columbus's direct inspiration seems to have been a letter and a map sent in 1474 by the Florentine astrologer Toscanelli to the Portuguese cleric Fernão Martins, who was eager for information about the world beyond Africa. In the letter Toscanelli, drawing on Marco, refers to the Great Khan, unaware that the Mongol khans had been expelled over a century before. It was as if the closure of the overland route had frozen the idea of China in European minds, immortalizing the Great Khan. Toscanelli estimates the distance westwards over the sea to China: 6,500 miles. In fact, the distance from Portugal to China is more than twice that.

Columbus knew Toscanelli's conclusions. His diary quotes from the letter,[7] speaking about 'a prince who is called Grand Khan'. His Big Idea – to sail west to get to the East – was in the air.

But that idea did not convince Afonso. He had invested too heavily in exploration round Africa to backtrack. In 1488, when the Portuguese explorer Bartholomew Diaz made it around the southern tip of Africa into the Indian Ocean, the way eastwards opened and Afonso's heir, John, decided against Columbus's trans-Atlantic venture.

Columbus, his hopes dashed, stormed off to Castile and presented his idea to the Spanish rulers, Ferdinand and Isabella. His timing was good: Spain was newly unified, and its two rulers ambitious for more power and influence. Seeing the Portuguese investment about to pay off, they felt under pressure to compete. The best way was to gamble on Columbus.

Of course, the Big Idea turned out to be both wrong and, by pure luck, also right beyond imagining because, luckily, America was in the way and Columbus's journey rather short, just five weeks. It still

---

[7] As always, academics dispute the nature of the evidence and the conclusions. I summarize the most widely accepted version. For details, see Larner, *Marco Polo and the Discovery of the World* who uses the translation by O. Dunn and J. E. Kelly in their edition of Columbus's *Diario*.

did not occur to him that he had stumbled on a new world. He thought one West Indian island had to be Japan. As he recorded in his diary, 'I have already decided to go to the mainland and . . . to give your Highness's letters to the Great Khan.' A few days later he was in Cuba and, despite the rather obvious lack of cities, thought it was China, referring to the 'city of Cathay' (which, given that Cathay was a kingdom not a city, suggests he had not yet read Marco's book).

Someone from Europe would have stumbled on America sooner or later, of course. But without Genghis, Kublai and the empire, who would have thought of heading west? And when? Almost certainly not Columbus, and not in 1492.

26

HOW TO SURVIVE DEATH

LET US APPROACH THE SUBJECT OF THIS CHAPTER AS PILGRIMS FROM THE north, crossing the Yellow River in mid-course. In this stretch, the river is a geographical oddity. Instead of flowing eastwards from the Tibetan highlands, it takes a huge diversion to the north, swinging in a vast loop before continuing on its way to the Pacific. The loop encloses a country-sized slab of semi-desert, sand, scrub, and ravines carved out by the sparse rain. This is the Ordos, which means 'tent-palaces' in old Mongolian, a reminder that it was once Mongolian territory before the arrival of Chinese roads and cities and mines. But it's not all arid. If you drive south from the top of the Great Bend, through the sparkling new tower-blocks of Ordos City, the regional capital, you cross a savannah of scattered trees and pastures. In the distance appears a fir-covered hill, and above the firs you glimpse three pink-and-blue domes, topped by little pillars, like cherries on cakes. The road leads uphill through a small town and into a giant courtyard lined with gift shops. A long flight of stairs climbs to a gallery of exhibition rooms topped by white crenellations. By now you are panting, probably sweating. That's as it should be. Pilgrims should suffer a little. Also, you are awed. You feel you are approaching something majestic. Ahead is a quadrangle of rough grass 100 metres across, and beyond lies the object of your journey: a long, pink, single-storey building, three squat pavilions linked by galleries and topped by blue-tiled roofs with upturned eves, which, like ballet skirts, circle the three pink-and-blue domes you saw from the countryside below.

You have arrived at the Mausoleum of Genghis Khan.

Here in the Lord's Enclosure, to translate the Mongolian name, Genghis has undergone the final and strangest part of his meta-morphosis from barbarian chief to demi-god. It is home to a religious sect that has evolved from historical roots, through legend, to create a community with a temple, rites and a belief-system that is beginning to show signs of a universal theology.

It started in 1227. Though buried obscurely in the mountains of Mongolia, Genghis had to be honoured, his possessions preserved, provision made for worship. His heir Ogedei decreed a solution that was original and appropriate for nomads. In the words of Sagang Tsetsen in the seventeenth century, 'white tents were raised for the purpose of veneration'. Each tent would have had its own object of worship – Genghis, his first three wives, his horse, mare's-milk bucket, bows, saddle and treasures. A clan – originally the Urianghai 'of the Woods' – was granted freedom from all other duties so that their 500 members could act as guardians in perpetuity, caring for the Lord's possessions and supervising the rituals of veneration. In this way, Genghis would watch over his people for ever.

At first, the focal point of veneration was, of course, the grave-site on or near Burkhan Khaldun. But there was an impermanence about the arrangements, since the secret location was deliberately over-grown. Years passed. The tents, originally nine but later eight, moved from place to place as a travelling shrine, wandering back and forth across the Gobi, from the Altai Mountains of the west to the eastern grasslands, until they settled here, at this well-watered spot on the eastern edge of the Ordos, in the mid-fifteenth century. Folklore improvised an explanation for the shrine's presence, until, with the passing of the generations, it seemed that this must have been the place where their Lord wished to be buried, though no one knew the exact spot. In the seventeenth century, the shrine acquired its present name – Edsen Khoroo,[1] the Lord's Enclosure.

The temple and its rituals were, and still are, controlled by the same group, now known as Darkhats (meaning 'exempt from taxation'). Their claim, more folklore than history, is that their families are all descended from Genghis's generals, two in particular: Boorchu (who as a teenager helped the future Genghis rescue his stolen horses) and Mukhali, viceroy of north China. In the words of one Darkhat, Surihu: ever since Genghis's death, 'we, the descendants of Boorchu, have been engaged in making offerings and guarding the mausoleum. And the duties have never been stopped. I am the thirty-ninth generation of Boorchu's family'.[2] The Darkhats who claim descent from Mukhali care for the war-standards – spears with shaggy circlets of yak-tail attached just below the point – and their ceremonies. Over the centuries these and other groups evolved ever more arcane and trivial tasks, such as caring for the horse-headed clappers, chanting, reading decrees, supervising liquor ceremonies, boiling sheep, carrying lanterns and butchering horses. These were all men, of course, and all the jobs were inherited from father to senior son.

From the early seventeenth century, shamanic elements gave way to Buddhist ones. Genghis became a reincarnation of the *bodhisattva* (or 'Buddha-to-be') Vajrapani, the Thunderbolt-bearer, who in Tibetan mythology fights demons to protect Buddhism. Rites settled into a series of thirty annual ceremonies, with four great seasonal observances, each with its songs, prayers and incantations, many beginning with words which, if the names were changed, could just as well be used by a priest invoking Christ: 'Heaven-born Genghis Khan, Born by the will of sublime Heaven, Your body provided with heavenly rank and name, You who took overlordship of the world's peoples . . .' Attributes, possessions, actions, looks, wives, children, horses, pastures: all are invoked as a means of assuring the Lord's blessing in

[1] As always, there are several transliterations of this from the Mongol. The Chinese version transcribes roughly as Yijin-huoluo.
[2] Rihu Su, 'The Chinggis Khan Mausoleum and Its Guardian Tribe', University of Pennsylvania dissertation, 2000.

the overcoming of obstacles, demons, illnesses, errors and discord.

Take one ceremony among many. This one happens once a year in front of the temple's main *ovoo*, the sacred pile of rocks that stands nearby. It is held in memory of the Golden Pole to which Genghis tied his horse, a horse of pure white, such as the ones allowed to wander around the temple today. It is said that a thief took the horse and as a punishment was made to represent the Golden Pole, standing all night holding the horse with his feet buried in the ground. In the mausoleum's ceremony, a man played the role of the thief. People threw loose change in front of him. Priests scattered milk, observed how it flowed and foretold how good the pastures would be, and how healthy the cattle. After the ceremony the man was released, gathered the cash and ran off, with people yelling 'Stop thief!' in ritual protest. That was fifty years ago. No man today stands out all night with his legs half buried. His place is taken by a real pole. Children and adults run back and forth between the pole and the *ovoo*, scattering milk on the pole.

The mausoleum and its web of ritual practice remained for Mongols a sort of *cosa nostra*, from which Chinese and other foreigners were excluded. Owen Lattimore, the great American Mongolist, was the first outsider to observe the Lord's Enclosure and its ceremonies. He came in April 1935, in time for the spring festival. Arriving for this 'Audience with Jenghis Khan', as he called his vivid account, he found five tents (not eight) flanked by two dozen *gers*, ox-carts, tethered horses and lines of poorer tents belonging to traders and servants. Inside the main tent was a low, silver-plated table, which was the altar, and a silver-plated wooden chest, the 'coffin'. This was supposed to contain the bones or ashes of Genghis himself, but Lattimore, with his excellent Mongol, noticed an inscription in the silver which suggested it was Manchu, no more than 300 years old. He had his doubts about the other items as well, given the frequency of rebellions and bandit raids.

There followed many offerings of silk scarves, a ninefold prostration, the drinking of milk-wine from silver cups, and many advances and retreats, all followed by the offering of a sacrificial sheep. Then came a procession around the other four tents, and prayers in the final one. Lattimore noted how much of a Mongol business this was; the Buddhist lamas performed only an insignificant role, their main task being to blow curved Tibetan trumpets, producing a sound like 'the splitting of gigantic trousers'. At the end of the ceremonies the following day, all five tents were lifted in their entirety on to carts drawn by two white camels and taken back to a walled enclosure nearby.

It was clear to Lattimore that the origins of the cult were back to front. Normally, you would expect a body, a burial, then the rituals. But there had been no body, this was no true mausoleum, the 'relics' were of dubious authenticity, and 'as for the tradition that the body of Jenghis is at Ejen Horo [sic], or his ashes, this is neither clear nor specific'. Somehow the rituals, based on a combination of thirteenth-century court observances and even older ancestor-worship, seemed to have come first, the beliefs following along later as rationalizations. Perhaps only then did the 'relics' appear, to provide a physical focus for worship.

War, which Lattimore just managed to avoid, changed everything. So far, the only contest to possess the legacy of Genghis had been between shaman and Buddhist, a rivalry hidden by the slow-motion nature of the Buddhist takeover. Now the story shifts gear. Since the turn of the twentieth century, Chinese officials had been encouraging Chinese peasants to colonize traditional Mongol lands, turning pasture into farmland, forcing herders into marginal pastures. At this point, three new elements intruded: Japan, expanding into Inner Asia from its colony in Manchuria, challenged by two Chinese rivals, the Nationalists under Chiang Kai-shek and Mao's Communists.

Japan sprang upon China rather as Genghis had done, but from the opposite side. In 1931–2 Manchuria became a Japanese puppet-state, Manchukuo, a prelude to expansion into Mongolia, China and Siberia. The first step was to take eastern and central Inner Mongolia, which acquired its own puppet-regime, the Mongolian Autonomous Government, complete with a revolutionary calendar which had as its founding date the year of Genghis's birth. Held back briefly by Chiang Kai-shek's Nationalist army, the Guomindang, Japanese troops advanced to the Yellow

River in 1937 and remained in control for the next eight years.[3]

In the autumn of 1937 an unexpected guest arrived at the Lord's Enclosure. He announced himself as a representative of the Royal Japanese Army based in Baotou, 100 kilometres to the north. Local officials were gathered. Demands were made. The officials were to declare themselves both against Chinese parties and for the Japanese; and to move the Eight White Tents and their contents into Japanese custody. The Japanese had realized that whoever ruled the Lord's Enclosure held the key to Mongolia and this part of China; and that whoever ruled Mongol lands had a fine base from which to secure the rest of China and Siberia. Suddenly Genghis's relics, Genghis's very soul, had become the key to empire in Asia.

A tricky position for the provincial chief, Shakhe. The relics had been there for 700 years, give or take, and the local Mongols were guarding them 'as if protecting their own eyes'. Besides, close by were Nationalist troops. Shakhe pointed out that if the mausoleum were moved there would be riots, which would not benefit the Japanese cause. The invaders saw the point, and backed off.

But the damage was done. Many Mongols in China turned to their own independence movement, while others approached the Nationalists for help in moving the relics to a place of safety, far from the reach of the enemy. The Guomindang government agreed, planning to move everything by truck and camel to the mountains south of Lanzhou on the Yellow River, 600 kilometres to the south-west. The area was chosen because it was safe, though the argument was also made that it was not far (well, only 150 kilometres) beyond the Liupan Mountains, where Genghis had spent his last summer.

On 17 May 1939, 200 Nationalist soldiers arrived unannounced at the mausoleum, to the astonishment of the confused locals, who blocked the way. A Nationalist official explained the need to protect the place against the 'East Ocean devils'. Panic gave way to negotiations. The Nationalists promised that all expenses would be paid,

[3] In 1941–4 the Japanese backed the construction of a Genghis Khan temple in Ulanhot. Its three white buildings, in a 6-hectare enclosure, were redeveloped in the 1980s, with a 3-tonne copper statue of the hero at its heart.

that some of the Darkhats could go along, and that all the ceremonies would be allowed to continue. The news spread fast. Hundreds, then thousands, came, spending the night in lantern-lit ceremonies, weeping and praying as the tents were struck and the carts loaded. At dawn the train of vehicles moved off. Across a 'sea of tears', in the words of a journalist, the carts slowly pulled out, heading south at walking pace towards Yan'an, Shaanxi province, almost 400 kilometres away.

Yan'an was the HQ of the Communist Party's Central Committee. By some unrecorded negotiation the Communists allowed the convoy, with its Nationalist contingent, to enter their territory. Because Genghis was, of course, a Chinese emperor and the whole mausoleum a Chinese relic, both sides in what would soon be a vicious civil war united in competing to praise Genghis as a symbol of Chinese resistance to the invader, seeing him not as the founder of the Mongol nation and empire, but as the founder of the Yuan dynasty. There was, therefore, a political subtext to this apparently altruistic gesture, based on the fact that Inner Mongolia was now part of China, and that its Mongolian people were officially Chinese. So the Mongols had better not forget that Genghis's conquests were not conquests at all, but a little difficulty that led to the Chinese majority being ruled, for a short while, not by foreigners but by a *Chinese* minority – i.e. the Mongols.

So, in mid-June, the Communists did Genghis proud. Camel-carts gave way to an eight-car convoy, one vehicle for each tent, the lead car bearing the coffin, which was draped in yellow satin. A crowd of 20,000 watched the convoy draw up at a room designated as a funeral hall. Here a huge scroll proclaimed Genghis 'The Giant of the World'. An arch hung with a sign – 'Welcome to Genghis Khan's coffin!' – led to a shrine laid with wreaths, one from Mao himself. A dozen senior party and army officials paid tribute to the convoy in a four-hour ceremony, the high point of which was a 'vehement and passionate' funeral oration by Secretary General Cao Liru. 'It praised Yuan Taizu [the Yuan dynasty's first emperor] as the world's hero', and instantly linked him to the Communist Party's cause, urging 'Mongolian and Chinese people to unite and resist to the end!'[4] Next day, the convoy moved on southwards, past another huge crowd of spectators. This was how to deal with a barbarian conqueror: confer upon him a retrospective change of nationality and turn him into a symbol of Chinese culture, fortitude and unity.

Three days later, the convoy again passed into Nationalist hands. In Xian, the Nationalists gave a reception that far outdid their rivals'. Here, 200,000 people packed the streets to greet the convoy. A cow and twenty-seven sheep were sacrificed in welcome. It was an astonishing display, given that this was the Chinese heartland, with few Mongols in evidence. Genghis had devastated the area. Yet ordinary people fell for his magic, because he had become a Chinese emperor, albeit posthumously. They were ancestor-worshippers, and Genghis was certainly a great ancestor, even if not theirs.

On 1 July, another 500 kilometres to the west, safe in the Xinglong Mountains south of Lanzhou, the convoy arrived at Dongshan Dafo Dian, the Buddhist temple that was to be the mausoleum's home for the next ten years. It's a glorious place, once hidden in towering forests, now opened by a winding road. A little river tumbles through a huddle of houses. Pagodas crown forested peaks. Daytrippers climb zigzag stairways to the temple, where they still remember Genghis. Inside, a golden statue of Genghis as a Buddhist deity is flanked by horsehair war-standards and a square tent. The original temple and its contents were destroyed by fire in 1968. It all dates from 1987. Nothing is authentic but landscape and memory.

In 1949, as communist troops approached to wrap up the civil war, the Nationalists shepherded the mausoleum away again, 200 kilometres further west to the great sixteenth-century Tibetan monastery of Ta'er Si, where monks welcomed it with chants and prayers. A month later the Communists won anyway. The Nationalists fled to Taiwan. The Japanese were gone, along with their puppet-regimes in Manchuria and Mongolia. Heaven, it seemed, had granted a new mandate – to Mao.

[4] Ju Naijun, 'The Coffin of Genghis Khan Passes Yenan', *National Unity*, Vol. 6, 1986; quoted in Rihu Su, 'The Chinggis Khan Mausoleum' (see Bibliography).

For the next five years, the Communist Party had its hands full with land reforms and other such revolutionary matters. Inner Mongolia was in the control of its own Communist warlord, Ulanhu. Once, before the war, the Communists had agreed that minority areas could secede from China if they wished. Not any more; not in the new China. But the Communists did recognize the right to some local autonomy, and Ulanhu pushed Mongolian claims to the limit. In the new Mongolian Autonomous Region, Mongolians made up only 15 per cent of the population – in a region that had once been theirs alone! – but dominated its administration. As post-revolutionary life returned to a semblance of normality, officials turned to the mausoleum. For Mongols and Chinese alike, Genghis deserved some prestigious and enduring memorial, something better than a few tents. A brand-new mausoleum was commissioned, to be built on the original site.

In spring 1954, by truck and train, the hero's bier and his relics returned to the Lord's Enclosure in time for the laying of the foundation stone on 20 April. Ulanhu himself did the honours. On 15 May, an auspicious day, the day of the most important observance, with *gers* crowding the surrounding pastures and sacrificial sheep piled in mounds, a memorial rite marked the mausoleum's renaissance.

In 1956 the new temple was complete, and remains largely unchanged today.

It seemed right, on my first visit in 2002, to enter as an ignorant outsider should enter any place of worship, with humility. I was with my Mongolian friend Jorigt. From one of the gift shops that lined the entrance courtyard we bought a length of blue silk – a *khatag* – a bottle of vodka and a brick of tea. We climbed the auspicious flight of ninety-nine steps – ninety-nine being the number of minor spirits subordinate to the overarching deity – through pines and cypresses to the temple's gateway, with its white crenellations. Beyond was a huge grassed courtyard, spilling across to the temple itself, its central dome flanked by two domed wings. They couldn't go too far wrong with a site like this. The temple is a jewel in a clasp of greenery, displayed on its hilltop like an offering to Blue Heaven.

After all those sweaty stairs, and the entrance gateway – which acts like the iconostasis in an Orthodox church, concealing then revealing the mystery within – and the huge courtyard, you feel yourself drawn towards something greater than the merely mortal.

Inside there was the divinity himself, as a vast and shadowy marble statue, a Buddha figure 4 metres high, beneath a frieze of dragons. Darkhat Mongols in suits and brown trilbies stood watch, dour as guard dogs. A sign warned against photography. I felt my scepticism retreating in the face of their seriousness. Perhaps it is the show of faith in others, not the literal truth of that faith, that induces a sense of the sacred.

A young Darkhat, Bulag, guided us past the looming marble presence, which was set against a huge map showing the full extent of the Mongol empire. Respectfully we trooped into a back room, where three tents stood beneath an array of banners, like rather tatty Christmas decorations. This was the Mourning Hall, the three tents being for Genghis himself, for his senior wife, Börte, and for Gurbelchin, the Tangut princess, reviled elsewhere as a murderess but here adored for her loyalty. We laid our *khatag* and our bottle down. We knelt. We lit incense. Bulag muttered a prayer, in Mongol: 'Holy Genghis Khan, John and Jorigt have come here today to pray at your tomb. We beg you to grant them good luck in their work.'

Then I regained my scepticism. I was amid relics as daft as any Splinter of the True Cross. Here were the Sacred Bow and Quiver, the Chamber of the Miraculous Milk Bucket, and the Holy Saddle, one of two on display, with pommels of chased silver. The one on the right, said Bulag – that was Genghis's. The one on the left was given in the seventeenth century by Ligdan Khan, the last of the emperors who ruled in Mongolia after being thrown out of China and before Mongolia fell to their successors, the Manchus. Both saddles looked in suspiciously good condition.

Murals display the glories of Genghis's rule in figures that reminded me of 1930s fashion plates, all suave elegance and fabrics falling in neat folds. Nothing mars the perfection of the costumes, the good looks of the men and women. Here Genghis presides over his united empire, there Kublai confers the title of dynastic founder upon his grandfather, who hovers, dragon-flanked, in the Blue Heaven. Musicians have never been happier to sing, maidens never prouder to present silk scarves. Foreigners cannot wait to offer tributes and products, for Genghis was the man who bridged east and west, stimulated a transfer of art, scholarship and trade, and assured the well-being of all.

Of dead bodies there is no trace.

For a decade, the temple served its purpose with increasing success, reaching a high point in the 1960s. In 1962 Mongolia declared the 800th anniversary of Genghis's birth and proposed a great celebration. In Mongolia itself, this proved a disaster. At the time, the country was a Soviet satellite. To Russians, Genghis was a reactionary, a destroyer of culture. The celebration came to a sudden halt. Their instigator was banished. But China knew very well the benefits to be had from the cult of Genghis, and in the same year the Lord's Enclosure hosted its largest rite ever: 30,000 people, mostly Mongols, participated in an excess of adoration that suited the official line perfectly. With the Mongols firmly behind the party, Inner Mongolia would be a stable bastion against the Soviet threat rolling its way across the Gobi.

But when Mao unleashed the Cultural Revolution in 1967, Genghis suddenly fell from grace. There could be no challenge from the past to the new ruler, who was about to usher in an era that would eclipse Genghis. In a wave of xenophobia, Mongols became victims, the prime political target being the so-called Inner Mongolian People's Revolutionary Party, which had, it was claimed, wanted total independence for Inner Mongolia, with the long-term aim of reuniting with Mongolia itself and establishing, presumably, a new Mongol empire. Now the masses must unite against the threat of 'pan-Mongolism'.

This was a hard time. In Cultural Revolutionary eyes, the mausoleum was a symbol of reactionary fervour, the seething heart of treason, the headquarters of pan-Mongolist plotters. In 1968 the Red Guards tore the place apart, destroying almost everything of value – the bow, the quiver, the miraculous milk bucket, the standards, the tents: all gone.

All these objects had a certain eminence, being at least a century, some perhaps several centuries old; but their destruction leaves the tantalizing thought that something among them might actually have dated right back to Genghis himself. Nachug, the head of the mausoleum's Institute of Genghis Khan Studies, certainly believed this to be so. What, for instance, of the contents of the silver coffin, which Lattimore had been told held the Lord's body, or ashes? Well, all Nachug knew was that it supposedly held 'the last breath of the Lord'.

'You mean – just . . .' I struggled. 'Just air?'

'No, no. Inside the box was a clump of hair from a white camel. And it was this hair that held the last breath of Genghis Khan.' I couldn't follow. It still sounded like nothing but air. 'You see, the hair had a little blood on it. And there was also the umbilical cord. That was what was in the coffin that we worshipped here.'

'Were they really in there?'

'Well, the box was never opened. Only worshipped.'

We were back to hearsay, legend, rumour, almost certainly myth. But perhaps there had been a little wisp of white camel-hair with its faint rusty stain and a shrivelled scrap of dried flesh – what tests might have been made, what theories spun. But now, as the result of revolutionary zeal, there would be no chance of DNA analysis and carbon-dating tests.

So the temple itself dates from the mid-1950s, the 'relics' were remade in the 1970s, the great marble statue finished in 1989 (as attested by the signature of the artist, Jiang Hun). It seemed that the only 'genuine' elements were the prayers, the songs, the rituals of the ceremonies themselves. Even these might have been lost, had it not been for the efforts of a few dedicated men, like Sainjirgal, once the chief researcher at the temple, now retired.

Sainjirgal was living in a nearby town, in a neat little house set round a tiny courtyard down a side-street. He made a charming contrast to the grim Darkhats at the temple, with twinkling eyes and a ready smile beneath a trilby which he wore permanently, even indoors. In his mid-seventies, he had the strength and looks of a man twenty years younger. He was from Shilingol, in the east of Inner

Mongolia, and had come as a teacher, but had become intrigued by the worship of Genghis Khan and had found his life's work as a local historian, collecting details of rites, prayers, songs and beliefs.

Sainjirgal's work was well under way when Mao unleashed the Red Guards. He saw the kids – young Mongolians, of all people – turn on the temple, destroying whatever they could, all the artefacts, tents, relics, the lot, all except the saddles, which were hidden in the top of the dome.

'What happened to you?'

'During the Cultural Revolution, I was arrested.' He said this as if he were describing a holiday, twinkling and smiling. 'I was in prison for over a year, then sent to do manual labour, and that was sometimes worse than prison. They tied me with arms outstretched, and beat me with canes. They made me stand close to fires and burned me.'

'But why?'

'Because I worshipped Genghis Khan, and this had become a crime! They also said I was a spy for Mongolian independence fighters, and for the Russians. That was when things were very bad with Russia.'

'You seem very relaxed about it. Do you feel no bitterness?'

He laughed. 'My experience during the Cultural Revolution was good for me.'

When he was finally freed in 1974, after six grim years, he was not broken, but inspired.

'Before, we had trusted that smaller nationalities would always have the same rights as everyone else. Now I saw the truth – that big nationalities can oppress little ones. That encouraged me. I knew I had to fight for our culture. I had to publish the history of my ancestor.'

It was an extraordinary commitment, given the state of the mausoleum in the 1970s, for it had been turned into a store for salt in case of war with Russia. But when Sainjirgal's book, *The Worship of the Golden Chamber*, finally appeared, he had already decided that he had done his subject less than justice. So he ditched it and began again, gathering yet more material, which when I visited had just been published in the book he now reached down from a shelf and signed for me. *Mongolian Worship* is his life's work, distilled between golden covers in 600 pages, beautifully printed in the old, vertical Mongolian script that is still used in Inner Mongolia. Forty years ago, Sainjirgal would have been lucky to survive if he had tried to publish this book. Some things do improve with time.

Most worshippers are content to make offerings and pray to Holy Genghis as if he were a god himself. But Genghisid theology is not that easy, as Nachug revealed on our return to the mausoleum. Strolling round the immense courtyard in front of the temple, we came to a platform on which fluttered yak-tail war-standards, the symbol of Mongol military prowess. Nachug told the story of how Genghis came by them, adding a whole new element to this strange set of beliefs.

'Once, when Holy Genghis was fighting to unite the Mongol tribes, he despaired, and addressed Heaven. "People call me the Son of God, but yet I fail! I beg Khökh Tenger, the Blue Sky, to give me the power to win!" At once, the heavens thundered, and something fell among some trees. He was unable to reach the object. So he commanded his generals to cut the trees and get it. It turned out to be a yak-tail standard. In thanks, Genghis sacrificed eighty-one sheep, leaving the remains for the "sky dogs" [wolves]. So the standard – the *sult* – became like a flag, a sign from the Blue Heaven uniting the Mongols, going before them in battle. That is why we worship the *sult* today.'

Then he added a conclusion that put the whole mausoleum and its ceremonies in a new light: 'This is a form of worship even higher than that of Genghis Khan. If Genghis Khan himself worshipped the standard, then it must be higher than him. It is a symbol of Heaven itself.' As such, it has a power of its own. Some people say that birds flying over it fall dead.

I had gained the impression in the Lord's Enclosure that Genghis was a god. Now I saw that he was not at the pinnacle, only near it, a demi-god. And perhaps with a hint of something even more mystical, a sort of Mongolian Trinity, with God the Father, Son and Holy Spirit mirrored by Blue Heaven, Genghis and Standard.

This was a subject for the temple's resident theologian, Sharaldai, who would be able to explain the next level of complexity. Sharaldai was in Ulaanbaatar, where, later, I found him.

Over our hotel tea, with the help of Erdene, an animal-husbandry expert, I tackled Sharaldai on the subject of Genghis's divinity. Sharaldai did not suffer me all that gladly. He is a Darkhat, with the cult in his blood over generations, and impatient with those, like me, who pretend to a little knowledge.

When I asked whether the Lord's Enclosure was ever associated with miracles, he became quite heated. My question implied a lowering of the purpose of the place. 'The worship of Genghis Khan is a way of connecting us to the Eternal Sky.'

'You mean he is an intermediary?' I was trying to find an equivalent from my own experience. Was the worship of Genghis comparable to Christian worship of, say, the statue of a saint? You direct your prayers to a statue; but the real object is the invisible spirit of the saint; and that is a gateway to God.

'Yes, there are three levels. Look—' He forced himself to be patient. 'The basic tenet of Eternal Heaven philosophy is that we on earth are part of Eternal Heaven, our system of nine planets. People say we human beings are the highest level of a hierarchy of life. That may be so in terms of biology. But in terms of philosophy, we are a part of Eternal Heaven. To think of ourselves as the top of a hierarchy is to separate ourselves from Eternal Heaven. Our task is to reintegrate ourselves with creation. That's what people don't appreciate today.'

'So when one worships Genghis Khan, does one worship Eternal Heaven through Genghis?'

'It is so. Also you can worship Eternal Heaven directly. You see, there are three components: Eternal Heaven, the *power* of Eternal Heaven and *being subject* to the power of Eternal Heaven.'

This was getting complicated. I had always been baffled by the Trinity.

'Christians say that God is three in one: Father, Spirit, Son.'

'There are similarities. But Eternal Heaven has real power. You can feel it, you can see its effects. That is the difference. Genghis knew that all living things owe their power to Eternal Heaven, and he was able to use it to lead. You can see how we Mongols did by looking at our three national sports, wrestling, horse racing and archery. A strong body, good horsemanship, accurate shooting. By these means, we conquered half the world.

'But to use power in such a way was not Eternal Heaven's true purpose. In conquering, we saw that this was not the way to live, bringing suffering to others. What we learned was that the time had come to stop fighting, and live by talking. Now we use our sports to sharpen our mentality, not to fight, but to talk.'

What does this mean for today?

'We are in the process of discovering. I think there are many things we Mongols have not yet understood in *The Secret History*. Some words, some things are still unclear. If we can understand more, we can discover a philosophy that will help the world.'

He was warming to his theme, forgetting me, speaking to his fellow Mongol, Erdene.

'In the world today, there is no philosophy of life! There is science, but science only looks at the surface of things. Science makes nuclear weapons – a stupid weapon, which cannot be used because the user destroys himself! Leaders use nuclear weapons to spread fear, but the power of the weapon does not prevent people like Bin Laden from doing what they want. All of them have forgotten about the existence of the power of Eternal Heaven.'

This was the real purpose of the mausoleum – to awaken not just Mongols but everyone to their place in the universe. 'It doesn't matter whether the objects are genuine or not. The real significance lies in the connection with the Eternal Sky. So in this sense, as I say in my book' – he pointed to the page for emphasis – 'Genghis Khan is a spirit for all of us. We are created by Eternal Heaven. If we follow the Way, then we shall all be eternal.'

It was an unlikely, extraordinary vision. I imagined a flow of priests through the mausoleum spreading the Word to the outside world, the formation of study groups and peace institutes and pressure groups, all the attributes of a new faith. If Sharaldai's message spreads, there will be those who will teach that Genghis's life was the first faltering line on a graph, which strengthens and soars over eight centuries to these astonishing conclusions: that violence, whatever its initial success, must ultimately fail; and that all conflict should be resolved in peaceful discussion.

This is surely the oddest of all Genghis's transformations: in life, from a 'louse' on a mountain to world conqueror; after death, to demi-god; and now to a spirit of universal harmony.

Afterword

BACK TO THE FUTURE

ONCE UPON A TIME, MONGOLIA WAS POOR AND UNKNOWN. THEN IT was rich and very well known indeed because it sucked in wealth from most of Asia and parts of Europe. Then it was poor again. Now it's richer by the day because of what lies beneath its grasslands, deserts and mountains. In 2013, Mongolia's economy was the fastest growing in the world (17 per cent per annum). This is *The Economist* in early 2012, in Ulaanbaatar, or UB as it is known:

> UB is a boom town on the frontier of global mining. Hotels are bursting; the Irish pubs, of which there are several, are heaving with foreign miners, investment bankers and young local women with very long legs and very short skirts. French bistros serve steaks the size of tabloid newspapers. Dozens of cranes punctuate the skyline. The streets, empty 20 years ago, are now clogged.

Most of it is down to the vast mineral wealth that lies beneath the desert.

The most impressive of many mines is in the south Gobi, only

80 kilometres from the Chinese border. It is a copper-and-gold mine, Oyu Tolgoi (Turquoise Hill), which should over the coming years become the world's third largest, contributing 30 per cent of Mongolia's GDP. Nearby is an equally staggering amount of coal (6.4 billion tonnes). Both copper and coal, plus as yet untold amounts of other minerals, head south to help fuel China's hungry economy, with interesting consequences that link directly back to Genghis, Kublai and the empire they created.

In Mongolia, of course, Genghis is resurrected. He symbolizes so much: the nation as an independent political entity; the nomadic, herding lifestyle; the spirit of rugged individuality; the feel of the landscape. The first time I attended a Naadam (National Day) celebration in 2002 – his 840th birthday – he led the parade round Ulaanbaatar's stadium, in the form of the opera singer Enkhbayar, who played the lead in an epic film about Genghis. Horsemen bore Genghis's yak-tail standards, black ones for war, white ones for peace. The great imperial tent-on-wheels, an ox-wagon 10 metres wide, made its cumbersome way round the track. A grandstand of troops displayed placards that spelled out a vast 'Genghis!' His face and name are on a grand hotel, a (German-made) beer, vodka, colleges and institutes. In 2012, the government celebrated his 850th anniversary with a conference and reception. A huge statue of him dominates a new wing of the parliament, backed by a 4-metre-high map of the empire on glass, reminding MPs of the glory days. On the once-open grasslands some 40 minutes east of the capital, the world's biggest equestrian statue – the mane of which is a stairway to a viewing platform on the horses's head – has him surveying his homeland. Babies bear his name. One day, Mongolia is going to be led by another Genghis.

In China, Genghis is also a symbol, but of very different values, because he is the Progenitor of the Great Yuan, the dynasty declared to be Chinese by his grandson Kublai. He stands for Chinese unity, imperial grandeur, national pride. A guide once told me: 'We are very proud of Genghis Khan, because he was the only Chinese to have conquered Europeans.' No point telling her that Genghis was not Chinese, that China was his prime enemy, that he never got as far as Europe himself. It would be like denying Mary's virginity to a Catholic.

The Chinese are on firmer historical ground pointing out that Mongolia and China were all one under Kublai's Yuan dynasty and again under the Manchus – the Qing dynasty – from 1691 until 1911. Both these dynasties were the creation of non-Han Chinese, so the conclusion drawn is rather less firm, namely that China and Mongolia should be one again, under Chinese rule. One of Mongolia's leading independent politicians, Oyun, was once in the Foreign Correspondents' Club in Beijing, and – as she told me – 'one young journalist actually said to me, "We have very confused feelings about Mongolia, because Mongolia is part of China!"'

Genghis's conquests, which were given their universalist ideology by Ogedei and extended by Kublai, still govern China's policies on its borderlands: Tibet sucked back into the fold, Mongol lands gradually absorbed – re-absorbed in Chinese eyes – making Inner Mongolia irrevocably part of China. Herders protest the loss of their lands to farmers and miners, and get abused, imprisoned and occasionally killed for their trouble.

What of Mongolia itself? It broke away in 1911 when China was weak, and fell into the Russian sphere of interest. In 1945, a plebiscite overwhelmingly 'confirmed' its 'independence' – the quotes reflecting its dubious nature in Chinese eyes.[1] The result was accepted only by the Nationalists, never by the Communists.

Officially, no one talks of repudiating the status quo. Unofficially, though, there is a wrong to be righted. If this ever comes to pass, it will be done in the name, naturally, of Genghis Khan, because it was his heirs who gave China its present borders (minus Mongolia itself, and a bit of Manchuria, now Russian).

Of course, no government accuses China of being a military threat, despite the occasional bit of scaremongering, like Samuel Huntington in *The Clash of Civilizations and the Remaking of*

---

[1] Actually they have a tiny point: the vote, organized by Mongolia's Stalin-figure, Choibalsan, was not just overwhelming but unanimous, with precisely *no one* voting to remain part of China.

World Order: 'Chinese expansion could also become military if China decided that it should attempt to reclaim Mongolia.'

There's no need for anything heavy-handed, because Chinese pressure is economic and social. For the last fifty years there has been one rail link between Mongolia and China, and one paved road which stops in mid-Gobi. But Oyu Tolgoi will change all that. Already there's a paved road for the trucks, and a railway is planned. The several thousand workers in what already counts as a new town will swell, with many Chinese immigrants. In Ulaanbaatar and elsewhere, Chinese are already creating shell companies to buy up land, property and mining rights, and more of the same will follow. It is not inconceivable that one day cash and immigration will turn the border porous, as thousands then tens of thousands trickle and then pour northwards, allowing China to exert ever more pressure on Mongolia, until – in the direst scenario – Mongolia is bought, pressurized and cajoled back into the bosom of the Chinese family.

That's a vision that fills most Mongols with horror. They were part of Qing-dynasty China for 220 years, and achieved enough independence under the Soviets to make themselves fully independent when the Soviet Union collapsed. The very idea of turning the clock back is a nightmare.

Officially, China and Mongolia get on fine. They have to – they're neighbours, and they need each other. But it's a marriage made in hell. Underneath, among ordinary people, there is a visceral distrust, as you would imagine, given that Mongols once ruled the Chinese and the Chinese once ruled the Mongols.

Where will it all end? Growth is erratic. It slowed dramatically in early 2014 as the government and Oyu Tolgoi's owners, Rio Tinto, haggled. It may all come to nothing. But the signs are that big changes are afoot, and Genghis and Kublai are the keys. If the Chinese take over Mongolia, they will do so in the names of Genghis and Kublai, who made Mongolia part of China. And if Mongols resist, they will do so in the name of Genghis and Kublai, who made China part of Mongolia.

BIBLIOGRAPHY

Mongolists, like the Mongol empire itself, span a formidable range of cultures and languages: Mongolian, Chinese, Persian, Tibetan, Korean, Japanese, Russian, Latin, Georgian, and several more. And those are just the primary sources. A full bibliography of the Mongol empire, including books and articles in all the different languages involved, would make a substantial volume. It does not exist. Two of the richest sources – the Chinese *Yuan Shi* and Rashid al-Din's *Collected Chronicles* in Persian – are still not fully accessible to English readers. Very few historians read both languages, let alone the material in a dozen others. We all depend on translations. The only Mongol source, *The Secret History*, exists in several versions, all superseded by the astonishingly erudite three-volume edition by de Rachewiltz, though its size and price make it unsuitable for non-specialists. The best bibliographies for English readers are in Ratchnevsky's *Genghis Khan* (in the English edition, superbly edited by Thomas Haining), Morgan's *The Mongols* (invaluable for his expertise in Islamic history), and Rossabi's *Khubilai Khan* (for Chinese sources). Mote is magnificent. So is Atwood.

I used the following – a small fraction of the whole:

Abu-Lughod, Janet L., *Before European Hegemony: The World System AD 1250 –1350*, Oxford: Oxford University Press, 1989.
Allsen, Thomas, *Culture and Conquest in Mongol Eurasia*, Cambridge:

Cambridge University Press, 2001.

Allsen, Thomas T., 'The Rise of the Mongolian Empire', see Franke and Twitchett.

Allsen, Thomas, 'Ever Closer Encounters: The Appropriation of Culture and the Apportionment of Peoples in the Mongol Empire', *Journal of Early Modern History*, Vol. 1, No. 1, Feb. 1997.

Amitai-Preiss, Reuven, and Morgan, David O. (eds), *The Mongol Empire and Its Legacy*, Leiden: Brill, 1999. Cf: Okada.

Atwood, Christopher, *Encyclopedia of Mongolia and the Mongol Empire*, New York: Facts on File, 2004.

Atwood, Christopher, 'The Date of the *Secret History of the Mongols* Reconsidered', *Journal of Song-Yuan Studies*, 37 (2007).

Barthold, Wilhelm (aka Vasili Vladimirovich), *Turkestan down to the Mongol Invasion*, London: E.J.W. Gibb Memorial Trust, 1928; with additional material, 1968.

Bartlett, W. B., *The Assassins: The Story of Medieval Islam's Secret Sect*, Stroud, Glos.: Sutton, 2001.

Batsaikhan, Z., Bor, J., and Davaa, N., 'Is Ikh Ovoo the Tomb of Genghis Khan?', unpublished paper (no date).

Bawden, Charles, *The Mongol Chronicle Altan Tobci*, Wiesbaden: Harrassowitz, 1955.

Bawden, Charles, *The Modern History of Mongolia*, London: Routledge, 1989.

Bazargur, Dambyn, *Chinggis Khaan Atlas*, Ulaanbaatar, 1996.

Bira, Sh., 'Mongolian Tenggerism and Modern Globalism: A Retrospective Outlook on Globalism', *Journal of the Royal Asiatic Society*, Vol. 14, 2004.

Bira, Sh., 'The Mongolian Ideology of Tenggerism and Khubilai Khan', unpublished paper, 2005.

Bira, Sh., *Studies in Mongolian History, Culture and Historiography*, Ulaanbaatar: International Association for Mongol Studies, 2001; esp. 'Khubilai Khan and Phags-pa bla-ma'.

Biran, Michal, *Qaidu and the Rise of the Independent Mongol State in Central Asia*, Richmond: Curzon, 1998.

Bretschneider, Emil, *Mediaeval Researches from Eastern Asiatic Sources*, 2 vols, London: Kegan Paul, 1888; in particular Vol. 1, Chap. III:

'Si Yu Ki', the translation of Li Zhichang's *Journey to the West* (Changchun's journey).

Bretschneider, Emil, *Archaeological and Historical Researches on Peking and Its Environs*, New York: Elibron (Adamant Media Corps.), 2005 (facsimile of the original, Shanghai and London: American and Presbyterian Mission Press, 1876).

Bulag, Uradyn E., *Nationalism and Hybridity in Mongolia*, Oxford: Oxford University Press, 1998.

Bulag, Uradyn E., *The Mongols at China's Edge*, Lanham, MD: Rowman and Littlefield, 2002.

Burns, James MacGregor, *Leadership*, New York, London: Harper & Row, 1978.

Bushell, S. W., 'Notes of a Journey Outside the Great Wall of China', *Journal of the Royal Geographical Society*, Vol. 44 (1874).

Campbell, C. W., 'Journeys in Mongolia', *Geographical Journal*, Vol. 22, No. 5, Nov. 1903.

Cannadine, David, and Price, Simon (eds), *Rituals of Royalty*, Cambridge: Cambridge University Press, 1992.

Chan, Hok-Lam, *China and the Mongols: History and Legend under the Yüan and Ming*, Farnham: Ashgate, 1999.

Ch'en, Paul Heng-chao, *Chinese Legal Tradition under the Mongols*, Princeton, NJ: Princeton University Press, 1979.

Ch'en Yüan, *Western and Central Asians in China under the Mongols*, Los Angeles: Monumenta Serica Monograph, UCLA, 1966.

Cleaves, Francis Woodman, 'The Historicity of the Baljuna Covenant', *Harvard Journal of Asiatic Studies*, Vol. 18, 1955.

Cleaves, Francis Woodman (trans.), *The Secret History of the Mongols*, Cambridge, MA: Harvard University Press, 1982.

Conlan, Thomas D. (trans. and interpretive essay), *In Little Need of Divine Intervention: Scrolls of the Mongol Invasions of Japan*, Ithaca, NY: Cornell University Press, 2001.

Crump, J. I., *Chinese Theatre in the Days of Kublai Khan*, Tucson: University of Arizona Press, 1980.

Damdinsuren, Ts., *Mongolin Nuuts Tovchoo* ('The Secret History of the Mongols'), Ulaanbaatar: 1990.

Davis, Richard L., *Wind against the Mountain: The Crisis of Politics and*

Culture in 13th-Century China, Cambridge, MA: Harvard University Press, 1996.

Delgado, James P., 'Relics of the Kamikaze', *Archaeology*, Vol. 56, No. 1, Jan.–Feb. 2003.

Delgado, James, *Khubilai Khan's Lost Fleet*, Vancouver: Douglas and MacIntyre, 2008, and London: The Bodley Head, 2009.

Denning, Stephen, *The Secret Language of Leadership: How Leaders Inspire Action through Narrative*, San Francisco: Jossey-Bass/Wiley, 2007.

Dunnell, Ruth, 'Hsi Hsia', in Franke and Twitchett.

Eckert, Carter J., et al., *Korea Old and New: A History*, Cambridge, MA: Ilchokak/Harvard University Press, 1990.

Farris, William Wayne, *Heavenly Warriors: The Evolution of Japan's Military, 500–1300*, Cambridge, MA: Harvard Council on East Asian Studies, 1992.

Fletcher, Joseph F., 'The Mongols: Ecological and Social Perspectives', in *Studies on Chinese and Islamic Inner Asia*, Aldershot: Variorum, 1995.

Franke, Herbert, 'Chia Ssu-tao (1213–1275): A "Bad Last Minister"?', in Arthur F. Wright and Denis Twitchett (eds), *Confucian Personalities*, Stanford, CA: Stanford University Press, 1962.

Franke, Herbert, 'Siege and Defence of Towns in Medieval China', in Frank A. Kierman and John K. Fairbank (eds), *Chinese Ways in Warfare*, Cambridge, MA: Harvard University Press, 1974.

Franke, Herbert, *From Tribal Chieftain to Universal Emperor and God: The Legitimation of the Dynasty*, Munich: Bayerische Akademie der Wissenschaften, 1978.

Franke, Herbert, *Studien und Texte zur Kriegsgeschichte der Südlichen Sungzeit* (esp. Ch. 4: 'Hsiang-yang: *Gelände und Befestigungen*'), Wiesbaden: Harrassowitz, 1987.

Franke, Herbert, *China under Mongol Rule*, Farnham: Ashgate, 1994.

Franke, Herbert, and Twitchett, Denis (eds), *The Cambridge History of China*, Vol. 6: *Alien Regimes and Border States*, esp. Thomas T. Allsen's chapter, 'The Rise of the Mongolian Empire', Cambridge: Cambridge University Press, 1994.

Goleman, Daniel, Boyatzis, Richard, and McKee, Annie, *The New Leaders: Transforming the Art of Leadership into the Science of Results*, London: Time Warner, 2002 (publ. in US as *Primal Leadership*).

Goodman, Jim, *The Exploration of Yunnan*, Yunnan People's Publishing House, 2000.

Grousset, René, *Conqueror of the World*, London: Oliver & Boyd, 1967.

Grousset, René, *The Empire of the Steppes*, New Brunswick, NJ: Rutgers University Press, 1970.

Haenisch, Erich, '*Die Letzten Feldzüge Cinggis Hans und Sein Tod*', *Asia Minor*, Vol. 9, 1933.

Halperin, Charles, *Russia and the Golden Horde*, Bloomington, Ind: Indiana University Press, 1985.

Harada, Yoshito, *Shang-tu, the Summer Capital of the Yuan Dynasty in Dolon Nor, Mongolia*, Tokyo: Far Eastern Archaeological Society, 1941.

Haw, Stephen G., *Marco Polo's China: A Venetian in the Realm of Khubilai Khan*, London: Routledge, 2006.

Heissig, Walther, *A Lost Civilization*, London: Thames and Hudson, 1966.

Heissig, Walther, *The Religions of Mongolia*, trans. Geoffrey Samuel, London: Routledge, 1980.

Hitti, Philip, *History of the Arabs*, London: Macmillan, 2002.

Hung, William, 'The Transmission of the Book Known as *The Secret History of the Mongols*', *Harvard Journal of Asiatic Studies*, Vol. 14, 1951.

Huntington, Samuel P., *The Clash of Civilizations and the Remaking of World Order*, New York and London: Simon & Schuster, 1996.

Impey, Lawrence, 'Shangtu, the Summer Capital of Kublai Khan', *Geographical Review*, Vol. 15, No. 4, Oct. 1925.

Jackson, Peter, *The Mongols and the West*, Harlow: Pearson Longman, 2005.

Jackson, Peter (trans. and ed., with David Morgan), *The Mission of Friar William of Rubruck*, London: Hakluyt Society, 1990.

Jagchid, Sechin, and Hyer, Paul, *Mongolia's Culture and Society*, Boulder, CO, and Folkestone: Westview Press/Dawson, 1979.

Jay, Jennifer W., *A Change in Dynasties: Loyalism in 13th-Century China*, Washington DC: Centre for East Asian Studies, 1991.

Juvaini, Ata-Malik, *Genghis Khan: The History of the World-Conqueror*, trans. and ed. J. A. Boyle, Manchester: Manchester University Press, 1958; 2nd edn 1997.

Kates, G. N., 'A New Date for the Origins of the Forbidden City', *Harvard Journal of Asiatic Studies*, Vol. 7, 1942–3.

Keegan, John, *A History of Warfare*, London: Random House, 1994.

Keegan, John, *The Mask of Command*, London: Jonathan Cape, 1987.

Khazanov, Anatoly, *Nomads and the Outside World*, Cambridge: Cambridge University Press, 1984.

Klopsteg, Paul E., *Turkish Archery and the Composite Bow*, Manchester: Simon Archery Foundation, 1987.

Kwanten, Luc, *Imperial Nomads: A History of Central Asia, 500–1500*, Philadelphia: University of Pennsylvania Press, 1979.

Lane, George, *Genghis Khan and Mongol Rule*, Westport CT and London: Greenwood Press, 2004

Lane, George, *Daily Life in the Mongol Empire*, Westport CT and London: Greenwood Press, 2006

Langlois, John D. (ed.), *China under Mongol Rule*, Princeton, NJ: Princeton University Press, 1981.

Larner, John, *Marco Polo and the Discovery of the World*, New Haven, CT: Yale University Press, 1999.

Lattimore, Owen, *Mongol Journeys*, London: Jonathan Cape, 1941.

Lattimore, Owen, *Studies in Frontier History*, Oxford: Oxford University Press, 1962.

Lewis, Bernard, *The Assassins: A Radical Sect in Islam*, London: Weidenfeld & Nicolson, 1967.

Li Zhichang (Li Chih-Ch'ang), cf. Waley and Bretschneider: *Medieval Researches*.

Liddell Hart, Basil, 'Jenghiz Khan and Sabutai', in *Great Captains Unveiled*, Edinburgh and London: Blackwood, 1927.

Lin Yutang, *Imperial Peking*, London: Elek, 1961.

Liu Jung-en, trans. and ed., *Six Yüan Plays* (includes *The Injustice Done to Tou Ngo*, aka *The Injustice to Dou E*), London: Penguin, 1972.

Lynn, Richard John (trans.), poems on Shangdu, personal communication.

Man, John, *Genghis Khan: Life, Death and Resurrection*, London: Transworld, 2011 (revised edn).

Man, John, *Kublai Khan: The Mongol King Who Remade China*, London: Transworld, 2007.

Man, John, *The Leadership Secrets of Genghis Khan*, London: Transworld, 2010.

Man, John, *Xanadu: Marco Polo and Europe's Discovery of the East*,

London: Transworld, 2009. Published in the US as *Marco Polo*, New York: HarperCollins, 2014.

Martin, H. Desmond, *The Rise of Chingis Khan and His Conquest of North China*, Baltimore, MD: Johns Hopkins Press, 1950.

Metternich, Hilary Roe, *Mongolian Folktales*, Boulder, CO: Avery, 1996.

Mongolian Academy of Sciences and the *Yomiuri Shimbun*, Japan, *A Report on the Joint Investigation under the Mongolian and Japanese Gurvan Gol Historic Relic Probe Project, 1990–3*.

Morgan, David, 'The Mongols in Syria, 1260–1300', in Peter Edbury (ed.), *Crusade and Settlement*, Cardiff: University College of Wales, 1985.

Morgan, David, *The Mongols*, Oxford: Blackwell, 1986.

Morgan, David, 'The "Great Yāsā of Chingiz Khān" and Mongol Law in the Īlkhānate', *Bulletin of the School of Oriental and African Studies*, 49: 1986.

Morgan, David, 'Marco Polo in China – or Not?', *Journal of the Royal Asiatic Society*, 3rd series, No. 6, 1996.

Mote, F. W., *Imperial China 900–1800*, Cambridge, MA: Harvard University Press, 1999.

Moule, A. C., and Pelliot, Paul, *Marco Polo: The Description of the World*, London: Routledge, 1938. Two vols, the second being the so-called 'Z text', found in Toledo in 1932.

Moule, A. C., *Quinsai, with other Notes on Marco Polo*, Cambridge: Cambridge University Press, 1957.

Mozai, Takao, 'Kublai Khan's Lost Fleet', *National Geographic*, Nov. 1982.

Needham, Joseph, *Science and Civilisation in China*, Vol. 4, Part III, *Civil Engineering and Nautics*, Cambridge: Cambridge University Press, 1971.

Nordby, Judith, *Mongolia*, Oxford, Santa Barbara and Denver: World Bibliographical Series, No. 156, 1993.

Okada, Hidehiro, 'China as a Successor State to the Mongol Empire', in Amitai-Preiss and Morgan.

Olbricht, Peter, *Das Postwesen in China unter der Mongolenherrschaft im 13. und 14. Jahrhundert*, Wiesbaden: Harrassowitz, 1954.

Olschki, Leonardo, *Marco Polo's Asia*, Berkeley and Los Angeles: University of California Press, and Cambridge: Cambridge University Press, 1960.

Onon, Urgunge (trans.), *The Secret History of the Mongols*, Leiden: Brill, 1990; new edn, Richmond: Curzon, 2001.

Pedersen, Neil, et al., 'Pluvials, Droughts, the Mongol Empire and Modern Mongolia', Proceedings of the National Academy of Sciences, March 2014 (online, pre-print).

Peers, Chris, *Medieval Chinese Armies, 1260–1520*, London: Osprey, 1992.

Peers, Chris, *Medieval Chinese Armies (2): 590–1260*, London: Osprey, 1996.

Pegg, Carole, *Mongolian Music, Dance, and Oral Narrative*, Seattle: University of Washington Press, 2001.

Pelliot, Paul, *Notes on Marco Polo*, ed. L. Hambis, Paris: Imprimerie Nationale, 1959–73.

Petech, Luciano, 'Tibetan Relations with Sung China and with the Mongols', in Morris Rossabi (ed.), *China among Equals*.

Polo, Marco, see Yule.

Rachewiltz, Igor de, *Papal Envoys to the Great Khans*, London: Faber, 1971.

Rachewiltz, Igor de, 'The Title Činggis qan/qagan Re-examined', in Walter Heissig and Klaus Sagaster (eds), *Gedanke und Wirkung: Festschrift zum 90. Geburtstag von Nikolaus Poppe*, Wiesbaden: Harrassowitz, 1989.

Rachewiltz, Igor de, et al., *In the Service of the Khan: Eminent Personalities of the Early Mongol–Yüan Period (1200–1300)*, Harrassowitz, Wiesbaden, 1993.

Rachewiltz, Igor de, 'Searching for Genghis Qan', *Rivista degli Studi Orientali*, Vol. 71, 1997.

Rachewiltz, Igor de, 'Marco Polo Went to China', *Zentralasiatische Studien*, Vols 27–8, 1997–8.

Rachewiltz, Igor de, 'Where is Genghis Khan Buried? Myths, Deceptions and Reality', unpublished paper, 2002.

Rachewiltz, Igor de, 'Heaven, Earth and the Mongols in the Time of Čingis Qan and his Immediate Successors (ca. 1160–1260) – A Preliminary Investigation', in *A Lifelong Dedication to the China Mission*, Leuven, 2007.

Rachewiltz, Igor de, 'The Dating of the Secret History of the Mongols – A Reinterpretation', *Ural-Altaische Jahrbücher*, Neue Folge, 22 (2008).

Rachewiltz, Igor de (trans. and ed.), *The Secret History of the Mongols: A Mongolian Epic Chronicle of the Thirteenth Century, translated with a historical and philological commentary*, 2 vols, Leiden, Boston and Cologne: Brill, 2004; supplementary volume, 2013.

Rashid al-Din, *The Successors of Genghis Khan*, trans. John Boyle, New York and London: Columbia University Press, 1971.

Ratchnevsky, Paul, *Genghis Khan: His Life and Legacy*, ed. Thomas Haining, Oxford: Blackwell, 1991.

Rihu Su, 'The Chinggis Khan Mausoleum and Its Guardian Tribe', dissertation, University of Pennsylvania, 2000.

Ronay, Gabriel, *The Tartar Khan's Englishman*, London: Cassell, 1978.

Rossabi, Morris, *Khubilai Khan: His Life and Times*, Berkeley: University of California, 1988.

Rossabi, Morris, *Voyager from Xanadu: Rabban Sauma and the First Journey from China to the West*, Tokyo: Kodansha, 1992.

Rossabi, Morris, ed., *China among Equals: The Middle Kingdom and Its Neighbours, 10th–14th Centuries*, Berkeley: University of California Press, 1983.

Roux, Jean-Paul, 'Tängri. Essai sur le ciel-dieu des peuples altaïques', *Revue de l'Histoire des Religions*, Vol. 149, Nos 1 &2 (1956).

Saunders, J. J., *A History of Medieval Islam*, London: Routledge, 1965.

Saunders, J. J., *The History of the Mongol Conquests*, London: Routledge, 1971.

Saunders, J. J., *Muslims and Mongols*, Christchurch, NZ: University of Canterbury, 1977.

Schubert, Johannes, *Ritt zum Burchan-chaldun*, Leipzig: Brockhaus, 1963.

Shiraishi, Noriyuki, et al., *Preliminary Report on Japan–Mongolia Joint Archaeological Expedition 'New Century Project'*, Niigata University and Institute of Archaeology, Mongolian Academy of Sciences, annually, 2001 onwards.

Silverberg, Robert, *The Realm of Prester John*, New York and London: Doubleday, 1972.

Spuler, Bertold, *History of the Mongols based on Eastern and Western Accounts of the 13th and 14th Centuries*, London: Routledge, 1972.

Ssanang Ssetsen, *Geschichte der Ost-Mongolen und Ihres Fürstentums*, trans. Isaac Schmidt, St Petersburg: 1829.

Steinhardt, Nancy, *Chinese Imperial City Planning*, Honolulu: University of Hawaii Press, 1990.

Strakosch-Grassmann, Gustav, *Der Einfall der Mongolen in Mitteleuropa in den Jahren 1241–2*, Innsbruck: 1893.

Sun Tzu (Sunzi), *The Art of War*, with Shang Yang, *The Book of Lord Shang*, Ware, Herts: Wordsworth, 1998.

Thorau, Peter, 'The Battle of Ayn Jalut: A Re-examination', in Peter Edbury (ed.), *Crusade and Settlement*, Cardiff: Cardiff University Press, 1985.

Turnbull, Stephen, *Siege Weapons of the Far East, (1) 612–1300 and (2) 960–1644*, London: Osprey, 2001.

Waldron, Arthur, *The Great Wall of China*, Cambridge: Cambridge University Press, 1997.

Waley, Arthur (trans.), *The Travels of an Alchemist: The Journey of the Taoist Ch'ang-Chun from China to the Hindukush at the Summons of Chingiz Khan, recorded by his disciple Li Chih-chang*, London: Routledge, 1934.

Weatherford, Jack, *Genghis Khan and the Making of the Modern World*, New York: Crown, 2004.

Wei Jian, *Yuan Shang Du* (in Chinese), Beijing: Encyclopedia of China Publishing House, 2008.

Williams, Peter, and Smith, Michael, *The Frozen Earth: Fundamentals of Geocryology*, Cambridge: Cambridge University Press, 1989.

Wood, Frances, *Did Marco Polo Go to China?*, London: Secker and Warburg, 1995.

Wylie, Turrell V., 'The First Mongol Conquest of Tibet Reinterpreted', *Harvard Journal of Asiatic Studies*, Vol. 37, No. 1, 1977.

Xu Cheng and Yu Jun, 'Genghis Khan's Palace in the Liupan Shan and the Official Residence of An-shi Wang' (in Chinese), *Journal of Ningxia University*, Vol. 3, 1993.

Yamada, Nabaka, *Ghenko: The Mongol Invasion of Japan*, London: Smith, Elder & Co., 1916.

Yule, Henry, and Cordier, Henri, *The Travels of Marco Polo: The Complete Yule-Cordier Edition*, 2 vols, New York: Dover Publications, 1993.

Zerjal, Tatiana, et al., 'The Genetic Legacy of the Mongols', *American Journal of Human Genetics*, Vol. 72, March 2003.

PICTURE ACKNOWLEDGEMENTS

Every effort has been made to contact copyright holders. Any we have omitted are invited to get in touch with the publishers.

Illustrations in the text
74: triple-bow crossbow catapult, woodcut from *Wu Ching Tsung Yao* (Ming edition); 134–5: Mongols transporting imperial tent, from *The Book of Ser Marco Polo* . . . by Henry Yule, 1903. © Ivy Close Images/Alamy; 206: Kublai Khan's howdah. © Corbis; 221: fire-lance containing broken porcelain, woodcut from *Huo Lung Ching* (Ming edition); Mongolian warriors in Japan, drawing after *Moko Shurai Ekotoba* (*Illustrated Account of the Mongol Invasion*), 1275–1293. © INTERFOTO/Alamy

Colour illustrations
Images are © John Man except for the following, and are listed clockwise from top-left corner:

First section
Western Xia imperial tombs: © Best View Stock/Alamy; ruins of the Great Kyz Kala Palace, Merv: © Dennis Cox/Alamy; Samanid Mausoleum, Bukhara, 892–943 : courtesy Helen Edwards; Genghis Khan on the steps of the mosque at Bukhara, illumination from Rashid-al-Din, *Jami al-Tawarikh* (*Compendium of Chronicles*), c.

1430: Suppl. Persan 1113, f. 90, bibliothèque nationale de France, Paris

Funeral of Genghis Khan, illumination from Rashid al-Din, *Jami al-Tawarikh* (*Compendium of Chronicles*), c. 1430: Suppl. Persan 1113, f. 98v, bibliothèque nationale de France, Paris

Genghis Khan, statue, Sükhbaatar Square, Ulaanbaatar: © James Caldwell/Alamy; Genghis statue and warriors, Mount Khan, Holingol: © Ren Junchuan/Xinhua Press/Corbis; Genghis Khan, equestrian statue, Tsonjin Boldog: © Nick Ledger/JAI/Corbis; Genghis Khan Mausoleum, Ordos: © TAO Images Limited/Alamy

Siege of Baghdad, illumination from the Diez Album, f. 70: Staatsbibliothek zu Berlin, Orientalabteilung/Ruth Schacht

Second section

Cloud Platform, Juyong Pass, Changping, Beijing, top and bottom left: © TAO Images Limited/Alamy

Cane palace reconstruction: © Ben Godber (Expedition), Tom Man, John Man; Kublai Khan hunting: National Palace Museum, Taipei

Bridge and entrance to the White Pagoda, Beijing (inset): © Alex Ekins/Alamy; Buddha tiles, White Pagoda: © Matt Humphrey/Alamy

Warship reconstruction: courtesy of ARIUA and Kinya Yamagata; Japanese defensive wall, detail from a Japanese scroll painting, c. 1293: The Granger Collection/Topfoto; embossed Mongol officer's helmet, Mongolian Invasion Memorial Museum, Fukuoka: James L. Stanfield/National Geographic Creative; Samurai Takezaki delivers the heads of two Mongol invaders to Adachi Morinume, 13th century: bibliothèque des arts decoratifs, Paris/Archives Charmet/The Bridgeman Art Library; Suenaga in battle: The Art Archive/Imperial Household Collection Kyoto/Granger Collection

Map by Fra Mauro Camaldolese: De Agostini/Getty Images

INDEX